Eyes Within the Diamond

About the Author

A baseball fanatic over the course of his life, Stacey Marc Goldman has compiled a collection of articles over a two-year period featuring his unique analysis and perspective about the game he loves.

Stacey Marc played representative baseball in Thornhill, Ontario, Canada for 6 years and played until the Junior Level. Mr. Goldman attended Spring Training in Florida from 1984-1987 and has traveled to Arizona for Spring Training likewise.

Stacey, to paraphrase Blue Jay Dave Stieb, is, "forever looking for tomorrow to be perfect." He is a huge fan of his hometown Toronto Blue Jays, and a fan of famed sportswriter and statistician Bill James. Stacey's contribution to the baseball literature includes an evaluation of over 700 baseball players using his own statistical formulae, and deep insights into the social aspect of the treatment of minorities within major league baseball.

Eyes Within the Diamond

Inside the Game, Outside the Box

By Stacey Marc Goldman

SUMMER
GAME
BOOKS

ISBN: 978-1-938545-77-1 (pbk)
ISBN: 978-1-938545-78-8 (ebook)

For permission requests, and for information regarding bulk purchases or additional distribution, write to the publisher at

info@summergamebooks.com

or to
Summer Game Books
Attn: Walter Friedman
PO Box 818
South Orange, NJ 07079

Dedications

To Oren Nuremberg, the best baseball player in Toronto, from 1967 - 1978, bar none. Oren once had five consecutive 5 for 5 games with at least 3 home runs in each game. Oren played all 9 positions at various points of his career and could hit a softball 550 feet, throw a softball 95 MPH, and played city-ball to boot.

Oren Nuremberg was a close personal friend of my dad and his teammates; he was a loyal husband to his wife; and he was a free spirit. I used to brag to my Dad when I had a good game that "I played like Oren today."

There is talk in Toronto to induct Oren Nuremberg into the Canadian Baseball Hall of Fame. He suffered from brain cancer towards the end of his life. He is sorely missed by many.

*   *   *

Jose Fernandez, perhaps the best pitcher in MLB, has just died tragically in a tragic boating accident at the age of 24 with two others. Fernandez was dominant in his 2013 NL Rookie of the Year season, in which he was 12-6 with an E.R.A of 2.19 and 187 K's in 172.2 IP. After injury plagued seasons in 2014 and 2015, Fernandez came back strong for 2016 going 16-8 with an E.R.A of 2.86. This year Jose struck out incredible 253 men in only 182.1 innings pitched. In Fernandez' career he was 38-17 (.691), and in 76 GS he pitched 471.1 Innings allowing only 357 hits and 140 BB's, while tallying an incredible 589 Strikeouts, with a WHIP of 1.054, 11.2 K's/9 Innings, and a strikeout to walk ratio of 4.21.

An argument could be made to elect Jose Fernandez into Cooperstown based on his quick rise to stardom. This J.R Richard-type assessment could be wrong. However, there should be a place in our hearts for players that were so rich with talent but whose careers ended in tragedy. Fernandez was perhaps the best pitcher to come out of Cuba.

R.I.P Jose Fernandez

Acknowledgments

During the compilation of articles for this book, I conferred with and received input from several of my friends and family. The dynamic of each relationship was different, but each was greatly appreciated and helpful to the writing process.

First, I'd like to thank my dad, Marty Goldman, for researching publishers for the book, as well as offering his baseball knowledge towards the research process. Then there was my friend, Walter Gula, and my uncle, Norm Goldman, who each gave me some information that led me to research into other areas that I hadn't thought to delve into (especially the International League teams in Toronto and Montreal.

Next I'd like to thank my friend from my old baseball days, Robbie Cooper (who was a standout ballplayer in his own right). Robbie offered some legal advice and was helpful with some abstract details of players that I hadn't thought of, and provided me with some feedback when I wrote the chapter "Players From Around the World."

Then there is my sister, Beth Goldman, who created the illustration for the cover—the iconic image of Willie Mays making "The Catch" in the 1954 World Series.

My neighbor Wadi (Wally) Qaqish, was always interested in talking about our Toronto Blue Jays and other baseball topics, and our conversations were very stimulating to the creative process. He and I like to joke that the rest of the teams in baseball are scared of our big, bad Blue Jays.

Finally, thanks and great appreciation to baseball-reference.com, the source for many of the statistics used in this book.

Contents

Eyes Within the Diamond

1
The Heart of the Game: Brief Essays

Baseball Is Everybody's Game

Moses Fleetwood Walker

Moses Fleetwood Walker was a standout Catcher in the American Association with the To-ledo Blue Stockings in Ohio (in 1884). He was travelling with the Team to Kentucky for a game and the Manager of the Kentucky squad, Cap Anson, drew attention to the fact that Walker was a "Black" man. He cited that the game be cancelled due to Kentucky's law of "Blacks" and "Whites" not being allowed to play on the same field (as was customary in schools across many Southern States - the Segregation Law). The Courts ruled in Anson's favour, and the game never took place. This essentially ended Walker's' Professional career. Many people today look at Anson as a blatant racist for not accepting what many Northern State Universities were trying to achieve, integration of African-Americans into Profession-al Sports.

Apartheid in Baseball

In the days of Babe Ruth, legends were born. Those that created an aura and were, for the most part, home run hitters.

In our modern day, stolen bases and home runs are equally revered. When Joe DiMaggio played, he only stole a few bases a year. During the integration of African Americans to the Majors in 1947, the league began assimilating five-tool players to the game. This was new to the Major Leagues, but not new to the Negro Leagues.

Even Willie Mays would have had a hard time making the Homestead Grays starting lineup. Henry Aaron played with the Indianapolis Clowns and wasn't the best player on the team. Jackie Robinson played in the Negro Leagues at the start of his baseball career and he wasn't even a starter.

As the game progresses, it's interesting to note that African-American ballplayers have had the most success in the Majors compared to other minorities, and Caucasians.

Why is it there have only been around ten African American Managers in the history of the Major Leagues?

Why is it there is only one African-American in a high ranking position for an organization? (Henry Aaron)

These gross inequities lead me to believe that there is a form of Apartheid that the Major League Owners have instilled among their brass to this day.

The Negro Leagues

In the sketchy history of the Negro Leagues from 1922-1950 there were at least thirteen organizations. Here are some of them:

1. Homestead Grays
2. Pittsburgh Crawfords
3. Kansas City Monarchs (later the Washington Monarchs)
4. St. Louis Stars (later the Philadelphia Stars and the Detroit Stars)
5. New York Cubans
6. Chicago American Giants
7. Birmingham Black Barons
8. Baltimore Black Sox
9. Cleveland Cubs
10. New York Black Yankees
11. Memphis Red Sox
12. Brooklyn Royal Giants (later the Lincoln Giants)
13. Indianapolis Clowns

Oscar Charleston

The Homestead Grays were the New York Yankees of the Negro Leagues, winning nine consecutive Negro National League Championships between 1937-1945. The Grays carried Josh Gibson (the all-time home runs Leader with 803 home runs) "Cool Papa" Bell, and Buck Leonard.

The best pitcher that came out of the Negro Leagues was Satchel Paige. In the 1932/1933 campaigns, Paige was in his prime with the Pittsburgh Crawfords. In 1932 Paige posted a 32-7 Won/Loss record and in 1933 he went 31-4.

Many of the great Negro Leaguers went to play abroad. For example, Josh Gibson played winter ball in Mexico, Cuba, Puerto Rico, the Dominican Republic, and Central America. In 1937 many of the stars of the Negro Leagues (Satchel Paige, Josh Gibson, and "Cool Papa"

Bell) went to the Dominican Republic to play on a team that was owned by "dictator" Rafael Trujilo.

The Negro Leagues' season was usually just under 200 Games. "Cool Papa" Bell once stole 175 bases in a year. Bell finished his career with a lifetime .341 Batting Average.

Josh Gibson played together with the Pittsburgh Crawfords between 1932-1936 and was the best hitter in the league over those years. Gibson hit 69 home runs in 1934, and in 1933 he played in 137 Games and batted .467 with 55 home runs.

Although Satchel Paige, Jackie Robinson, Willie Mays and Henry Aaron were players that made the adjustment from the Negro Leagues to the Major Leagues, these players were few and far between from the masses. Had Negro Leagues' organizations been instituted into the Majors, this would have been a truer test to the African-American ballplayer and would have created front office positions for African-Americans. It would also have promoted African-American ownership of Professional Sports Franchises in the U.S.A.

The 1955 Brooklyn Dodgers

In 1955 something happened on the baseball diamond that had never happened before in the Major Leagues. A team fielded more African-Americans than Caucasians in their starting lineup. It was in 1947 that Dodger Owner Branch Rickey brought Jackie Robinson into the Majors to integrate African-Americans into the Major Leagues. On that fateful day in '55, the Brooklyn Dodgers Manager – Walter Alston, penciled Junior Gilliam at Second, Sandy Amoros in Leftfield, Roy Campanella as Catcher, Duke Snider in Centerfield, Gil Hodges at First, Jackie Robinson at Third Base, Pee Wee Reese at Shortstop, Carl Furillo in Rightfield, and Don Newcombe on the hill.

Some say that this was the greatest team of the 1950's, and this is hard to argue.

Roy Campanella was heads above the other Catchers who played at that time (aside from Yogi Berra). Duke Snider was a perennial 40 HR man. Jackie Robinson was probably the most versatile ballplayer in the Majors. Don Newcombe was well established and ended up winning the first Cy Young Award in 1956. They also had Pee Wee Reese around to keep things loose. There was a mystique surrounding Ebbots Field and was surmounted by the Dodgers willingness to truly integrate African-Americans into the Major Leagues.

For this reason I would have to say that the most important roster of any Major League Baseball Team in the history of the Majors would have to be the World Series Champion '55 Brooklyn Dodgers;

1. Jim "Junior" Gilliam (2B)
2. Jackie Robinson (3B)
3. Duke Snider (CF)
4. Roy Campanella (C)
5. Gil Hodges (1B)
6. Carl Furillo (RF)
7. Sandy Amoros (LF)
8. Pee Wee Reese (SS)
9. Don Newcombe (P)

Accomplished Jewish Ballplayers

1. **Sandy Koufax** (Sanford Braun; 1955-1966) - Won three National League Cy Young Awards (1963, 1965, and 1966), and the 1963 NL MVP Award. Won four World Series with the Dodgers Chain - 1955, 1959, 1963, and 1965. Won three National League Pitching Triple Crown's; 1963, 1965, and 1966. Threw 4 No-Hitters (one a perfect game). Was awarded the World Series MVP Awards in 1963 and 1965. Was inducted into the Baseball Hall of Fame on his first ballot.

2. **Hank Greenberg** (Henry Benjamin Greenberg; 1930-1947) - Hit 58 home runs in one year (1938). Had 183 RBI's in one year (1937). Won two World Series with the Detroit Tigers; 1935 and 1945. Won two AL MVP Awards with the Detroit Tigers; 1935 and 1940. Was inducted into the Baseball Hall of Fame on his first ballot.

3. **Rod Carew** (Rodney Cline Carew; 1967-1985) - Won the 1977 AL MVP Award by batting .388 with 14 HRs, 100 RBI's, and 238 base-hits. Finished his career with 3053 base hits. Won Seven Batting Titles; 1969, 1972, 1973, 1974, 1975, 1977, 1978. Had four 200+ base-hits/year seasons and was inducted into the Baseball Hall of Fame on his first ballot.

4. **Mordecai "Three Finger" Brown** (Mordecai "Miner" Braun; 1903-1916) - six consecutive 20+ Win Years (1906-1911), seven consecutive 18+ Win Years, eight consecutive 15+ Win Years, six Years with sub-1.87 ERA (five consecutive from 1906-1910), eight years with sub-2.18 ERA, led in Saves four years

in a row (1908-1911), eleven years with 201.0 +IP (nine in a row from 1903-1911), eight consecutive Years with 20+ Complete Games in a Year (1904-1911) - a ninth with 19 CG (1903), Won two World Series for the Chicago Cubs, the only years they ever won the World Series, and won three World Series matches in those two 'Series against the Detroit Tigers. Surely would have won the 1908 World Series MVP had they issued such an Award in that year. Was duly elected into the Baseball Hall of Fame in Cooperstown in 1949, the year after he died.

5. **Lou Boudreau** (Louis Boudreau; 1938-1952 and 1942-1960 as a Manager) - Won the AL MVP Award in 1948. Won the 1948 World Series Title with the Cleveland Indians. Was the top Shortstop in the Majors when he played and Boudreau finished his career with 519 Extra-Base Hits and 1779 Hits, with a .295 Avg and a lifetime OPS of .795. Was voted into Cooperstown in 1970.

6. **Ryan Braun** (Ryan Joseph Braun "The Hebrew Hammer"; 2007 - Present) - Won the NL Rookie of the Year in 2007 with the Milwaukee Brewers. Won the NL MVP Award in 2011 with the Milwaukee Brewers. Has had two 30+HR/30+SB seasons to this point of his career. Nickname is "The Hebrew Hammer".

7. **Shawn Green** (Shawn David Green; 1993-2007) - Had four consecutive 20+HR/ 20+SB campaigns (1998-2001). Had one 35+HR/35+SB campaign (1998). Had three 42+ HR/ 114+RBI seasons. Hit four home runs in a game once. Won a Gold Glove in 1999 with the Toronto Blue Jays.

8. **Ken Holtzman** (Kenneth Dale Holtzman; 1965-1979) - Won three World Series Titles with the Oakland A's in their three-peat from 1972-1974. Threw two no-hitters with the Cubs before moving to the Athletics. Has the most career wins of all Jewish pitchers with a record of 174-150 with an ERA of 3.49. Won 20 games in a year once and had six 17+ win campaigns. Was a standout in Post-Season play with a 6-4 record and an ERA of 2.30. Has the most Games pitched of any Jewish ballplayer with 451 Games.

9. **Larry Sherry** (Lawrence Sherry; 1958-1968) - Had the second most appearences of any Jewish pitcher with 416 Games. Won the 1959 World Series MVP for the Los Angeles Dodgers, playing alongside fellow Hebrew Sandy Koufax. Was 2-0 with two saves for the Dodgers in that World Series.

10. **Al Rosen** (Albert Leonard Rosen; 1947-1956) - Won the 1953 AL MVP Award and narrowly missed winning the Triple Crown that year (winning the home run and RBI titles and losing the Batting Title by one point to Washington

Senators Mickey Vernon). Had five consecutive 24+ HRs/102+ RBI campaigns between 1950-1954. Won a World Series with the 1948 Cleveland Indians.

11. **Ian Kinsler** (Ian Michael Kinsler; 2006-Present) - Has had two seasons of 30+HR's/30+SB's. Has averaged 22 HR's a year, 23 SB's a year, with 111 runs scored a year, to this point of his career.

Al Rosen.

12. **Kevin Youkilis** (Kevin Edmund Youkilis; 2004-2013) - Won a Gold Glove at 1st Base with the Boston Red Sox in 2007, likewise a World Series Championship that year. Was known as a solid clutch bat in the Red Sox batting order.

13. **Steve Yeager** (Stephen Wayne Yeager; 1972-1986) - Won a World Series with the Los Angeles Dodgers in 1981 taking home the World Series MVP along the way. Was known to have a cannon of an arm at the Catcher position and Lou Brock said he was the hardest man to steal a base on. He threw out 38% of the attempted steals on him over the duration of his career.

14. **Walt Weiss** (Walter William Weiss; 1987-2000) - Won the 1988 Rookie of the Year Award. Won the 1989 World Series with the Oakland A's and finished his career with 1207 Hits.

15. **Steve Braun** (Steven Russell Braun; 1971-1985) - Won a World Series with the St. Louis Cardinals in 1982. Was a pinch-hitting machine over the duration of his career.

16. **Ryan Zimmerman** (Ryan Wallace Zimmerman; 2005-Present) - Finished second in the Rookie of the Year vote in 2006, a year that saw him club 20 HR's with 110 RBI's, with 47 Doubles, a .287 Avg and an OPS of .822. Zimmerman has had four more all-star years to this point of his career, taking home two Silver Slugger Awards and one Gold Glove to date. We'll see how Zimmerman pans out as he was moved to 1st Base for the Washington Natiuonals last year, a move that took him away from his original spot at 3rd Base at the start of his career...

17. (a) **Steve Stone** (Steven Michael Stone; 1971-1981) - Won the 1980 AL Cy Young Award with the Baltimore Orioles.

(b) **Bo Belinsky** (Robert Belinsky; 1962-1970) - Pitched a No-Hitter in his Rookie Season in the bigs. Was known to be a California Playboy during his days with the Angels. Many people in the Baseball World thought that Belinsky was a wasted talent.

18. **Elliott Maddox** (Elliott Maddox; 1970-1980) - Converted to Judaism like Rod Carew. Was a solid ballplayer for both the New York Yankees and the New York Metropolitans. Was mainly a Center-Fielder during his days in the 'bigs (although he played 3rd Base in his last year with the Mets in 1980).

19. **Mark Clear** (Mark Alan Clear; 1979-1990) - Was an outstanding set-up man starting out for the California Angels and later the Boston Red Sox and the Milwaukee Brewers. Finished his career with 83 Saves and was 71-49 along the way. Finished his career with 804 Strikeouts in 804.1 IP. In 1986 with the Brewers, Clear was 5-5 with a 2.20 ERA and had 85 strikeouts in 73.2 IP.

20. (a) **Mike Epstein** (Michael Peter Epstein a.k.a Superjew; 1966-1974) - Was a lefthanded hitting First Baseman for the Washington Senators for the bulk of his career. Hammered 30 home runs in the 1969 season with an OPS of .965 for the Senators that year.

(b) **Kevin Pillar** (Kevin Andrew Pillar a.k.a Superman; 2013-Present) - Came into his own last year and made several highlight reel catches In Center-Field for the Toronto Blue Jays. Is the front-runner for a Gold Glove in Center-Field this year alongside Kevin Kiermaier. Could very well become an all-star for years' to come.

Sandy Koufax (Sanford Braun)

In 1955 the Brooklyn Dodgers employed the services of one 19-year-old southpaw by the name of Sandy Koufax. They won the World Series that year. It wasn't until 1961, after the Dodgers move to Los Angeles, that Koufax reached superstar status. In 1961 Koufax had his breakout season going 18-13 with a 3.52 and 269 K's in 255 2/3 innings pitched, leading the National League in Strikeouts. The following year Koufax went 14-7 with an ERA of 2.54 and 216 K's in 184 1/3rd innings pitched, and never looked back. In 1963 Koufax won the NL Cy Young Award and the NL MVP Award alongside the World Series MVP Award. His numbers that year were astounding, leading him to a NL Pitching Triple Crown; 25-5 1.88 ERA and 306 Strikeouts. In 1964 Sandy Koufax went 19-5 with an ERA of 1.74 and 223 Strikeouts, finshing third in the NL Cy Young voting. The next year of 1965, Koufax won the NL Pitching Triple Crown again going 26-8 with an ERA of

2.04, likewise the NL Cy Young Award for a second time. He shattered the single season record of strikeouts in one season, bettering his own mark established in 1963, with an astounding 382 K's. He also won the World Series MVP Award for the second time in 1965. The following year of 1966 Koufax took home the NL Pitching Triple Crown again, going 27-9 with an ERA of 1.73 and 317 Strikeouts and his third Cy Young Award in four years.

Ironically, it was a game that Koufax didn't pitch for which he is best known. In the 1965 World Series, Koufax was scheduled to pitch on the Jewish High Holiday of Yom Kippur. He refused, sitting out Game 1. Koufax dominated Games 5 and 7, taking home the World Series MVP Award.

Koufax had previously led his Dodgers to a World Series win in 1963, and captured the World Series MVP Award in that post-season. It was following the 1966 campaign that the torque on his left arm took its toll, and he had to give up the game he loved.

A Baseball Demi-G-d, Koufax will surely be remembered as, perhaps, the greatest pitcher who ever played the game. At the end of his career Koufax recorded 4 no-hitters (one was a perfect game), and held the record for most Strikeouts in a single season (with 382 K's in 1965 - bettered only by the great Nolan Ryan - 383).

A role model to many, Koufax is special to Jews in a way he is not to Gentiles. Being Jewish in America in 1963 was not the same as being Jewish in America today. We take for granted not hearing racial slurs and threats, as were common in the early 1960's across America. For Koufax to observe perhaps the holiest of all Jewish ceremonies helped change the perception and predudices that Jewish people faced in Koufax' time. As a result we saw a much more liberal and tolerant 60's. This societal indifference to religion in America as a result of Koufax' actions, raised the spirits of every North American Jew and gave us a role model who was the elite of America's Pastime. Our role model was real, his name was Sandy Koufax.

Famous and Accomplished Italian Ballplayers

1. **George Herman Ruth** (Babe Ruth "The Bambino" "The Sultan of Swat"; 1914-1935) - AL MVP in 1923, hit 54+ HR's in a year four times, hit 41+ HR's in a year eleven times (seven in a row 1926-1932), had 34+ HR's in a year thirteen times, led the AL in HR's twelve times, had 104+ RBI's in a year thirteen times (eight years in a row 1926-1933), had 130+ RBI's in a year ten times (including seven years in a row with 137+ RBI's 1926-1932), had 153+ RBI's six times, led the AL in RBI's five times, eight

years batting .356+, scored 150+ runs in a year six times, led the AL in runs scored eight times, lifetime OPS of 1.164. Won seven World Series and was one of the first men to be voted into the Baseball Hall of Fame in Cooperstown.

The Bambino was half Italian and half German. He grew up on the sandlots in Baltimore living in an orphanage in his early years. "The Babe" was a standout pitcher with the Boston Red Sox who won 23 games in 1916 and 24 games in 1917. In the mid-teens of the 20th Century, Ruth led his Red Sox to three World Series Titles (mainly as a star Pitcher) before being traded to the New York Yankees before the 1920 season for a princely sum of $100,000. He ended his career bashing 714 home runs and held the all-time single season mark of 60 home runs (in 1927) for 34 years. His 714 career home runs were the record until Henry Aaron bettered the mark in 1974. He became so famous in New York that the new Yankee Stadium was called 'the House that Ruth Built' and he even had a chocolate bar made in his name ("Baby Ruth"). Ruth won four World Series Titles in his years with the Bronx Bombers, and was the main focus of "Murderer's Row".

2. **Joe DiMaggio** (Giuseppe Paolo DiMaggio "Joltin Joe" "The Yankee Clipper"; 1936-1951) - AL MVP in 1939, 1941, and 1947, had seven years with 30+ HR's, had eleven years with 20+ HR's, batted .301+ eleven times, batted .323+ six years in a row (1936-1941), seven years in a row with 114+ RBI's (1936-1942), nine years with 114+ RBI's, his lifetime OPS was .977. One of the greatest Center-Fielders of all-time. Won nine World Series Titles, HOF inductee on his first ballot.

3. **Yogi Berra** (Lawrence Peter Berra; 1946-1965) - AL MVP in 1951, 1954, and 1955, had 105+ RBI's in a year five times, had eleven years with 20+ HR's, was integral to the success of the Yankee dynasty of the late forties through the mid-sixties winning ten World Series and was voted into Cooperstown on his first Hall of Fame Ballot.

4. **Mike Piazza** (Michael Joseph Piazza; 1992-2007) - 1993 NL Rookie of the Year Award, won ten Silver Slugger Awards, nine years with 32+ HR's, six years with 105+ RBI's, ten years batting .300+, finished his career with 427 HR's, his lifetime OPS was .922. Duly enshrined in Cooperstown.

5. **Tony Lazzeri** (Anthony Michael Lazzeri; 1926-1939) - Had 102+ RBI's in a year seven times. Won five World Series with the Bronx Bombers and was voted into the Baseball Hall of Fame.

6. **Joe Torre** (Joseph Paul Torre; 1960-1977 and 1977-2010 as a Manager) - NL MVP in 1971, won one Gold Glove Award, was a standout Catcher who finished his illustrious career with 2342 base-hits. Topped 100 RBI's in a year five times, topped .282+ in average eleven times, had 20+ HR's in a year six times. Won 1996 and 1998 AL Manager of the Year Award, won four World Series Titles as a Manager. Was voted into the Baseball Hall of Fame by the Veteren's Committee as a Manager in 2014.

7. **Jason Giambi** (Jason Gilbert Giambi; 1995-2014) - AL MVP in 2000, won two Silver Slugger Awards, had eight years with 32+ HR's, had seven years with 107+ RBI's, finished his career with 440 HR's, 1441 RBI's, and 2010 Hits. His lifetime OPS was .916.

8. **Joey Votto** (Joseph Daniel Votto; 2007-2015) - NL MVP in 2010, won 2011 Gold Glove Award, lifetime OPS of .957 to date...

9. **Rocky Colavito** (Rocco Domenico Colavito; 1955-1968) - Had seven seasons hitting 30+ HR's, six years with 102+ RBI's, finished his career with 374 HR's, lifetime OPS of .848.

10. **Jake Arrieta** (Jacob Joseph Arrieta; 2010-2015) - A standout pitcher for the Chicago Cubs, Arrieta came into his own last year posting a record of 22-6 with a 1.77 ERA and an incredibly low 0.865 WHIP, taking home the NL Cy Young Award.

11. **Tony Conigliaro** (Anthony Richard Conigliaro; 1964-1975) - Had six 20+ HR seasons. Would have achieved greater things had he not been struck by a ball to the head during a game. As was he still finished his career with a lifetime OPS of .803.

12. **Johnny Antonelli** (John August Antonelli; 1948-1961) - Won 20+ games in a year twice and came third in the NL MVP voting in 1954, leading the NL in ERA with a mark of 2.30.

13. **Dave Giusti** (David John Giusti; 1962-1977) - Had 145 Saves in his career (one of the pioneers of the Closer Role). Won the 1971 World Series with the Pittsburgh Pirates.

14. **Lou Piniella** (Louis Victor Piniella; 1964-1984) - "Sweet Lou" took home the AL Rookie of the Year in 1969 with the Kansas City Royals, and when he joined the New York Yankees in 1974 helped turn around the Franchise to their glory years evidenced by his Yanks winning the 1977 and 1978 World Series Titles. His lifetime OPS was .741.

15. (a) **Dom DiMaggio** (Dominic Paul DiMaggio "The Little Professor"; 1940-1953) - A standout defensive Center-Fielder for the Boston Red Sox from 1940-1953. Dom also had six campaigns with 110+ runs scored. He rivaled his older brother Joe on many occasions and many thought Dom's defense was at least on a par with brother Joe.

    (b) **Vince DiMaggio** (Vincent Paul DiMaggio; 1937-1946) - The oldest of the DiMaggio brothers, Vincent was also a Center-Fielder and played all over the National League starting with the Boston Bees, then the Cincinnati Reds, the Pittsburgh Pirates, the Philadelphia Phillies, and finally the New York Giants. In 1941 Vince had a 100 RBI season with the Pittsburgh Pirates.

16. **Carl Furillo** (Carl Anthony Furillo; 1946-1960) - Was a main cog in the offense of the Brooklyn Dodgers of the fifties. His best year came in 1953 when he batted .344 with an OPS of .973. "Skoonj" finished his career with a lifetime batting average of .299 and his lifetime OPS was .813. Furillo was also nicknamed "The Reading Rifle" for his ability to throw guys out at the plate from Right-Field.

17. **Rico Petrocelli** (Americo Peter Petrocelli; 1963-1976) - Became the second Shortstop (after Ernie Banks) to hammer 40+ HR's in a year (with 40 in 1969). Was moved to Third Base in 1971 with the Boston Red Sox to accomodate Luis Aparicio and had a couple of good years there as well. His lifetime OPS was .752.

18. **Sal Maglie** (Salvatore Anthony Maglie; 1945-1958) - A great pitcher for the New York Giants early in Maglie's career. Was a swingman early on and moved into the starting rotation for the Giants in 1951. Played for the Cleveland Indians, the Brooklyn Dodgers, the New York Yankees and the St. Louis Cardinals later in his career. Won the World Series with the New York Giants in 1954.

19. **Ernie Broglio** (Ernest Gilbert Broglio; 1959-1966) - A standout pitcher with the St. Louis Cardinals. Was 21-9 with an ERA of 2.74 in 1960 with the 'Cards. Was dealt to the Cubs (with others) in '64 for Lou Brock (and others).

20. **Anthony Rizzo**. An outstanding power-hitting first baseman for the Chicago Cubs, who regularly contributes 30 home runs and 100 RBI to his team's offense.

21. **Joe Girardi** (Joseph Elliott Girardi; 1989-2003) - Was a Catcher in the bigs playing with the Chicago Cubs, New York Yankees, Colorado Rockies, and

the St. Louis Cardinals. Won three World Series Titles with the Yankees in the nineties. Is currently the Manager of the New York Yankees and he won the World Series as the Yankees skipper in 2009.

22. **Chris Colabello** (Chrisopher Adrian Colabello; 2013-Present) - Had a break-out year with the Toronto Blue Jays in 2015, carrying an OPS of .886 and batting .321 along the way. Looks to be a Major Leaguer for years to come.

Anointments for African American Ownership of Baseball Franchises in North America – New Owners Under Affirmative Action

Henry Aaron – Atlanta Braves

Qualifications; Played in both the Negro Leagues and the Major Leagues for a total just over 20 years. President of Baseball Operations of the Atlanta Braves for 20 years. His lifetime playing statistics in the Majors include a .305 Avg, 755 home runs and one MVP Award. Has one World Series Ring to his name. Was inducted into the Baseball Hall of Fame in Cooperstown, New York.

Other notable statistics; greatest one year home run total – 47. Hammered 44 home runs in a season 4 times.

Frank Robinson and Joe Morgan – Homestead Grays (Greatest Negro League Team of All Time)

Qualifications; Frank Robinson - Played in the Major Leagues for over 20 years. Became the first African American Manager with the Cleveland Indians in 1976. Managed in the Major Leagues for more than 15 years. His lifetime playing statistics in the Majors include 586 home runs and he's the only Major Leaguer to ever win an MVP in both the National and American Leagues. Has two World Series rings to his name. Was inducted into Cooperstown.

Other notable statistics; Won the World Series with both an American League and National League team.

Qualifications; Joe Morgan - Played in the Major Leagues for over 20 years. Has been a Baseball Commentator for 25 years. Played with the expansion Houston Colt 45's, later the Houston Astros before being traded to the Cincinnati Reds (a team Robinson played on likewise). Won the MVP trophy twice (in 1975 and 1976), where he likewise won two World Series rings. Was inducted into Cooperstown.

Other notable statistics; 1976 Stats - .320 avg 27 home runs 111 RBI 60 SB 11 CS.

Willie Mays, Willie McCovey, and Barry Bonds - San Francisco Giants

Qualifications; Willie Mays - Played in both the Negro Leagues and the Major Leagues for over 20 years. Is known as the greatest center fielder of all time. Won 12 Gold Glove Awards and 2 MVP Awards. His lifetime statistics also include 660 home runs, a .302 BA, and one World Series ring. Has a grandstand at the Giants Park in San Francisco named after him. Was inducted into Cooperstown.

Other notable statistics; Hit 50+ home runs in a year twice. Had two 30HR/30SB Campaigns.

Qualifications; Willie McCovey - Played in the Major Leagues for over 20 years. Was known to hit the ball farther than any man in the majors when he played. At San Francisco's home park, they named beyond the right field grandstand "McCovey Cove" (the water in which the balls end up, if hit far enough). His lifetime statistics include 1 MVP Award and 521 lifetime home runs. Was inducted into Cooperstown.

Other notable statistics; MVP Campaign of 1969 - .320 avg 45 HR 126 RBI.

Qualifications; Barry Bonds - Played in the Major Leagues for just over 20 years. Played for the Pittsburgh Pirates and the San Francisco Giants. Won 8 Gold Gloves. Hammered 762 home runs, the all-time mark. Deserved a World Series ring in 2002 when his Giants were winning the 6th game (that would have won them the Series), yet ended up losing games 6 and 7 to the Anaheim Angels. Won 7 MVP Awards in his storied career. Barry Bonds' Godfather is Willie Mays.

Other notable statistics; One 40+ HR / 40+ SB season. Five 30+ HR / 30+ SB seasons. Holds the all-time single season home run mark with 73 HR (in 2001).

Cito Gaston and Dave Winfield - Toronto Blue Jays

Qualifications; Cito Gaston - Played in the Major Leagues for almost ten years. Served as Batting Coach for the Toronto Blue Jays under Bobby Cox in 1983. Was instrumental in orchastrating perhaps the best offense in the Majors in his time there. Was promoted to Manager in 1989 and proceeded to guide the Jays to the playoffs in 4 of his first 7 years as Manager. Returned as the Blue Jays Manager for the 2009 after a 14 year hiatis. Gaston became the first African-American to win the World Series as a Manager (and has won two rings as Manager to date). He will surely be enshrined into Cooperstown once his Managerial Career ends.

Other notable statistics - Helped Dave Winfield enormously when Winfield joined the San Diego Padres in 1974. Gaston was picked as a representative of the Padres in the 1970 All Star game.

Qualifications; Dave Winfield - Played in the Majors for over 20 years. Played a storied career which encompassed tours in 5 cities including Toronto in 1992. 1992 was the year Winfield won his only World Series ring, playing under former teamate Cito Gaston. Winfields' lifetime statistics include 465 home runs and 5 consecutive 100+ RBI campaigns with the New York Yankees. Was inducted into Cooperstown.

Other notable statistics - Finished his playing career with his hometown Minnesota Twins.

Ozzie Smith and Bob Gibson - St. Louis Cardinals

Qualifications; Ozzie Smith - Played in the Majors for around 20 years almost exclusively with the Cardinals. Was ironically traded after his rookie season in San Diego for a fellow shortstop, Gary Templeton (most people thought that San Diego got the better of the deal). As he left the Padres in the trade to St. Louis, he dispelled the sentiment of being the lesser shortstop and went on to win 13 consecutive Gold Glove Awards. He won 1 World Series ring with St. Louis, and was duly inducted into Cooperstown.

Other notable statistics - Stole 30+ bases in 11 separate campaigns.

Qualifications; Bob Gibson - A standout Right-handed pitcher for the 'Cards for the duration of his career. Recorded the lowest Modern Day Yearly ERA with a mark of 1.12 in 1968. Won the 1964 World Series winning 2 and losing one, 1967 World Series MVP winning three games in a seven game set against the Boston Red Sox. Won the 1968 NL MVP Award. Won two Cy Young Awards; in 1968 and 1970. Would have probably taken home a third World Series MVP in 1968 had the 'Cards taken game seven in that World Series.

Other notable statistics - struck out 204+ in a year nine times.

Ken Griffey Jr./Ken Griffey Sr. - Seattle Mariners

Qualifications; Ken Griffey Jr.- Played in the Majors for over 20 years. Won 10 consecutive Gold Glove Awards with the Mariners from 1990-1999. Griffey Jr. won the American League MVP in 1997 and finished his career with 632 home runs. Many would argue that Griffey Jr. was as great a Centerfielder as Willie Mays.

Other noteable statistics; Hit 40+ HRs in seven of eight seasons between 1993-2000.

Qualifications; Ken Griffey Sr. - Played in the Majors for about twenty years and won two World Series with the Cincinnati Reds in 1975 and 1976. Won the NL Batting Title in 1977. Played on the same team as his son with the Seattle Mariners in 1990/1991, the first time Father and Son were teammates in the 'bigs.

Other noteable statistics; Had seven seasons batting .300+. Lifetime OPS was .790.

2
All-Time Best Players by Position

50 Greatest Managers of All-Time

1. **Casey Stengel (1905-1842 Record)** - 10 AL Pennants, 7 World Series Titles, HOF
2. **Joe Torre (2329-1997 Record) -** 1996 and 1998 A,L Manager of the Year, 6 AL Pennants, 4 World Series Titles, HOF
3. **Cum Posey** - Manager of the famed "Homestead Grays" of the Negro Leagues, HOF
4. **Billy Martin (1253-1013 Record)** - 2 AL Pennants, 1 World Series Title, HOF
5. **Sparky Anderson (2194-1834 Record) -** 1984 and 1987 AL Manager of the Year, 4 NL Pennants, 1 AL Pennant, 3 World Series Titles, HOF
6. **Dick Williams (1571-1451 Record) -** 3 AL Pennants, 1 NL Pennant, 2 World Series Titles, HOF
7. Cito Gaston (894-837 Record) - 2 AL Pennants, 2 World Series Titles
8. **Tony La Russa (2728-2365 Record)** - 1983, 1988, and 1992 AL Manager of the Year, 2002 NL Manager of the Year, 3 AL Pennants, 3 NL Pennants, 3 World Series Titles, HOF
9. **Connie Mack (3731-3948 Record)** - 9 AL Pennants, 5 World Series Titles, HOF
10. **Walter Alston (2040-1613 Record**) - 7 NL Pennants, 4 World Series Titles, HOF
11. **John McGraw (2763-1948 Record)** - 10 NL Pennants, 3 World Series Titles, HOF
12. **Bobby Cox (2504-2001 Record) -** 1985 AL Manager of the Year, 1991, 2004, and 2005 NL Manager of the Year, 5 NL Pennants, 1 World Series Title, HOF
13. **Tommy Lasorda (1599-1439 Record)** - 1983 and 1988 NL Manager of the Year, 4 NL Pennants, 2 World Series Titles, HOF
14. **Earl Weaver (1480-1060 Record)** - 4 AL Pennants, 1 World Series Title, HOF

15. **Bruce Bochy (1702-1682 Record)** - 1996 NL Manager of the Year, 4 NL Pennants, 3 World Series Titles to date*

16. **Leo Durocher (2008-1709 Record)** - 3 NL Pennants, 1 World Series Title, HOF

17. **Danny Murtaugh (1115-950 Record)** - 2 NL Pennants, 2 World Series Titles

18. **Dick Howser (507-425 Record)** - 1 AL Pennant, 1 World Series Title

19. **Terry Francona (1287-1142 Record)** - 2013 AL Manager of the Year, 2 AL Pennants, 2 World Series Titles to date*

20. **Tom Kelly (1140-1244 Record)** - 1991 AL Manager of the Year, 2 AL Pennants, 2 World Series Titles

21. **Whitey Herzog (1281-1125 Record)** - 1985 NL Manager of the Year, 3 NL Pennants, 1 World Series Title, HOF

22. **Johnny Keane (398-350 Record)** - 1 NL Pennant, 1 World Series Title

23. **Cap Anson (1295-947 Record)** - 5 Pennants (with the Chicago White Sox - later the Chicago Colts)

24. **Felipe Alou (1033-1021 Record)** - 1994 NL Manager of the Year

25. **Davey Johnson (1372-1071 Record)** - 1997 AL Manager of the Year, 2012 NL Manager of the Year, 1 NL Pennant, 1 World Series Title

26. **Buck Showalter (1340-1242 Record)** - 1994, 2004, and 2014 AL Manager of the Year to date*

27. **Mike Scoscia (1416-1176 Record)** - 2002 and 2009 AL Manager of the Year, 1 AL Pennant, 1 World Series Title to date*

28. **Charlie Manuel (1000-826 Record)** - 2 NL Pennants, 1 World Series Title

29. **Dusty Baker (1671-1504 Record)** - 1993, 1997, and 2000 NL Manager of the Year, 1 NL Pennant

30. **Chuck Tanner (1352-1381 Record)** - 1 NL Pennant, 1 World Series Title

31. **Joe Girardi (813-645 Record)** - 1996 NL Manager of the Year, 1 AL Pennant, 1 World Series Title to date*

32. **Ned Yost (925-971 Record)** - 2 AL Pennants, 1 World Series Title to date*

33. **Jim Leyland (1769-1728 Record)** - 1990 and 1992 NL Manager of the Year, 2006 AL Manager of the Year, 1 NL Pennant, 1 World Series Title, 2 AL Pennants

34. **Jack McKeon (1051-990 Record)** - 1999 and 2003 NL Manager of the Year, 1 NL Pennant, 1 World Series Title

35. **Ralph Houk (1619-1531 Record)** - 3 AL Pennants, 2 World Series Titles

36. **Joe Maddon (979-851 Record)** - 1 AL Pennant

37. **Lou Piniella (1835-1713 Record)** - 1995 and 2001 AL Manager of the Year, 2008 NL Manager of the Year, 1 NL Pennant, 1 World Series Title

38. **Joe Altobelli (437-407 Record)** - 1 AL Pennant, 1 World Series Title
39. **Ron Washington (664-611 Record)** - 2 AL Pennants
40. **Gene Mauch (1902-2037 Record)**
41. **Frank Robinson (1065-1176 Record)** - 1989 AL Manager of the Year, HOF
42. **Gil Hodges (660-753 Record)** - 1 NL Pennant, 1 World Series Title
43. **Jimmy Collins (455-376 Record)** - 2 AL Pennants, 1 World Series Title, HOF
44. **Mike Hargrove (1188-1173 Record)** - 2 AL Pennants
45. **Birdie Tebbetts (748-705 Record)**
46. **John Farrell (400-410 Record)** - 1 AL Pennant, 1 World Series Title to date*
47. **George Stallings (879-898 Record)** - 1 NL Pennant, 1 World Series Title
48. **Danny Ozark (618-542 Record)**
49. **Don Zimmer (885-858 Record)** - 1989 NL Manager of the Year
50. **Dallas Green (454-478)**

Honorable Mention: Bill Virdon, Jim Frey (1 AL Pennant), Pete Rose, John Gibbons, Hal Lanier (1986 NL Manager of the Year), Jimy Williams (1999 AL Manager of the Year), Don Baylor (1995 NL Manager of the Year), and Art Howe.

50 Greatest Catchers of All Time

No.	Catcher	Career Highlights
1	Josh Gibson	803 HR's in Negro-League play, HOF
2	Roy Campanella	NL MVP in 1951, 1953, and 1955, 242 HR's, 438 Extra-Base Hits, 856 RBI's, .860 OPS, 1 World Series Title, HOF
3	Ivan Rodriguez	AL MVP in 1999, 2003 NLCS MVP, 13 Gold Glove Awards (10 consecutive; 1992-2001), 7 Silver Slugger Awards, 311 HR's, 934 Extra-Base Hits, 1332 RBI's, 1354 Runs, 2844 Hits, .296 Avg, .798 OPS, 1 World Series Title
4	Johnny Bench	1968 NL Rookie of the Year, NL MVP in 1970 and 1972, 1976 World Series MVP, 10 consecutive Gold Glove Awards (1968-1977), 389 HR's, 794 Extra-Base Hits, 1376 RBI's, 1091 Runs, 2048 Hits, .817 OPS, 2 World Series Titles, HOF
5	Yogi Berra	AL MVP in 1951, 1954, and 1955, 358 HR's, 728 Extra-Base Hits, 1430 RBI's, 1175 Runs, 2150 Hits, .830 OPS, 10 World Series Titles, HOF
6	Mickey Cochrane	AL MVP in 1928 and 1934, 516 Extra-Base Hits, 830 RBI's, 1041 Runs, 1652 Hits, .320 Avg, .897 OPS, 3 World Series Titles, HOF
7	Mike Piazza	1993 NL Rookie of the Year, 10 Silver Slugger Awards, 427 HR's, 779 Extra-Base Hits, 1335 RBI's, 1048 Runs, 2127 Hits, .308 Avg, .922 OPS, HOF
8	Carlton Fisk	1972 AL Rookie of the Year, 1 Gold Glove Award, 3 Silver Slugger Awards, 376 HR's, 844 Extra-Base Hits, 1330 RBI's, 1276 Runs, 2356 Hits, .797 OPS, HOF
9	Thurman Munson	1970 AL Rookie of the Year, AL MVP in 1976, 3 Gold Glove Awards, 374 Extra-Base Hits, 701 RBI's, 696 Runs, 1558 Hits, .756 OPS, 2 World Series Titles

No.	Catcher	Career Highlights
10	Gary Carter	3 Gold Glove Awards, 5 Silver Slugger Awards, 324 HR's, 726 Extra-Base Hits, 1225 RBI's, 1025 Runs, 2092 Hits, .773 OPS, 1 World Series Title, HOF
11	Buster Posey	2010 NL Rookie of the Year, NL MVP in 2012, 3 Silver Slugger Awards, .310 Avg, .859 OPS, 3 World Series Titles to date*
12	Jorge Posada	5 Silver Slugger Awards, 275 HR's, 664 Extra-Base Hits, 1065 RBI's, 900 Runs, 1664 Hits, .848 OPS, 4 World Series Titles
13	Bill Dickey	617 Extra-Base Hits, 1209 RBI's, 930 Runs, 1969 Hits, .313 Avg, .868 OPS, 7 World Series Titles, HOF
14	Yadier Molina	8 consecutive Gold Glove Awards (2008-2015), 1 Silver Slugger Award, .733 OPS, 2 World Series Titles to date*
15	Elston Howard	AL MVP in 1963, 2 Gold Glove Awards, 167 HR's, 435 Extra-Base Hits, 762 RBI's, .749 OPS, 4 World Series Titles
16	Lance Parrish	3 Gold Glove Awards, 6 Silver Slugger Awards, 324 HR's, 656 Extra-Base Hits, 1070 RBI's, 856 Runs, 1782 Hits, .753 OPS, 1 World Series Title
17	Brian McCann	6 Silver Slugger Awards, 225 HR's, 486 Extra-Base Hits, 830 RBI's, 1293 Hits, .803 OPS to date*
18	Joe Torre	NL MVP in 1971, 1 Gold Glove Award, 252 HR's, 655 Extra-Base Hits, 1185 RBI's, 996 Runs, 2342 Hits, .817 OPS, HOF (as Manager)
19	Russell Martin	1 Gold Glove Award, 1 Silver Slugger Award, .757 OPS to date*
20	Javier Lopez	1 Silver Slugger Award, 1996 NLCS MVP, 260 HR's, 546 Extra-Base Hits, 864 RBI's, 674 Runs, 1527 Hits, .828 OPS, 1 World Series Title
21	Joe Mauer	AL MVP in 2009, 3 Gold Glove Awards, 5 Silver Slugger Awards, 486 Extra-Base Hits, 755 RBI's, 817 Runs, 1697 Hits, .313 Avg, .845 OPS to date*
22	Bob Boone	7 Gold Glove Awards, 434 Extra-Base Hits, 826 RBI's, 1838 Hits, .661 OPS, 1 World Series Title
23	Bill Freehan	5 consecutive Gold Glove Awards (1965-1969), 200 HR's, 476 Extra-Base Hits, 758 RBI's, 706 Runs, 1591 Hits, .752 OPS, 1 World Series Title
24	Salvador Perez	2015 World Series MVP, 3 consecutive Gold Glove Awards (2013-2015), .737 OPS, 1 World Series Title to date*
25	Manny Sanguillen	1500 Hits, .296 Avg, .724 OPS, 2 World Series Titles
26	Tony Pena	4 Gold Glove Awards, 432 Extra-Base Hits, 708 RBI's, 667 Runs, 1687 Hits, .673 OPS
27	Mickey Tettleton	3 Silver Slugger Awards, 245 HR's, 471 Extra-Base Hits, 732 RBI's, 711 Runs, .818 OPS
28	Benito Santiago	1987 NL Rookie of the Year, 2002 NLCS MVP, 3 Gold Glove Awards, 4 Silver Slugger Awards, 217 HR's, 581 Extra-Base Hits, 920 RBI's, 755 Runs, 1830 Hits, .722 OPS
29	Charles Johnson	4 consecutive Gold Glove Awards (1995-1998), 167 HR's, 382 Extra-Base Hits, .762 OPS, 1 World Series Title

(Continued)

No.	Catcher	Career Highlights
30	Todd Hundley	202 HR's, 376 Extra-Base Hits, 599 RBI's, .763 OPS
31	Ted Simmons	248 HR's, 678 Extra-Base Hits, 1389 RBI's, 1074 Runs, 2472 Hits, .785 OPS
32	Gene Tenace	1972 World Series MVP, 201 HR's, 400 Extra-Base Hits, .817 OPS, 4 World Series Titles
33	Jason Varitek	1 Gold Glove Award, 1 Silver Slugger Award, 193 HR's, 513 Extra-Base Hits, 757 RBI's, .776 OPS, 2 World Series Titles
34	Ray Fosse	2 Gold Glove Awards, .673 OPS, 2 World Series Titles
35	Jim Sundberg	6 consecutive Gold Glove Awards (1976-1981), 1493 Hits, .674 OPS, 1 World Series Title
36	Terry Steinbach	162 HR's, 456 Extra-Base Hits, 745 RBI's, 638 Runs, 1453 Hits, .746 OPS, 1 World Series Title
37	Jason Kendall	504 Extra-Base Hits, 744 RBI's, 1030 Runs, 2195 Hits, 189 SB's, .744 OPS
38	Jonathan Lucroy	770 OPS to date*
39	Brian Downing	275 HR's, 663 Extra-Base Hits, 1073 RBI's, 1188 Runs, 2099 Hits, .796 OPS
40	Darrell Porter	1982 NLCS MVP, 1982 World Series MVP, 188 HR's, 473 Extra-Base Hits, .763 OPS, 1 World Series Title
41	Tim McCarver	396 Extra-Base Hits, 1501 Hits, .725 OPS, 2 World Series Titles
42	Rick Dempsey	1983 World Series MVP, .666 OPS, 2 World Series Titles
43	Pat Borders	1992 World Series MVP, .663 OPS, 2 World Series Titles
44	Carlos Santana	.798 OPS to date*
45	Mike Scoscia	.700 OPS, 2 World Series Titles
46	Mike Matheny	4 Gold Glove Awards, .637 OPS
47	Sandy Alomar	1990 AL Rookie of the Year, 1 Gold Glove Award, .716 OPS
48	Darrin Fletcher	.740 OPS
49	Bengie Molina	2 Gold Glove Awards, 367 Extra-Base Hits, 711 RBI's, .718 OPS, 1 World Series Title
50	Joe Girardi	.666 OPS, 3 World Series Titles

Buck Leonard

10 Greatest Switch-Hitting Catchers

1. Ted Simmons
2. Mickey Tettleton
3. Todd Hundley
4. Jorge Posada
5. Jason Varitek

6. Butch Wynegar
7. Carlos Santana*
8. Dioner Navarro
9. Alan Ashby
10. Buck Rodgers

50 Greatest First Basemen of All Time

No.	First Baseman	Career Highlights
1	Buck Leonard	Negro Leagues Great, HOF
2	Lou Gehrig	AL MVP in 1927 and 1936, 493 HR's, 1190 Extra-Base Hits, 1995 RBI's, 1888 Runs, 2721 Hits, .340 Avg, 1.080 OPS, 2130 consecutive games played, second longest streak in history, 6 World Series Titles, HOF
3	Jimmie Foxx	AL MVP in 1932, 1933, and 1938, 534 HR's, 1117 Extra-Base Hits, 1922 RBI's, 1751 Runs, 2646 Hits, .325 Avg, 1.038 OPS, 2 World Series Titles, HOF
4	Albert Pujols	2001 NL Rookie of the Year, NL MVP in 2005, 2008 and 2009, NLCS MVP in 2004, 2 Gold Gloves Awards, 5 Silver Slugger Awards, 560 HR's, 1159 Extra-Base Hits, 1698 RBI's, 1599 Runs, 2666 Hits, .312 Avg, .977 OPS, 2 World Series Titles to date*
5	Henry Greenberg	AL MVP in 1935 and 1940, 331 HR's, 781 Extra-Base Hits, 1274 RBI's, 1046 Runs, 1628 Hits, .313 Avg, 1.017 OPS, 2 World Series Titles, HOF
6	Eddie Murray	1977 AL Rookie of the Year, 3 Gold Glove Awards, 3 Silver Slugger Awards, 504 HRs, 1099 Extra-Base Hits, 1917 RBI's, 1627 Runs, 3255 Hits, .836 OPS, 1 World Series Title, HOF
7	George Sisler	102 HR's, 689 Extra-Base Hits, 1178 RBI's, 1284 Runs, 2812 Hits, .340 Avg, 375 SB's, .847 OPS, HOF
8	Willie Stargell	NL MVP in 1979, World Series MVP in 1979, 475 HR's, 953 Extra-Base Hits, 1540 RBI's, 1194 Runs, 2232 Hits, .889 OPS, 2 World Series Titles (1 in LF, and 1 at 1B), HOF
9	Willie McCovey	1959 NL Rookie of the Year, NL MVP in 1969, 521 HR's, 920 Extra-Base Hits, 1555 RBI's, 1229 Runs, .889 OPS, HOF
10	Stan Musial	NL MVP in 1943, 1946, and 1948, 475 HR's, 1377 Extra-Base Hits, 1951 RBI's, 1949 Runs, 3630 Hits, .331 Avg, .976 OPS, 3 WS Titles, HOF

(Continued)

No.	First Baseman	Career Highlights
11	Rod Carew	1967 AL Rookie of the Year (at 2nd), AL MVP in 1977 (at 1st), 649 Extra-Base Hits, 1015 RBI's, 1424 Runs, 3053 Hits, .328 Avg, 353 SB's, .822 OPS, HOF
12	Miguel Cabrera	AL Triple Crown in 2012, AL MVP in 2012 and 2013, 6 Silver Slugger Awards, 408 HR's, 916 Extra-Base Hits, 1445 RBI's, 1229 Runs, 2331 Hits, .321 Avg, .961 OPS, 1 World Series Title to date*
13	Mark McGwire	1987 AL Rookie of the Year, 1 Gold Glove Award, 3 Silver Slugger Awards, 583 HR's, 841 Extra-Base Hits, 1414 RBI's, 1167 Runs, 1626 Hits, .982 OPS, 1 World Series Title
14	Frank Thomas	AL MVP in 1993 and 1994, 4 Silver Slugger Awards, 521 HR's, 1028 Extra-Base Hits, 1704 RBI's, 1494 Runs, 2468 Hits, .301 Avg, .974 OPS, HOF
15	Todd Helton	3 Gold Glove Awards, 4 Silver Slugger Awards, 369 HR's, 998 Extra-Base Hits, 1406 RBI's, 1401 Runs, 2519 Hits, .316 Avg, .953 OPS
16	Carlos Delgado	3 Silver Slugger Awards , 473 HR's, 974 Extra-Base Hits, 1512 RBI's, 1241 Runs, 2038 Hits, .929 OPS
17	Orlando Cepeda	1958 NL Rookie of the Year, NL MVP in 1967, 379 HR's, 823 Extra-Base Hits, 1365 RBI's, 1131 Runs, 2351 Hits, .297 Avg, .849 OPS, 1 World Series title, HOF
18	Jim Thome	612 HR's, 1089 Extra-Base Hits, 1699 RBI's, 1583 Runs, 2328 Hits, .956 OPS
19	Jeff Bagwell	1991 NL Rookie of the Year, NL MVP in 1994, 3 Silver Slugger Awards, 449 HR's, 969 Extra-Base Hits, 1529 RBI's, 1517 Runs, 2314 Hits, .297 Avg, .948 OPS
20	Bill Terry	154 HR's, 639 Extra-Base Hits, 1078 RBI's, 1120 Runs, 2193 Hits, .341 Avg, .899 OPS, 1 World Series Title, HOF
21	Don Mattingly	AL MVP in 1985, 9 Gold Glove Awards, 3 Silver Slugger Awards, 222 HR's, 684 Extra-Base Hits, 1099 RBI's, 1007 Runs, 2153 Hits, .307 Avg, .830 OPS
22	Will Clark	1989 NLCS MVP, 1 Gold Glove Award, 2 Silver Slugger Awards, 284 HR's, 767 Extra-Base Hits, 1205 RBI's, 1186 Runs, 2176 Hits, .303 Avg, .880 OPS
23	Rafael Palmeiro	3 Gold Glove Awards, 2 Silver Slugger Awards, 569 HR's, 1192 Extra-Base Hits, 1835 RBI's, 1663 Runs, 3020 Hits, .885 OPS
24	Jason Giambi	AL MVP in 2000, 2 Silver Slugger Awards, 440 HR's, 854 Extra-Base Hits, 1441 RBI's, 1227 Runs, 2010 Hits, .916 OPS
25	Keith Hernandez	NL MVP in 1979, 11 Gold Glove Awards, 2 Silver Slugger Awards, 648 Extra-Base Hits, 1071 RBI's, 1124 Runs, 2182 Hits, .821 OPS, 2 World Series Titles
26	Mark Teixeira	5 Gold Glove Awards, 3 Silver Slugger Awards, 394 HR's, 804 Extra-Base Hits, 1254 RBI's, 1056 Runs, 1783 Hits, .882 OPS, 1 World Series Title to date*

No.	First Baseman	Career Highlights
27	Cap Anson	97 HR's, 821 Extra-Base Hits, 2075 RBI's, 1999 Runs, 3435 Hits, .334 Avg, 277 SB's, .841 OPS, 1 World Series Title, HOF
28	John Olerud	3 Gold Glove Awards, 255 HR's, 768 Extra-Base Hits, 1230 RBI's, 1139 Runs, 2239 Hits, .863 OPS, 2 World Series Titles
29	Gil Hodges	3 Gold Glove Awards, 370 HR's, 713 Extra-Base Hits, 1274 RBI's, 1105 Runs, 1921 Hits, .846 OPS, 2 World Series Titles
30	Jackie Robinson	1947 NL Rookie of the Year (1B), NL MVP in 1949 (2B), 137 HR's, 464 Extra-Base Hits, .311 Avg, 197 SB's, .883 OPS, 1 World Series Title, HOF
31	Ernie Banks	NL MVP in 1958 (SS) and 1959 (SS), 512 HR's, 1009 Extra-Base Hits, 1636 RBI's, 1305 Runs, 2583 Hits, .830 OPS, HOF
32	Steve Garvey	NL MVP in 1974, 1978 NLCS MVP, 4 Gold Glove Awards, 272 HR's, 755 Extra-Base Hits, 1308 RBI's, 1143 Runs, 2599 Hits, .775 OPS, Holds the NL Mark For Most Consecutive Games Played With a Streak of 1207 Games Played, 1 World Series Title
33	Tony Perez	379 HR's, 963 Extra-Base Hits, 1652 RBI's, 1272 Runs, 2732 Hits, .804 OPS, 2 World Series Titles, HOF
34	Dick Allen	1964 NL Rookie of the Year, AL MVP in 1972, 351 HR's, 750 Extra-Base Hits, 1119 RBI's, 1099 Runs, .912 OPS
35	Joey Votto	NL MVP in 2010, 1 Gold Glove Award, .957 OPS to date*
36	Fred McGriff	3 Silver Slugger Awards, 493 HR's, 958 Extra-Base Hits, 1550 RBI's, 1349 Runs, 2490 Hits, .886 OPS, 1 World Series Titles
37	Tino Martinez	1 Silver Slugger Award, 339 HR's, 725 Extra-Base Hits, 1271 RBI's, 1009 Runs, .815 OPS, 4 World Series Titles
38	Mo Vaughn	AL MVP in 1995, 1 Silver Slugger Award, 328 HR's, 608 Extra-Base Hits, 1064 RBI's, 861 Runs, .906 OPS
39	Paul Konerko	439 HR's, 857 Extra-Base Hits, 1412 RBI's, 1162 Runs, 2340 Hits, .841 OPS and Cecil Fielder - 2 Silver Slugger Awards, 319 HR's , 526 Extra-Base Hits, 1008 RBI's, 744 Runs, .827 OPS
40	Andres Galarraga	2 Gold Glove Awards, 2 Silver Slugger Awards, 399 HR's, 875 Extra-Base Hits, 1425 RBI's, 1195 Runs, 2333 Hits, 128 SB's, .846 OPS
41	Prince Fielder	3 Silver Slugger Awards, 311 HR's, 626 Extra-Base Hits, 984 RBI's, 833 Runs, 1576 Hits, .903 OPS to date*
42	George Scott	8 Gold Glove Awards, 271 HR's, 637 Extra-Base Hits, 1051 RBI's, 957 Runs, 1992 Hits, .767 OPS
43	Ryan Howard	2005 NL Rookie of the Year, NL MVP in 2006, NLCS MVP in 2009, 1 Silver Slugger Award, 357 HR's, 645 Extra-Base Hits, 1135 RBI's, 813 Runs, 1410 Hits, .868 OPS, 1 World Series Award to date*
44	Paul Goldschmidt	2 Gold Glove Awards, 2 Silver Slugger Awards, .930 OPS to date*

No.	First Baseman	Career Highlights
45	Mark Grace	4 Gold Glove Awards, 173 HR's, 729 Extra-Base Hits, 1146 RBI's, 1179 Runs, 2445 Hits, .303 Avg, .825 OPS
46	Justin Morneau	AL MVP in 2006, 2 Silver Slugger Awards, .832 OPS to date*
47	Adrian Gonzalez	4 Gold Glove Awards, 2 Silver Slugger Awards, 290 HR's, 686 Extra-Base Hits, 1056 RBI's, 899 Runs, .860 OPS to date*
48	Norm Cash	377 HR's, 659 Extra-Base Hits, 1104 RBI's, 1045 Runs, 1820 Hits, .862 OPS, 1 World Series Title
49	J. T. Snow	6 Gold Glove Awards, .784 OPS
50	Jose Abreu	Jose Abreu - 2014 AL Rookie of the Year, 1 Silver Slugger Award, .904 OPS to date*

Honorable Mention: Frank Chance, Jim Bottomley, Joe Adcock, Rudy York, Pete Rose, Boog Powell, Chris Chambliss, Cecil Cooper, Kent Hrbek, Cecil Fielder, Mike Sweeney, Darin Erstad, Michael Young, Edwin Encarnacion*, Anthony Rizzo*, and Eric Hosmer*

50 Greatest Second Basemen of All Time

No.	Second Baseman	Career Highlights
1	Jackie Robinson	1947 NL Rookie of the Year (1B), NL MVP in 1949 (2B), 137 HR's, 464 Extra-Base Hits, .311 Avg, 197 SB's, .883 OPS, 1 World Series Title, HOF
2	Rogers Hornsby	NL Triple Crown in 1922, NL MVP in 1925 and 1929, 2930 Hits, 301 HR's, 1011 Extra-Base Hits, 1584 RBI's, 1579 Runs, .358 Avg, 1.010 OPS, 3 Yrs with .400+, 7 Yrs with 203+ Hits, 1 World Series Title, HOF
3	Joe Morgan	NL MVP in 1975 and 1976, 5 Gold Glove Awards, 1 Silver Slugger Awards, 268 HR's, 813 Extra-Base Hits, 1133 RBI's, 1650 Runs, 2517 Hits, 1865 BB, .818 OPS, 689 SB's, 2 World Series Titles, HOF
4	Roberto Alomar	1992 ALCS MVP, 10 Gold Glove Awards, 4 Silver Slugger Awards, 210 HR's, 794 Extra-Base Hits, 1134 RBI's, 1508 Runs, 2724 Hits, .814 OPS, 474 SB's, 2 World Series Titles, HOF
5	Ryne Sandberg	NL MVP in 1984, 9 Gold Glove Awards, 7 Silver Slugger Awards, 282 HR's, 761 Extra-Base Hits, 1061 RBI's, 1318 Runs, 2386 Hits, .795 OPS, 344 SB's, HOF
6	Eddie Collins	AL MVP in 1914, 672 Extra-Base Hits, 1300 RBI's, 1821 Runs, 3315 Hits, .853 OPS, 741 SB's, 4 World Series Titles, HOF
7	Charlie Gehringer	AL MVP in 1937, 904 Extra-Base Hits, 1427 RBI's, 1775 Runs, 2839 Hits, .884 OPS, 1 World Series Title, HOF

(Continued)

No.	Second Baseman	Career Highlights
8	Alfonso Soriano	3 Silver Slugger Awards (a fourth in OF), 412 HR's, 1024 Extra-Base Hits, 1159 RBI's, 1152 Runs, .819 OPS, 289 SB's
9	Nap Lajoie	Led Majors with a .426 Avg in 1901 (first year of the American League), 902 Extra-Base Hits, 1599 RBI's, 1504 Runs, 3243 Hits, .847 OPS, 380 SB's, HOF
10	Robinson Cano	2 Gold Gloves, 5 Silver Slugger Awards, 239 HR's, 716 Extra-Base Hits, 983 RBI's, 958 Runs, .850 OPS, 1 World Series Title to date*
11	Jeff Kent	NL MVP in 2000, 4 Silver Slugger Awards, 377 HR's, 984 Extra-Base Hits, 1518 RBI's, 1320 Runs, 2461 Hits, .855 OPS
12	Craig Biggio	4 Gold Glove Awards, 5 Silver Slugger Awards, 291 HR's, 1014 Extra-Base Hits, 1175 RBI's, 1844 Runs, 3060 Hits, .796 OPS, 414 SB's, HOF
13	Chuck Knoblauch	1991 AL Rookie of the Year, 1 Gold Glove Award, 2 Silver Slugger Awards, 1839 Hits, .783 OPS, 407 SB's, 4 World Series Titles
14	Paul Molitor	1993 World Series MVP Award, 4 Silver Slugger Awards, 234 HR's, 953 Extra-Base Hits, 1307 RBI's, 1782 Runs, 3319 Hits, .306 Avg, .817 OPS, 504 SB's, 1 World Series Title (DH), HOF
15	Frankie Frisch	NL MVP in 1931, 105 HR's, 709 Extra-Base Hits, 1244 RBI's, 1532 Runs, 2880 Hits, .316 Avg, 419 SB's, .801 OPS, 4 World Series Titles, HOF
16	Frank White	8 Gold Glove Awards, 1 Silver Slugger Awards, ALCS MVP in 1980, 625 Extra-Base Hits, 2006 Hits, .675 OPS, 1 World Series Title
17	Willie Randolph	1 Silver Slugger Award, HAD MORE BB THAN SO IN EVERY YEAR PLAYED, .724 OPS, 1 World Series Title
18	Lou Whitaker	1978 AL Rookie of the Year, 3 Gold Gloves Awards, 4 Silver Slugger Awards, 244 HR's, 729 Extra-Base Hits, 1084 RBI's, 1386 Runs, 2369 Hits, .789 OPS, 1 World Series Title
19	Nellie Fox	AL MVP in 1959, 3 Gold Glove Awards, HAD MORE BB THAN SO IN EVERY YEAR PLAYED, 502 Extra-Base Hits, 2663 Hits, .710 OPS, HOF
20	Rod Carew	1967 AL Rookie of the Year (at 2nd), AL MVP in 1977 (at 1st), 649 Extra-Base Hits, 1015 RBI's, 1424 Runs, 3053 Hits, .328 Avg, 353 SB's, 822 OPS, HOF
21	Bill Mazeroski	8 Gold Glove Awards, 494 Extra-Base Hits, 2016 Hits, .667 OPS, 2 World Series Titles, HOF
22	Bobby Grich	4 Gold Glove Awards, 1 Silver Slugger Award, 224 HR's, 595 Extra-Base Hits, 864 RBI's, 1033 Runs, .794 OPS
23	Dustin Pedroia	2007 AL Rookie of the Year, AL MVP in 2008, 4 Gold Glove Awards, 1 Silver Slugger Award, 471 Extra-Base Hits, 769 Runs, 1482 Hits, .809 OPS, 2 World Series Titles to date*
24	Davey Lopes	1 Gold Glove Award, 1024 Runs, .737 OPS, 557 SB's, 1 World Series Title
25	Bret Boone	4 Gold Glove Awards, 2 Silver Slugger Awards, 252 HR's, 646 Extra-Base Hits, 1021 RBI's, 927 Runs, 1775 Hits, .767 OPS

No.	Second Baseman	Career Highlights
26	Julio Franco	4 Silver Slugger Awards (a fifth at DH), 173 HR's, 634 Extra-Base Hits, 1194 RBI's, 1285 RBI's, 2586 Hits, .782 OPS
27	Chase Utley	4 Silver Slugger Awards, 236 HR's, 641 Extra-Base Hits, 925 RBI's, 963 Runs, 1648 Hits, .843 OPS, 1 World Series Title to date*
28	Brandon Phillips	4 Gold Glove Awards, 1 Silver Slugger Award, 187 HR's, 524 Extra-Base Hits, 831 RBI's, 853 Runs, 1718 Hits, 186 SB's, .742 OPS to date*
29	Delino DeShields	1548 Hits, .729 OPS, 463 SB's
30	Tony Lazzeri	178 HR's, 627 Extra-Base Hits, 1194 RBI's, 986 Runs, 1840 Hits, 148 SB's, .846 OPS, 5 World Series Titles, HOF
31	Michael Young	185 HR's, 686 Extra-Base Hits, 1030 RBI's, 1137 Runs, 2375 Hits, .300 Avg, .787 OPS
32	Red Schoendienst	589 Extra-Base Hits, 1223 Runs, 2449 Hits, .724 OPS, 2 World Series Titles, HOF
33	Jose Vidro	1 Silver Slugger Award, 481 Extra-Base Hits, 1524 Hits, .298 Avg, .804 OPS
34	Jim "Junior" Gilliam	1953 NL Rookie of the Year (HAD MORE BB THAN SO IN EVERY YEAR PLAYED), 440 Extra-Base Hits, 1163 Runs, 1889 Hits, 203 SB's, .715 OPS, 4 World Series Titles
35	Pete Rose	1963 NL Rookie of the Year (2B), 1975 World Series MVP (3B), NL MVP in 1973 (LF), 2 Gold Gloves Awards, (LF), 1 Silver Slugger Award (1B), 1041 Extra-Base Hits, 2165 Runs, 4256 Hits (ALL-TIME RECORD), .784 OPS, 2 World Series Titles at 3B, 1 World Series Title at 1B
36	Bobby Doerr	223 HR's, 693 Extra-Base Hits, 1247 RBI's, 1094 Runs, 2042 Hits, .823 OPS, HOF
37	Steve Sax	1982 NL Rookie of the Year, 1 Silver Slugger Award, 379 Extra-Base Hits, 913 Runs, 1949 Hits, 444 SB's, .692 OPS, 2 World Series Titles
38	Jay Bell	1 Gold Glove Award, 1 Silver Slugger Award, 195 HR's, 656 Extra-Base Hits, 1963 Hits, .759 OPS
39	Juan Samuel	1 Silver Slugger Award, 161 HR's, 550 Extra-Base Hits, 703 RBI's, 873 Runs, 1578 Hits, 396 SB's, .735 OPS
40	Tony Phillips	160 HR's, 570 Extra-Base Hits, 819 RBI's, 1300 Runs, 2023 Hits, 177 SB's, .763 OPS
41	Ian Kinsler	184 HR's, 542 Extra-Base Hits, 704 RBI's, 942 Runs, 1518 Hits, 197 SB's .791 OPS to date*
42	Davey Johnson	3 Gold Glove Awards, .744 OPS, 2 World Series Titles
43	Jose Altuve	1 Gold Glove Award, 2 Silver Slugger Awards, 169 SB's, .305 Avg, .758 OPS to date*
44	Bobby Richardson	1960 World Series MVP, 5 consecutive Gold Glove Awards, 1432 Hits, .634 OPS, 3 World Series Titles

(Continued)

No.	Second Baseman	Career Highlights
45	Mark Grudzielanek	1 Gold Glove Award, 517 Extra-Base Hits, 946 Runs, 2040 Hits, .725 OPS
46	Manny Trillo	1980 NLCS MVP, 3 Gold Glove Awards, 2 Silver Slugger Awards, 1562 Hits, .660 OPS, 1 World Series Title
47	Dee Gordon	1 Gold Glove Award, 1 Silver Slugger Award, 188 SB's, .698 OPS to date*
48	Harold Reynolds	3 Gold Glove Awards, .668 OPS, 250 SB's
49	Pokey Reese	2 Gold Glove Awards, .659 OPS, 1 World Series Title
50	Eddie Stanky	.758 OPS - Brooklyn Dodgers' 2B from 1944-1947

Honorable Mention: Rennie Stennett, Dave Cash, Phil Garner, Jim Gantner, Damaso Garcia, Tony Bernazard, Mariano Duncan, Billy Doran, Manny Lee, Jose Lind, Brian Dozier*, and Ryan Goins*

50 Greatest Third Basemen of All Time

No.	Third Baseman	Career Highlights
1	Mike Schmidt	NL MVP in 1980,1981, and 1986, 10 Gold Glove Awards, 6 Silver Slugger Awards, 548 HR's, 1015 Extra-Base Hits, 1595 RBI's, 1506 Runs, 2234 Hits, 174 SB's, .908 OPS, 1 World Series Title, HOF
2	George Brett	AL MVP in 1980, 1 Gold Glove Award, 3 Silver Slugger Award, 317 HR's, 1119 Extra-Base Hits, 1596 RBI's, 1583 Runs, 3154 Hits, .305 Avg, 201 SB's, .857 OPS, 1 World Series Title, HOF
3	Brooks Robinson	1970 World Series MVP, AL MVP in 1964, 16 consecutive Gold Glove Awards, 268 HR's, 818 Extra-Base Hits, 1357 RBI's, 1232 Runs, 2848 Hits, .723 OPS, 2 World Series Titles, HOF
4	Chipper Jones	468 HR's, 1055 Extra Base Hits, 1619 Runs, 1623 RBI's, 150 SB's, 2726 Hits, .303 Avg, .930 OPS
5	Alex Rodriguez Includes 2016 stats.	AL MVP in 2005 and 2007 (AL MVP in 2003 as a SS), 3 Silver Slugger Awards (7 more as a Shortstop), 696 HRs, 1275 Extra Base Hits, 2086 RBI's, 2021 Runs, 3115 Hits, 329 SB's, .295 Average, .930 OPS, one World Series title.*
6	Harmon Killebrew	AL MVP in 1969, 573 HR's, 887 Extra-Base Hits, 1584 RBI's, 1283 Runs, .884 OPS, HOF
7	Eddie Mathews	512 HR's, 1453 RBI's, 1509 Runs, 2315 Hits, .885 OPS, 2 World Series Titles, HOF
8	Pie Traynor	593 Extra-Base Hits, 1273 RBI's, 1183 Runs, 2416 Hits, .320 Avg, 158 SB's, .797 OPS, 1 World Series Title, HOF
9	Wade Boggs	2 Gold Glove Awards, 8 Silver Slugger Awards, 757 Extra-Base Hits, 1014 RBI's, 1513 Runs, 3010 Hits, .328 Avg, .858 OPS, 1 World Series Title, HOF
10	Ron Santo	5 Gold Glove Awards, 342 HR's, 774 Extra-Base Hits, 1331 RBI's, 1138 Runs, 2254 Hits, .826 OPS, HOF

No.	Third Baseman	Career Highlights
11	"Bullet" Joe Rogan	"Negro League" Great at Third Base and as a Pitcher, HOF
12	Adrian Beltre	4 Gold Glove Awards, 4 Silver Slugger Awards, 413 HR's, 1008 Extra-Base Hits, 1467 RBI's, 1339 Runs, 2767 Hits, 118 SB's, .814 OPS to date*
13	Edgar Martinez	1 Silver Slugger Award (4 more as DH), 309 HR's, 838 Extra-Base Hits, 1261 RBI's, 1219 Runs, 2247 Hits, .312 Avg, .933 OPS
14	Howard Johnson	2 Silver Slugger Awards, 228 HR's, 497 Extra-Base Hits, 231 SB's, .786 OPS, 2 World Series Titles
15	Graig Nettles	2 Gold Glove Awards, 1981 ALCS MVP, 390 HR's, 746 Extra-Base Hits, 1314 RBI's, 1193 Runs, 2225 Hits, .750 OPS, 2 World Series Titles
16	Bill Madlock	163 HR's, 545 Extra-Base Hits, 860 RBI's, 920 Runs, 2008 Hits, .305 Avg, .807 OPS, 174 SB's, 4 Batting Titles 1 World Series Title
17	Troy Glaus	2002 World Series MVP, 2 Silver Slugger Awards, 320 HR's, 623 Extra-Base Hits, 950 RBI's, 889 Runs, .847 OPS, 1 World Series Title
18	David Wright	2 Gold Glove Awards, 2 Silver Slugger Awards, 235 HR's, 643 Extra-Base Hits, 956 RBI's, 931 Runs, 1746 Hits, .869 OPS to date*
19	Matt Williams	4 Gold Glove Awards, 4 Silver Slugger Awards, 378 HR's, 751 Extra-Base Hits, 1218 RBI's, 997 Runs, 1878 Hits, .805 OPS, 1 World Series Title
20	Scott Rolen	1997 NL Rookie of the Year, 8 Gold Glove Awards, 1 Silver Slugger Award, 316 HR's, 876 Extra-Base Hits, 1287 RBI's, 1211 Runs, 118 SB's, 2077 Hits .855 OPS, 1 World Series Title
21	Robin Ventura	6 Gold Glove Awards, 294 HR's, 646 Extra-Base Hits, 1182 RBI's, 1006 Runs, 1885 Hits, .806 OPS
22	Gary Gaetti	1987 ALCS MVP, 4 Gold Glove Awards, 1 Silver Slugger Award, 360 HR's, 842 Extra-Base Hits, 1341 RBI's, 1130 Runs, 2280 Hits, .741 OPS, 1 World Series Title
23	Vinny Castilla	3 Silver Slugger Awards, 320 HR's, 697 Extra-Base Hits, 1105 RBI's, 902 Runs, 1884 Hits, .797 OPS
24	Al Rosen	AL MVP in 1953 (one point shy in Avg from winning the elusive Triple Crown that year), .879 OPS, 1 World Series Title
25	Ken Boyer	NL MVP in 1964, 5 Gold Glove Awards, 282 HR's, 668 Extra-Base Hits, 1141 RBI's, 1104 Runs, 2143 Hits, .810 OPS, 1 World Series Title
26	Josh Donaldson	AL MVP in 2015, 1 Silver Slugger Award, .844 OPS to date*
27	Pete Rose	1963 NL Rookie of the Year (2B), 1975 World Series MVP (3B), NL MVP in 1973 (LF), 2 Gold Glove Awards (LF), 1 Silver Slugger Award (1B), 1041 Extra-Base Hits, 2165 Runs, 4256 Hits (ALL-TIME RECORD), .784 OPS, 2 World Series Titles at 3B, 1 World Series Title at 1B
28	Buddy Bell	6 Gold Glove Awards, 1 Silver Slugger Award, 201 HR's, 682 Extra-Base Hits, 1106 RBI's, 1151 Runs, 2514 Hits, .747 OPS

(Continued)

No.	Third Baseman	Career Highlights
29	Sal Bando	242 HR's, 569 Extra-Base Hits, 1039 RBI's, 982 Runs, 1790 Hits, 1790 Hits, .760 OPS, 3 World Series Titles
30	Eric Chavez	6 Gold Glove Awards, 1 Silver Slugger Award, 260 HR's, 602 Extra-Base Hits, 902 RBI's, 816 Runs, .818 OPS
31	Jim Thome	1 Silver Slugger Award at 3rd Base, 612 HR's, 1089 Extra-Base Hits, 1699 RBI's, 1583 Runs, 2328 Hits, .956 OPS
32	Manny Machado	2 Gold Glove Awards, .787 OPS to date*
33	Ken Caminiti	NL MVP in 1996, 3 Gold Glove Awards, 1 Silver Slugger Award, 239 HR's, 604 Extra-Base Hits, 983 RBI's, 894 Runs, .794 OPS
34	Evan Longoria	2008 AL Rookie of the Year, 2 Gold Glove Awards, 1 Silver Slugger Award, 205 HR's, 479 Extra-Base Hits, .833 OPS to date*
35	Terry Pendleton	NL MVP in 1991, 3 Gold Glove Awards, 535 Extra-Base Hits, 946 RBI's, 851 Runs, 1897 Hits, .707 OPS
36	Nolan Arenado	3 Gold Glove Awards, 1 Silver Slugger Award, .818 OPS to date*
37	Gary Sheffield	1 Silver Slugger Award at Third (4 more in OF), 509 HR's, 1003 Extra-Base Hits, 1676 RBI's, 1636 Runs, 2689 Hits, 253 SB's, .907 OPS, 1 World Series Title (OF)
38	Tim Wallach	3 Gold Glove Awards, 2 Silver Slugger Awards, 260 HR's, 728 Extra-Base Hits, 1125 RBI's, 908 Runs, 2085 Hits, .732 OPS
39	Toby Harrah	195 HR's, 542 Extra-Base Hits, 918 RBI's, 1115 Runs, 1954 Hits, .760 OPS
40	Carney Lansford	1 Silver Slugger Award, 151 HR's, 523 Extra-Base Hits, 874 RBI's, 1007 Runs, 2074 Hits, 224 SB's, .753 OPS
41	Doug DeCinces	1 Silver Slugger Award, 237 HR's, 578 Extra-Base Hits, 879 RBI's, 778 Runs, 1505 Hits, .774 OPS
42	Ron Cey	1981 World Series MVP, 316 HR's, 665 Extra-Base Hits, 1139 RBI's, 977 Runs, 1868 Hits, .799 OPS, 1 World Series Title
43	Michael Young	185 HR's, 686 Extra-Base Hits, 1030 RBI's, 1137 Runs, 2375 Hits, .300 Avg, .787 OPS
44	Frankie Frisch	NL MVP in 1931, 105 HR's, 709 Extra-Base Hits, 1244 RBI's, 1532 Runs, 2880 Hits, .316 Avg, 419 SB's, .801 OPS, 4 World Series Titles, HOF
45	Pablo Sandoval	2012 World Series MVP, .791 OPS, 3 World Series Titles to date*
46	Kris Bryant	2015 NL Rookie of Year Award, .853 OPS to date*
47	Tony Fernandez	4 consecutive Gold Glove Awards at Shortstop, 600 Extra-Base Hits, 844 RBI's, 1057 RBI's, 2276 Hits, .746 OPS, 246 SB's, 1 World Series Title (SS)
48	Pedro Guerrero	1 Silver Slugger Award, 215 HR's, 511 Extra-Base Hits, 898 RBI's, 730 Runs, 1618 Hits, .300 Avg, .850 OPS
49	Jim "Junior" Gilliam	1953 NL Rookie of the Year (HAD MORE BB THAN SO IN EVERY YEAR PLAYED) , 440 Extra-Base Hits, 1163 Runs, 1889 Hits, 203 SB's, .715 OPS, 4 World Series Titles

No.	Third Baseman	Career Highlights
50	Ryan Zimmerman	1 Gold Glove Award, 2 Silver Slugger Awards, 200 HR's, 539 Extra-Base Hits, .824 OPS to date*

Honorable Mention: George Kell, Aaron and Ray Boone, Johnny Pesky, Clete Boyer, Rico Petrocelli, Darrell Evans, Larry Parrish, Ray Knight, Kevin Seitzer, Rance Mulliniks, Kelly Gruber, Kevin Mitchell, Ed Sprague, and Mike Moustakas*

50 Greatest Shortstops of All Time

No.	Shortstop	Career Highlights
1	Derek Jeter	1996 AL Rookie of the Year, 2000 World Series MVP, 5 Gold Glove Awards, 5 Silver Slugger Awards, 260 HR's, 870 Extra-Base Hits, 1311 RBI's, 1923 Runs, 3465 Hits, 358 SB's, .310 Avg, .817 OPS, 5 World Series Titles
2	Ozzie Smith	1985 NLCS MVP, 13 consecutive Gold Glove Awards, 1 Silver Slugger Awards, 499 Extra-Base Hits, 1257 Runs, 2460 Hits, 580 SB's, .666 OPS, 1 World Series Title, HOF
3	Alex Rodriguez Includes 2016 stats.	AL MVP in 2005 and 2007 at Third, AL MVP in 2003 as a SS, 10 Silver Slugger Awards (7 as a Shortstop), 696 HRs, 1275 Extra Base Hits, 2086 RBI's, 2021 Runs, 3115 Hits, 329 SB's, .295 Average, .930 OPS, one World Series title.
4	Barry Larkin	NL MVP in 1995, 3 Gold Glove Awards, 9 Silver Slugger Awards, 198 HR's, 715 Extra-Base Hits, 960 RBI's, 1329 Runs, 2340 Hits, 379 SB's, .295 Avg, .815 OPS, 1 World Series Title, HOF
5	Ernie Banks	NL MVP in 1958 and 1959, 1 Gold Glove Award, 512 HR's, 1636 RBI's, 2583 Hits, .830 OPS, HOF
6	Cal Ripken, Jr.	1982 AL Rookie of the Year, AL MVP in 1983 and 1991, 2 Gold Glove Awards, 8 Silver Slugger Awards, Set Record for Most Consecutive Games Played Streak with 2632 Games Played in a Row, 431 HR's, 1078 Extra-Base Hits, 1695 RBI's, 1647 Runs, 3184 Hits, .788 OPS, 1 World Series Title, HOF
7	Nomar Garciaparra	1997 AL Rookie of the Year, 1 Silver Slugger Award, 229 HR's, 651 Extra-Base Hits, 936 RBI's, 927 Runs, 1747 Hits, .313 Avg, .882 OPS
8	Honus Wagner	996 Extra-Base Hits, 1732 RBI's, 1739 Runs, 3420 Hits, 723 SB's, .328 Avg, .858 OPS, 1 World Series Title
9	Omar Vizquel	11 Gold Glove Awards (nine in a row), 613 Extra-Base Hits, 951 RBI's, 1445 Runs, 2877 Hits, 404 SB's, .688 OPS
10	Tony Fernandez	4 consecutive Gold Glove Awards at Shortstop, 600 Extra-Base Hits, 844 RBI's, 1057 Runs, 2276 Hits, .746 OPS, 246 SB's, 1 World Series Title (SS)

(Continued)

No.	Shortstop	Career Highlights
11	Luis Aparicio	1956 AL Rookie of the Year, 9 Gold Glove Awards, 569 Extra-Base Hits, 791 RBI's, 1335 Runs, 2677 Hits, 506 SB's, .653 OPS
12	Alan Trammell	1984 World Series MVP, 4 Gold Glove Awards, 3 Silver Slugger Awards, 185 HR's, 652 Extra-Base Hits, 1003 RBI's, 1231 Runs, 2365 Hits, .767 OPS, 1 World Series Title
13	Robin Yount	AL MVP in 1982 (1989 AL MVP in CF), 1 Gold Glove Award, 2 Silver Slugger Awards (1 more Silver Slugger in CF), 251 HR's, 960 Extra-Base Hits, 1406 RBI's, 1632 Runs, 3142 Hits, 271 SB's, .772 OPS
14	Jimmy Rollins	NL MVP in 2007, 4 Gold Glove Awards, 1 Silver Slugger Award, 229 HR's, 846 Extra-Base Hits, 928 RBI's, 1396 Runs, 2422 Hits, 465 SB's, .745 OPS, 1 World Series Title to date*
15	Troy Tulowitzki	2 Gold Glove Awards, 2 Silver Slugger Awards, 193 HR's, 449 Extra-Base Hits, 674 RBI's, 691 Runs, 1204 Hits, .877 OPS to date*
16	Miguel Tejada	AL MVP in 2002, 2 Silver Slugger Awards, 307 HR's, 798 Extra-Base Hits, 1302 RBI's, 1230 Runs, 2407 Hits, .791 OPS, 1152 Consecutive Games Played
17	Joe Sewell	553 Extra-Base Hits, 1054 RBI's, 1141 Runs, 2226 Hits, .312 Avg, .804 OPS, 2 World Series Titles, HOF
18	Luke Appling	587 Extra-Base Hits, 1116 RBI's, 1319 Runs, 2749 Hits, .310 Average, 179 SB's, .798 OPS, HOF
19	Edgar Renteria	2010 World Series MVP, 2 Gold Glove Awards, 3 Silver Slugger Awards, 605 Extra-Base Hits, 923 RBI's, 1200 Runs, 2327 Hits, 294 SB's, .741 OPS, 2 World Series Titles
20	Dave Concepcion	5 Gold Glove Awards, 2 Silver Slugger Awards, 538 Extra-Base Hits, 950 RBI's, 993 Runs, 2326 Hits, 321 SB's, .679 OPS, 2 World Series Titles
21	Julio Franco	4 Silver Sluggers at 2nd Base (one more as DH), 173 HR's, 634 Extra-Base Hits, 1194 RBI's, 1285 Runs, 2586 Hits, 281 SB's, .298 Avg, .782 OPS
22	Jose Reyes	1 Silver Slugger Award, 572 Extra-Base Hits, 621 RBI's, 1030 Runs, 1904 Hits, 479 SB's, .290 Avg, .770 OPS to date*
23	Bert Campaneris	478 Extra-Base Hits, 646 RBI's, 1181 Runs, 2249 Hits, 649 SB, .653 OPS, 3 World Series Titles
24	Lou Boudreau	AL MVP in 1948, 519 Extra-Base Hits, 789 RBI's, 861 Runs, 1779 Hits, .295 Avg, .795 OPS, 1 World Series Title, HOF
25	Xander Bogaerts	Enjoyed breakout season in 2016 at age 23, with 21 HR, 89 RBI, 115 RS, and a BA of .293
26	Rabbit Maranville	585 Extra-Base Hits, 884 RBI's, 1256 Runs, 2605 Hits, 291 SB's, .658 OPS, 1 World Series Title, HOF
27	Michael Young	1 Gold Glove Award, 185 HR's, 686 Extra-Base Hits, 1030 RBI's, 1137 Runs, 2375 Hits, .300 Avg, .787 OPS

No.	Shortstop	Career Highlights
28	Johnny Pesky	.307 Avg, .780 OPS, "Pesky Pole" (in right-field) at Fenway Park in Boston is named after him, as it was the only place in the park where he could reach the fences
29	Jay Bell	1 Gold Glove Award, 1 Silver Slugger Award, 195 HR's, 656 Extra-Base Hits, 1963 Hits, .759 OPS
30	Rico Petrocelli	210 HR's, 469 Extra-Base Hits, .752 OPS
31	Pee Wee Reese	Led the NL in SB in 1952, 536 Extra-Base Hits, 885 RBI's, 1338 Runs, 2170 Hits, 232 SB,s, .743 OPS, 1 World Series Title
32	Freddie Patek	385 SB,s, Stole 32+ bases in a year 8 years' consecutive, .633 OPS
33	Alcides Escobar	1 Gold Glove Award, 145 SB's, .642 OPS, 1 World Series Title to date*
34	Orlando Cabrera	2 Gold Glove Awards, 614 Extra-Base Hits, 854 RBI's, 985 Runs, 2055 Hits, 216 SB's, .707 OPS, 1 World Series Title
35	Zoilo Versalles	AL MVP in 1965, 2 Gold Glove Awards, 1246 Hits, .657 OPS
36	Brandon Crawford	1 Gold Glove Award, 1 Silver Slugger Award, .696 OPS, 2 World Series Titles to date*
37	Mark Belanger	8 Gold Glove Awards, .580 OPS, 1 World Series Title
38	Garry Templeton	2 Silver Slugger Awards, 505 Extra-Base Hits, 728 RBI's, 893 Runs, 2096 Hits, 242 SB's, .673 OPS
39	J. J. Hardy	3 Gold Glove Awards, 1 Silver Slugger Award, 175 HR's, 437 Extra-Base Hits, 616 RBI's, 651 Runs, 1324 Hits, .720 OPS to date*
40	Tony Kubek	1957 AL Rookie of the Year, .667 OPS, 3 World Series Titles
41	Bill Russell	1926 Hits, 167 SB's, .648 OPS, 1 World Series Title
42	Andrelton Simmons	2 Gold Glove Awards, .666 OPS to date*
43	Hubie Brooks	2 Silver Slugger Awards, 149 HR's, 470 Extra-Base Hits, 1608 Hits, .717 OPS
44	Roy Smalley	163 HR's, 432 Extra-Base Hits, 1454 Hits, .740 OPS
45	Alfredo Griffin	1979 AL Rookie of the Year, 1 Gold Glove Award, 1688 Hits, 759 Runs, 192 SB's, .604 OPS, 3 World Series Titles (two for an AL team and one with an NL team)
46	Larry Bowa	2 Gold Glove Awards, 987 Runs, 2191 Hits, 318 SB'S, .620 OPS, 1 World Series Title
47	Rick Burleson	1 Gold Glove Award, 1 Silver Slugger Award, 1401 Hits, .689 OPS
48	Phil Rizzuto	AL MVP in 1950, 877 Runs, 1588 Hits, 149 SB's, .706 OPS, Won 7 World Series, 5 in a row 1949-1953, HOF
49	Ozzie Guillen	1 Gold Glove Award, 1764 Hits, 169 SB's, .626 OPS

No.	Shortstop	Career Highlights
50	Frank Taveras	1029 Hits, 300 SB's, .614 OPS

Honorable Mention: Bucky Dent, U.L Washington, Rafael Ramirez, Greg Gagne, Manny Lee, Marco Scutaro, Dickie Thon, Carlos Correa*, Didi Gregorius*.

50 Greatest Outfields of All Time (1947 – Present)

No.	Team	Year	Left Field	Center Field	Right Field
1	St. Louis Cardinals	1985	Vince Coleman	Willie McGee	Andy Van Slyke
2	Pittsburgh Pirates	1990	Barry Bonds	Andy Van Slyke	Bobby Bonilla
3	Cleveland Indians	1995	Albert Belle	Kenny Lofton	Manny Ramirez
4	Montreal Expos	1994	Moises Alou	Marquis Grissom	Larry Walker
5	Toronto Blue Jays	1987	George Bell	Lloyd Moseby	Jesse Barfield
6	Cleveland Indians	1998	Manny Ramirez	Kenny Lofton	David Justice
7	Boston Red Sox	1979	Jim Rice	Fred Lynn	Dwight Evans
8	Oakland A's	1990	Rickey Henderson	Dave Henderson	Jose Canseco
9	New York Yankees	1996	Tim Raines	Bernie Williams	Paul O'Neill
10	New York Yankees	1961	Yogi Berra	Mickey Mantle	Roger Maris
11	San Francisco Giants	1962	W.McCovey/H.Kuenn	Willie Mays	Felipe Alou
12	Oakland A's	1980	Rickey Henderson	Dwayne Murphy	Tony Armas
13	New York Giants	1954	D.Rhodes/M.Irvin	Willie Mays	Don Mueller
14	Brooklyn Dodgers	1953	Jackie Robinson	Duke Snider	Carl Furillo
15	Boston Red Sox	1984	Jim Rice	Tony Armas	Dwight Evans
16	Pittsburgh Pirates	1969	Willie Stargell	Matty Alou	Roberto Clemente
17	St. Louis Cardinals	1982	Lonnie Smith	Willie McGee	George Hendrick
18	Anaheim Angels	1997	Garrett Anderson	Jim Edmonds	Tim Salmon
19	Anaheim Angels	2004	Jose Guillen	Garrett Anderson	Vladimir Guerrero
20	Pittsburgh Pirates	1971	Willie Stargell	Al Oliver	Roberto Clemente
21	Kansas City Royals	1999	Johnny Damon	Carlos Beltran	Jermaine Dye
22	Seattle Mariners	1997	Jose Cruz Jr.	Ken Griffey Jr.	Jay Buhner

No.	Team	Year	Left Field	Center Field	Right Field
23	Boston Red Sox	1975	J.Rice/C Yastrzemski	Fred Lynn	Dwight Evans
24	Colorado Rockies	1997	Dante Bichette	Ellis Burks	Larry Walker
25	Montreal Expos	1983	Tim Raines	Andre Dawson	Warren Cromartie
26	St. Louis Cardinals	1967	Lou Brock	Curt Flood	Roger Maris
27	Anaheim Angels	2002	Garrett Anderson	Darin Erstad	Tim Salmon
28	Montreal Expos	1980	Ron LeFlore	Andre Dawson	Ellis Valentine
29	Oakland A's	1973	Joe Rudi	Bill North	Reggie Jackson
30	Philadelphia Phillies	1977	Greg Luzinski	Garry Maddox	B.McBride/ J. Johnstone
31	Brooklyn Dodgers	1955	Sandy Amoros	Duke Snider	Carl Furillo
32	PhiladelphiaPhillies	1980	L. Smith/G. Luzinski	Garry Maddox	Bake McBride
33	Los Angeles Dodgers	1977	Dusty Baker	Rick Monday	Reggie Smith
34	New York Yankees	1977	Roy White	Mickey Rivers	Reggie Jackson
35	Toronto Blue Jays	2015	B.Revere/D. Pompey	Kevin Pillar	Jose Bautista
36	Toronto Blue Jays	1992	Candy Maldonado	Devon White	J.Carter/ D.Winfield
37	Milwaukee Brewers	1979	Ben Oglivie	Gorman Thomas	Sixto Lezcano
38	Boston Red Sox	1967	Carl Yastrzemski	Reggie Smith	Tony Conigliaro
39	Cincinnati Reds	1976	George Foster	Cesar Geronimo	Ken Griffey Sr.
40	Philadelphia Phillies	2009	Raul Ibanez	Shane Victorino	Jayson Werth
41	Baltimore Orioles	1996	B. J. Surhoff	Brady Anderson	Bobby Bonilla
42	New York Yankees	1985	Ken Griffey Sr.	Rickey Henderson	Dave Winfield
43	Atlanta Braves	1991	Ron Gant	Otis Nixon	David Justice
44	San Francisco Giants	2003	Barry Bonds	Marquis Grissom	Jose Cruz, Jr.
45	Boston Red Sox	1986	Jim Rice	Dave Henderson	Dwight Evans
46	Cincinnati Reds	1990	Billy Hatcher	Eric Davis	Paul O'Neill
47	Milwaukee Braves	1964	Rico Carty	Lee Maye	Henry Aaron
48	Atlanta Braves	1970	Rico Carty	Tony Gonzalez	Henry Aaron
49	Baltimore Orioles	1971	Don Buford	Paul Blair	Frank Robinson
50	Chicago Cubs	1998	Henry Rodriguez	Brent Brown	Sammy Sosa

100 Greatest Outfielders of All Time

No.	Outfielder	Career Highlights
1	"Cool Papa" Bell and Oscar Charleston	Negro Leagues Greats, both were inducted into the Hall of Fame in Cooperstown
2	Barry Bonds	7 NL MVP Awards (1990, 1992, 1993, 2001-2004), 8 Gold Glove Awards, 12 Silver Slugger Awards, 762 HR's, 1440 Extra-Base Hits, 1996 RBI's, 2227 Runs, 2935 Hits, .298 Avg, 514 SB's, 1.051 OPS
3	Willie Mays	1951 NL Rookie of the Year, NL MVP in 1954 and 1965, 12 consecutive Gold Glove Awards, 660 HR's, 1323 Extra-Base Hits, 1903 RBI's, 2062 Runs, 3283 Hits, .302 Avg, 338 SB's, .941 OPS, 1 World Series Title, HOF
4	Henry Aaron	NL MVP in 1957, 3 Gold Glove Awards, 755 HR's, 1477 Extra-Base Hits, 2297 RBI's, 2174 Runs, 3771 Hits, .305 Avg, 240 SB's, .928 OPS, 1 World Series Title, HOF
5	Roberto Clemente	NL MVP in 1966, 1971 World Series MVP, 12 consecutive Gold Glove Awards, 240 HR's, 846 Extra-Base Hits, 1305 RBI's, 1416 Runs, 3000 Hits, .317 Avg, .834 OPS, 2 World Series Titles, HOF
6	Ted Williams	AL Triple Crown Years (1942 and 1947), AL MVP in 1946 and 1949, 521 HR's, 1117 Extra-Base Hits, 1839 RBI's, 1798 Runs, 2654 Hits, .344 Avg, 1.116 OPS, HOF
7	Babe Ruth	AL MVP in 1923, 714 HR's, 1356 Extra-Base Hits, 2214 RBI's, 2174 Runs, 2873 Hits, .342 Avg, 1.164 OPS, 7 World Series Titles, HOF
8	Ken Griffey, Jr.	AL MVP in 1997, 10 consecutive Gold Glove Awards, 7 Silver Slugger Awards, 630 HR's, 1192 Extra-Base Hits, 1836 RBI's, 1662 Runs, 2781 Hits, 184 SB's, .907 OPS, HOF
9	Joe DiMaggio	AL MVP in 1939, 1941, and 1947, 361 HR's, 881 Extra-Base Hits, 1537 RBI's, 1390 Runs, 2214 Hits, .325 Avg, .977 OPS, 9 World Series Titles. HOF
10	Kirby Puckett	6 Gold Glove Awards, 6 Silver Slugger Awards, 1991 ALCS MVP, 207 HR's, 678 Extra-Base Hits, 1085 RBI's, 1071 Runs, 2304 Hits, .318 Avg, 134 SB's, .837 OPS, 2 World Series Titles, HOF
11	Frank Robinson	1956 NL Rookie of the Year, NL MVP in 1961, AL MVP in 1966, 1966 AL Triple Crown, 1966 World Series MVP, 586 HR's, 1186 Extra-Base Hits, 1812 RBI's, 1829 Runs, 2943 Hits, .294 Avg, 204 SB's, .926 OPS, 2 World Series Titles (one for an NL team, one for an AL team), HOF
12	Stan Musial	NL MVP in 1943, 1946, and 1948, 475 HR's, 1377 Extra-Base Hits, 1951 RBI's, 1949 Runs, 3630 Hits, .331 Avg, .976 OPS, 3 World Series Titles, HOF
13	Larry Walker	NL MVP in 1997, 7 Gold Glove Awards, 3 Silver Slugger Awards, 383 HR's, 916 Extra-Base Hits, 1311 RBI's, 1355 Runs, 2160 Hits, .313 Avg, .965 OPS

No.	Outfielder	Career Highlights
14	Ty Cobb	AL MVP in 1911, 117 HR's, 1136 Extra-Base Hits, 1933 RBI's, 2244 Runs, 4189 Hits ,.366 Avg, 897 SB's, .945 OPS, HOF
15	"Shoeless" Joe Jackson	"Shoeless" Joe Jackson - 529 Extra-Base Hits, 785 RBI's, 873 Runs, 1772 Hits, .356 Avg, 202 SB's, .940 OPS, 1 World Series Title
16	Mickey Mantle	AL MVP in 1956, 1957, and 1962, 1956 AL Triple Crown, 1 Gold Glove Award, 536 HR's, 952 Extra-Base Hits, 1509 RBI's, 1676 Runs, 2415 Hits, .298 Avg, 153 SB's, .977 OPS, 7 World Series Titles, HOF
17	Sammy Sosa	NL MVP in 1998, 6 Silver Slugger Awards, 609 HR's, 1033 Extra-Base Hits, 1667 RBI's, 1475 Runs, 2408 Hits, 234 SB's, .878 OPS
18	Vladimir Guerrero	AL MVP in 2004, 8 Silver Slugger Awards, 449 HR's, 972 Extra-Base Hits, 1496 RBI's, 1328 Runs, 2590 Hits, .318 Avg, 181 SB's, .931 OPS
19	Ichiro Suzuki Includes 2016 stats.	2001 AL Rookie of the Year, AL MVP in 2001, 10 consecutive Gold Glove Awards, 3 Silver Slugger Awards, 114 HR's, 566 Extra-Base Hits, 760 RBI's, 1396 Runs, 3030 Hits, 508 SB, .313 Avg, .761 OPS.*
20	Carl Yastrzemski	AL Triple Crown in 1967, AL MVP in 1967, 7 Gold Glove Awards, 452 HR's, 1157 Extra-Base Hits, 1844 RBI's, 1816 Runs, 3419 Hits, 168 SB's, .841 OPS, HOF
21	Andruw Jones	10 consecutive Gold Glove Awards, 1 Silver Slugger Award, 434 HR's, 853 Extra-Base Hits, 1289 RBI's, 1204 Runs, 1933 Hits, 152 SB's, .823 OPS
22	Dave Winfield	7 Gold Glove Awards, 6 Silver Slugger Awards, 465 HR's, 1093 Extra-Base Hits, 1833 RBI's, 1669 Runs, 3110 Hits, 223 SB's, .827 OPS, 1 World Series Title, HOF
23	Andre Dawson	1977 NL Rookie of the Year, NL MVP in 1987, 8 Gold Glove Awards, 4 Silver Slugger Awards, 438 HR's, 1039 Extra-Base Hits, 1591 RBI's, 1373 Runs, 2774 Hits, 314 SB's, .806 OPS, HOF
24	Reggie Jackson	AL MVP in 1973, World Series MVP in 1973 and 1977, 2 Silver Slugger Awards, 563 HR's, 1075 Extra-Base Hits, 1702 RBI's, 1551 Runs, 2584 Hits, 228 SB's, .846 OPS, 5 World Series Titles, HOF
25	Rickey Henderson	AL MVP in 1990, 1989 ALCS MVP, 1 Gold Glove Award, 3 Silver Slugger Awards, 297 HR's, 873 Extra-Base Hits, 1115 RBI's, 2295 Runs, 1406 SB's, .820 OPS, 2 World Series Titles, HOF
26	Lou Brock	149 HR's, 776 Extra-Base Hits, 900 RBI's, 1610 Runs, 3023 Hits, .293 Avg, 938 SB's, .753 OPS, 2 World Series Titles, HOF
27	Al Simmons	307 HR's, 995 Extra-Base Hits, 1828 RBI's, 1507 Runs, 2927 Hits, .334 Avg, .915 OPS, 2 World Series Titles, HOF
28	Manny Ramirez	2004 World Series MVP, 9 Silver Slugger Awards (8 in a row), 555 HR's, 1122 Extra-Base Hits, 1831 RBI's, 1544 Runs, 2574 Hits, .312 Avg, .996 OPS, 2 World Series Titles

(Continued)

No.	Outfielder	Career Highlights
29	Duke Snider	407 HR's, 850 Extra-Base Hits, 1333 RBI's, 1259 Runs, 2116 Hits, .295 Avg, .919 OPS, 2 World Series Titles, HOF
30	Tony Gwynn	5 Gold Glove Awards, 7 Silver Slugger Awards, 135 HR's, 763 Extra-Base Hits, 1138 RBI's, 1383 Runs, 3141 Hits, .338 Avg, 319 SB's, .847 OPS, HOF
31	Juan Gonzalez	AL MVP in 1996 and 1998, 6 Silver Slugger Awards, 434 HR's, 847 Extra-Base Hits, 1404 RBI's, 1061 Runs, 1936 Hits, .295 Avg, .904 OPS
32	Bobby Abreu	1 Gold Glove Award, 1 Silver Slugger Award, 288 HR's, 921 Extra-Base Hits, 1363 RBI's, 1453 Runs, 2470 Hits, .291 Avg, 400 SB's, .870 OPS
33	Jim Edmonds	8 Gold Glove Awards (6 consecutive), 1 Silver Slugger Award, 393 HR's, 855 Extra-Base Hits, 1199 RBI's, 1251 Runs, 1949 Hits, .903 OPS, 1 World Series Title
34	Willie Keeler	419 Extra-Base Hits, 810 RBI's, 1719 Runs, Keeler 'Hit'em where they Ain't' 2932 times, Had 8 consecutive years with 202+ Hits, .341 Avg, 495 SB's, .802 OPS
35	Tim Raines	1 Silver Slugger Award, 170 HR's, 713 Extra-Base Hits, 980 RBI's, 1571 Runs, 2605 Hits, .294 Avg, 808 SB's, .810 OPS, 1 World Series Title
36	Bernie Williams	1996 ALCS MVP, 4 consecutive Gold Glove Awards, 1 Silver Slugger Award, 287 HR's, 791 Extra-Base Hits, 1257 RBI's, 1366 Runs, 2336 Hits, .297 Avg, 147 SB's, .858 OPS, 4 World Series Awards
37	Willie Stargell	NL MVP in 1979 (1B), 1979 World Series MVP (1B), 2 World Series Titles (1 in LF, and 1 at 1B), 475 HR's, 953 Extra-Base Hits, 1540 RBI's, 1194 Runs, 2232 Hits, .889 OPS, HOF
38	Kenny Lofton	4 consecutive Gold Glove Awards, 130 HR's, 629 Extra-Base Hits, 781 RBI's, 1528 Runs, 2428 Hits, .299 Avg, 622 SB's, .794 OPS
39	Fred Lynn	1975 AL Rookie of the Year, AL MVP in 1975, 1982 ALCS MVP, 4 Gold Glove Awards, 306 HR's, 737 Extra-Base Hits, 1111 RBI's, 1063 Runs, 1960 Hits, .845 OPS
40	Al Kaline	10 Gold Glove Awards (7 in a row), 399 HR's, 972 Extra-Base Hits, 1582 RBI's, 1622 Runs, 3007 Hits, .297 Avg, 137 SB's, .855 OPS, 1 World Series Title
41	Mike Trout	2012 AL Rookie of the Year, AL MVP in 2014, 4 consecutive Silver Slugger Awards, .304 Avg, .956 OPS to date*
42	Jim Rice	AL MVP in 1978, 2 Silver Slugger Awards, 382 HR's, 834 Extra-Base Hits, 1451 RBI's, 1249 Runs, 2452 Hits, .298 Avg, .854 OPS, HOF
43	Andrew McCutchen	NL MVP in 2013, 1 Gold Glove Award, 4 consecutive Silver Slugger Awards, .298 Avg, .884 OPS to date*
44	Dave Parker	NL MVP in 1978, 3 Gold Glove Awads in a row, 3 Silver Slugger Awards, 339 HR's, 940 Extra-Base Hits, 1493 RBI's, 1272 Runs, 2712 Hits, .290 Avg, 154 SB's, .810 OPS, 2 World Series Titles (one for an NL team and 1 with an AL team)

No.	Outfielder	Career Highlights
45	Billy Williams	1961 NL Rookie of the Year, 1117 consecutive games played, 426 HR's, 948 Extra-Base Hits, 1475 RBI's, 1410 Runs, 2711 Hits, .290 Avg, .853 OPS, HOF
46	Harry Heilmann	183 HR's, 876 Extra-Base Hits, 1540 RBI's, 1291 Runs, 2660 Hits, .342 Avg, .930 OPS, HOF
47	Paul Waner	NL MVP in 1927, 113 HR's, 909 Extra-Base Hits, 1309 RBI's, 1627 Runs, 3152 Hits, .333 Avg, .878 OPS, HOF
48	Luis Gonzalez	1 Silver Slugger Award, 354 HR's, 1018 Extra-Base Hits, 1439 RBI's, 1412 Runs, 2591 Hits, 128 SB's, .845 OPS, 1 World Series Title
49	Moises Alou	2 Silver Slugger Awards, 332 HR's, 792 Extra-Base Hits, 1287 RBI's, 1109 Runs, 2134 Hits, .303 Avg, .885 OPS, 1 World Series Title
50	Torii Hunter	9 consecutive Gold Glove Awards, 2 Silver Slugger Awards, 353 HR's, 890 Extra-Base Hits, 1391 RBI's, 1296 Runs, 2452 Hits, 195 SB's, .793 OPS to date
51	Devon White	7 Gold Glove Awards, 208 HR's, 657 Extra-Base Hits, 846 RBI's, 1125 Runs, 1934 Hits, 346 SB's, .739 OPS, 3 World Series Titles (2 for an AL team, 1 with an NL team)
52	Dwight Evans	8 Gold Glove Awards, 2 Silver Slugger Awards, 385 HR's, 941 Extra-Base Hits, 1384 RBI's, 1470 Runs, 2446 Hits, .840 OPS
53	Jose Bautista	3 Silver Slugger Awards, 286 HR's, 546 Extra-Base Hits, 793 RBI's, 810 Runs, 1212 Hits, .865 OPS to date*
54	David Justice	1990 NL Rookie of the Year, 2 Silver Slugger Awards, 2000 NLCS MVP, 305 HR's, 609 Extra-Base Hits, 1017 RBI's, 929 Runs, 929 Runs, 1571 Hits, .878 OPS, 2 World Series Titles (one for an NL team and one for an AL team)
55	Reggie Smith	1 Gold Glove Award, 314 HR's, 734 Extra-Base Hits, 1092 RBI's, 1123 Runs, 2020 Hits, .287 Avg, .855 OPS, 1 World Series Title
56	Andy Van Slyke	5 consecutive Gold Glove Awards, 2 Silver Slugger Awards, 164 HR's, 548 Extra-Base Hits, 792 RBI's, 835 Runs, 1562 Hits, 245 SB's, .792 OPS
57	Gary Sheffield	Gary Sheffield - 5 Silver Slugger Awards (4 in OF, 1 at 3B), 509 HR's, 1003 Extra-Base Hits, 1676 RBI's, 1636 Runs, 2689 Hits, 253 SB's, .907 OPS, 1 World Series Title (OF)
58	Shawn Green	1 Gold Glove Award, 1 Silver Slugger Award, 328 HR's, 808 Extra-Base Hits, 1070 RBI's, 1129 Runs, 2003 Hits, 162 SB's, .850 OPS
59	Robin Yount	AL MVP in 1982 (1989 AL MVP in CF), 1 Gold Glove Award, 2 Silver Slugger Awards (1 more Silver Slugger in CF), 251 HR's, 960 Extra-Base Hits, 1406 RBI's, 1632 Runs, 3142 Hits, 271 SB's, .772 OPS, HOF
60	Bryce Harper	Bryce Harper - 2012 Rookie of the Year, NL MVP in 2015, 1 Silver Slugger Award, .902 OPS to date*

(Continued)

No.	Outfielder	Career Highlights
61	Dale Murphy	NL MVP in 1982 and 1983, 1982-1986 Gold Glove Award Winner (five in total), 1982-1985 Silver Slugger Award Winner (four in total), 398 HR's, 787 Extra-Base Hits, 1266 RBI's, 1197 Runs, 2111 Hits, 161 SB's, .815 OPS
62	Bobby Bonds	3 Gold Glove Awards, 332 HR's, 700 Extra-Base Hits, 1024 RBI's, 1258 Runs, 1886 Hits, 461 SB's, .824 OPS
63	Paul O'Neill	281 HR's, 753 Extra-Base Hits, 1269 RBI's, 1041 Runs, 2105 Hits, 141 SB's, .833 OPS, 5 World Series Titles (one for an NL team, four with an AL team)
64	Ryan Braun	2007 NL Rookie of the Year, NL MVP in 2011, 5 consecutive Silver Slugger Awards, 255 HR's, 589 Extra-Base Hits, 846 RBI's, 799 Runs, 1441 Hits, .304 Avg, 165 SB's, .911 OPS to date*
65	Carlos Beltran	1999 AL Rookie of the Year, 3 Gold Gloves in a row, back to back Silver Slugger Awards, 392 HR's, 973 Extra-Base Hits, 1443 RBI's, 1449 Runs, 2454 Hits, 311 SB's, .845 OPS to date*
66	Hack Wilson	244 HR's, 577 Extra-Base Hits, 1063 RBI's, 884 Runs, 1461 Hits, .307 Avg, .940 OPS, HOF
67	Joe Carter	2 Silver Slugger Awards, 396 HR's, 881 Extra-Base Hits, 1445 RBI's, 1170 Runs, 2184 Hits, 231 SB's, .771 OPS, 2 World Series Titles
68	Paul Blair	8 Gold Glove Awards (8 in 9 years), 134 HR's, 471 Extra-Base Hits, 1513 Hits, 171 SB's, .684 OPS, 4 World Series Titles (2 with each team he donned jersey's in the Fall Classic)
69	Steve Finley	5 Gold Glove Awards, 304 HR's, 877 Extra-Base Hits, 1167 RBI's, 1443 Runs, 2548 Hits, 320 SB's, .775 OPS, 1 World Series Title
70	Kirk Gibson	NL MVP in 1988, 1984 ALCS MVP, 1 Silver Slugger Award, 255 HR's, 569 Extra-Base Hits, 870 RBI's, 985 Runs, 1553 Hits, .815 OPS, 2 World Series Titles
71	Curt Flood	7 consecutive Gold Glove Awards, 1861 Hits, .293 Avg, .732 OPS, 2 World Series Titles
72	Vince Coleman	1985 NL Rookie of the Year, 752 SB's, .668 OPS
73	Josh Hamilton	AL MVP in 2010, 2010 ALCS MVP, 3 Silver Slugger Awards, 200 HR's, 458 Extra-Base Hits, 701 RBI's, 609 Runs, 1134 Hits, .290 Avg, .865 OPS to date*
74	Cesar Cedeno	5 consecutive Gold Glove Awards, 199 HR's, 695 Extra-Base Hits, 976 RBI's, 1084 Runs, 2087 Hits, 550 SB's, .790 OPS
75	Darin Erstad	3 Gold Glove Awards, 1 Silver Slugger Award, 124 HR's, 473 Extra-Base Hits, 699 RBI's, 913 Runs, 179 SB's, .743 OPS, 1 World Series Title
76	Jose Canseco	1986 AL Rookie of the Year, AL MVP in 1988, 4 Silver Slugger Awards, 462 HR's, 816 Extra-Base Hits, 1407 RBI's, 1186 Runs, 1877 Hits, 200 SB's, .867 OPS, 2 World Series Titles

No.	Outfielder	Career Highlights
77	Eric Davis	3 Gold Glove Awards, 2 Silver Slugger Awards, 282 HR's, 547 Extra-Base Hits, 934 RBI's, 938 Runs, 1430 Hits, 349 SB's, .841 OPS, 1 World Series Title
78	Vernon Wells	3 Gold Glove Awards in a row, 1 Silver Slugger Award, 270 HR's, 683 Extra-Base Hits, 958 RBI's, 930 Runs, 1794 Hits, 109 SB's, .778 OPS
79	Amos Otis	3 Gold Glove Awards, 193 HR's, 633 Extra-Base Hits, 1007 RBI's, 1092 Runs, 2020 Hits, 341 SB's, .768 OPS
80	Ken Williams	196 HR's, 558 Extra-Base Hits, 916 RBI's, 860 Runs, 1552 Hits, .319 Avg, 154 SB's, .924 OPS
81	Larry Doby	253 HR's, 548 Extra-Base Hits, 970 RBI's, 960 Runs, 1515 Hits, .876 OPS
82	Jacoby Ellsbury	1 Gold Glove Award, 1 Silver Slugger Award, 301 SB's, .289 Avg, .768 OPS, 2 World Series Titles to date*
83	Gary Pettis	5 Gold Glove Awards (5 in 6 years), 354 SB's, .642 OPS
84	Kevin Mitchell	NL MVP in 1989, 1 Silver Slugger Award, 234 HR's, 483 Extra-Base Hits, 760 RBI's, 630 Runs, 1173 Hits, .880 OPS, 1 World Series Title
85	Adam Jones	4 Gold Glove Awards, 196 HR's, 447 Extra-Base Hits, 659 RBI's, 675 Runs, 1316 Hits, .781 OPS to date*
86	Albert "Joey" Belle	Albert "Joey" Belle - 5 Silver Slugger Awards (5 in 6 years), 381 HR's, 791 Extra-Base Hits, 1239 RBI's, 974 Runs, 1726 Hits, .295 Avg, .933 OPS
87	Vada Pinson	1 Gold Glove Award, 256 HR's, 868 Extra-Base Hits, 1169 RBI's, 1365 Runs, 2757 Hits, 305 SB's, .769 OPS
88	Raul Mondesi	1994 NL Rookie of the Year, 2 Gold Glove Awards, 271 HR's, 639 Extra-Base Hits, 860 RBI's, 909 Runs, 1589 Hits, 229 SB's, .815 OPS
89	Richie Ashburn	455 Extra-Base Hits, 1322 Runs, 2574 Hits, .308 Avg, 234 SB's, .778 OPS, HOF Add in defensive numbers
90	Matt Kemp	2 Gold Glove Awards, 2 Silver Slugger Awards, 205 HR's, 487 Extra-Base Hits, 748 RBI's, 730 Runs, 1346 Hits, 182 SB's, .289 Avg, .833 OPS to date*
91	Jose Cruz, Sr.	2 Silver Slugger Awards, 165 HR's, 650 Extra-Base Hits, 1077 RBI's, 1036 Runs, 2251 Hits, 317 SB's, .774 OPS
92	Jesse Barfield	2 Gold Glove Awards, 1 Silver Slugger Award, 241 HR's, 487 Extra-Base Hits, 716 RBI's, 715 Runs, 1219 Hits, .802 OPS
93	Willie Wilson	1 Gold Glove Award, 2 Silver Slugger Award, 469 Extra-Base Hits, 1169 Runs, 2207 Hits, 668 SB's, .702 OPS, 1 World Series Title
94	Jackie Jensen	AL MVP in 1958, 1 Gold Glove Award, 199 HR's, 503 Extra-Base Hits, 929 RBI's, 810 Runs, 1463 Hits, 143 SB's, .829 OPS

(Continued)

No.	Outfielder	Career Highlights
95	Curtis Granderson	1 Silver Slugger Award, 263 HR's, 606 Extra-Base Hits, 742 RBI's, 951 Runs, 1435 Hits, 141 SB's, .816 OPS to date*
96	Johnny Damon	235 HR's, 866 Extra-Base Hits, 1139 RBI's, 1668 Runs, 2769 Hits, 408 SB's, .785 OPS, 2 World Series Titles
97	Willie Davis	3 Gold Glove Awards, 182 HR's, 715 Extra-Base Hits, 1053 RBI's, 1217 Runs, 2561 Hits, 398 SB's, .723 OPS, 2 World Series Titles
98	Brady Anderson	210 HR's, 615 Extra-Base Hits, 761 RBI's, 1062 Runs, 1661 Hits, 315 SB's, .787 OPS
99	Ken Griffey, Sr.	152 HR's, 593 Extra-Base Hits, 859 RBI's, 1129 Runs, 2143 Hits, 200 SB's, .296 Avg, .790 OPS, 2 World Series Titles
100	Pete Rose	1963 NL Rookie of the Year (2B), 1975 World Series MVP (3B), NL MVP in 1973 (LF), 2 Gold Glove Awards (LF), 1 Silver Slugger Award (1B), 1041 Extra-Base Hits, 2165 Runs, 4256 Hits (ALL-TIME RECORD), .784 OPS, 2 World Series Titles at 3B, 1 World Series Title at 1B

Honorable Mention: Gus Bell, Frank Howard, Rocky Colavito, Tony Oliva, Rico Carty, Jimmy Wynn, Richie Zisk, Mickey Rivers, Al Bumbry, Bake McBride, Ron LeFlore, Gorman Thomas, Lonnie Smith, Pedro Guerrero, Lloyd Moseby, George Bell, Chili Davis, Mookie Wilson and Lenny Dykstra, Magglio Ordonez, Nelson Cruz*, Michael Brantley*, Lorenzo Cain*, Giancarlo Stanton*, Mookie Betts*

The Designated Hitter

At the start of the 1973 MLB season the designated hitter rule came into effect. What it meant was that one player from the lineup card (usually a Pitcher) could be replaced for his at-bats during the game by another player. It only came into effect in the American League, and to the baseball purist the National League did the right thing in rejecting this new rule. Since 1976, the World Series has employed the DH in some fashion or another.

"Big Papi" David Ortiz

Some of the top notch DH's (besides blue chip stocks like David Ortiz, Frank Thomas, and Edgar Martinez) throughout major league history include Gene Tenace, Rico Carty, Cliff Johnson, Andre Thornton, Larry Parrish, Ken Phelps, Chili Davis, Mike Sweeney, and Michael Young. What makes a Designated Hitter the all more productive is being able to hit in clutch situations. The aforementioned were all pretty good RBI men in these situations. It's a much appreciated relief to the fan of a team when your DH is up to bat instead of your pitcher.

To the baseball purist, however, the game should never have deviated into more of an offensive-minded one. The National League fan will tell you having no DH tests the manager to a greater degree. What do you do if your team's pitcher is throwing a no-hitter in a meaningful game of the year, and it's the 8th inning with a man on third, one out, and your pitcher is due up. Do you pinch hit for him to try and bring in the guy from third, or do you opt for the pitcher hitting, hoping he continues what he started on the hill for the ninth, with the off-chance that he'll knock in the winning run?

50 Greatest Designated Hitters of All Time

No.	Designated Hitter	Career Highlights
1	David Ortiz	2013 World Series MVP, 2004 ALCS MVP, 6 Silver Slugger Awards, 541 HR's, 1193 Extra-Base Hits, 1768 RBI's, 1419 Runs, 2472 Hits, .286 Avg, .931 OPS, 3 World Series Titles to date*
2	Frank Thomas	AL MVP in 1993 and 1994, 4 Silver Slugger Awards, 521 HR's, 1028 Extra-Base Hits, 1704 RBI's, 1494 Runs, 2468 Hits, .301 Avg, .974 OPS, HOF
3	Edgar Martinez	5 Silver Slugger Awards, 309 HR's, 838 Extra-Base Hits, 1261 RBI's, 1219 Runs, 2247 Hits, .312 Avg, .933 OPS
4	Paul Molitor	1993 World Series MVP Award, 4 Silver Slugger Awards, 234 HR's, 953 Extra-Base Hits, 1307 RBI's, 1782 Runs, 3319 Hits, .306 Avg, 504 SB's, .817 OPS, 1 World Series Title (DH), HOF
5	Jim Rice	A.L MVP in 1978, 2 Silver Slugger Awards, 382 HR's, 834 Extra-Base Hits, 1451 RBI's, 1249 Runs, 2452 Hits, .854 OPS, HOF
6	Edwin Encarnacion	268 HR's, 553 Extra-Base Hits, 815 RBI's, 1281 Hits, .846 OPS to date*
7	Dave Winfield	1 Silver Slugger as DH, 465 HR's, 1093 Extra-Base Hits, 1833 RBI's, 1669 Runs, 3110 Hits, 223 SB's, .827 OPS, 1 World Series Title, HOF
8	Hal McRae	1 Silver Slugger Award, 191 HR's, 741 Extra-Base Hits, 1097 RBI's, 940 Runs, 2091 Hits, .805 OPS, 1 World Series Title
9	Gary Sheffield	1 Silver Slugger Award at Third (4 more in OF), 509 HR's, 1003 Extra-Base Hits, 1676 RBI's, 1636 Runs, 2689 Hits, 253 SB's, .907 OPS, 1 World Series Title (OF)
10	Albert "Joey" Belle	5 Silver Slugger Awards, 381 HR's, 791 Extra-Base Hits, 1239 RBI's, 974 Runs, 1726 Hits, .933 OPS

No.	Designated Hitter	Career Highlights
11	Jose Canseco	1986 A.L Rookie of the Year, A.L MVP in 1988, 4 Silver Slugger Awards, one 40+HR/40+SB year, three 42+/26+ years, 462 HR's, 816 Extra-Base Hits, 1407 RBI's, 1186 Runs, 1877 Hits, 200 SB's, .867 OPS, 1 World Series Title
12	George Bell	A.L MVP in 1987, 3 Silver Slugger Awards, 265 HR's, 607 Extra-Base Hits, 1002 RBI's, 814 Runs, 1702 Hits, .785 OPS
13	Nelson Cruz	1 Silver Slugger Award, 241 HR's, 478 Extra-Base Hits, 690 RBI's, 581 Runs, .844 OPS to date*
14	Travis Haffner	213 HR's, 476 Extra-Base Hits, 731 RBI's, 619 Runs, 1107 Hits, .874 OPS
15	Jason Giambi	A.L MVP in 2000, 2 Silver Slugger Awards, 440 HR's, 854 Extra-Base Hits, 1441 RBI's, 1227 Runs, 2010 Hits, .916 OPS
16	Don Baylor	A.L MVP in 1979, 3 Silver Slugger Awards, 338 HR's, 732 Extra Base Hits, 1276 RBI's, 1236 Runs, 2135 Hits, 285 SB's, .777 OPS, 1 World Series Title
17	Eddie Murray	1977 A.L Rookie of the Year, 3 Gold Glove Awards, 3 Silver Slugger Awards, 504 HRs, 1917 RBI's, 1627 Runs, 3255 Hits, .836 OPS, 1 World Series Title, HOF
18	Cliff Johnson	196 HR's, 394 Extra-Base Hits, .815 OPS, 2 World Series Titles
19	Jack Clark	2 Silver Slugger Awards, 340 HR's, 711 Extra-Base Hits, 1180 RBI's, 1118 Runs, 1826 Hits, .854 OPS
20	Mike Sweeney	215 HR's, 545 Extra-Base Hits, 909 RBI's, 759 Runs, 1540 Hits, .297 Avg, .851 OPS
21	Dave Kingman	442 HR's, 707 Extra-Base Hits, 1210 RBI's, 901 Runs, 1575 Hits, .780 OPS
22	Al Oliver	3 Silver Slugger Awards, 219 HR's, 825 Extra-Base Hits, 1326 RBI's, 1189 Runs, 2743 Hits, .303 Avg, .795 OPS, 1 World Series Title
23	Greg Luzinski	307 HR's, 675 Extra-Base Hits, 1128 RBI's, 880 Runs, 1795 Hits, .840 OPS
24	Rusty Staub	292 HR's, 838 Extra-Base Hits, 1466 RBI's, 1189 Runs, 2716 Hits, .793 OPS
25	Chili Davis	350 HR's, 804 Extra-Base Hits, 1372 RBI's, 1240 Runs, 2380 Hits, .811 OPS, 3 World Series Titles
26	Andre Thornton	1 Silver Slugger Award, 253 HR's, 519 Extra-Base hits, 895 RBI's, 792 Runs, .811 OPS
27	Gene Tenace	1972 World Series MVP, 201 HR's, .817 OPS, 4 World Series Titles
28	Willie Horton	325 HR's, 649 Extra-Base Hits, 1163 RBI's, 873 Runs, 1993 Hits, .789 OPS, 1 World Series Title
29	Rico Carty	204 HR's, 499 Extra-Base Hits, 890 RBI's, 712 Runs, 1677 Hits, .833 OPS

No.	Designated Hitter	Career Highlights
30	Ken Phelps	.854 OPS
31	Ruben Sierra	1 Silver Slugger Award, 306 HR's, 793 Extra-Base Hits, 1322 RBI's, 1084 Runs, 2152 Hits, 142 SB's, .765 OPS
32	Rich Zisk	207 HR's, 478 Extra-Base Hits, .818 OPS
33	Hideki Matsui	175 HR's, 436 Extra-Base Hits, .822 OPS, 1 World Series Title
34	Ken Singleton	246 HR's, 588 Extra-Base Hits, 1065 RBI's, 985 Runs, 2029 Hits, .824 OPS, 1 World Series Title
35	Brad Fullmer	.822 OPS, 1 World Series Title
36	Vladimir Guerrero	A.L MVP in 2004, 8 Silver Slugger Awards, 449 HR's, 972 Extra-Base Hits, 1496 RBI's, 1328 Runs, 2590 Hits, 181 SB's, .931 OPS
37	Carl Yastrzemski	A.L MVP in 1967, Triple Crown in 1967, 452 HR's, 1157 Extra-Base Hits, 1844 RBI's, 1816 Runs, 3419 Hits, 168 SB's, .841 OPS, HOF
38	Larry Hisle	166 HR's, 391 Extra-Base Hits, 128 SB's, .799 OPS
39	Mo Vaughn	A.L MVP in 1995, 1 Silver Slugger Award, 328 HR's, 608 Extra-Base Hits, 1064 RBI's, 861 Runs, 1620 Hits, .906 OPS
40	Reggie Jackson	A.L MVP in 1973, 1973 World Series MVP, 1977 World Series MVP, 2 Silver Slugger Awards, 563 HR's, 1075 Extra-Base Hits, 1702 RBI's, 1551 Runs, 2584 Hits, 228 SB's, .846 OPS, HOF
41	Matt Stairs	265 HR's, 572 Extra-Base Hits, 899 RBI's, 770 Runs, 1366 Hits, .832 OPS, 1 World Series Title
42	Darrell Evans	414 HR's, 779 Extra-Base Hits, 1354 RBI's, 1344 Runs, 2223 Hits, .792 OPS, 1 World Series Title
43	Otto Velez	810 OPS
44	Cecil Fielder	319 HR's, 526 Extra-Base Hits, 1008 RBI's, 744 Runs, 1313 Hits, .827 OPS, 1 World Series Title
45	Mike Easler	.804 OPS, 1 World Series Title
46	B. J. Surhoff	188 HR's, 670 Extra-Base Hits, 1153 RBI's, 1062 Runs, 2326 Hits, 141 SB's, .745 OPS
47	Oscar Gamble	200 HR's, .811 OPS
48	Larry Parrish	256 HR's, 649 Extra-Base Hits, 992 RBI's, 850 Runs, 1789 Hits, .757 OPS
49	Erubiel Durazo	.868 OPS
50	Michael Young	185 HR's, 686 Extra-Base Hits, 1030 RBI's, 1137 Runs, 2375 Hits, .300 Avg, .787 OPS

Honorable Mention: Frank Howard, Jorge Orta, Manny Ramirez, and Carlos Santana*

50 Greatest Pinch Hitters of All Time

1. Dusty Rhodes
2. Matt Stairs
3. Willie McCovey
4. Cliff Johnson
5. Rusty Staub
6. Manny Mota
7. Gates Brown
8. Jerry Lynch
9. Joe Cronin
10. Harold Baines
11. Kirk Gibson
12. Smoky Burgess
13. Dave Hansen
14. Craig Wilson
15. Ken Phelps
16. Lenny Harris
17. Mike Stanley
18. Rich Reese
19. Jose Morales
20. David Bergman
21. Mark Sweeney
22. Denny Walling
23. Hal McRae
24. Greg Colbrunn
25. Seth Smith
26. Merv Rettenmund
27. Oscar Gamble
28. Wes Helms
29. Johnny Grubb
30. John Vander Wal
31. Erubiel Durazo
32. Ben Broussard
33. Jerry Turner
34. Terry Crowley
35. Steve Braun
36. David Dellucci
37. Willie McGee
38. Pat Kelly
39. Dwight Smith
40. Orlando Merced
41. Lou Piniella
42. Candy Maldonado
43. Tony Clark
44. Carlos Baerga
45. Thad Bosley
46. Don Baylor
47. Bernie Carbo
48. Alex Arias
49. Gerald Perry
50. Nippy Jones

Honorable Mention: Chuck Tanner and Alvin Woods (both homered in their first Major League at bat, as pinch hitters.)

50 Greatest Pitching Rotations of All-Time (1947 - Present)

1. **Cleveland Indians – 1954** - Bob Feller, Early Wynn, Bob Lemon, Dave Garcia, Art Houtteman
2. **Atlanta Braves – 1998** – Greg Maddux, John Smoltz, Tom Glavine, Kevin Millwood, Denny Neagle, Dennis Martinez
3. **Baltimore Orioles – 1971** - Jim Palmer, Mike Cuellar, Pat Dobson, Dave McNally

4. **Houston Astros - 1986** - Mike Scott, Nolan Ryan, Bob Knepper, Jim Deshaies, Danny Darwin, Matt Keough

5. **Los Angeles Dodgers – 1963** - Sandy Koufax, Don Drysdale, Johnny Podres

6. **New York Yankees – 1999** - Roger Clemens, Andy Pettite, David Cone, Orlando Hernandez

7. **Atlanta Braves - 1993** - Greg Maddux, Tom Glavine, John Smoltz, Steve Avery

8. **Toronto Blue Jays – 2015** - David Price, Marcus Stroman, Marco Estrada, Mark Buehrle, R.A. Dickey, Drew Hutchison, Aaron Sanchez

9. **Toronto Blue Jays – 1985** - Dave Stieb, Jimmy Key, Doyle Alexander, Jim Clancy, Luis Leal, Tom Filer

10. **Baltimore Orioles – 1979** - Mike Flanagan, Jim Palmer, Scott McGregor, Dennis Martinez, Steve Stone

11. **Oakland A's – 1972** - Vida Blue, Jim "Catfish" Hunter, "Blue Moon" Odom, Ken Holtzman

12. **Toronto Blue Jays – 1992** - Jack Morris, Juan Guzman, Jimmy Key, David Cone, Todd Stottlemyre, David Wells, Dave Stieb

13. **Houston Astros – 1980** - J.R. Richard, Nolan Ryan, Joe Niekro, Ken Forsch, Vern Ruhle, Joaquin Andujar

14. **Los Angeles Dodgers - 1974** - Andy Messersmith, Don Sutton, Doug Rau, Tommy John, Geoff Zahn

15. **Baltimore Orioles – 1980** - Scott McGregor, Steve Stone, Jim Palmer, Mike Flanagan

16. **Montreal Expos -1980** - Steve Rogers, Bill Gullickson, Scott Sanderson, David Palmer, Charlie Lea

17. **Boston Red Sox – 2004** - Curt Schilling, Pedro Martinez, Tim Wakefield, Derek Lowe

18. **Kansas City Royals – 1985** - Bret Saberhagen, Charlie Liebrandt, Danny Jackson, Mark Gubicza

19. **Baltimore Orioles – 1983** - Mike Boddicker, Scott McGregor, Jim Palmer, Mike Flanagan

20. **Philadelphia Phillies - 2011** - Roy Halladay, Cliff Lee, Cole Hamels, Roy Oswalt, Vance Worley

21. **Detroit Tigers - 2013** - Justin Verlander, Max Scherzer, Doug Fister, Anibal Sanchez, Rick Porcello

22. **Los Angeles Dodgers - 1966** - Sandy Koufax, Don Drysdale, Claude Osteen, Don Sutton

23. **Los Angeles Dodgers - 1985** - Fernando Valenzuela, Orel Hershiser, Bob Welch, Jerry Reuss, Rick Honeycutt

24. **Los Angeles Dodgers - 1965** - Sandy Koufax, Don Drysdale, Claude Osteen, Johnny Podres
25. **Oakland Athletics - 1990** - Dave Stewart, Bob Welch, Scott Sanderson, Mike Moore
26. **Montreal Expos - 1979** - Steve Rogers, Bill "Spaceman" Lee, Scott Sanderson, Dan Schatzeder, Ross Grimsley, David Palmer
27. **New York Mets - 1969** - Tom Seaver, Jerry Koosman, Gary Gentry, Nolan Ryan
28. **Houston Astros – 2005** - Roger Clemens, Roy Oswalt, Andy Pettite
29. **St. Louis Cardinals – 1985 -** John Tudor, Juaquin Andujar, Danny Cox
30. **Philadelphia Phillies - 1976** - Steve Carlton, Jim Lonberg, Jim Kaat, Larry Christenson, Tom Underwood
31. **St. Louis Cardinals - 1968** - Bob Gibson, Steve Carlton, Nelson Briles, Ray Washburn, Larry Jaster
32. **Chicago White Sox - 1983** - LaMarr Hoyt, Richard Dotson, Floyd Bannister, Britt Burns, Jerry Koosman
33. **Detroit Tigers - 1984** - Jack Morris, Dan Petry, Milt Wilcox, Juan Berenguer, Dave Rozema
34. **Chicago Cubs - 1989** - Greg Maddux, Rick Sutcliffe, Mike Bielecki, Scott Sanderson
35. **Los Angeles Dodgers – 1977** - Don Sutton, Bert Hooton, Doug Rau, Jerry Reuss
36. **New York Mets – 1986** - Dwight Gooden, Ron Darling, Walt Terrell, Sid Fernandez
37. **Chicago Cubs - 2003** - Carlos Zambrano, Mark Prior, Kerry Wood, Matt Clement
38. **Chicago White Sox - 2005** - Mark Buehrle, Freddy Garcia, Jon Garland, Jose Contreras, Orlando Hernandez
39. **St. Louis Cardinals - 1964** - Bob Gibson, Curt Simmons, Ray Sadecki, Ernie Broglio, Roger Craig
40. **Brooklyn Dodgers - 1955** - Don Newcombe, Carl Erskine, Johnny Podres, Sandy Koufax
41. **Seattle Mariners - 2001** - Freddy Garcia, Aaron Sele, Jamie Moyer, Paul Abbott, John Halama, Joel Pineiro
42. **New York Yankees - 1961** - Whitey Ford, Bill Stafford, Ralph Terry, Rollie Sheldon
43. **Washington Nationals - 2014** - Stephen Strasburg, Jordan Zimmermann, Tanner Roark, Doug Fister, Gio Gonzalez
44. **Cleveland Indians - 1968** - Luis Tiant, Sam McDowell, Sonny Seibert, Stan Williams, Steve Hargan

45. **Detroit Tigers - 1987** - Jack Morris, Doyle Alexander, Walt Terrell, Frank Tanana, Dan Petry
46. **Oakland Athletics - 1989** - Dave Stewart, Mike Moore, Bob Welch, Storm Davis, Curt Young
47. **New York Yankees - 1956** - Whitey Ford, Johnny Kucks, Don Larson, Tom Sturdivant, Bob Turley
48. **Minnesota Twins - 1991** - Jack Morris, Kevin Tapani, Scott Erickson, Allan Anderson
49. **Chicago Cubs - 2008** - Ryan Dempster, Ted Lilly, Carlos Zambrano, Jason Marquis, Rich Harden
50. **Detroit Tigers - 1968** - Denny McLain, Mickey Lolich, Earl Wilson, Joe Sparma

Honorable Mention

2016 Toronto Blue Jays - Marcus Stroman, Marco Estrada, R.A Dickey, Aaron Sanchez, J.A Happ, Francisco Liriano

1967 San Francisco Giants - Gaylord Perry, Mike McCormick, Juan Marichal, Ray Sadecki, Ron Herbel, Joe Gibbon

1977 New York Yankees - Ron Guidry, Jim "Catfish" Hunter, Don Gullett, Ed Figueroa, Mike Torrez, Ken Holtzman

1992 Atlanta Braves - John Smoltz, Steve Avery, Tom Glavine, Charlie Liebrandt, Mike Bielecki, Pete Smith

1975 Los Angeles Dodgers - Andy Messersmith, Don Sutton, Doug Rau, Burt Hooton, Juan Marichal, Rick Rhoden, Charlie Hough

1988 Los Angeles Dodgers - Orel Hershiser, John Tudor, Tim Leary, Tim Belcher, Fernando Valenzuela, Ramon Martinez, Don Sutton

2016 Washington Nationals - Max Scherzer, Stephen Strasburg, Gio Gonzalez, Tanner Roark, Joe Ross

2016 New York Mets - Noah Syndergaard, Jacob DeGrom, Matt Harvey, Steven Matz, Bartolo Colon, Logan Verrette

1977 Texas Rangers - Gaylord Perry, Doyle Alexander, Bert Blyleven, Dock Ellis, Len Barker, Nelson Briles

1968 Detroit Tigers - Denny McLain, Mickey Lolich, Earl Wilson, Joe Sparma, John Hiller, Pat Dobson

1976 New York Mets - Tom Seaver, Jerry Koosman, Jon Matlock, Mickey Lolich, Craig Swan

50 Greatest Left-Handed Pitchers of All-Time

1. Sandy Koufax
2. Randy Johnson
3. Steve Carlton
4. Lefty Grove
5. Warren Spahn
6. Clayton Kershaw*
7. Hal Newhouser
8. Whitey Ford
9. Tom Glavine
10. Ron Guidry
11. Fernando Valenzuela
12. Johan Santana
13. Madison Bumgarner*
14. Billy Wagner
15. David Price*
16. Aroldis Chapman*
17. Carl Hubbell
18. Rube Waddell
19. John Tudor
20. Babe Ruth
21. Lefty Gomez
22. Tommy John
23. Don Gullet
24. Andrew Miller
25. Sparky Lyle
26. Mike Cuellar
27. John Franco
28. Jimmy Key
29. Mickey Lolich
30. Randy Myers
31. Mark Langston
32. C. C. Sabathia
33. Cole Hamels*
34. Mike Flanagan
35. Jesse Orosco
36. Vida Blue
37. David Wells
38. Guillermo "Willie" Hernandez
39. Jamie Moyer
40. Mark Buehrle
41. Al Leiter
42. Frank Tanana
43. John Candalaria
44. Jerry Reuss
45. Kenny Rogers
46. John Lester*
47. Charlie Leibrandt
48. Frank Viola
49. Mike Hampton
50. Teddy Higuera

Honorable Mention: Johnny Vander Meer, Bill "Spaceman" Lee, Sid Fernandez, Norm Charlton, Tippy Martinez.

50 Greatest Right-Handed Pitchers

1. Satchel Paige
2. Roger Clemens
3. Christy Mathewson
4. Walter Johnson
5. Bob Gibson
6. Tom Seaver
7. Jim Palmer
8. Mariano Rivera
9. Pedro Martinez
10. Greg Maddux

11. Jim "Catfish" Hunter
12. John Smoltz
13. Dennis Eckersley
14. Nolan Ryan
15. Trevor Hoffman
16. Juan Marichal
17. Don Sutton
18. Charles "Hoss" Radbourne
19. Cy Young
20. Grover Alexander
21. Tommy Bond
22. Dizzy Dean
23. Robin Roberts
24. Roy Halladay
25. Mordecai "Three Finger" Brown
26. Craig Kimbrel*
27. Dazzy Vance
28. Bob Feller
29. Curt Schilling
30. Orel Hershiser
31. Don Drysdale
32. Rich "Goose" Gossage
33. Rollie Fingers
34. Gaylord Perry
35. J. R. Richard
36. "Smoky" Joe Wood and "Bullet" Joe Rogan
37. Dave Stewart
38. Jack Morris
39. Luis Tiant
40. Bruce Sutter
41. Dan Quisenberry
42. Lee Smith
43. Hoyt Wilhelm
44. Early Wynn
45. Ferguson Jenkins
46. Phil Niekro
47. David Cone
48. Mike Mussina
49. Dwight Gooden
50. Zack Greinke

Honorable Mention: Bob Lemon, Bert Blyleven, Mel Stottlemyre, Mike Marshall, Andy Messersmith, Justin Verlander*, Max Scherzer*, Jake Arrieta*, and Jake Arrieta.*

50 Greatest Swingmen of All-Time

1. Lefty Grove and Satchel Paige
2. Luis Tiant
3. Christy Mathewson
4. Mordecai "Three Finger" Brown
5. Walter Johnson
6. Dennis Eckersley
7. Phil Niekro
8. Wilbur Wood
9. Tom Gordon
10. John Smoltz
11. Dennis Martinez
12. "Smoky" Joe Wood
13. Mike Garcia
14. Al Leiter
15. Derek Lowe
16. Jim Perry
17. Jim Kaat
18. Ernie Broglio
19. Danny Darwin
20. Sal Maglie
21. Rudy May

22. Dennis Lamp
23. Woodie Fryman
24. Bill "Spaceman" Lee
25. Joe Niekro
26. David Palmer
27. Hoyt Wilhelm
28. Dan Schatzeder
29. Ray Sadecki
30. Larry Gura
31. Curt Schilling
32. Dean Chance
33. Tim Wakefield
34. Mike Cuellar
35. Larry Demery
36. Bob Turley
37. David Wells
38. Gaylord Perry
39. Dick Tidrow
40. Jerry Reuss
41. Rick Aguilera
42. Charlie Hough
43. John Hiller
44. Don Gullett
45. Dave Giusti
46. Dickie Kerr
47. Doyle Alexander
48. Ted Lyons
49. Luke Walker
50. Alejandro Pena

Honorable Mention: Preacher Roe, Don Larsen, Roger Craig, Mike McCormick, Jim Lonborg, Ken Brett, Rich "Goose" Gossage, Reggie Cleveland , Pete Vuckovich, Geoff Zahn, Don Aase, Juaquin Andujar, Rick Langford, Bruce Kison, Juan Berenguer, and John Cerutti

The Role of the Set-Up Man and Closers

The "Closer" really didn't surface in MLB until the early 70's. There were only a handful of guys chosen to close games out in the Fifties and Sixties; Elroy Face, Hoyt Wilhelm, and Dave Giusti come to mind from this era. The era was based on having a couple of swingmen in the bullpen. To spot start for the team when needed. As most rotations back then were a four-man, this necessitated that most starters could "finish what they started" and pitch nine inning affairs. As for set-up men, they never really existed from the 50's to the 70's, as most starters were averaging over seven innings a start.

It was the Pittsburgh Pirates with Dave Giusti, the Oakland A's with Rollie Fingers, the Mets with Tug McGraw, the Dodgers with Mike Marshall, and the Yankees with Sparky Lyle that started the trend and even at that it was skewed from what we see today, as most closers in the seventies were used for more than one inning per outing.

The first team to implement set-up man AND closer was the '77 Pittsburgh Pirates. They had Kent Tekulve as their set-up man (he was 10-1) and Rich "Goose" Gossage as their closer (he had 26 saves to go along with a 1.62 ERA. My second ranking of set-up man and closer would have to go to the Toronto Blue Jays in the early 90's when they had Duane Ward as the set-up man and Tom Henke as their closer. 3rd in ranking would be the 2014/15 Kansas City Royals with Kelvin Herrera, Wade Davis, and Greg Holland.

In the game today we see the set-up man/closer as a necessity as the average starter pitches six innings a start. The need to have a dominating pitcher in the role of set-up man and closer in there because of the intensity of the game in the late innings. This level of specialization has become a fixture of the game. When will relief pitchers eventually be recognized by Cooperstown? Sparky Lyle, Tug McGraw, Mike Marshall, Lee Smith, Tom Henke, and Trevor Hoffman...to name but a few guys that should be inaugarated into Cooperstown by this writer's account.

50 Greatest Closers of All Time

1. Mariano Rivera
2. Craig Kimbrel*
3. Aroldis Chapman*
4. Trevor Hoffman
5. Dennis Eckersley
6. Billy Wagner
7. Jonathan Papelbon*
8. John Wetteland
9. John Franco
10. Francisco Rodriguez
11. Rich "Goose" Gossage
12. Lee Smith
13. Tom Henke
14. John Smoltz
15. Bruce Sutter
16. Rollie Fingers
17. Rany Myers
18. Joe Nathan*
19. Brian Wilson
20. Elroy Face
21. Sparky Lyle
22. Eric Gagne
23. Kenley Jansen*
24. Dan Quisenberry
25. Kent Tekulve
26. Dave Giusti
27. Tug McGraw
28. Bobby Thigpen
29. Wade Davis*
30. Hoyt Wilhelm
31. Jesse Orosco
32. Rob Nenn
33. Todd Worrell
34. Duane Ward
35. Rick Aguilera
36. Jeff Reardon
37. Steve Bedrosian
38. Guillermo "Willie" Hernandez
39. Doug Jones
40. Jason Isringhausen
41. Roberto Hernandez
42. Trevor Rosenthal
43. Francisco Cordero
44. Rob Dibble
45. Jose Mesa
46. Heath Bell
47. Mike Marshall
48. Rafael Soriano
49. Bill Campbell
50. Michael Jackson

Honorable Mention: Frank Linzy, Tippy Martinez, Bill Caudill and Donnie Moore, B.J Ryan, Billy Koch, Jose Valverde, Brad Lidge, Neftali Feliz*, and Andrew Miller*

50 Greatest Set-Up Men of All-Time

1. Mariano Rivera
2. Wade Davis*
3. Duane Ward
4. Andrew Miller*
5. Rob Dibble*
6. Michael Jackson
7. Pedro Martinez
8. Kent Tekulve
9. Mark Eichhorn
10. John Hiller
11. Kelvin Herrera*
12. Jesse Orosco
13. Gary Lavelle
14. Larry Sherry
15. Norm Charlton
16. Dennis Lamp
17. Dellin Betances*
18. Mike Marshall
19. Darren Oliver
20. Mark Clear
21. Larry Anderson
22. Hoyt Wilhelm
23. Tippy Martinez
24. Mike Timlin
25. Sparky Lyle
26. Charlie Hough
27. Alejandro Pena
28. Kevin Siegrist*
29. Gene Garber
30. Mel Rojas
31. Clem Labine
32. Rudy May
33. Tug McGraw
34. Woodie Fryman
35. Jim Kern
36. Bob Stanley
37. David Wells
38. Mike Stanton
39. Casey Janssen
40. Aaron Sanchez
41. Jay Howell
42. Tim Burke
43. Ryan Madsen*
44. Ron Reed
45. Jeff Parrett
46. Sid Monge
47. Doug Bair
48. Terry Forster
49. Scott Downs
50. Greg Minton

3
Other Greats, Other Lists

75 Greatest Position Players

No.	Player
1	Josh Gibson
2	"Cool Papa" Bell
3	Buck Leonard
4	Barry Bonds
5	Willie Mays
6	Henry Aaron
7	Babe Ruth
8	Roberto Clemente
9	Derek Jeter
10	Jackie Robinson
11	Roy Campanella
12	Reggie Jackson
13	Lou Gehrig
14	Ted Williams
15	Jimmie Foxx
16	Rogers Hornsby
17	Stan Musial
18	Alex Rodriguez
19	Frank Robinson
20	Mike Schmidt
21	Ivan Rodriguez
22	Joe Morgan
23	Ozzie Smith

No.	Player
24	Ernie Banks
25	Ty Cobb
26	Johnny Bench
27	Mark McGwire
28	Carl Yastrzemski
29	Ken Griffey Jr.
30	Mickey Cochrane
31	Joe DiMaggio
32	Mickey Mantle
33	Kirby Puckett
34	Yogi Berra
35	Sammy Sosa
36	George Brett
37	Rickey Henderson
38	Cal Ripken, Jr.
39	Henry Greenberg
40	Roberto Alomar
41	Ryne Sandberg
42	Larry Walker
43	Eddie Collins
44	Charlie Gehringer
45	Albert Pujols
46	"Shoeless" Joe Jackson

No.	Player
47	Eddie Murray
48	Keith Hernandez
49	Honus Wagner
50	Brooks Robinson
51	Vladimir Guerrero
52	Dave Winfield
53	Lou Brock
54	Andre Dawson
55	Willie McCovey
56	Eddie Murray
57	Willie Stargell
58	Robin Yount
59	Pete Rose
60	Duke Snider
61	Mike Piazza

No.	Player
62	Tony Gwynn
63	Manny Ramirez
64	Barry Larkin
65	Eddie Mathews
66	Ichiro Suzuki
67	Tony Gwynn
68	Andy Van Slyke
69	David Ortiz
70	Jim Rice
71	Mike Trout*
72	Bryce Harper*
73	Jose Bautista*
74	Josh Donaldson*
75	Salvador Perez*/ Lorenzo Cain*

75 Greatest Pitchers of All Time

No.	Pitcher
1	Satchel Paige
2	Sandy Koufax
3	Roger Clemens
4	Christy Mathewson
5	Walter Johnson
6	Bob Gibson
7	Tom Seaver
8	Jim Palmer
9	Randy Johnson
10	Warren Spahn
11	Mariano Rivera
12	Pedro Martinez
13	Greg Maddux
14	Jim "Catfish" Hunter
15	Lefty Grove

No.	Pitcher
16	John Smoltz
17	Tom Glavine
18	Steve Carlton
19	Dennis Eckersley
20	Nolan Ryan
21	Trevor Hoffman
22	Juan Marichal
23	Don Sutton
24	Charles "Hoss" Radbourne
25	Cy Young
26	Grover Alexander
27	Tommy Bond
28	Dizzy Dean
29	Whitey Ford
30	Carl Hubbell

No.	Pitcher
31	Robin Roberts
32	Roy Halladay
33	Mordecai "Three Finger" Brown
34	Ron Guidry
35	Hal Newhouser
36	Dazzy Vance
37	John Franco
38	Bob Feller
39	Curt Schilling
40	Clayton Kershaw*
41	Orel Hershiser
42	Don Drysdale
43	Rich "Goose" Gossage
44	Rollie Fingers
45	Gaylord Perry
46	J. R. Richard
47	"Smoky" Joe Wood
48	Dave Stewart
49	Jack Morris
50	Luis Tiant
51	Mickey Lolich
52	Bruce Sutter
53	Dan Quisenberry

No.	Pitcher
54	Lee Smith
55	Lefty Gomez
56	Hoyt Wilhelm
57	Bob Lemon
58	Ferguson Jenkins
59	Phil Niekro
60	Sparky Lyle
61	David Cone
62	Mike Mussina
63	Billy Wagner
64	Babe Ruth
65	Johan Santana
66	Dwight Gooden
67	Zach Greinke
68	John Tudor
69	Mike Marshall
70	Vida Blue
71	Bert Blyleven
72	Fernando Valenzuela
73	Jimmy Key
74	Francisco Rodriguez*
75	Craig Kimbrell*/Rube Waddell

75 Greatest Defensive Players of All Time

No.	Player	Primary Position
1	Roberto Clemente	RF
2	Brooks Robinson	3B
3	Josh Gibson	C
4	Ozzie Smith	SS
5	Ivan Rodriguez	C
6	Garry Pettis	CF

No.	Player	Primary Position
7	Willie Mays	CF
8	"Cool Papa" Bell	CF
9	Roberto Alomar	2B
10	Keith Hernandez	1B
11	Ken Griffey, Jr.	CF
12	Jim Kaat	P

No.	Player	Primary Position
13	Roy Campanella	C
14	Jackie Robinson	2B/1B
15	Devon White	CF
16	Johnny Bench	C
17	Jesse Barfield	RF
18	Andrew Jones	CF
19	Dave Winfield	RF/CF/LF
20	Paul Blair	CF
21	Luis Aparico	SS
22	Andre Dawson	RF
23	Larry Walker	RF
24	Bob Gibson	P
25	Ryne Sandberg	2B
26	Kirby Puckett	CF
27	Ken Boyer	3B
28	Derek Jeter	SS
29	Andy Van Slyke	CF
30	Tony Fernandez	SS/2B/3B
31	Barry Larkin	SS
32	Greg Maddux	P
33	Bernie Williams	CF
34	Ichiro Suzuki	RF
35	Jim Edmonds	CF
36	Scott Rolen	3B
37	Barry Bonds	LF
38	Tony Gwynn	RF
39	Don Mattingly	1B
40	Joe DiMaggio	CF
41	Vernon Wells	CF
42	Mark Belanger	SS
43	Darrin Erstad	CF/1B
44	Curt Flood	CF

No.	Player	Primary Position
45	Eric Chavez	3B
46	Honus Wagner	SS
47	Jim Palmer	P
48	Joe Morgan	2B
49	Dwight Evans	RF
50	Willie McGee	CF
51	Steve Carlton	P
52	Mike Schmidt	3B
53	Willie McCovey	1B
54	Lenny Dykstra	CF
55	Mark Langston	P
56	George Scott	1B
57	Al Kaline	RF
58	Bill Mazeroski	2B
59	Nellie Foxx	2B
60	Cal Ripken, Jr.	SS
61	Henry Aaron	RF
62	Frank White	2B
63	Charlie Gehringer	2B
64	Lou Whitaker	2B
65	Alfredo Griffin	SS
66	Stan Musial	LF/1B
67	Lloyd Moseby	CF
68	Ozzie Guillen	SS
69	Mookie Wilson	CF
70	Mickey Mantle	CF
71	Jose Bautista	RF
72	Robin Yount	SS/CF
73	Alan Trammell	SS
74	Willie Wilson	CF
75	Pee Wee Reese	SS

50 Greatest Base Stealers of All Time

No.	Player	SB	CS	Pct
1	"Cool Papa" Bell	N/A	N/A	N/A
2	Rickey Henderson	1406	335	80.8%
3	Tim Raines	808	146	84.7%
4	Vince Coleman	752	177	81.0%
5	Lou Brock	938	307	75.3%
6	Willie Wilson	668	134	83.3%
7	Ty Cobb	897	N/A	N/A
8	Joe Morgan	689	162	81.0%
9	Davey Lopes	557	114	83.0%
10	Kenny Lofton	622	160	79.5%
11	Ozzie Smith	580	148	79.7%
12	Luis Aparicio	506	136	78.8%
13	Otis Nixon	620	186	76.9%
14	Ichiro Suzuki	508	116	81.4%
15a	Max Carey	738	N/A	N/A
15b	Eddie Collins	741	N/A	N/A
15c	Honus Wagner	723	N/A	N/A
16	Roberto Alomar	474	114	80.6%
17	Jose Reyes	488	119	80.4%
18	Paul Molitor	504	131	79.4%
19	Barry Bonds	514	141	78.5%
20	Bert Campaneris	649	199	76.5%
21	Cesar Cedeno	550	179	75.4%
22	Maury Wills	586	208	73.8%
23	Marquis Grissom	429	116	78.7%
24	Carlos Beltran	311	49	86.4%
25	Ron LeFlore	455	142	76.2%
26	Delino DeShields	463	147	75.9%
27	Omar Moreno	487	182	72.8%
28	Bobby Bonds	461	169	73.2%
29	Barry Larkin	379	77	83.1%
30	Eric Davis	349	66	84.1%

No.	Player	SB	CS	Pct
31	Jacoby Ellsbury	321	68	82.5%
32	Tommy Harper	408	116	77.9%
33	Chuck Knoblauch	407	117	77.7%
34	Amos Otis	341	93	78.6%
35	Freddie Patek	414	124	74.6%
36	Mookie Wilson	385	98	76.9%
37	Willie Mays	338	103	76.6%
38	Bobby Abreu	400	128	75.8%
39	Jackie Robinson	197	N/A	N/A
40	Willie Davis	398	131	75.2%
41	Willie McGee	352	121	74.4%
42	Juan Samuel	396	143	73.5%
43	Brett Butler	558	257	68.5%
44	Gary Pettis	354	104	77.3%
45	Dave Collins	395	139	74.0%
46	Lonnie Smith	370	140	72.5%
47	Frank Taveras	300	106	73.9%
48	Tony Gwynn	319	125	71.8%
49	Bill North	395	162	70.5%
50a	Jose Altuve*	199	59	77.1%
50b	Dee Gordon*	218	65	77.0%

Honorable Mention: Willie Keeler, Frank Chance, George Sisler, Frankie Frisch, Rod Carew, Mickey Rivers, Andre Dawson, Rodney Scott, Damaso Garcia, Lloyd Moseby, Von Hayes, Lenny Dykstra, Gary Redus, Brady Anderson, Deion Sanders, Derek Jeter, Johnny Damon, Alex Rodriguez.

10 Greatest Knuckleballers of All-Time

1. Eddie Cicotte
2. Hoyt Wilhelm
3. Phil Niekro
4. Wilbur Wood
5. Joe Niekro
6. Jesse Haines
7. Charlie Hough
8. Dutch Leonard
9. Ted Lyons
10. R. A. Dickey*

Honorable Mention: Tom Candiotti and Tim Wakefield

Thirty Greatest Switch-Hitters of All Time

1. "Cool Papa" Bell
2. Mickey Mantle
3. Eddie Murray
4. Chipper Jones
5. Tim Raines
6. Roberto Alomar
7. Pete Rose
8. Lance Berkman
9. Bernie Williams
10. Carlos Beltran
11. Reggie Smith
12. Mark Teixeira
13. Jose Reyes
14. Howard Johnson
15. Bobby Bonilla
16. Ken Singleton
17. Melky Cabrera
18. Willie McGee
19. Tony Fernandez
20. Jorge Posada
21. Chili Davis
22. Red Schoendienst
23. Roy White
24. Ted Simmons
25. Willie Wilson
26. Ruben Sierra
27. Frank Frisch
28. Ozzie Smith
29. Richie Ashburn
30. Gary Templeton

Great Baseball Dynasties

1. New York Yankees (1947-1963)
2. New York Yankees (in the 1920's)
3. Homestead Grays (in the 1920's)
4. Oakland Athletics (1972-1974)
5. Atlanta Braves (1991-2000)
6. Cincinnati Reds (1972-1977)
7. Pittsburgh Crawfords (1932-1934)
8. New York Yankees (1976-1978)
9. St. Louis Cardinals (1964-1968)
10. Pittsburgh Pirates (1970-1979)
11. Brooklyn Dodgers (1950's)
12. San Francisco Giants (2010-2014)
13. Boston Red Sox (2004-2007)
14. Los Angeles Dodgers (1962-1966)
15. Toronto Blue Jays (1983-1993)
16. Boston Red Sox (1967-1979)
17. New York Yankees (1996-2009)
18. Los Angeles Dodgers (1974-1981)
19. Minnesota Twins (1984-1991)
20. Kansas City Royals (1976-1985)

The Greatest Ballplayers of All Time All in One List

Position Players	Pitchers
1. Josh Gibson	1. Satchel Paige
2. "Cool Papa" Bell	2. Sandy Koufax
3. Buck Leonard	3. Roger Clemens
4. Barry Bonds	4. Christy Mathewson
5. Willie Mays	5. Walter Johnson
6. Henry Aaron	6. Bob Gibson
7. Babe Ruth	7. Tom Seaver
8. Roberto Clemente	8. Jim Palmer
9. Derek Jeter	9. Randy Johnson
10. Jackie Robinson	10. Warren Spahn
11. Roy Campanella	11. Mariano Rivera
12. Reggie Jackson	12. Pedro Martinez
13. Lou Gehrig	13. Greg Maddux
14. Ted Williams	14. Jim "Catfish" Hunter
15. Jimmie Foxx	15. Lefty Grove
16. Rogers Hornsby	16. John Smoltz
17. Stan Musial	17. Tom Glavine
18. Alex Rodriguez*	18. Steve Carlton
19. Frank Robinson	19. Dennis Eckersley
20. Mike Schmidt	20. Nolan Ryan
21. Ivan Rodriguez	21. Trevor Hoffman
22. Joe Morgan	22. Juan Marichal
23. Ozzie Smith	23. Don Sutton
24. Ernie Banks	24. Charley "Hoss" Radbourne
25. Ty Cobb	25. Cy Young
26. Johnny Bench	26. Pete "Grover" Alexander
27. Mark McGwire	27. Tommy Bond
28. Carl Yastrzemski	28. Dizzy Dean
29. Ken Griffey Jr.	29. Whitey Ford
30. Mickey Cochrane	30. Carl Hubbell
31. Joe DiMaggio	31. Robin Roberts
32. Mickey Mantle	32. Roy "Doc" Halladay
33. Kirby Puckett	33. Mordecai "Three Finger" Brown

Position Players	Pitchers
34. Yogi Berra	34. Ron Guidry
35. Sammy Sosa	35. Hal Newhouser
36. George Brett	36. Dazzy Vance
37. Rickey Henderson	37. John Franco
38. Cal Ripken Jr	38. Bob Feller
39. Henry Greenberg	39. Curt Schilling
40. Roberto Alomar	40. Clayton Kershaw*
41. Ryne Sandberg	41. Orel Hershiser
42. Larry Walker	42. Don Drysdale
43. Eddie Collins	43. Rich "Goose" Gossage
44. Charlie Gehringer	44. Rollie Fingers
45. Albert Pujols	45. Gaylord Perry
46. "Shoeless" Joe Jackson	46. J.R. Richard
47. Eddie Murray	47. "Smoky" Joe Wood
48. Keith Hernandez	48. Dave Stewart
49. Honus Wagner	49. Jack Morris
50. Brooks Robinson	50. Luis Tiant
51. Vladimir Guerrero	51. Mickey Lolich
52. Dave Winfield	52. Bruce Sutter
53. Lou Brock	53. Dan Quisenberry
54. Andre Dawson	54. Lee Smith
55. Willie McCovey	55. Lefty Gomez
56. Eddie Murray	56. Hoyt Wilhelm
57. Willie Stargell	57. Bob Lemon
58. Robin Yount	58. Ferguson Jenkins
59. Pete Rose	59. Phil Niekro
60. Duke Snider	60. Sparky Lyle
61. Mike Piazza	61. David Cone
62. Tony Gwynn	62. Mike Mussina
63. Manny Ramirez	63. Billy Wagner
64. Barry Larkin	64. Babe Ruth
65. Eddie Mathews	65. Johan Santana*
66. Ichiro Suzuki*	66. Dwight Gooden
67. Tony Gwynn	67. Zack Greinke*

Position Players	Pitchers
68. Andy Van Slyke	68. John Tudor
69. David Ortiz	69. Mike Marshall
70. Jim Rice	70. Vida Blue
71. Mike Trout*	71. Bert Blyleven
72. Bryce Harper*	72. Fernando Valenzuela
73. Jose Bautista*	73. Jimmy Key
74. Josh Donaldson*	74. Francisco Rodriguez*
75. Salvador Perez* / Lorenzo Cain*	75. Craig Kimbrel*/ Rube Waddell

Baseball's All-Time Roster

No.	Position	Starting Lineup
1	CF	"Cool Papa" Bell
2	SS	Derek Jeter
3	LF	Barry Bonds
4	C	Josh Gibson
5	RF	Ted Williams
6	DH	Babe Ruth
7	1B	Buck Leonard
8	3B	George Brett
9	2B	Jackie Robinson
	Position	Pitching Staff
	StP/Rel	Satchel Paige (R)
	StP	Sandy Koufax (L)
	StP	Roger Clemens (R)
	StP	Randy Johnson (L)
	StP	Bob Gibson (R)
	StP	Pedro Martinez (R)
	StP	Lefty Grove (L)
	Rel	John Franco (L)
	Rel/St	John Smoltz (R)
	Closer	Mariano Rivera (R)

Position	Substitutes
C	Johnny Bench
1B	Lou Gehrig
2B/SS	Ozzie Smith
SS/3B	Alex Rodriguez
OF	Willie Mays
OF	Henry Aaron

Great First Basemen in 1937

1. Buck Leonard
2. Lou Gehrig
3. Jimmie Foxx
4. Henry Greenberg
5. Johnny Mize

Buck Leonard

Greatest First Basemen 1977/78

1. Rod Carew
2. Steve Garvey
3. Willie Stargell
4. Willie McCovey
5. Pete Rose
6. Eddie Murray
7. Tony Perez
8. George Scott
9. Chris Chambliss
10. Mike Hargrove
11. Dan Driessen
12. Keith Hernandez
13. Jack Clark
14. Jason Thompson
15. Andre Thornton
16. Cecil Cooper
17. John Mayberry
18. Bill Robinson
19. Lee Maye
20. Willie Montanez

Honorable Mention; Dan Meyer, Doug Ault, and Ron Fairly

Greatest First Basemen 1983/84

1. Eddie Murray
2. Don Mattingly
3. Keith Hernandez
4. Cecil Cooper
5. Willie Upshaw
6. Kent Hrbek

7. Rod Carew
8. Jack Clark
9. Alvin Davis
10. Pete O'Brien
11. Darrell Evans
12. Pete Rose
13. Al Oliver
14. Steve Garvey
15. Tony Perez
16. Chris Chambliss
17. Bill Buckner
18. Dan Driessen
19. Steve Balboni
20. Ray Knight

Honorable Mention; Leon Durham, David Green, and Dave Kingman

50 Greatest Multi-Positional and Versatile Ballplayers

1. Jackie Robinson (1B/2B/3B/LF)
2. Tony Fernandez (SS/2B/3B)
3. Babe Ruth (P/RF)
4. Pete Rose (2B/LF/3B/1B)
5. Robin Yount (SS/CF)
6. Alex Rodriguez (3B/SS)
7. Henry Greenberg (1B/LF)
8. Darin Erstad (1B/CF)
9. Stan Musial (LF/1B)
10. Alfonso Soriano (2B/OF)
11. Junior Gilliam (2B/3B/LF)
12. Julio Franco (SS/2B/1B)
13. Dale Murphy (C/1B/OF)
14. Tony Phillips (2B/3B/OF)
15. Craig Biggio (C/2B)
16. Michael Young (2B/SS/3B/DH/1B)
17. Joe Sewell (SS/3B)
18. Marco Scutaro (2B/SS/3B)
19. Johnny Pesky (SS/3B/2B)
20. Joe Mauer (C/1B)*
21. Frankie Frisch (3B/2B)

22. Paul Molitor (2B/3B/1B/DH)
23. Howard Johnson (3B/LF)
24. Rico Petrocelli (SS/3B)
25. Pedro Guerrero (OF/3B/1B)
26. Denny Walling (OF/PH/1B/3B)
27. Miguel Cabrera (OF/3B/1B)
28. Albert Pujols (LF/1B)
29. Andre Dawson (CF/RF)
30. Al Oliver (OF/1B)
31. Jay Bell (SS/2B/SS)
32. Juan Samuel (2B/CF)
33. Yogi Berra (C/LF)
34. B.J. Surhoff (C/3B/OF)
35. Ray Boone (SS/3B/1B)
36. Rick Ankiel (P/OF)
37. Hubie Brooks (3B/SS/RF)
38. Brian Downing (C/OF/DH)
39. Mike Sweeney (C/1B/DH)
40. Buster Posey (C/1B)*
41. George Sisler (P/1B)
42. Rod Carew (2B/1B)
43. Joe Carter (OF/1B)
44. Willie Stargell (LF/1B)
45. Boog Powell (OF/1B)
46. Phil Garner (2B/3B)
47. John Olerud (P/1B)
48. Don Money (SS/3B/2B)
49. Jose Bautista (3B/RF)*
50. Carl Yastrzemski (LF/1B/DH)

Honorable Mention; Harry Heilmann (1B/OF), Cesar Cedeno (CF/1B), Dave Winfield (OF/DH), Greg Luzinski (LF/DH), Lee Lacy (2B/OF), Mickey Stanley (CF/SS), Mike Schmidt (3B/1B), Don Baylor (OF/DH), Jim Rice (DH/LF), Rick Rhoden (P/OF), Eddie Murray (DH/1B), Jim Gantner (2B/3B), Dave Stieb (OF/P), Manny Lee (2B/SS), Kevin Mitchell (LF/3B), Jeff Kent (3B/2B/1B), Mike Stanley (C/1B/DH), Carlos Santana (C/1B)*, and Ryan Goins (2B/SS)*

25 Greatest Multi-Sport Athletes (MLB included)

1. Bo Jackson - Played for the Kansas City Royals and the Oakland Raiders
2. Deion Sanders - Played for the Atlanta Braves and the Atlanta Falcons (only man to have appeared in a World Series and a Super-Bowl)
3. Michael Jordan - Played in the High Minors for the Chicago White Sox
4. Jim Thorpe - Played for the New York Giants, Boston Braves, Canton Bulldogs to name a few...
5. Dave Winfield - Drafted by teams in MLB, NFL, and NBA
6. Frank Thomas - Played Fullback for Auburn Universtiy alongside Bo Jackson
7. John Elway [a] - Was a standout Baseball Player and played in the High Minors
8. Bob Gibson - Played for the St. Louis Cardinals and the Harlem Globetrotters
9. Kirk Gibson - Was a standout Wide-Receiver on the '78 All-American Team, played for the Detroit Tigers and the Los Angeles Dodgers

10. Danny Ainge - Played for the Toronto Blue Jays and the Boston Celtics
11. Jackie Jensen - Was a Running Back and Defensive Back at University of Southern California
12. Frank Howard - Was an All-American Forward at Ohio State in Basketball
13. D.J Dozier - Played NFL Football as a Running Back and a year with the Mets
14. Vic Janowicz - 1950 Heisman Trophy winner who played for the Washington Redskins and the Pittsburgh Pirates
15. Dick Groat - Played in the NBA for the Fort Wayne Pistons in 1952
16. Tony Gwynn - Drafted by both the San Diego Padres and the San Diego Clippers
17. Tom Glavine - Drafted by the Los Angeles Kings
18. Rick Leach - Was Quarterback for the Michigan Wolverines
19. Todd Helton - Played Quarterback at the University of Tennessee
20. Ferguson Jenkins - Played for the Harlem Globetrotters
21. Ron Reed - Played in the NBA for the Detroit Pistons
22. Cumberland Posey [b]
23. Matt Kinzer - Played for the Detroit Lions and the Detroit Tigers
24. Brian Jordan - Was a Defensive Back for the Atlanta Falcons
25. Steve Hamilton - Played for the Minneapolis Lakers

a Signed by the New York Yankees, but never played a game with them.

b Played for and owned the Negro-League Baseball team the Homestead Gray's. Cum Posey was known as an elite basketballer at the turn of the 20th Century until about 1920. Posey is in both the Major League Baseball Hall of Fame in Cooperstown, and the NBA Hall of Fame.

Joe DiMaggio and
Ted Williams

Players with More Walks than Strikeouts in a Season Since 1947 (Minimum 10 Consecutive Seasons)

1. Joe DiMaggio
2. Ted Williams*
3. Stan Musial
4. Bill Dickey

5. Eddie Stanky
6. Johnny Pesky
7. Yogi Berra
8. Lou Boudreau*
9. George Kell
10. Jackie Robinson*
11. Red Schoendienst*
12. Richie Ashburn*
13. Jim "Junior" Gilliam*
14. Carl Yastrzemski
15. Nellie Fox*
16. Al Kaline
17. Pete Rose
18. Rusty Staub
19. Joe Morgan
20. Rod Carew
21. George Brett
22. Willie Randolph*
23. Brian Downing
24. Ozzie Smith*
25. Rickey Henderson
26. Wade Boggs
27. Tony Gwynn
28. Barry Bonds
29. Mark Grace*
30. Frank Thomas
31. John Olerud
32. Albert Pujols

* Signifies a ballplayer who had more BB than SO in EVERY YEAR PLAYED in his Major League career.

Honorable Mention; Frank Chance, Babe Ruth, Jim Bottomley, Zachariah "Buck" Wheat, Bill Terry, Luke Sewell, Nemo Leibold, Bobby Doerr, Ray Boone, Birdie Tebbetts, Phil Rizzuto, Harry Walker, Carl Furillo, Ted Kluszewski, Willie Mays, Mickey Mantle, Jackie Jensen, Billy Williams, Roy White, Sal Bando, Dave Cash, Ted Simmons, Bob Boone, Bill Madlock, John Mayberry, Ken Singleton, Darrell Evans, Steve Braun, Terry Puhl, Don Mattingly, and Lenny Dykstra

30 Monumental Trades in Baseball History

1. Babe Ruth from the Boston Red Sox to the New York Yankees for $100,000 U.S.D (1919/1920).
2. Frank Robinson from the Cincinnati Reds to the Baltimore Orioles for Milt Pappas, Jack Baldschen, and Dick Simpson (1965/66).
3. Jimmie Foxx from the Philadelphia A's to the Boston Red Sox for Gordon Rhodes, George Savinop, and $150,000 U.S.D (1935/36).
4. Harvey Kuenn from the Detroit Tigers to the Cleveland Indians for Rocky Colavito (1959/60).
5. Doyle Alexander from the Atlanta Braves to the Detroit Tigers for John Smoltz (at the 1987 trade deadline).
6. Roberto Clemente from the Brooklyn Dodgers (left unprotected in the Rule V draft). Drafted by the Pittsburgh Pirates as a free-agent (1955).

7. Nolan Ryan, Don Rose, Frank Estrada, and Leroy Stanton from the New York Mets to the California Angels for Jim Fregosi (1971/72)

8. Ozzie Smith from the San Diego Padres to the St. Louis Cardinals for Gary Templeton (1981/82).

9. Mark McGwire from the Oakland A's to the St. Louis Cardinals for T.J. Matthews, Blake Stein, and Eric Ludwick (at the 1997 trade deadline)

10. Roberto Alomar and Joe Carter from the San Diego Padres to the Toronto Blue Jays for Fred McGriff and Tony Fernandez. (1990/91).

11. Mickey Rivers and Ed Figueroa from the California Angels to the New York Yankees for Bobby Bonds (1975/76).

12. Gary Carter from the Montreal Expos to the New York Mets for Floyd Youmans, Hubie Brooks, Tom Fitzgerald (1984/85).

13. Ron Darling, Howard Johnson, and Walt Terrell from the Detroit Tigers to the New York Mets for Lee Mazzilli and drafts (1984/85).

14. Roy Halladay from the Toronto Blue Jays to the Philadelphia Phillies for Travis d'Arnaud, Kyle Drabek, and Michael Taylor (eventually traded for Anthony Gose - 2009/2010).

15. Curt Schilling, Pete Harnisch, and Steve Finley from the Baltimore Orioles to the Houston Astros for 1st Baseman Glenn Davis (1990/91).

16. Jose Reyes, Mark Buehrle, Josh Johnson, John Buck, Emilio Bonifacio, and cash from the Florida (Miami) Marlins to the Toronto Blue Jays for Yunel Escobar, Adeiny Hechavarria, Henderson Alvarez, Jake Marisnick, Justin Nicolino, Jeff Mathis and Anthony DeSclafani (2012/13).

17. Josh Donaldson from the Oakland A's to the Toronto Blue Jays for Brett Lawrie, Kendall Graveman, Franklin Barreto and Sean Nolin (2014/15).

18. John Franco from the Cincinnati Reds to the New York Mets for Randy Myers (1989/90).

19. Lou Brock, Jack Spring, and Paul Toth from the Chicago Cubs to the St. Louis Cardinals for Ernie Broglio, Doug Clemens, and Bobby Shantz (1964).

20. Noah Syndergaard and Travis d'Arnaud from the Toronto Blue Jays to the New York Mets for R.A. Dickey (2012/13).

21. Jose Reyes from the Toronto Blue Jays to the Colorado Rockies for Troy Tulowitzki (at the 2015 trade deadline).

22. C.C. Sabathia from the Cleveland Indians to the Milwaukee Brewers for Matt LaPorte, Zach Jackson, Rob Bryson, and a player to be named later (Michael Brantley - at the 2008 trade deadline).

23. Bob Turley, Don Larson, Billy Hunter, Dick Kryhoski, Mike Blyzka, Darrell Johnson, and Jim Fridley from the Baltimore Orioles to the New York Yankees for Harry Byrd, Jim McDonald, Hal Smith, Gus Triandos, Gene Woodling, Willie

Miranda, Bill Miller, Kal Segrist, Don Leppert, and Ted Del Guercio + (a player to be named later that never occurred - 1954/55).

24. Roger Maris, Kent Hedley, and Joe DeMaestri from the Kansas City Athletics to the New York Yankees for Marv Throneberry, Norm Siebern, Hank Bauer, and Don Larsen (1959/1960)

25. Shoeless Joe Jackson from the Cleveland Indians to the Chicago White Sox for Braggo Roth, Larry Chappell, Ed Klepfer, and $31,500 cash (at the 1915 trade deadline).

26. Rich "Goose" Gossage and Terry Forster from the Chicago White Sox to the Pittsburgh Pirates for Richie Zisk and Silvio Martinez (1976/77).

27. Tom Seaver from the New York Mets to the Cincinnati Reds for Pat Zachary, Doug Flynn, Steve Henderson, and Dan Norman (1977).

28. Alfredo Griffin and Dave Collins from the Toronto Blue Jays to the Oakland A's for Bill Caudill (1984/85).

29. Jeff Bagwell from the Boston Red Sox to the Houston Astros for Larry Anderson (at the 1990 trade deadline).

30. Randy Johnson from the Seattle Mariners to the Houston Astros for Freddy Garcia, Carlos Guillen, and John Halama (at the 1998 trade deadline).

Ten Most Impressive Seasons

Player	Year	Team	Avg	HR	RBI	SB	OBP	Slg%
1. Josh Gibson	1934	Pittsburgh Crawfords	.440	69	N/A	–	N/A	N/A
2. Barry Bonds	2001	San Francisco Giants	.328	73	137	13	.515	.863
3. Barry Bonds	2002	San Francisco Giants	.370	46	110	–	.582	.799
4. Barry Bonds	2004	San Francisco Giants	.362	45	101	–	.609	.812
5. Babe Ruth	1921	New York Yankees	.378	59	171	17	.512	.846
6. Barry Bonds	1996	San Francisco Giants	.308	42	129	40	.461	.615
7. Jimmie Foxx	1932	Philadelphia A's	.364	58	169	–	.469	.749
8a. Rogers Hornsby	1922	St Louis Cardinals	.401	42	152	17	.459	.722
8b. Rogers Hornsby	1925	St. Louis Cardinals	.403	39	143	5	.489	.756
9a. Sammy Sosa	2001	Chicago Cubs	.328	64	160	–	.437	.737
9b. Mark McGuire	1998	St. Louis Cardinals	.299	70	147	–	.470	.752
10. Sammy Sosa	1998	Chicago Cubs	.308	66	158	18	.377	.647

50 Home Run Seasons, and Near Misses

Player	HR	Year
Barry Bonds	73	2001
Mark McGwire	70	1998
Sammy Sosa	66	1998
Mark McGwire	65	1999
Sammy Sosa	64	2001
Sammy Sosa	63	1999
Roger Maris	61	1961
Babe Ruth	60	1927
Babe Ruth	59	1921
Jimmie Foxx	58	1932
Hank Greenberg	58	1938
Mark McGwire	58	1997
Ryan Howard	58	2006
Luis Gonzalez	57	2001
Alex Rodriguez	57	2002
Hack Wilson	56	1930
Ken Griffey Jr.	56	1997
Ken Griffey Jr.	56	1998
Babe Ruth	54	1920
Babe Ruth	54	1928
Ralph Kiner	54	1949
Mickey Mantle	54	1961
David Ortiz	54	2006
Alex Rodriguez	54	2007
Jose Bautista	54	2010
Chris Davis	53	2013
Mickey Mantle	52	1956
Willie Mays	52	1965
George Foster	52	1977
Mark McGwire	52	1996
Alex Rodriguez	52	2001

Player	HR	Year
Jim Thome	52	2002
Ralph Kiner	51	1947
Johnny Mize	51	1947
Willie Mays	51	1955
Cecil Fielder	51	1990
Andruw Jones	51	2005
Jimmie Foxx	50	1938
Albert Belle	50	1995
Brady Anderson	50	1996
Greg Vaughn	50	1998
Sammy Sosa	50	2000
Prince Fielder	50	2007
Babe Ruth	49	1930
Lou Gehrig	49	1934
Lou Gehrig	49	1936
Ted Kluszewski	49	1954
Willie Mays	49	1962
Harmon Killebrew	49	1964
Frank Robinson	49	1966
Harmon Killebrew	49	1969
Mark McGwire	49	1987
Andre Dawson	49	1987
Ken Griffey Jr.	49	1996
Larry Walker	49	1997
Albert Belle	49	1998
Barry Bonds	49	2000
Todd Helton	49	2001
Jim Thome	49	2001
Shawn Green	49	2001
Sammy Sosa	49	2002
Albert Pujols	49	2006

MVP Votes Worth Ruminating Over

1974 NL MVP

Steve Garvey (had 111 RBI's and won the Gold Glove at 1st Base - the eventual NL MVP) versus Lou Brock (set the single-season stolen base record with 118 SB) versus Mike Marshall (set the all-time single season games pitched record with 106 games) versus Johnny Bench (the best Catcher of his day, led the NL in RBI's with 129, belted 33 HR's and won a Gold Glove that year) versus Mike Schmidt (belted 36 home runs that year leading the NL, and stealing 23 bases) versus Joe Morgan (belted 22 HR's, stole 58 bases, and his OPS was .921winning the Gold Glove that year).

1978 AL MVP

Jim Rice versus Ron Guidry - Since I used to be a big Red Sox fan during this year in MLB, there was a bias towards Rice in my mind. The guy hammered 46 dingers, had 139 RBI's, a .315 Batting Average, and 16 of his home runs either tied or was the Game Winning RBI for the "Sox. The argument when the voting began stemmed from the insurmountable lead that Boston squandered to the Yankees in September of 1978. Guidry was a focal point of the Yanks" comeback. All Louisiana Lightening achieved during the "78 campaign was a 25-3 record with an ERA of 1.74, alongside 248 strikeouts. He also had an uncanny nine shutouts through the year. The MVP vote was close and the nod went to Rice. The merit of a position player versus a pitcher came up to many of the traditional voters and this cost Guidry. Both would have been deserving recipients of the AL MVP voting for this year.

1979 AL MVP

Don Baylor (36 HR's, led the AL with 139 RBI's, and had an OPS of .901 - the eventual AL MVP) versus Ken Singleton (35 HR's, 111 RBI's and an OPS of .938) versus George Brett (42 doubles, 20 triples, 23 HR's, 107 RBI's, 119 Runs, 212 Hits, 17 SB's, .329 Avg, .939 OPS) versus Fred Lynn (42 doubles, 39 HR's, led the AL in Avg .333, OBP - .423, and SLG% with a mark of .637 and OPS 1.059, had 122 RBI's, 116 Runs, won a Gold Glove that year) versus Jim Rice (39 HR's, 130 RBI's, .325 Avg, had 201 Hits, his OPS was .977) versus Mike Flanagan (23-9, won the Cy Young that year) versus Gorman Thomas (led the AL with 45 HR's, OPS of .895) versus Bobby Grich (led all second basemen with 30 HR's and had 101 RBI's with an OPS of .903)) versus Darrell Porter (had 112 RBI's leading all AL Catchers, led the AL in BB with 121, and had an OPS of .905) versus Jim Kern (the best AL Reliever that year).

1979 NL MVP

Willie Stargell versus Keith Hernandez - A virtual tie. Two First Basemen who had outstanding years in a year that saw the first and only occurance of a dead heat in the voting. "Pops" led his Pirates to their first World Series win since 1971, while Hernandez batted .344 exhibiting Gold Glove defense in his banner season. There was no determining factor between these two greats of the game, merits on both sides, hence the deadlock.

1998 NL MVP

Sammy Sosa versus Mark McGwire - All that happened this year was Roger Maris' single season home run record of 61 was shattered by these two greats of the game. When all was said and done, McGuire hit an astonishing 70 home runs alongside 147 RBI's with a Major League leading 1.222 OPS. Sosa wasn't far behind, obligerating Maris' old mark with 66 home runs. Sosa's 158 RBI's and 134 Runs Scored led the Majors in 1998. To be honest, I felt that Big Mac was the deserving candidate for the 1998 MVP, just for his leading in home runs and his incredible OPS mark. Sosa may have gotten the extra vote for taking his Cubs into the playoffs, but a tie would have been just, to say the least. What's incredible about these two ballplayers prowess in hitting the long ball is the fact that Sosa had 4 consecutive 50+HR/138+RBI seasons, while McGwire had 4 consecutive 52+HR/113+RBI campaigns mishmashed around 1998.

1999 AL MVP

Ivan Rodriguez (Seven 1st Place Votes - the eventual AL MVP) versus Pedro Martinez (Eight 1st Place Votes) versus Roberto Alomar (Four 1st Place Votes) versus Manny Ramirez (Four 1st Place Votes) versus Rafael Palmeiro (Four 1st Place Votes) versus Derek Jeter (One 1st Place Vote) versus Nomar Garciaparra versus Jason Giambi versus Shawn Green versus Ken Griffey Jr. versus Bernie Williams versus Carlos Delgado versus Juan Gonzalez versus Mariano Rivera versus Alex Rodriguez... They all had GREAT YEARS

2000 AL MVP

This year in the American League was filled with a truly remarkable offensive output. There were ten players that in my mind whose statistics would qualify as the 2000 AL MVP from an offensive standpoint. There were three 1st Basemen; Jason Giambi (the eventual winner), Carlos Delgado, and Mike Sweeney. There were three shortstops; Derek Jeter, Nomar Garciaparra, and Alex Rodriguez in the mix. There were two outfielders; Darin Erstad and

Manny Ramirez. Finally, there were two Designated Hitters that were lights out likewise; Edgar Martinez and Frank Thomas. To break down the statistics in this mix would be mind boggling. Take my word for it that any of the ten would have been worthy recipients of the 2000 AL MVP Award. Let's just call it a ten-way tie.

Post Season MLB Stars

Babe Ruth

Player	AB	H	R	2B	3B	HR	RBI	SB	CS	BB	K	BA	OBA	SA
Ruth	129	42	37	5	2	15	33	4	3	33	30	.326	.470	.744

Player	G	GS	W	L	IP	H	BB	K	ERA	CG	SHO	SV
Ruth	3	3	3	0	31.0	19	10	8	0.87	2	1	0

Won 7 World Series with the Boston Red Sox and the New York Yankees.

Sandy Koufax

Player	G	GS	W	L	IP	H	BB	K	ERA	CG	SHO	SV
Koufax	8	7	4	3	57.0	36	11	61	0.95	4	2	0

Won 4 World Series with the Brooklyn Dodgers and the Los Angeles Dodgers. Was the 1963 and 1965 World Series MVP .

Mariano Rivera

Player	G	GS	W	L	IP	H	BB	K	ERA	CG	SHO	SV
Rivera	98	-	8	1	141.0	86	21	110	0.70	-	-	42

Won 5 World Series with the New York Yankees. Was the 1999 World Series MVP and the 2003 ALCS MVP.

Curt Schilling

Player	G	GS	W	L	IP	H	BB	K	ERA	CG	SHO	SV
Schilling	19	19	11	2	133.1	104	25	120	2.23	4	2	-

Won 1 World Series with the Arizona Diamondbacks and 2 World Series with the Boston Red Sox. Was the 2001 World Series MVP.

Derek Jeter

Player	AB	H	R	2B	3B	HR	RBI	SB	CS	BB	K	BA	OBA	SA
Jeter	650	200	111	32	5	20	61	18	5	66	135	.308	.374	.465

Won 5 World Series with the New York Yankees. Was the 2000 World Series MVP.

David Ortiz

Player	AB	H	R	2B	3B	HR	RBI	SB	CS	BB	K	BA	OBA	SA
Ortiz	304	88	22	2	17	61	0	1	59	72	.289	.404	.543	.947

Won 3 World Series with the Boston Red Sox. Was the 2013 World Series MVP and the 2004 ALCS MVP.

Reggie Jackson

Player	AB	H	R	2B	3B	HR	RBI	SB	CS	BB	K	BA	OBA	SA
Jackson	281	78	41	14	1	18	48	5	2	33	70	.278	.358	.527

Won 3 World Series with the Oakland A's and 2 World Series with the New York Yankees. Won the World Series MVP in both 1973 and 1977.

Bob Gibson

Player	G	GS	W	L	IP	H	BB	K	ERA	CG	SHO	SV
Gibson	9	9	7	2	81.0	55	17	92	1.89	8	2	-

Won 2 World Series with the St. Louis Cardinals. Won the World Series MVP in both 1964 and 1967.

Manny Ramirez

Player	AB	H	R	2B	3B	HR	RBI	SB	CS	BB	K	BA	OBA	SA
Ramirez	410	117	67	19	0	29	78	1	1	72	91	.285	.394	.544

Won 2 World Series with the Boston Red Sox. Was the 2004 World Series MVP.

Mickey Mantle

Player	AB	H	R	2B	3B	HR	RBI	SB	CS	BB	K	BA	OBA	SA
Mantle	230	59	42	6	2	18	40	3	4	43	54	.257	.374	.535

Won 7 World Series with the New York Yankees.

Madison Bumgarner

Player	G	GS	W	L	IP	H	BB	K	ERA	CG	SHO	SV
Bumgarner	16	14	8	3	102.1	74	18	87	2.11	3	3	1

Won 3 World Series to date with the San Francisco Giants. Won the 2014 NLCS MVP and the 2014 World Series MVP.

Paul Molitor

Player	AB	H	R	2B	3B	HR	RBI	SB	CS	BB	K	BA	OBA	SA
Molitor	117	43	28	5	3	6	22	3	2	12	15	.368	.435	.615

Won 1 World Series with the Toronto Blue Jays. Was named the 1993 World Series MVP.

Bernie Williams

Player	AB	H	R	2B	3B	HR	RBI	SB	CS	BB	K	BA	OBA	SA
Williams	465	128	83	29	0	22	80	8	5	71	85	.275	.371	.480

Won 4 World Series with the New York Yankees. Was the 1996 ALCS MVP.

Christy Mathewson

Player	G	GS	W	L	IP	H	BB	K	ERA	CG	SHO	SV
Mathewson	11	11	5	5	101.2	75	10	48	0.97	10	4	-

Won 1 World Series with the New York Giants.

Randy Johnson

Player	G	GS	W	L	IP	H	BB	K	ERA	CG	SHO	SV
Johnson	19	16	7	9	121.0	106	32	132	3.50	3	2	0

Won 1 World Series with the Arizona Diamondbacks. Was named 2001 World Series MVP. Keep in mind that Johnson was 2-8 in Division Series with an ERA around 5.00 and his record in ALCS/NLCS/World Series play was 5-1 with an ERA around 1.50.

George Brett

Player	AB	H	R	2B	3B	HR	RBI	SB	CS	BB	K	BA	OBA	SA
Brett	166	56	30	8	5	10	23	2	3	17	20	.337	.397	.627

Won 1 World Series with the Kansas City Royals. Won the 1985 ALCS MVP.

Whitey Ford

Player	G	GS	W	L	IP	H	BB	K	ERA	CG	SHO	SV
Ford	22	22	10	8	146.0	132	34	94	2.71	7	3	-

Won 6 World Series Titles with the New York Yankees. Was named World Series MVP in 1961.

Chipper Jones

Player	AB	H	R	2B	3B	HR	RBI	SB	CS	BB	K	BA	OBA	SA
Jones	338	97	58	18	0	13	47	8	3	72	61	.287	.409	.456

Won 1 World Series with the Atlanta Braves.

Rollie Fingers

Player	G	GS	W	L	IP	H	BB	K	ERA	CG	SHO	SV
Fingers	30	0	4	4	57.1	50	17	45	2.35	-	-	9

Won three World Series with the Oakland A's. Won the 1974 World Series MVP Award.

Pedro Martinez

Player	G	GS	W	L	IP	H	BB	K	ERA	CG	SHO	SV
Martinez	16	14	6	4	96.1	74	30	96	3.46	0	0	0

Won 1 World Series with the Boston Red Sox.

Albert Pujols

Player	AB	H	R	2B	3B	HR	RBI	SB	CS	BB	K	BA	OBA	SA
Pujols	279	90	55	18	1	19	54	1	2	49	40	.323	.431	.599

Won 2 World Series with the St. Louis Cardinals. Was named the 2004 NLCS MVP. Would rank higher but he hit for a low average in the two World Series in which he participated.

Johnny Bench

Player	AB	H	R	2B	3B	HR	RBI	SB	CS	BB	K	BA	OBA	SA
Bench	169	45	27	8	3	10	20	6	1	18	29	.266	.335	.527

Won 2 World Series with the Cincinnati Reds. Was named the 1976 World Series MVP .

Roberto Alomar

Player	AB	H	R	2B	3B	HR	RBI	SB	CS	BB	K	BA	OBA	SA
Alomar	230	72	32	17	1	4	33	20	2	27	32	.313	.381	.448

Won 2 World Series Titles with the Toronto Blue Jays. Was named the 1992 ALCS MVP.

Carlos Beltran

Player	AB	H	R	2B	3B	HR	RBI	SB	CS	BB	K	BA	OBA	SA
Beltran	180	60	45	13	1	16	40	11	0	35	24	.333	.445	.683

His numbers are lights out, but he still hasn't won a World Series to date...

Dusty Rhodes

Player	AB	H	R	2B	3B	HR	RBI	SB	CS	BB	K	BA	OBA	SA
Rhodes	6	4	2	0	0	2	7	0	0	1	2	.667	.714	1.667

Won 1 World Series with the New York Giants. Was a pinch hitting machine during the 1954 World Series.

Mike Scott

Player	G	GS	W	L	IP	H	BB	K	ERA	CG	SHO	SV
Scott	2	2	2	0	18.0	8	1	19	0.50	2	1	-

Was the star of the 1986 NLCS Series. Topped the great Dwight Gooden in the Series. Would have taken home the NLCS MVP had the Astros pulled off the upset against the Mets

Chris Chambliss

Player	AB	H	R	2B	3B	HR	RBI	SB	CS	BB	K	BA	OBA	SA
Chambliss	114	32	12	4	1	3	15	2	0	5	14	.281	.314	.412

Won 2 World Series with the Yankees. Single handedly took his 'Yanks to the World Series in 1976 performing like the ALCS MVP in 1976.

Ron Guidry

Player	G	GS	W	L	IP	H	BB	K	ERA	CG	SHO	SV
Guidry	10	10	5	2	62.2	52	25	51	3.02	3	0	-

Won 2 World Series with the New York Yankees. "Louisana Lightening" was the arm the ,Yanks needed to win the '77 and '78 World Series.

Thurman Munson

Player	AB	H	R	2B	3B	HR	RBI	SB	CS	BB	K	BA	OBA	SA
Munson	129	46	19	9	0	3	22	1	1	5	19	.357	.378	.496

Won 2 World Series with the New York Yankees. Munson was integral towards the 'Yanks winning the '77 and '78 World Series.   People forget that he batted .529 in the '76 World Series against the Reds.

Don Larsen

Player	G	GS	W	L	IP	H	BB	K	ERA	CG	SHO	SV
Larsen	10	6	4	2	36.0	24	19	24	2.75	1	1	0

Won 2 World Series with the New York Yankees. The 1956 World Series MVP as he pitched the only Perfect Game in post-season history.

Carl Yastrzemski

Player	AB	H	R	2B	3B	HR	RBI	SB	CS	BB	K	BA	OBA	SA
Yastrzemski	65	24	15	3	0	4	11	0	0	9	3	.369	.447	.600

Yastrzemski surely would have taken home the 1967 World Series MVP had the Red Sox beaten the Cards that year, as he belted 3 Home-Runs and 5 RBI's in that Series to go along with a .400 Avg.

Fred Lynn

Player	AB	H	R	2B	3B	HR	RBI	SB	CS	BB	K	BA	OBA	SA
Lynn	54	22	8	4	0	2	13	0	0	5	8	.407	.450	.593

Never won the coveted World Series, however, Lynn won the 1982 ALCS MVP playing with the California Angels (even though they lost the Series to the Brewers).

Ryan Howard

Player	AB	H	R	2B	3B	HR	RBI	SB	CS	BB	K	BA	OBA	SA
Howard	170	44	22	13	1	8	33	1	1	26	67	.259	.357	.488

Won 1 World Series with the Philadelphia Phillies, took home the 2009 NLCS MVP, and performed admirably in the 2008 World Series when the Phillies won their first World Series Title since 1980.

Pete Rose

Player	AB	H	R	2B	3B	HR	RBI	SB	CS	BB	K	BA	OBA	SA
Rose	268	86	30	13	2	5	22	2	5	28	22	.321	.388	.440

Won 3 World Series Titles during his storybook career, two with the "Big Red Machine" of Cincy and one with the Philadelphia Phillies in 1983. Was the 1975 World Series MVP. In this writer's opinion, Rose should be granted Hall of Fame status in Cooperstown.

Kirk Gibson

Player	AB	H	R	2B	3B	HR	RBI	SB	CS	BB	K	BA	OBA	SA
Gibson	78	22	13	2	0	7	22	9	1	12	19	.282	.380	.557

Won 2 World Series in his fabled career, one with the Detroit Tigers in 1984 and one with the Los Angeles Dodgers in 1988. Was the shining light behind the Dodgers magical win against the powerful Oakland A's in the 1988 World Series. His pinch hit against Dennis Eckersley in the ninth inning of game 1 proved to be a demoralizing blow for the A's. Took home the ALCS MVP for his efforts with the Detroit Tigers in 1984.

Orel Hershiser

Player	G	GS	W	L	IP	H	BB	K	ERA	CG	SHO	SV
Hershiser	22	18	8	3	132.0	103	43	97	2.59	4	2	1

Won 1 World Series Title. Was the 1988 NLCS AND World Series MVP, took home the 1995 ALCS MVP with the Cleveland Indians. A true great of the game.

Joe Carter

Player	AB	H	R	2B	3B	HR	RBI	SB	CS	BB	K	BA	OBA	SA
Carter	119	30	15	5	0	6	20	3	1	7	20	.252	.282	.445

Won 2 World Series with the Toronto Blue Jays (their first in team's' history). Was the man who delivered the final nail in the coffin defeating the Philadelphia Phillies in the 1993 World Series as he clubbed a three-run Home-Run against Mitch Williams in the ninth inning of game six (the second Walk-off homer in World Series history, along with Bill Mazeroski's to end the 1960 World Series).

David Cone

Player	G	GS	W	L	IP	H	BB	K	ERA	CG	SHO	SV
Cone	21	18	8	3	111.1	93	58	94	3.80	1	0	0

Won 5 World Series Titles. Was a hired gun for the Blue Jays in 1992. Cone was integral to the New York Yankees reign in the late nineties-early 2000's, winning 4 World Series with the Bronx Bombers.

Mickey Lolich

Player	G	GS	W	L	IP	H	BB	K	ERA	CG	SHO	SV
Lolich	5	5	3	1	46.0	34	11	31	1.57	3	0	-

Won 1 World Series Title with the Detroit Tigers. Single handedly won the World Series for the Detroit Tigers in 1968. Outshined Bob Gibson and Denny McClain taking home the World Series MVP honors that year.

Jim "Catfish" Hunter

Player	G	GS	W	L	IP	H	BB	K	ERA	CG	SHO	SV
Hunter	22	19	9	6	132.1	114	35	70	3.26	4	1	1

Won 5 World Series Titles, three with the A's and two with the Yankees during the 1970's. A true great of the game.

Jim Palmer

Player	G	GS	W	L	IP	H	BB	K	ERA	CG	SHO	SV
Palmer	17	15	8	3	124.1	101	50	90	2.61	6	2	0

Won 2 World Series Titles with the Orioles.   Was always clutch in Post-Season games.

Alex Rodriguez

Player	AB	H	R	2B	3B	HR	RBI	SB	CS	BB	K	BA	OBA	SA
Rodriguez	278	72	43	16	0	13	41	8	3	39	77	.259	.365	.457

Won 1 World Series Title with the New York Yankees. A-Rod, while not dominating in Post-Season play has put up good numbers, winning a coveted World Series Title in 2009.

Andruw Jones

Player	AB	H	R	2B	3B	HR	RBI	SB	CS	BB	K	BA	OBA	SA
Jones	238	65	43	8	0	10	34	5	5	34	50	.273	.363	.433

Although Jones never won the World Series over the course of his career, he put up good numbers in post-season play.

Jim Edmonds

Player	AB	H	R	2B	3B	HR	RBI	SB	CS	BB	K	BA	OBA	SA
Edmonds	260	63	33	16	0	13	42	2	2	30	72	.274	.361	.513

Won 1 World Series Title with the St. Louis Cardinals in 2006. Edmonds was a Post-Season standout.

Troy Glaus

Player	AB	H	R	2B	3B	HR	RBI	SB	CS	BB	K	BA	OBA	SA
Glaus	78	25	18	5	1	9	16	0	0	9	20	.321	.398	.756

Won 1 World Series Title with the Anaheim Angels in 2002. Was the World Series MVP that year.

Darin Erstad

Player	AB	H	R	2B	3B	HR	RBI	SB	CS	BB	K	BA	OBA	SA
Erstad	118	40	18	9	0	3	12	4	0	5	17	.339	.368	.492

Won 1 World Series Title with the Anahein Angels.

Steve Garvey

Player	AB	H	R	2B	3B	HR	RBI	SB	CS	BB	K	BA	OBA	SA
Garvey	222	75	32	8	3	11	31	2	2	8	32	.338	.361	.550

Won 1 World Series Title with the Dodgers in '81. Garvey was the 1978 NLCS MVP with the Dodgers and the NLCS MVP for the San Diego Padres in 1984.

Yogi Berra

Player	AB	H	R	2B	3B	HR	RBI	SB	CS	BB	K	BA	OBA	SA
Berra	259	71	41	10	0	12	39	0	2	32	17	.274	.359	.452

Won 10 World Series Championships with the dynasty New York Yankees of the forties and fifties.

Henry Greenberg

Player	AB	H	R	2B	3B	HR	RBI	SB	CS	BB	K	BA	OBA	SA
Greenberg	85	27	17	7	2	5	22	1	0	13	19	.318	.420	.624

Won 2 World Series Titles with the Detroit Tigers in 1935 and 1940. One of the greatest Jewish ballplayers of all-time.

Hideki Matsui

Player	AB	H	R	2B	3B	HR	RBI	SB	CS	BB	K	BA	OBA	SA
Matsui	205	64	32	15	1	10	39	0	0	27	33	.312	.391	.541

Won 1 World Series Title with the New York Yankees in 2009. Was the 2009 World Series MVP. One of the great Japanese exports.

Honorable Mention; a) Ryan Braun b) Bill Mazeroski c) Fred McGriff d) Rusty Staub e) Bobby Richardson f) Henry Aaron g) Roberto Clemente h) Ken Griffey Jr. i) Joe DiMaggio j) Kirby Puckett k) Lou Brock l) Duke Snider m) Al Kaline n) Mike Sweeney (the only man in Post-Season history to have a 1.000 Batting Average 1 for 1) o) Jose Bautista p) Will Clark q) Lenny Dykstra r) Jimmie Foxx s) Mordecai "Three Finger" Brown a.k.a "Miner" t) Walter "Barney" Johnson a.k.a "The Big Train" u) David Wells v) Al Simmons w) Juan Guzman x) Ken Holtzman

Ten Underrated Power/Speed Guys

Player	Score*
1. Bobby Bonds	386.01
2. Andre Dawson	365.78
3. Paul Molitor	319.61
4. Steve Finley	311.93

5. Don Baylor	309.25
6. Cesar Cedeno	292.26
7. Kirk Gibson	268.72
8. Devon White	259.81
9. Amos Otis	246.49
10. Brady Anderson	231.57
*The Power/Speed Number, developed by Bill James. Equal to 2 x (Home Runs x Stolen Bases)/(Stolen Bases + Home Runs).	

1. Bobby Bonds was a true baseball traveler. Starting out with the San Francisco Giants in 1968, he seemed poised for greatness. By the time his career was over, Bonds had successful campaigns in San Fran, New York (with the Yanks), California, Texas, and Cleveland. He finished his career as a journeyman ball-player with the St. Louis Cardinals, and finally the Chicago Cubs.

   Make no mistake, Bobby Bonds had enormous talent and amazingly seemed to be passed over by every team he played with. Numbers do not lie though, and Bonds posted five 30+HR/30+SB seasons throughout his career, and eleven 20+HR/20SB years (seven consecutive). Had he remained with the Giants, he probably would have been voted into the Baseball Hall of Fame. As was, all Bonds did was poke 332 home runs and steal 461 bases.

   Here is Bonds' average yearly line;

AB	R	H	2B	3B	HR	RBI	SB	CS	BB	SO	AVG	OBP	Slg%
617	110	165	26	6	29	90	40	15	80	154	.268	.353	.471

2. Andre Dawson started his career with the Montreal Expos in 1977. There was no doubt that he would have success at the Major League level. He was a consistent 20+/20+SB producer in each of his first 10 seasons with the Expos. Ironically, it wasn't until he got out of Montreal to play a more one-dimensional game with the Cubs in 1987 (belting 49 HR's with only a couple of stolen bases) that Dawson became recognized by the average fan of the game. Baseball insiders knew better.

3. What is there to say about Paul Molitor? The man finished his career with over 3000 hits and had good pop out of his bat. The only weak spot of his game was that his defense wasn't extraordinary. After his tenure with the Milwaukee Brewers Molitor moved on to Toronto and finally Minnesota to play for his hometown Twins.

4. Steve Finley, bar none, was the most underrated ballplayer of the nineties -2000's. A dominant defensive Centerfielder winning 5 Gold Glove Awards,

Finley was also a dynamo with the bat. Hammering 304 home runs was not all of what he was made of offensively. Finley also stole 320 bases in his illustrious career. His lifetime average year shows that Finley hit 19 home runs and 20 Stolen Bases, almost achieving the laudable 20/20 mark.

5. Baylor began his career with the Baltimore Orioles and moved to the Oakland A's in 1976 claiming a 50+ Stolen Base season in his lone year with the A's. Baylor became a home run hitter with the California Angels the following year. In 1979, Baylor belted out 36 home runs and had 139 RBI's, winning the MVP that year. He moved to the Yankees and had continued success for the rest of his playing career. He became the third African-American to manage a Major League team (after Frank Robinson and Cito Gaston).

6. Truly underrated, Cesar Cedeno was a legitimate 20+HR/20SB threat every year he played. He started his career with the Houston Astros, and had his last productive year with the Cincinnati Reds. Cedeno had stolen over 50 bases in a year six times in succession (with the Astros between 1972-1977), and had three years in a row (1972-1974) posting 20+ home runs/ 20+ Stolen Bases.

7. Gibson started his career with the Tigers in '81 and was a 5-tool ballplayer until 1987. The following campaign Gibson joined the Dodgers and became a household name hitting a game-winning home run in game 1 of the series against Dennis Eckersley. Gibson sustained a long tenure as one of the best power/speed players over the duration of his career.

8. When 'Zelle started his career with the California Angels in 1987, he looked poised to be a standout of the game for years to come. He didn't really come into his own until the Toronto Blue Jays signed him in 1991. White is probably the best defensive ballplayer on this list, neigh Andre Dawson.

9. Amos Otis was a true 5-tool ballplayer. Playing for the highly successful Kansas City Royals' ball-clubs of the Seventies, Otis played table setter (stealing bases at a 90%+ rate). Amos was only a 15 home run/year hitter but provided the Royals with a clutch bat and excellent defense.

10. Brady Anderson is the only ballplayer in MLB history to have a season with 50+ home runs/20+Stolen Bases and a season with 20+home runs / 50+Stolen Bases.

Other Underappreciated Ballplayers

a. **Reggie Smith** - 1 Gold Glove Award, 2020 Hits, 314 home runs, 1123 Runs Scored, 1092 RBI's, 1 World Series title (1981)

b. **Tony Fernandez** - 4 consecutive Gold Glove Awards at shortstop, played as a starter at SS/2B/3B, 2276 Hits, 1057 Runs Scored, 1 World Series Title (1993)

c. **Vada Pinson** - 1 Gold Glove Award, 2757 Hits, five 20HR/20SB years, four 204+ Hit campaigns, 1365 Runs Scored, 1169 RBI's

d. **Dwight Evans** - 8 Gold Glove Awards, 2446 Hits, eleven 20+ HR campaigns, 385 home runs, 1470 Runs Scored, 1384 RBI's

e. **Lloyd Moseby** - Two 20+HR/20+SB campaigns, four consecutive 18+HR/32+SB seasons, 169 home runs, 280 Stolen Bases

f. **Andy Van Slyke** - 5 Gold Glove Awards, 164 home runs, 245 Stolen Bases, two 21+HR/30+SB campaigns

g. **Richie "Dick" Allen** - 1964 NL Rookie of the Year, 1972 AL MVP Award, ten 20+ HR years (nine consecutive), six 32+HR years, lifetime OPS of .912

h. **Julio Franco** - Won 5 Silver Slugger Awards, 2586 Hits, eight years batting .300+, 173 home runs, 281 Stolen Bases

i. **Jesse Barfield** - 2 Gold Glove Awards, six 23+ HR seasons, one 20+HR/20+SB year, 241 home runs, AL HR Leader in 1986

j. **George Foster** - 1977 NL MVP, ten 21+ home run seasons, NL HR Leader (1977/1978), led NL in RBI in 1976/77/78, 348 home runs, 2 World Series ('75/'76)

k. **Dave Stieb** - 176 wins-137 losses 3.44 E.RA, six 16+ win seasons, nine seasons with 205+ innings pitched, led AL in ERA in 1985, 1669 Strikeouts

l. **Gene Tenace** - 201 home runs, five years of 20+ HR's, six years with 101+BB, 4 World Series (1972-74, 1982), 1972 World Series MVP with the Oakland A's

m. **Dusty Baker** - 1977 NLCS Award, 1 Gold Glove Award, 2 S.S Awards, 1981 Hits, six years 20+ home runs, 242 HR's, 1013 RBI's, 1 World Series (1981)

n. **Davey Johnson** - 3 Gold Glove Awards, won two World Series (1966/70 w/ the Baltimore Orioles), hit 43 home runs in 1973

o. **Nellie Fox** - 1959 AL MVP, 3 Gold Gloves, AL Hit Leader 4 times, 187+ Hits/ Year eight times (10 years in a row with 175+ Hits), 2663 Hits, 1279 Runs Scored

p. **Bake McBride** - 1974 NL Rookie of the Year, 183 Stolen Bases, six years w/ 25+ Stolen Bases, six season Batting .300+, Lifetime Average of .299

q. **Lonnie Smith** - 4 years in a row 43+ Stolen Bases (1982-85), 8 years with 21+ Stolen Bases, 370 Stolen Bases, 5 years Batting .305+, 3 World Series (80/82/85)

r. **Nomar Garciaparra** - 1997 AL Rookie of the Year, 9 years .301+, six years 190+ Hits, 6 years 101+ Runs, 7 years 93+ RBI's, AL Batting Champ in 1999 and 2000

s. **Willie Randolph** - 2210 Hits, 4 years 30+ Stolen Bases, 271 Stolen Bases, 14 years in a row more BB than K's, Won the 1977 World Series (New York Yankees)

t. **Frank White** - 8 Gold Glove Awards, 1980 ALCS MVP, 2006 Hits, 4 years 19+ Stolen Bases, 160 home runs, 178 Stolen Bases, Won 1985 World Series (K.C)

u. **Rance Mulliniks** - Batted .300+ three times, a favorite prodigy of famed batting instructor Charlie Lau, keen eye at the plate

v. **Duke Snider** - Led NL in Runs 1953-55, 2116 Hits, 407 HR's, 1259 Runs, 1339 RBI's, 7 yrs .303+, 6 yrs 101+ RBI's, 5 yrs in a row 40+HR's, 2 W.S with Dodgers

w. **Richie Ashburn** - 2574 Hits, 234 Stolen Bases, 205+ Hits a year 3 times (leading NL all 3 years), 1322 Runs Scored, had more BB than K's in all 15 yrs played

x. **Bill Mazeroski** - 8 Gold Glove Awards, 2016 Hits, 2 World Series (with the Pittsburgh Pirates in 1960/71), known for W.S walkoff HR vs the Yankees in 1960

y. **George Scott** - 8 Gold Glove Awards, 1992 Hits, 271 home runs, 1051 RBI's, 5 years 20+home runs/88+RBI's, 9 years 17+HR's/77+RBI's

z. **Tim Raines** - 2605 hits, 1571 Runs, 170 home runs, 808 Stolen Bases, 14 of 15 years more BB than K's, 7 yrs in a row 50+ Stolen Bases, 11 yrs 40+SB, W.S (1996)

Honorable Mention; C- Joe Torre, Gary Carter, Darrin Fletcher, and Russell Martin 1B- Mike Sweeney, Fred McGriff, Cecil Fielder, and Carlos Delgado 2B- Tony Phillips, Jose Vidro, Billy

Doran and Jim "Junior" Gilliam 3B- Toby Harrah, Buddy Bell, Eric Chavez, and Ron Santo SS- Omar Vizquel, Alan Trammell, Alfredo Griffin, and Luis Aparicio LF- Jim Rice, Ron Le-Flore, Pedro Guerrero, and George Bell CF- Mickey Rivers, Tony Armas, Lenny Dykstra and Mookie Wilson, RF- Jackie Jensen, Tony Oliva, Raul Mondesi and Shawn Green DH- Jim Rice, Eddie Murray, Cliff Johnson, and Dave Phelps Starting Pitchers- Ferguson Jenkins, Jimmy Key, Mark Buehrle, Frank Tanana and Bert Blyleven Swingmen- Hoyt Wilhelm, Luis Tiant and Dennis Eckersley Set-Up Men- Kent Tekulve, Michael Jackson and Duane Ward Closers-Jeff Reardon and Tom Henke (The Canadian "Terminators")

20+ 2B's/ 20+ 3B's/ 20+ HR Seasons

Year	Player	Hits	2B	3B	HR	Runs	RBI	Avg	OBP	SLG%	OPS	TB	SB	MVP
1911	Schulte	173	30	21	*21*	105	*107*	.300	.384	*.534*	.918	*308*	23	Yes
1928	Bottomley	187	42	*20*	*31*	123	*136*	.325	.402	.628	1.030	*362*	10	Yes
1941	Heath	199	32	*20*	24	89	123	.340	.396	.586	.982	343	18	No
1957	Mays	195	26	*20*	35	112	97	.333	.407	*.627*	1.033	366	38	No
1979	Brett	*212*	42	*20*	23	119	107	.329	.376	.563	.939	363	17	No
2007	Granderson	185	38	*23*	23	122	74	.302	.361	.552	.913	338	26	No
2007	Rollins	212	38	20	30	*139*	94	.296	.344	.531	.875	380	41	Yes

Baseball Families

Brothers in MLB History

1. Christy and Henry Mathewson
2. Zach and Mack Wheat
3. Ike and Dan Boone
4. Joe, Luke, and Tommy Sewell
5. Dizzy and Paul Dean
6. Vince, Joe, and Dom DiMaggio
7. Dick and Dave Sisler
8. Dixie Jr. and Harry Walker
9. George and Skeeter Kell
10. Gaylord and Jim Perry
11. Phil and Joe Niekro
12. Norm and Larry Sherry
13. Felipe, Matty, and Jesus Alou
14. Tony and Billy Conigliaro
15. Jose, Hector and Tommy Cruz
16. Joe and Frank Torre
17. Cal Jr. and Billy Ripken
18. Mike and Greg Maddux
19. Pascual, Melido, and Carlos Perez
20. Sandy Jr. and Roberto Alomar

21. Ramon and Pedro Martinez
22. Aaron and Bret Boone
23. Rob and Rich Butler
24. David and Mike Bell
25. Orlando and Livan Hernandez
26. Jose, Bengie, and Yadier Molina

Vince, Joe, and Dom DiMaggio

Fathers-Sons in MLB History

1. Bob and Ray Boone
2. Dick, Dave and George Sisler
3. Harry, Dixie Jr. and Dixie Walker Sr.
4. Buddy and Gus Bell
5. Billy, Cal Jr., and Cal Ripken Sr.
6. Pete Rose Jr. and Sr.
7. Dick Schofield Jr. and Sr.
8. Barry and Bobby Bonds
9. Roberto, Sandy Jr., and Sandy Alomar Sr.
10. Moises and Felipe Alou
11. Todd and Mel Stottlemyre
12. Ken Griffey Jr. and Sr.
13. Aaron, Bret, and Bob Boone
14. Jose Cruz Jr. and Sr.
15. John Mayberry Jr. and Sr.
16. Tony Armas Jr. and Sr.
17. Tim Raines Jr. and Sr.
18. Mike, David, and Buddy Bell
19. Robinson and Jose Cano
20. Prince and Cecil Fielder
21. Kyle and Doug Drabek
22. Dee and Tom Gordon

The Journeyman Ballplayer (a.k.a "Field of Dreams")

The "Journeyman Ballplayer" was named such, as in the early days of professional Baseball (the late 19th Century) a ballplayer travelled from town to town to play in semi-pro and Professional Leagues. Many people considered other Professional Leagues, such as the Piedmont League and the International League (Leagues that had no affiliation to a Major League Team), to be on par to the National League of the Majors (the only League within the Majors at that time). The jorneyman ballplayer, many times played in a number of different Leagues, let alone teams. A ballplayer that I would refer to in Modern Day time would be Elston Howard, who started out in the independant Internantional League and moved on play many years in the Majors. Many times it would be a ballplayer earning stripes, and many times it would be a ballplayer who either prolonging his playing career, or gaining experience as a Manager. Sparky Anderson was a good example of that as he played the infield with the Toronto Maple Leafs (of the International League) after his lone year in the Bigs, and went on to Manage in the Major Leagues after his playing career. Bill Lajoie is a player who toiled in the Minors as a traditional "Journeyman Ballplayer" for ten years. He played for 16 teams overall.

In today's age we see many ballplayers moving from team to team within the Major Leagues. Such players include

1. **Bruce Chen** (11 Teams) - Played for the Atlanta Braves, Philadelphia Phillies, New York Metropolitans, Montreal Expos, Cincinnati Reds, Houston Astros, Boston Red Sox, Baltimore Orioles, Texas Rangers, Kansas City Royals, and the Cleveland Indians

2. **Roberto Hernandez** (10 Teams) - Played for the Chicago White Sox, San Francisco Giants, Tampa Bay Devil Rays, Kansas City Royals, Atlanta Braves, Philadelphia Phillies, New York Metropolitans, Pittsburgh Pirates, Cleveland Indians, and the Los Angeles Dodgers

3. **Jesse Orosco** (9 teams) - New York Mets, Los Angeles Dodgers, Cleveland Indians, Milwaukee Brewers, Baltimore Orioles, St. Louis Cardinals, San Diego Padres, New York Yankees, Minnesota Twins

4. **Rickey Henderson** (9 Teams) - Played for the Oakland Athletics, New York Yankees, Toronto Blue Jays, San Diego Padres, Anaheim Angels, New York Metropolitans, Seattle Mariners, Boston Red Sox, and the Los Angeles Dodgers

5. **Jason Grilli** (9 Teams) Florida Marlins, Chicago White Sox, Detroit Tigers, Pittsburgh Pirates, Los Angeles Angels, Atlanta Braves, and the Toronto Blue Jays

6. **Bobby Bonds** (8 Teams) - Played for the San Francisco Giants, New Yok Yankees, California Angels, Chicago White Sox, Texas Rangers, Cleveland Indians, St. Louis Cardinals, and the Chicago Cubs

7. **Doyle Alexander** (8 Teams) - Played for the Los Angeles Dodgers, Baltimore Orioles, New York Yankees, Texas Rangers, Atlanta Braves, San Francisco Giants, Toronto Blue Jays, and the Detroit Tigers

8. **Lee Smith** (8 Teams) - Played for the Chicago Cubs, Boston Red Sox, St. Louis Cardinals, New York Yankees, Baltimore Orioles, California Angels, Cincinnati Reds, and the Montreal Expos

Intriguing Teams (That Could Have Won the World Series With Any Luck)

The Boston Red Sox and Their World Series Losses in Seven Games:

1. 1946 - lost to the St. Louis Cardinals in Seven
2. 1967 - lost to the St. Louis Cardinals in Seven
3. 1975 - lost to the Cincinnati Reds in Seven
4. 1986 - lost to the New York Metropolitans in Seven

The 1974 Los Angeles Dodgers 102-60 (Lost in World Series in five games)

Manager - Tommy Lasorda

Starting Rotation

1. Andy Messersmith (RHP)
2. Don Sutton (RHP)
3. Doug Rau (LHP)
4. Tommy John (LHP)
5. Al Downing (LHP)
6. Geoff Zahn (LHP)

Bullpen

1. Rick Rhoden (RHP)
2. Geoff Zahn (LHP)
3. Jim Brewer (LHP)
4. Charlie Hough (RHP)

5. Mike Marshall (RHP)

Catcher

1. Steve Yeager
2. Joe Ferguson

First Base

1. Steve Garvey
2. Tom Paciorek

Second Base

1. Davey Lopes
2. Lee Lacy

Third Base

1. Ron Cey
2. Lee Lacy

Shortstop

1. Bill Russell
2. Lee Lacy

Left Field

1. Bill Buckner

2. Tom Paciorek
3. Manny Mota

Center Field

1. Jimmy Wynn
2. Von Joshua

Right Field

1. Willie Crawford
2. Tom Paciorek

The 1979 Houston Astros 89-73 (Finished 2nd in N.L West)

Manager - Bill Virdon

Starting Rotation

1. J.R. Richard (RHP)
2. Joe Niekro (RHP)
3. Ken Forsch (RHP)
4. Joaquin Andujar (RHP)
5. Rick Williams (RHP)
6. Vern Ruhle (RHP)

Bullpen

1. Joaquin Andujar (RHP)
2. Bobby Sprowl (LHP)
3. Randy Niemann (LHP)
4. Bret Roberge (RHP)
5. Joe Sambito (LHP)

Catcher

1. Alan Ashby
2. Bruce Bochy
3. Luis Pujols

First Base

1. Cesar Cedeno

2. Bob Watson

Second Base

1. Rafael Landestoy
2. Art Howe

Third Base

1. Enos Cabell
2. Art Howe

Shortstop

1. Craig Reynolds
2. Julio Gonzalez

Left Field

1. Jose Cruz Sr.
2. Denny Walling

Center Field

1. Terry Puhl
2. Denny Walling

Right Field

1. Jeffrey Leonard
2. Denny Walling

The 1980 Houston Astros 93-70 (Lost NLCS in five games)

Manager - Bill Virdon

Starting Rotation

1. Joe Niekro (RHP)
2. Nolan Ryan (RHP)
3. J.R. Richard (RHP)
4. Ken Forsch (RHP)
5. Vern Ruhle (RHP)
6. Joaquin Andujar (RHP)

Bullpen

1. Bobby Sprowl (LHP)
2. Joaquin Andujar (RHP)
3. Frank LaCorte (RHP)
4. Dave Smith (RHP)
5. Joe Sambito (LHP)

Catcher

1. Alan Ashby
2. Luis Pujols

First Base

1. Art Howe
2. Denny Walling
3. Dave Bergman

Second Base

1. Joe Morgan
2. Rafael Landestoy

Third Base

1. Enos Cabell
2. Art Howe

Shortstop

1. Craig Reynolds
2. Rafael Landestoy

Left Field

1. Jose Cruz Sr.
2. Jeffrey Leonard
3. Gary Woods

Center Field

1. Cesar Cedeno
2. Jeffrey Leonard

Right Field

1. Terry Puhl
2. Jeffrey Leonard

The 1986 Houston Astros 96-66 (Lost NLCS in six games)

Manager - Hal Lanier

Starting Rotation

1. Mike Scott (RHP)
2. Nolan Ryan (RHP)

3. Bob Knepper (LHP)
4. Jim Deshaies (LHP)
5. Danny Darwin (RHP)
6. Matt Keough (RHP)

Bullpen

1. Jeff Calhoun (LHP) *
2. Mike Madden (LHP) *
3. Frank DiPino (LHP)
4. Larry Andersen (RHP)
5. Aurelio Lopez (RHP)
6. Charlie Kerfeld (RHP)
7. Dave Smith (RHP

Catcher

1. Alan Ashby
2. Mark Bailey

First Base

1. Glenn Davis
2. Dan Driessen

Second Base

1. Billy Doran
2. Davey Lopes

Third Base

1. Denny Walling
2. Phil Garner

Shortstop

1. Dickie Thon
2. Craig Reynolds

Left Field

1. Jose Cruz Sr.
2. Terry Puhl

Center Field

1. Billy Hatcher
2. Terry Puhl

Right Field

1. Kevin Bass
2. Terry Puhl

The 1990 Pittsburgh Pirates 95-67 (Lost NLCS in six games)

Manager - Jim Leyland

Starting Rotation

1. Doug Drabek (RHP)
2. John Smiley (LHP)
3. Zane Smith (LHP)
4. Neal Heaton (LHP)
5. Bob Walk (RHP)
6. Randy Tomlin (LHP)

7. Bob Patterson (LHP)

Relievers

1. Bob Patterson (LHP)
2. Bob Kipper (LHP)
3. Stan Belinda (RHP)
4. Scott Ruskin (LHP)
5. Bill Landrum (RHP)

Catcher

1. Mike LaValliere
2. Don Slaught

First Base

1. Sid Bream
2. Gary Redus

Second Base

1. Jose Lind
2. Wally Backman

Third Base

1. Wally Backman
2. Jeff King

Shortstop

1. Jay Bell
2. Rafael Belliard

Left Field

1. Barry Bonds
2. Gary Redus

Center Field

1. Andy Van Slyke
2. John Cangelosi
3. Moises Alou

Right Field

1. Bobby Bonilla
2. Gary Redus

The 1998 Atlanta Braves 106-56 (Lost NLCS in six games)

Manager - Bobby Cox

Starting Rotation

1. Greg Maddux
2. Tom Glavine
3. John Smoltz
4. Danny Neagle
5. Kevin Millwood
6. Dennis Martinez
7. Bruce Chen

Relievers

1. Dennis Martinez
2. Mike Cather
3. Rudy Seanez
4. Mark Wohlers

5. John Rocker
6. Kerry Ligtenberg

Catcher

1. Javy Lopez
2. Eddie Perez

First Base

1. Andres Galarraga
2. Greg Colbrunn

Second Base

1. Keith Lockhart
2. Tony Graffanino

Third Base

1. Chipper Jones
2. Wes Helms

Shortstop

1. Walt Weiss
2. Ozzie Guillen

Left Field

1. Ryan Klesko
2. Danny Bautista
3. Gerald Williams

Center Field

1. Andruw Jones
2. Gerald Williams

Right Field

1. Michael Tucker
2. Gerald Williams

The 2011 Texas Rangers 96-66 (Lost World Series in seven games)

Manager - Ron Washington

Starting Rotation

1. C.J. Wilson (LHP)
2. Colby Lewis (RHP)
3. Derek Holland (LHP)
4. Matt Harrison (LHP)
5. Alexi Ogando (RHP)

Bullpen

1. Mike Adams (RHP)
2. Arthur Rhodes (LHP)
3. Koji Uehara (RHP)
4. Yoshinori Tateyama (RHP)
5. Mark Lowe (RHP)
6. Darren Oliver (LHP)
7. Neftali Feliz (RHP)

Catchers

1. Yorvit Torrealba
2. Taylor Teagarden
3. Matt Treanor

First Base

1. Mitch Moreland
2. Mike Napoli

Second Base

1. Ian Kinsler
2. Michael Young
3. Andres Blanco

Third Base

1. Adrian Beltre
2. Michael Young
3. Mike Napoli

Shortstop

1. Elvis Andrus
2. Andres Blanco
3. Michael Young

Left Field

1. Josh Hamilton
2. David Murphy

Center Field

1. Endy Chavez

2. Craig Gentry
3. Julio Borbon

Right Field

1. Nelson Cruz
2. David Murphy

Designated Hitter

1. Michael Young
2. Mike Napoli

The 2015 Toronto Blue Jays 93-69 (Lost in ALCS in six games)

Manager: John Gibbons

Starting Rotation

1. David Price (LHP)
2. Marcus Stroman (RHP)
3. Marco Estrada (RHP)
4. R.A. Dickey (RHP)
5. Mark Buehrle (LHP)
6. Drew Hutchison (RHP)
7. Aaron Sanchez (RHP)

Bullpen

1. LaTroy Hawkins (RHP)
2. Aaron Loup (LHP)
3. Bo Schultz (RHP)
4. Liam Hendriks (RHP)
5. Brett Cecil (LHP)
6. Aaron Sanchez (RHP)
7. Roberto Osuna (RHP

Catcher

1. Russell Martin
2. Dioner Navarro

First Base

1. Edwin Encarnacion
2. Justin Smoak
3. Chris Colabello

Second Base

1. Ryan Goins
2. Cliff Pennington
3. Devon Travis

Third Base

1. Josh Donaldson
2. Cliff Pennington

Left Field

1. Ben Revere
2. Dalton Pompey
3. Ezequiel Carrera

Center Field

1. Kevin Pillar
2. Dalton Pompey

Right Field

1. Jose Bautista
2. Dalton Pompey
3. Ezequiel Carrera

Designated Hitter

1. Edwin Encarnacion
2. Chris Colabello
3. Dioner Navarro

The 2016 Toronto Blue Jays 89-73 (Lost in ALCS in five games)

Manager: John Gibbons

Starting Rotation

1. Aaron Sanchez
2. J. A. Happ
3. Marco Estrada
4. Marcus Stroman
5. Francisco Liriano
6. R. A. Dickey

Bullpen

1. Ryan Tepera
2. Aaron Loup
3. Joe Biagini
4. Brett Cecil
5. Jason Grilli
6. Roberto Osuna

Lineup

1. Devon Travis (2B)
2. Josh Donaldson (3B)
3. Edwin Encarnacion (1B)
4. Jose Bautista (RF)
5. Troy Tulowitzki (SS)
6. Russell Martin (C)
7. Michael Saunders (LF)
8. Kevin Pillar
9. Ezequiel Carrera
10. Dioner Navarro (C)
11. Ryan Goins (2B/SS)
12. Darwin Barney (2B/3B)
13. Justin Smoak (1B)
14. Melvin Upton, Jr. (OF)
15. Dalton Pompey (OF)

Bet You Didn't Know...

1. 1954/1955 - Brooklyn Dodgers carried 5 men that went on to manage in the Major Leagues; Gil Hodges, Don Zimmer, Dick Williams, Roger Craig, Tommy Lasorda.

2. 1979/1980 - Chicago Cubs Rosters carried 5 men that went on to have 30+save years; Lee Smith, Bruce Sutter, Bill Caudill, Donnie Moore, Guillermo Hernandez.

3. Two men were traded by the Boston Red Sox to the New York Yankees and won awards with the Yankees: Sparky Lyle (Cy Young) and Babe Ruth (Chalmers Award).

4. Two teams in the history of the game had a 4-man rotation where each pitcher won 20+ games; Jim Palmer, Mike Cuellar, Pat Dobson, and Dave McNally of the 1971 Baltimore Orioles; and Red Faber, Eddie Cicotte, Lefty Williams, and Dickey Kerr of the 1920 Chicago White Sox.

5. The first Major Leagues was called the Piedmont League.

6. The last switch hitting American League MVP was pitcher Vida Blue (1971).

7. The first World Series was won by the Boston Red Sox in 1903, managed by Jimmy Collins.

8. The only man in Professional Baseball to hit 3 home runs in one inning was Eugene Marcerelli (Gene Rye) with El Paso (in 'A' Ball - the highest Minor League level at that time).

9. The only man in MLB history to hit 50+ HR and 20+ SB in one year and 50+ SB and 20+ HR in another season - Brady Anderson.

10. The only teams with four 30+ HR hitters in their lineup; 1977 Los Angeles Dodgers (Steve Garvey, Dusty Baker, Reggie Smith, and Ron Cey) and the 1998 Atlanta Braves (Andres Galarraga, Chipper Jones, Javy Lopez, and Andruw Jones).

4
Profiles of the Greats

Josh Gibson

Josh Gibson is probably the best ballplayer Baseball has ever seen, and ever will see.

When Gibson started out in the Negro Leagues with the Homestead Grays in 1930, he helped carry them to a playoff win over the New York Lincoln Giants. He batted an incredible .461 in his rookie campaign. Defensively, Gibson was equally as talented with his glove as with his bat.

Gibson moved to the Pittsburgh Crawfords in 1932 and teamed with Satchel Paige to bring the Crawfords to the top of the American League. Josh hammered 69 home runs in 1934 and in 1933, in just 137 games, Gibson hit 55 home runs batting .467 that year.

Over Gibson's career he hit 803 home runs in Negro League play. This was a huge accomplishment considering that he played the toughest position, backstop. Had Gibson not died at the age of 35 he probably would have put up another five years of stellar ball. It's a shame that he didn't get the opportunity to shine in the Major Leagues.

It is said that Gibson could hit the ball farther than Babe Ruth.

In 1937, the Dominican Republic "Dictator", Rafael Trujillo, signed Gibson. Playing alongside Satchel Paige and "Cool Papa" Bell, Gibson managed to bat .453, to lead the League, and Trujillo's team won the championship.

From 1936 – 1944, Gibson played for the Homestead Grays in the Negro Leagues and they won the National League Pennant each year, winning five World Series along the way.

When compiling Josh's lifetime totals (including his tours in Mexico, Cuba, Puerto Rico, Dominican Republic, Central America, and Canada) his lifetime home run total is at a staggering 962.

Gibson had a nervous breakdown in 1943 but returned to play until 1946. It was at this point that Josh developed a brain tumor. On January 20th, 1947 Gibson passed on.

Josh Gibson was finally recognized for his accomplishments on February 8th, 1972 as he was finally included in the Major League Baseball Hall of Fame – Cooperstown.

As testament to his statistics, had the Negro Leagues instituted a Baseball Hall of Fame, Josh most certainly would have been included the day he died.

Gibson's lifetime batting average was .391.

Satchel Paige

Satch Paige has been said to have been the greatest Pitcher of all-time (in any professional baseball league).

Paige began his career in 1926 with the Birmingham Black Barons. Satch established himself as the best Pitcher in the Negro Leagues when he moved to the Pittsburgh Crawfords. In 1932 Paige posted a 32-7 record, and in 1933 with the Crawfords he went an incredible 31-4.

In 1937 Paige and Josh Gibson went to play in the Dominican Republic (which was under rule by Dictator Rafael Trujillo). In 1938, Satchel was pitching in Mexico when he developed a sore arm.

Even still, Paige came back to "America" to pitch for the Kansas City Monarchs. The Monarchs won 4 consecutive American League Pennants, culminated by a World Series win in 1942. In that series Paige won 3 games and was selected World Series MVP.

Satch will always be remembered for an incident in the 1933 campaign. In one of his starts an opposing player was showboating. The next inning, when he came up to bat, Paige called all the position players to the mound and told them to sit down and proceeded to walk the bases loaded with two out. With just his battery mate (Josh Gibson), Paige proceeded to throw three consecutive strikes to record the strikeout.

When African-Americans were allowed to play in the Major Leagues, Paige was coveted by many teams. The Cleveland Indians signed Paige for the 1948 season. Satch was 42 years of age that year and incredibly managed to put up good numbers until 1953, the year he retired. At his retirement Paige was 48 years old. Paige came out of retirement in 1965, and ironically was signed by the Kansas City A's. At the age of 59 Paige pitched 3 innings of shutout ball to close his career.

"Cool Papa" Bell

"Cool Papa" was a Center-Fielder in the Negro-Leagues from 1922-1946. He played for the St Louis Stars, Kansas City Monarchs, Chicago American Giants, Pittsburgh Crawfords, and the Homestead Grays. When Bell played with the Grays he played alongside Josh Gibson, and Buck Leonard. Bell played with Satchel Paige when he was with the Pittsburgh Craw-fords.

"Cool Papa" was so fast that it was said when he hit the ball, he was on second base be-fore the ball hit the ground. That may be a slight exaggeration. However, Bell was document-ed to have run the bases in 12 seconds flat.

Had "Cool Papa" been ten years younger he most certainly would have been handpicked for the Major Leagues. As such, Bell's stardom was retarded by racism. Even though Bell was elected into the Baseball Hall of Fame in 1974 his contribution to the game is still not fully recognized. Bell's lifetime batting average in Negro-League play was .341. Bell once stole 175 bases in a 200 game season.

Bell was the table setter for the Homestead Gray's offense. The Gray's became a team of fabled folklore, due to their uncanny ability to score runs. Bell was the leader in runs for them.

"Cool Papa"s' defense has also been documented to have been extraordinary. Had Bell played in today's age he most certainly would win Gold Glove after Gold Glove.

I would have to say that "Cool Papa" Bell is the greatest Center-Fielder of all-time (even ahead of Willie Mays and Gary Pettis).

Jackie Robinson

Jackie Robinson began his professional baseball career as a back-up infielder for the Wash-ington Monarchs. After being schooled by Negro-League Great "Cool Papa" Bell, Robinson moved from Shortstop to 2nd Base in his formative years.

In 1946, Branch Rickey (Owner of the Dodgers) signed Robinson to a minor league contract with the Montreal Royals. The rest is history. All Robinson did was make the se-nior squad for good in '47. Rickey had no choice but to act. Robinson was an early call up in May of '47 and recorded Rookie of the Year honors. In '49 Robinson took home the MVP Award (his first full season at 2B, after two years at 1st Base) batting .342 with 16 home runs and 124 RBI's. Having lost 8 years in his early prime due to bigotry, Robinson showcased his diver-sity as both a dynamic offensive player, yet extreme-ly versatile in the field – playing 2nd base, 3rd base, 1st base, and Left-Field, at various points in his Major League career. Jackie was usually good for 20+ Stolen Bases, and 100 Runs Scored each year.

Jackie Robinson heard constant racial profiling and bigoted slurs from the fans, and even fellow ballplayers (some from Brooklyn). This made his success all that more remarkable.

In 1949, Robinson was moved to his natural position of 2nd base and may very well be the greatest defensive Second Basemen of All-Time. Jackie's best year may very well be his 1951 campaign in which he batted .338 with 25 stolen bases. It was in this year that he posted a Major League Record .992 Fielding %, committing an incredibly low seven errors all season.

Robinson took the Dodgers to the World Series; 1947, 1949, 1952, 1953, 1955, and 1956. The Dodgers won the '55 World Series in seven games against the fabled dynasty of the 'Bronx Bombers' featuring Mantle, Berra, and Whitey Ford. Brooklyn in those days were the Atlanta Braves of our day, sort of a championship team with only one World Series Title to show for it. A team that carried Jackie, Roy Campanella, Duke Snider, Gil Hodges, Carl Furillo, Al Gianfranco, Don Newcombe, Carl Erskine, Pee Wee Reese, Junior Gilliam, Sam Jethroe, and even Ralph Branca (the man who gave up the "shot heard around the world" to Bobby Thomson) vividly come to mind.

Over the course of his ten year career, Robinson batted .308+ in 6 consecutive years (1949-1954). He also stole 22+ Bases, in five of his first six years.

Not only was Robinson a great hitter and glove, he may very well be the most versatile ballplayer the game has ever seen, the most diverse as one of the 5-tool pioneers (alongside Willie Mays, Henry Aaron, and Roberto Clemente).

Henry Aaron

Henry Aaron may very well have been the greatest hitter to have played the game. Aaron posted fifteen seasons of 30+home runs/Year. He also batted .300+ fourteen times in his career. Aaron finished his career with the most lifetime home runs with 755 and had 3771 lifetime hits, with a .305 lifetime batting average, and 2297 RBI, still the most all time.

What made Aaron so special was that he was truly consistent over the years he played. From 1957–1973 he failed to hit 30+home runs only twice.

Hank Aaron started his career with the Indianapolis Clowns of the Negro-Leagues and fared well as a prospective Shortstop. He was signed by the Milwaukee Braves on this premise. While in the Braves chain Aaron was moved to his post in Right-Field which he served for 23 years. In his minor league days, starting in 1952, Aaron played alongside Wes Covington whom he claimed was a "Negro" too colourful for the Braves organization. Aaron always considered Covington to be a better player than himself and although Covington was called up to play with the Braves, he never reached the status that Aaron thought he deserved.

Aaron's professional career actually started in 1952 with the Indianapolis Clowns in the Negro Leagues. He was a standout Shortstop. Had the Major Leagues truly integrated African American Teams and players into the game, Worldwide Media would have integrated African-American Ownership in North American sport. In truth, while the Dominican Republic, Mexico, Puerto Rico, and Cuba are top Leagues in the World, the U.S.A market for Baseball has far too much bigotry when it comes to changing economic times.

When Aaron reached the Majors in 1954, he joined a great team. With Spahn, Sain, and Lou Burdette in the rotation, and Joe Adcock and Eddie Mathews in the lineup, the Braves were peaking when Aaron joined them. It all came together in 1957, with Aaron leading the way. Aaron won the MVP that year and led Milwaukee to their first World Series Title, the organization's first since their days in Boston. They looked poised to win more but were defeated the next year against the New York Yankees in a rematch of the '57 Series. They never won another World Series Title in Milwaukee.

The team relocated to Atlanta in 1966, but didn't win a Series in the remainder of Aaron's career.

Aaron did however have another goal in mind (although I'm sure he'd have taken another World Series Title instead): his pursuit of Babe Ruth's Career home run record of 714.

When Aaron started to get close in 1973 he received hate letters and death threats in large numbers. This hatred was nothing more than ignorance. Aaron passed Babe Ruth early in the season of 1974, and then went back to Milwaukee to finish his career with the expansion Milwaukee Brewers.

Henry Aaron is now the only African-American President of Operations and has held this position with the Atlanta Braves since 1988. It would stand to reason that America's pastime would promote African-American ownership at three levels;

1. The MLBPA (Major League Baseball Players Association)
2. Ownership of specific franchises
3. Major League Executive positions

It was 1936, in Berlin, Germany, when Jesse Owens defeated Nazi-ism by winning four Gold Medals. In 1947 Jackie Robinson broke the color barrier in MLB.

In 2008 there are zero African-American Owners in Major League Baseball. There has never been an African-American named Commissioner.

This was why the British and the Americans fought WWII?

Alex Rodriguez

A great of the game who is still playing today. Not only has Rodriguez dominated with his bat, but he was a standout defensive shortstop in his own right earlier in his career, taking home two Gold Glove Awards. A-Rod has won ten Silver Slugger Awards to this point of his career (seven from the shortstop position and three at third base once he arrived in New York with the Yankees). A-Rod has won the illustrious MVP Award three times to this point of his career, and although it looks like his better days are behind him, he's still a capable bat in any batting order in the game today. Going into the 2016 campaign, Rodriguez had 687 home runs, and looks poised to top the great Babe Ruth in career home runs (714) once his playing career ends. Time will tell if A-Rod will catch up to the Major League record 762 home runs set by the great Barry Bonds. To this point of his career Alex Rodriguez has mashed out a lifetime OPS score of .936. He will surely be enshrined in Cooperstown, unless blackballed for steroid use earlier in his career. The only dark mark in his career is that he only won one World Series Title, doing so with the 2009 New York Yankees.

Babe Ruth

Babe Ruth started his career in 1914 with the Boston Red Sox. He was a pitcher and thought of, at the time, to be the man to replace "Smoky" Joe Wood. In Ruth's third season he not only won 23 games, he also had 9 shutouts that season. This led the Red Sox to a World Series title. He also won 2 games as a starting pitcher in the 1918 World Series.

Proven as a pitcher, the Red Sox also had their eye on Ruth's bat. He belted 11 home runs in 1918 (which was a substantial amount for the Major Leagues back then – it led the league). In 1919, not only did Ruth flourish as the Red Sox right fielder, he led the Majors in home runs again with 29. This was only a sign of things to come.

The New York Yankees bought Ruth's contract from the Red Sox for what was thought to be too much for any one player (in excess of $300,000). Ruth not only superceded expectations, he was also responsible for the home run style of play that revolutionized how the game was played. Up to that point in the game, Batting Average and stolen bases were the foundation for the offense of the game.

Ruth's yearly home run totals from 1920 – 1934 were; 54, 59, 35, 41, 46, 25, 47, 60, 54, 46, 49, 46, 41, 34, 22. Ironically, Ruth finished his career back in Boston in 1935 where he hit 6 home runs for the Boston Braves.

Barry Bonds

When Bonds started his career with the Pittsburgh Pirates, he was 21, fresh out of Arizona State University. Bonds started his career as a five-tool player. By 1990, Bonds captured his first MVP Trophy. He won seven Most Valuable Player Awards (including 4 in a row 2001– 2004) over a storybook career. The only thing missing was a World Series Title.

From 1990 – 1999 Bonds was a 20HR/20SB man every year but one. As well, he posted 5 30HR/30SB seasons in the 90's and even had the elusive 40+HR's/40SB's campaign. The scary thing was, Bonds just got better with age and started hitting the long ball with greater proficiency, topping out at 73 in 2001. Bonds finished his playing career with the Major League Record in home runs in a single season with 73, and the Major League Record for lifetime home runs with 762.

Bonds' had 45+ home runs every year from 2001 to 2004. During that stretch, his numbers were stratospheric, leaving all historical figures behind.

Year	AB	Hits	Avg	Run	2B	3B	HR	RBI	Slg%	OBP	SB	BB	SO
2001	476	156	.328	129	32	2	73	137	.863	.515	13	177	93
2002	403	149	.370	117	31	2	46	110	.799	.582	9	198	47
2003	390	133	.341	111	22	1	45	90	.749	.529	7	148	58
2004	373	135	.362	128	27	3	45	101	.817	.609	6	232	41

Taking each statistical average; Here's what our computer said should have happened for Barry for '05.

Bonds	406	141	.348	119	27	2	51	106	.795	.553	8	181	60
Ruth	544	186	.342	141	33	9	46	143	.690	.474	8	133	86

In comparing Bonds' average year for his best 5-year stretch with Ruth's average top 5 seasons, we see that Bonds is 105 points up in Slugging %, and 79 points higher in On Base %. The OPS average for Bonds is 1.348 (1348 points). The OPS average for Ruth is 1.164 (1164 points).

After sitting out the 2005 due to having surgery on his knee, Bonds came back strong for the '06 campaign and bashed out 26 home runs in only 367 At-Bats carrying an OPS of .999. Bond finished his career in 2007 and this time he slugged 28 home runs in only 340 At-Bats, with an OPS of 1.045. Although Bonds didn't reach the lofty projections previously speculated, it was still not bad for a 42 year old.

Up until 1993 Bonds was the franchise player for the Pittsburgh Pirates. In '93 he moved to the San Francisco Giants where he has continued his dominance. Having moved to left-field while in Pittsburgh (to accommodate Andy Van Slyke), all Barry did was win eight consecutive Gold Gloves, the majority of them with San Francisco.

Over the course of his career Bonds bashed 762 home runs (for the home run record) and had a lofty 514 Stolen Bases to boot. His lifetime batting average was .298. He had nine consecutive 31.6+Power\Speed numbers from 1990-1998. Bonds was one in intentional walks 11 times in his career, reaching an astounding peak of 120 in 2004. Bonds has ten first place years for adjusted on-Base%/Slugging%, with a high of 275 in 2002. Bonds had 16 consecutive campaigns of .406+ O.B.P.

Other noteworthy Bonds' statistics;

1. 11 campaigns with a .609+ Slugging %
2. Won 12 Silver Slugger Awards
3. Seven campaigns with a .456+ O.B.P
4. 12 seasons posting 104+ runs scored
5. 12 seasons posting 101+ RBI's
6. Eleven years posting a .301+ Batting Average
7. 14 seasons of 33+ home runs
8. Eight seasons posting 40+home runs
9. Nine seasons of 31+ Stolen Bases
10. 12 seasons posting 28+ Stolen Bases

It's official. After the 2007 campaign Bonds retired with 762 lifetime home runs. In forty years baseball historians will look back at Barry Bonds career in sheer awe. Bonds is a true legend. In our time today players are being scrutinized regarding steroids. The question regarding steroid use that will be asked in 40 years will be this. When was the ban on steroids policy integrated? If beer was illegal in the time of Ruth (which it was), why desecrate Bonds' accomplishments if he did use a legal performance enhancing drug? Likewise any pitcher that used the spitball before it became an illegal pitch in 1920.

What should be remembered are Bonds' accomplishments as a ballplayer, playing the game he loved to play, and at the ultimate highest peak.

Bob Gibson

Gibby was a lifetimer with the St. Louis Cardinals. He was a standout with the Cards in 1964 winning two games in the 1964 World Series, taking home the World Series MVP that year. He led St. Louis to another World Series in 1967 winning three games in that World Series, again claiming the World Series MVP Award. He was a standout in the 1968 World Series winning two games, but he lost game seven against Mickey Lolich and the Detroit Tigers; otherwise he probably would have won a third World Series MVP as his numbers were stellar.

"Hoot" won the National League Cy Young Award twice in his illustrious career (1968 and 1970) and posted the lowest modern day ERA in 1968 with an ERA of 1.12. He was 22-9 that year with 28 Complete Games in 34 Games Started. He had an incredible 13 shutouts in 1968 and struck out 268 batters alongside only 62 Walks, in 304.2 Innings Pitched. In fact Gibson had five years with 20+ Wins, eight years with 18+ Wins, and ten years with 15+ Wins. He also had nine consecutive Gold Glove Awards from 1965-1973. In Post-Season play the famed Bob Gibson was 7-2 with a 1.89 ERA, and in nine games started he had eight complete games and two shutouts. Alongside Tom Seaver, he was the best that the Majors had to offer when he played the game. His lifetime numbers show that he was 251-174 and in 482 games started he completed 255 games with 56 shutouts, a 2.91 ERA, a 1.188 WHIP, and 3117 strikeouts. Gibson was duly named to the Baseball Hall of Fame in Cooperstown on his first ballot.

Bobby Bonds, Willie Mays, and Barry Bonds

When Willie Mays was already established as a Major-league superstar (for the San Francisco Giants), the Giants brought up a rookie prodigy to Mays. His name was Bobby Bonds.

Bobby Bonds looked to be poised to be the next Willie Mays; Bonds exhibited raw power with a penchant for stealing bases. In just Bonds' second year (1969), Bobby hit 32 home runs and had 45 Stolen Bases (caught only four times).

Unfortunately, Bobby Bonds couldn't seem to shake the tag the media put on him (that he was moody and a selfish ballplayer). He bounced from team to team his entire career. He went from the San Francisco Giants to the New York Yankees to the California Angels to the Chicago White Sox to the Texas Rangers to the Cleveland Indians to the St. Louis Cardinals and finally to the Chicago Cubs. Even so, Bobby still managed to post five seasons of 30+home runs/ 30+Stolen Bases equaled by only one man, his son Barry Bonds.

When Barry Bonds was born, Bobby went to his teammate and friend Willie Mays to make him his son's Godfather.

The pool of talent and knowledge that was passed down to Barry has made him, in my estimation, the greatest ballplayer the game has ever seen, along with Josh Gibson.

Brooks Robinson

Brooks Robinson is simply the greatest defensive 3rd Baseman of all-time. He won 16 consecutive Gold Glove Awards for the Baltimore Orioles from 1960-1975. In the 1970 World Series Robinson was stellar and showed he could hit the ball in clutch situations. He took home the 1970 World Series MVP for his efforts. In fact that was his second World Series Title with the O's (as they won the Series in '66). Robinson was also an accomplished bat in a dangerous Baltimore lineup featuring Frank Robinson and Boog Powell. Brooks won the AL MVP in 1964 with an AL leading 118 RBI's and of course a Gold Glove that year. Robinson had five seasons with 20+HR's/84+RBI's and finished his career with 268 HR's, 1357 RBI's, 1232 Runs, and a .723 OPS. Of course Brooks was voted into Cooperstown in his first year of eligibility. There will never be a performance like that of the 1970 World Series when Robinson was sprawling all over the place making big time plays seem easy and natural. The one and only Brooks Robinson.

Cal Ripken Jr.

Not only was Cal Ripken Jr. one of the greatest shortstops in the history of Baseball both offensively and defensively, he also is the all-time iron man (topping the great Lou Gehrig's mark of 2130 consecutive games played streak by 502 games) compiling a mark of 2632 consecutive games played. He also hold the record for most consecutive innings played with 8243 innings in a row.

When Ripken Jr. joined the Orioles in 1981 he showed plenty of promise. In his rookie year of 1982 he took home the AL Rookie of the Year Award, and the following year of 1983 he won the AL MVP, guiding his Orioles to a World Series Title. In fact, throughout baseball circles Ripken was considered one of the game's great students in playing the demanding position of shortstop. Without the quickness and speed of a player like Ozzie Smith or Tony Fernandez, Ripken relied on positioning himself as the pitch was thrown and was a master of the position defensively, showcased by his record season mark of .996, commiting only 3 errors in 1990. The following year of 1991 Cal took home his second AL MVP award and over his illustrious career he won 2 Gold Glove Awards and 8 Silver Slugger Awards. In the 80's and 90's (before Derek Jeter arrived) there was much competition as to who the best short-stop in the American League was (Ozzie Smith in the NL was simply the best of the time), but Cal Ripken will be remembered as perhaps the best all-round shortstop of his day.

He finished his career with 431 HR's, 1078 Extra-Base Hits, 1695 RBI's, 1647 Runs, .788 OPS, and a lifetime fielding % at shortstop of .979. Cal was voted into the Baseball Hall of Fame on his first ballot scoring 537 of a possible 545 votes.

Cap Anson

Finished his career with 3435 Hits. From 1879-1898 was a Player/Manager winning 5 Pennants (known in todays' age as 5 World Series Titles. Was duly inaugurated into Cooperstown in 1939. Was a known racist of his day and was truly anti-semitic.

Christy Mathewson (a.k.a "Big Six" or "Matty")

Had twelve consecutive seasons with 22+ Wins (1903-1914). Inducted into Cooperstown in 1936 alongside Babe Ruth, Ty Cobb, Cy Young, and Walter Johnson.

Curt Schilling

Curt Schilling was a standout Minor-Leaguer in the Orioles chain in the late-eighties. He was traded to the Houston Astros after appearing in a handful of games with Baltimore, and believe it or not the Astros used him as a reliever in his lone season in the Lone Star state. He only surfaced as a bona-fide starter when he reached the Philadelphia Phillies in 1992 (as a swingman at that). He led his Phillies to the World Series in 1993, and although Philly lost to the Toronto Blue Jays in that World Series, Schilling showed alot of moxie in his playoff starts that year taking home the 1993 NLCS MVP for his efforts.

When he moved to the Arizona Diamondbacks in 2000 Schilling was already a bonafide superstar having already posted back to back 300+ strikeout year (1997/98-319, 300 K's respectively), and he showcased his abilities in 2001 and 2002 with back to back 22+ win years. His stat line for the 2001, 2002, and 2004 (when he moved to the Boston Red Sox) are as follows;

Year	Wins	Losses	ERA	IP	BB	SO	WHIP	SO/9	SO/BB
2001	22	6	2.98	256.2	39	293	1.075	10.3	7.51
2002	23	7	3.23	259.1	33	316	0.968	11.0	9.58
2004	21	6	3.26	226.2	35	203	1.063	8.1	5.8

Alongside Randy Johnson, Schilling led his Diamondbacks to their first World Series Title in 2001 taking home the World Series co-MVP with Johnson. His playoff statistics are on par with Bob Gibson's numbers. Here is a look at both of their playoff statistics;

Pitcher	W	L	ERA	GS	CG	SHO	IP	H	BB	SO	WHIP	SO/9	SO/BB
Curt Schilling	11	2	2.23	19	4	2	133.1	104	25	120	0.968	8.1	4.8
Bob Gibson	7	2	1.89	9	8	2	81.0	55	17	92	0.889	10.2	5.41

Schilling took home his second and third World Series Titles in 2004 and 2007 with the Boston Red Sox. Although he never won the coveted Cy Young Award, Schilling will surely be inducted into Cooperstown, as evidenced by his lifetime marks of 216 Wins -146 Losses .597 W% 3.46 ERA 1.137 WHIP and 3116 SO, 4.38 SO/BB ratio, and post-season prowess.

Cy Young

This great pitcher from the turn of the 20th Century recorded 511 lifetime wins (the all-time career record) and was voted into Cooperstown in 1937.

Dave Winfield

Dave Winfield is probably the biggest enigma the game of baseball has ever seen. Winfield was drafted in three sports drafts after his senior year at the University of Minnesota (MLB, NBA, and NFL). Winfield had a world of talent and chose to play for the San Diego Padres, signing with a huge bonus in 1973.

Playing for the parent club in his first year of professional baseball didn't seem to faze Winfield as he managed a .277 average in 141 at-bats.

Dave Winfield harnessed his abilities both offensively and defensively. He was known to have the strongest arm in the Majors, and he also had the legs to get to balls most outfielders couldn't get to. This led to seven Gold Gloves for Dave over his career.

Dave's bat was truly consistent throughout his career. When he signed as a free agent with the Yankees after the '80 season, it looked as though this would lead Winfield to several World Series Championships. In his first year with New York they won the American League Pennant and were winning the Series 2 games-0 only to lose the last 4 in succession.

Although Winfield couldn't seem to lead his Yankees to World Series Championships, he could be counted on to provide his team with 25+ home runs/ 100+ RBI's every year he played with them. The constant feuding that he had to endure with George Steinbrenner taxed Winfield's statistics. He could very well have had a few 40+ HR/Year under more peaceful circumstances. Winfield had the power that punished many Major League pitchers.

It was when Dave left the Yankees in 1990 (in an approved trade as he was a 10/5 man) in a mid-season trade with the California Angels that he discovered team success. Winfield spent two years with the Angels, putting up decent numbers, before signing with the Toronto Blue Jays for the 1992 campaign. He was reunited with former teammate and Blue Jay Manager Cito Gaston. This was the year that the Blue Jays (and Winfield) won their first World Series Title. Appropriately enough it was Winfield who was credited with the final game's game winning RBI, a ninth inning double that hit the chalk down the 3rd base line.

Dave Winfield finished his career with 3110 base hits, 465 home runs, 1833 RBI's, 225 stolen bases, and a lifetime batting average of .283. There is no telling how much better his numbers would have been had Winfield been able to avoid Steinbrenner's chaotic nature.

Dave was duly enshrined in the Baseball Hall of Fame in his first appearance on the ballot.

Dennis Eckersley

Ace Starter/Closer. Finished his illustrious career with 197 Wins and 390 Saves. Inducted into Cooperstown in his first year of eligibility.

Derek Jeter (Mr. November, The Captain, Captain Clutch)

Derek Jeter wore number 2 in pinstripes for the duration of his career (1995-2014). The greatest #2 of all-time.

Here is a list of accomplishments from a man that dominated the sport at the most demanding position:

1. 13 seasons of 102+ runs scored in a season
2. 8 years of 202+ basehits in a season

3. 11 years of 190+ basehits in a season
4. 13 years of 183+ basehits in a season
5. 15 years of 179+ basehits in a season
6. Two years with 20+Hr's/20+ SB's
7. 4 seasons of 30+ SB's
8. 8 seasons of 22+ SB's
9. 5 Gold Glove Awards
10. 5 Silver Slugger Awards
11. Finished his career with 3465 basehits
12. 12) Went 5 for 5 in the game in which he collected his 3000'th hit (a home run naturally)
13. 13) Scored 1923 in his storied career
14. 14) Had 15 consecutive years of hitting 10+ home runs/10+ Stolen Bases
15. 15) Had an incredible 200 basehits in post-season play
16. 16) Had 20 Post-Season home runs (3rd of All-Time next to Manny Ramirez and Bernie Williams)
17. 17) Had 18 Stolen Bases in Post-Season play
18. Was the Yankee Captain for the majority of his career
19. His lifetime fielding % was .976
20. Won the 1996 AL Rookie of the Year Award
21. Was the 2000 All-Star MVP and the 2000 World Series MVP
22. Won the 2000 AL Babe Ruth Award
23. Won the 2006 and 2009 AL Hank Aaron Awards
24. Won the 2009 Roberto Clemente Award
25. Won the 2010 Lou Gehrig Memorial Award
26. Won 5 World Series, all with the only organization he ever played with, the New York Yankees

In my estimation, Jeter is the greatest shortstop to have ever played the game (including the Negro Leagues, the Cuban League, the Japanese League, and the Dominican League). He posed fear into the pitchers that he faced. It didn't matter if the game was under the magnifying glass of post-season, Derek Jeter showed up 110% of the time. He played hurt, and he played shortstop with reckless abandon, making plays that even the great Ozzie Smith couldn't make. The nickname Captain Clutch suited Jeter's ability to step up when called upon. Alongside Bernie Williams and Mariano Rivera, Jeter guided his Yanks to 5 World Series Titles. His unparalleled leadership made everyone he played with that much better. The question I have for baseball fans is this; Did Derek Jeter earn every dollar he made? The answer in my mind is, "and then some."

Don Newcombe

Won the first Cy Young Award in 1956. Was a main cog of the Brooklyn Dodgers dynasty of the 50's, culminated by a World Series Title in 1955.

Eddie Murray

Steady Eddie was simply a great player, perhaps the best first baseman of his day.

Starting out with the Baltimore Orioles in 1977, Eddie had no trouble adjusting to big-league pitching belting 27 home runs and had 88 RBI's and batting .283 winning Rookie of the Year Honors.

Eddie's numbers only got better and from 1977-1993, during which he hit a minimum 16 home runs and 78 RBI's. He had four 30+ HR's/110+ RBI's campaigns. Murray also had twelve seasons in which he hit 25+ home runs. Murray was also renowned for his defense, winning three consecutive Gold Glove Awards from 1982-1984.

Eddie Murray was the major cog of the Orioles offense and he led them to two World Series Appearances. In 1979, the Orioles took a commanding 3-1 game lead in the series, only to see the Pittsburgh Pirates reel off three straight wins to capture the Title. Murray didn't fare well at the plate in the '79 series, batting only .154. He did however lead his Orioles to a World Series win against the Philadelphia Phillies in 1983. Eddie had perhaps his best season in 1983. He hit 33 home runs, had 111 RBI's, 115 runs scored, and a .306 Average. In the regular season MVP voting Murray finished second behind teammate Cal Ripken Jr. (many baseball people thought that Murray deserved to win it). All Eddie did during the series that year against the Phillies was bang out 2 home runs and 3 RBI's in the 5-game series win.

To impress how successful Murray was during his career defensively, let's look at his career Range Factor and compare it to the League average. Over his career Eddie's Range Factor at 1st Base was 9.55. The League average was 8.41. It seemed that when Don Mattingly came into the League he automatically received recognition for his defense, and proceeded to win seven consecutive Gold Glove Awards. This is a joke, and making educated fans of the game abhorrent of this travesty. Murray deserved more Gold Gloves from 1985-1988.

In 1989, Murray was signed by the Los Angeles Dodgers through Free Agency, and played three solid years there. In 1992 and 1993 Steady Eddie was just that, while playing for the New York Mets.

'94 saw Murray in an Indians' uniform, and Cleveland is where Eddie finished his illustrious career retiring his spikes at the end of the 1997 season.

Over his career Murray amassed 3255 hits, 504 home runs, 1917 RBI's, with a lifetime batting average of .287. Eddie was a true gentleman of the game of baseball when he played and he has since worked as Batting Instructor in two organizations.

Ernie Banks

Ernie Banks will forever be remembered as the man who said "Let's play two!"

Ernie Banks was a Chicago Cub his entire career. He quickly established as a superstar, belting 44 home runs in 1955 setting the record for most home runs be a shortstop in a single season.

He went on to better his mark in 1958 hitting 47 out of the yard. In fact, Banks hit 41+ home runs in five of six seasons from 1955-1960. Banks won back to back MVP Awards in 1957 and 1958.

Although Banks won a Gold Glove Award at the shortstop position in 1960, he was moved to first base to start the 1962 campaign. He went on to post six 20+HR/80+RBI years at 1st.

Banks was the pinnacle of the Cubs offense and even though they didn't win the World Series when he was there, Banks would have been as dominant had he played for a championship team.

In total Banks had 13 seasons of 23+ home runs/80+RBI's. He also had six seasons of 32+ home runs/102+ RBI's.

Frank Robinson

Last year watching the Washington Nationals' game highlights, the presence of skipper Frank Robinson was seen and felt by all baseball fans. The first player to win MVP awards in both leagues and the first African American to Manage in the Major Leagues, Robinson is a great baseball mind. The years of playing the game at an elite level has to be respected. Too many ex-players that performed well during their playing career aren't recognized as great baseball minds, even though they're studious. Frank Robinson is just that, studious.

When Robinson joined the Cincinnati Reds in 1956 (signed in 1953) great things were expected of him. Sure enough, Robinson had harnessed his ability and after three years of seasoning in the minors won the National League Rookie of the Year Award for 1956. He hammered 38 home runs, batted .290, and scored 122 runs that year. If you thought there was a drop-off after his rookie campaign (a sophomore jinx sort of speak) there wasn't.

From 1956-1967, Robinson had eleven seasons of 29+ home runs, batted .306+ seven times, had 113+RBI's five times, and along the way posted three seasons of 20+HR's/20+SB\s. Robinson won the MVP twice during these years, and in style won the MVP in both leagues (1961 with Cincy, and 1966 with the Baltimore Orioles).

After the '65 campaign the Cincy GM thought that Robinson was past his prime. All Robinson did was to win the Triple Crown belting 49 home runs, score and record 122 RBI's, while batting .316 along the way. He led his new team, the Orioles, to their first World Series Title that year (1966), winning the World Series MVP to boot. He also led Baltimore to a second World Series win in 1970 over, you guessed it, Cincinnati. That moment was short lived however as Robinson began setting his sights on the home run Record, sitting with 475 home runs and still at the reasonably young age of 35. There was no doubt that he'd reach the 500 home run Milestone and quite possibly challenge for the All-time mark of 714. Robinson put up three reasonably good seasons, but came up short with a very respectable 586 lifetime home runs, putting him fourth behind Aaron, Ruth, and Mays. With Barry Bonds and Sammy Sosa in the game today Robinson has fallen to sixth. Keep in mind though that in today's age it's a hitter's game and that when Robinson played there were fewer teams and better pitching. It was a pitcher's game when he played. To summarize Robinson's career numbers, they include a lifetime batting average of .294, a .389 OBP, and a lifetime Slugging % of .537 with nearly 3000 lifetime hits.

Robinson was vocal about the lack of African-American managers in baseball, and his outspokenness earned him a trade from the Angels to the Indians during the 1974 season. The next year, Robinson was named player-manager of the Indians, and he proceeded to homer in his first at bat. The rest is history.

Gaylord Perry

Was the first Pitcher in the history of the game to win the Cy Young Award in both Leagues.

George Brett

Perhaps the greatest batter of his day.

Greg Maddux

Maddux was perhaps the greatest pitcher of his era, alongside Pedro Martinez, Roger Clemens, Randy Johnson, Curt Schilling, and teammates John Smoltz and Tom Glavine. Winning four consecutive Cy Young Awards from 1992-1995, he became the first pitcher in MLB history to accomplish this feat. Maddux won 13 consecutive Gold Glove Awards, and in 18 of 19 years had 202.0+ innings pitched (14 years in a row). In fact, he threw 199.1 innings pitched in all 19 of those years. Greg Maddux was so consistent that he had 20 years pitching 198.0+innings and 21 seasons in which he threw 194.0+ innings.

"Mad Dog" won 4 ERA Titles and led the National League in WHIP 4 times likewise. He finished his illustrious career with 355 Wins and 3371 Strikeouts and was inducted into Cooperstown in his first year of eligibility. On the next page is a look at Maddux's career numbers and the other pitchers named earlier in this bio, followed by their average yearly lines;

Jim "Catfish" Hunter

Won 21+ Games in a Year from 1971-1975 (5 years in a row). An integral piece of the Oakland A's Dynasty of 1972-1974.

Jim Palmer

Jim Palmer was a standout pitcher for the Baltimore Orioles. Palmer started his career as a swingman in the Orioles pitching staff in 1965. He was promoted to the starting rotation the following year, during which he shined going 15-10 with a 3.46 ERA over 208.1 IP. "Cakes" won his first post-season game that year, throwing a complete game four hit shutout. After a couple of years battling a sore arm, Palmer came back strong in 1969 with a 16-4 record and a 2.34 ERA over 181.0 IP. Many baseball insiders questioned Palmer's ability to play a full season, but "Cakes" proved his cynics wrong in 1970 leading the American League in innings pitched with 305, and compiling a 20-10 W-L record and 2.71 ERA. This led Baltimore to its second World Series victory in which Palmer again performed admirably.

Palmer was so dominating in the seventies that he strung together four consecutive 20 win seasons TWICE, winning three Cy Young Awards along the way. He guided his Orioles to their third World Series Title in 1983, and became a men's underwear model as a prop to his endowment for the women that enjoy a good game of ball.

Palmer had 8 20-win seasons in his career, nine years posting a sub 3.00 ERA, and 12 years with a .615+ winning %. He won the Cy Young Award in 1973, 1975, and 1976, and could have easily been selected as the Cy Young Award winner another 5 times. Palmer also won four consecutive Gold Glove Awards from '76-'79, and was 8-3 with a 2.61 ERA in post-season affairs. A true great of the game, Palmer will be remembered as one of the greatest Righties to have pitched in Major League history as evidenced by a 268-152 cord, to go along with a lifetime ERA of 2.86. His average year in the Majors shows a mark of 17-10, a 2.86 ERA, and he totaled 211 complete games, and 53 shutouts. He was duly voted into Cooperstown on his first ballot.

Pitcher	Games	GS	CG	SH	Saves	IP	Hits	BB	SO	SO/9	SO/BB	Wins	Losses	Winning %	ERA	WHIP
Greg Maddux	744	740	109	35	-	5008.1	4726	999	3371	6.1	3.37	355	227	.610	3.16	1.143
Avg Year	34	34	5	2	-	229.0	217	46	154	6.1	3.37	16	10	.610	3.16	1.143
Pedro Martinez	476	409	46	17	3	2827.1	2221	760	3154	10.0	4.15	219	100	.687	2.93	1.054
Avg Year	37	31	4	1	0	217.0	171	58	242	10.0	4.15	17	8	.687	2.93	1.054
Roger Clemens	709	707	118	46	-	4916.2	4185	1580	4672	8.6	2.96	354	184	.658	3.12	1.173
Avg Year	34	34	6	2	-	236.0	201	76	224	8.6	2.96	17	9	.658	3.12	1.173
Randy Johnson	618	603	100	37	2	4135.1	3346	1497	4875	10.6	3.26	303	166	.646	3.29	1.171
Avg Year	34	34	6	2	-	230.0	186	83	271	10.6	3.26	17	9	.646	3.29	1.171
John Smoltz	723	481	53	16	154	3473.0	3074	1010	3084	8.0	3.05	213	155	.579	3.33	1.176
Avg Year	41	27	3	1	9	196.0	174	57	174	8.0	3.05	12	9	.579	3.33	1.176
Tom Glavine	682	682	56	25	-	4413.1	4298	1500	2607	5.3	1.74	305	203	.600	3.54	1.314
Avg Year	34	34	3	1	-	220.0	214	75	130	5.3	1.74	15	10	.600	3.54	1.314
Curt Schilling	569	436	83	20	22	3261.0	2998	711	3116	8.6	4.38	216	146	.597	3.46	1.137
Avg Year	38	30	6	1	1	221.0	203	48	211	8.6	4.38	15	10	.597	3.46	1.137

Jim Rice and Tony Fernandez

These two ballplayers were my favorites growing up. I was always torn between the Toronto Blue Jays and the Boston Red Sox, although I am a Toronto boy. The Red Sox were my first favorite team. My earliest recollections are of the 1978 Major League season. In that year I collected cards with my friends Andreas Agathagolos and Randy Himmelstein. One day in the school year of September – June 77/78, I took our collection to our School – Ernest Public School, and was confronted by the older Grade 6 students. I was 7 at the time and I was very nervous as the older kids were curious about my collection of cards. I took them out of the box that they were in and held a large pile of cards in my hands. I decided to have some fun and I threw all the cards in the air. You should have seen all the children running to "get some".

In 1978, the Boston Red Sox and the New York Yankees were the best teams (alongside the Kansas City Royals) out of the American League and they both played out of the Eastern Division. I was a huge Red Sox fan when the 1978 O-Pee-Chee set came out, featuring All-Stars Carlton Fisk and Carl Yastremski. My favorite Red Sox player though was Jim Rice. During the season Rice managed to hit 16 Game winning/Game tying home runs, finishing the year with a Major League leading 46 home runs, with 139 RBI's and 213 hits (batting .315 along the way). He led that Boston's offense, and they looked poised to win the Eastern Division as they were up by 10.5 games entering September. The Yankees had won the World Series the year before but looked overmatched, as aside from Ron Guidry (who had a Cy Young year) they didn't seem to have the pitching to come back.

My heart truly sank when the Yankees came fully back and overtook the Red Sox in a 1 game playoff as the season had ended in a tie.

Although I loved the Jays when they joined the American League in 1977, my first "favorite team" will always be of those Red Sox players imprinted on the 1978 set.

In 1983, the Toronto Blue Jays brought up a young rookie for a very brief stint in September. His name was Antonio Octavio Fernandez. Tony was a wizard with the glove playing a demanding shortstop and he finally made starting shortstop for the Jays in 1985 (as in the '84 off-season the Jays had traded their former starting shortstop, Alfredo Griffin). In September of 1985 our family took a trip to New York City to spend time with my Mother's first cousin, Brian Kaufman, and his family. Brian got tickets to the Jays/Yankees series (for the last three games). As we drove into the city the Jays were winning the first game by three runs. When we got to their house the Yankees had come back in the eighth, scoring 4 runs winning the game.

Brian took us to the next three games at Yankee Stadium for one of the most special times of my life. In game Two we were walking back from the Babe Ruth, Lou Gehrig, and Joe

DiMaggio Monuments when a fan at the ballpark had a heart attack. Brian, being a Doctor, (and a heart specialist at that) rushed to the man's aid and saved his life.

In that game, Tony Fernandez made a play that will forever be etched in my memory. Don Baylor hit a groundball deep in the hole between short and third. Tony retrieved it, and then, from behind third base threw out Baylor at first.

The fans at Yankee Stadium were unruly. At one point my sister's "B.J Birdy" doll was taken from her by a Yankees' fan, and the fans started throwing it around. I intervened and got the doll back for her.

As Tony Fernandez defense shone, so did the rest of the Jays. They went on to win those three games at Yankee Stadium that early September and won their first American League East Division Title, in Tony's first year.

I was heartbroken in the 90-91 off season when Fernandez and McGriff were traded to the San Diego Padres for Roberto Alomar and Joe Carter. It was, however, a nice touch when the Jays brought Tony back to Toronto, in 1993, to be apart of their latter World Series of 1992/1993.

In looking at Tony Fernandez's career, he moved on to Cleveland to play 2nd base for the Indians and led them to the World Series in 1995 against the Atlanta Braves, losing a tight 6-game series. Tony was the type of player that had an impact on the teams he played with both offensively and defensively. Had the Jays have had Tony for the last 7 games of the 1987 campaign they most surely would have won the American League East that year. Fernandez was a .300 hitter, usually stole 20-30 bases a year, and he could lay down a bunt or slap the ball through the infield if he wanted. Defensively, Tony's only rival defensively was Ozzie Smith. When Tony played 2nd base for the Indians, he established himself as one of the better defensive players at that position as well. Fernandez finished his career in 1998 with the Jays as a Third baseman. In fact, Tony holds the mark for best fielding % in a single season at third base, when during the 1994 strike season he committed just two errors in 87 games started for the Cincinnati Reds. He finished the year with an unheard of mark of .991 at third base (topping even the great Brooks Robinson). Not a bad resume, one that shows 2000+ career hits and a lifetime batting average of .288. To boot, Fernandez took home 4 consecutive Gold Glove Awards at shortstop in the American League from 1986-1989.

Jim Rice while not known to be the greatest leftfielder in his day, was perhaps the greatest Boston Red Sox leftfielder at handling the Green Monster.

Rice was known as being the best hitter in the Major Leagues from 1977-1986. In those ten years he averaged roughly 35 home runs/year, and 100+RBI's/year with a .310 Average. He had an impact on the '75 Red Sox team that lost the World Series to the Cincinnati Reds in 7 games, the '78 Red Sox, and the '86 Boston team that narrowly lost the World Series to the Mets in Seven games (the Bill Buckner Series).

If I had my choice, both Rice and Fernandez would be enshrined in Cooperstown. Rice was voted in a few years back, and let's just say Fernandez is on the bubble based on his career numbers. Ironically only Tony Fernandez (of the two) won a World Series Title (with the Jays in 1993), although Rice was robbed of a World Series Title in 1986 when Bill Buckner booted the third out leading to a miraculous N.Y Mets comeback. I'm keeping my fingers crossed.

Jimmie Foxx

There were many ballplayers that made an impact on the game. Those through innovation like a Babe Ruth, or Ty Cobb, Rickey Henderson, Josh Gibson, Barry Bonds, and Satch Paige were always, and will always be, remembered.

Players that benefited from the advent of the long ball in the days of Gibson and Ruth include Foxx.

Jimmie Foxx was a young man from Maryland who began his professional career at the age of 17 with the Philadelphia Athletics in 1925.

Jimmie flourished in 1932/1933. In those 2 years Foxx won the Triple Crown once and had 2 MVP trophies to show for it. The year he won the Triple Crown he hit 48 Home Runs, had 163 RBI's, had a .356 batting average and scored 125 runs.

The year prior, Foxx had hit .364 with 58 home runs, 169 RBI's, scoring 151 runs. In 1936 Foxx moved to the Boston Red Sox and continued to feast on American League Pitchers. He had his second 50 + home run season in 1938 (with 175 RBI's to boot).

Over the course of Foxx' career, he posted 11 seasons of 35 + home runs (9 consecutive), as well as posting 13 consecutive years with 100 + RBI's.

An argument could be made that Foxx was every bit as talented at first base as Buck Leonard of the Homestead Grays' (known within the baseball community to be the greatest hitter, neigh Josh Gibson, in the Negro Leagues).

An argument could be made that Foxx was every bit as durable as Lou Gehrig. Having played in 14 consecutive seasons of 100+ games played – 10 consecutive seasons of 139+ games played.

Joe, Dom, and Vince DiMaggio

Joe DiMaggio was perhaps the most graceful of all ballplayers when he played. The way he swung a bat, shagged down a fly-ball, ran the bases, he was consummate and graceful in the way he played the game. DiMaggio started out with the Yankees in 1936 and surely would have taken home the AL Rookie of the Year Award if it had been given out. He ended up finishing 8th in the MVP voting, hammering 29 home runs, 88 Extra-Base Hits, 125 RBI's, 132 Runs, 206 Hits, a .323 Avg and a .923 OPS. DiMaggio was just starting to peak. The next year of 1937 he smashed 46 home runs, with 96 Extra-Base Hits, alongside 167 RBI's with 151 Runs, and a .346 Avg. Although he came second in the MVP voting, DiMagg established himself as the best Center-Fielder in the game. He ended up winning three MVP Awards during his illustrious career (1939, 1941, 1947). In fact it was in 1941 that the Yankee Clipper set the all-time mark for most consecutive games with a base-hit doing so in 56 straight contests. Joltin' Joe led his Yankees to 9 World Series Titles, and even though he only played in 13 years in the Majors (as his career was interrupted by WW2), he put up astronomical numbers that led to him being inducted into the Baseball Hall of Fame on his first ballot. His lifetime numbers include a .325 Avg, a .977 OPS, 361 HR's, 881 Extra-Base Hits, 1537 RBI's, 1390 Runs, and 2214 Hits.

In fact Joltin Joe averaged 143 RBI's a year with 207 Hits a year to boot.

Dom DiMaggio (Dominic Paul DiMaggio "The Little Professor"; 1940-1953) was a stand-out defensive Center-Fielder for the Boston Red Sox from 1940-1953. Dom had six campaigns with 110+ runs scored. He rivaled his older brother Joe on many game occasions between the Yankees and the Red Sox, and many thought their defense to be on-par.

Vince DiMaggio (Vincent Paul DiMaggio; 1937-1946) was the oldest of the DiMaggio brothers, Vincent was also a Center-Fielder and played throughout the National League starting with the Boston Bees, then the Cincinnati Reds, the Pittsburgh Pirates, the Philadelphia Phillies, and finally the New York Giants. In 1941 Vince had a 100 RBI season.

From 1940-1945 Major League Baseball saw three DiMaggio's starting in Center-Field for their respective teams; Joe DiMaggio - the New York Yankees, Dom DiMaggio - the Boston Red Sox, and Vince DiMaggio - the Pittsburgh Pirates (and the Philadelphia Phillies).

Joe Morgan

Joe Morgan began his career in 1963 with the old Houston Colt 45's of the first expansion. A terrific talent, Joe came into his own in the 1965 campaign, his rookie year. Although Joe didn't capture the Rookie of the Year honours, he did have an excellent year. He scored 100 runs, had 14 home runs, and stole 20 bases. In the following year of 1966, the Colt 45's moved to the first dome in the history of the game (commonplace now) and changed their team name to the Astros. Morgan continued to put up good numbers. The following year of 1966 he batted .285, and .275 in '67 with 29 stolen bases. Morgan was only 5 feet 7 inches in height and had a keen eye at the plate, this attributed to his excellent walks/strikeout ratio.

While he managed to be a useful offensive player, and was great defensively, he still hadn't reached superstar status by any means. Although he stole 49 bases in the 1969 campaign, he batted a paltry .236 along the way.

Morgan caught a break following the '71 season. He was dealt to the ever-tough "Big Red Machine" in Cincinnati. Playing alongside Johnny Bench, Tony Perez, Pete Rose and the other members of the "Big Red Machine" boosted Morgan's statistics significantly as pitchers now had to come into him with more fastballs. This becomes obvious when we see the numbers Joe put up in his inaugural season of 1972 in Cincy. Morgan's '72 set career highs in runs scored, home runs, stolen bases (with 58), RBI's (with 73), Bases on Balls (with 115), and batting average (.292).

Let's also include the fact that he was the igniter of that "Big Red Machine" offense. Nobody set the table as well as Morgan did. From 1969-1977 (9 years), he had 40+ stolen bases each year. From 1972-1976 (5 years), he had 58+ stolen bases each year. From 1972 -1977 (6 years), Morgan had 107+ runs scored each year.

It was Morgan who won back-back MVP Awards (in 1975/1976), the same years in which Cincinnati won back-to-back World Series Titles. If you look at the defense that Morgan provided throughout his career, it's obvious that Morgan was one of best defensive second baseman in his day, and perhaps of all-time. Joe won a Gold Glove at second base five years in a row from 1973-1977.

In perhaps Morgan's best year, 1976, he amazingly led the National League in slugging % with a mark of .576, and he finished the year second in stolen bases, stealing 60 that year. Along the way he had 27 home runs, 111 RBI's, and 113 runs scored, in just 472 At-Bats. He almost had a 3:1 BB/K ratio, and finished the year batting .327.

Although Morgan didn't put up terrific post-season numbers throughout his career, he was a dangerous bat in the 1976 World Series, slugging a homer and batting .333 in a four game series against the Yankees.

Joe Morgan was, until recently, a baseball commentator for ESPN who gave excellent and useful analysis of the game in which he dominated. Morgan would make an excellent choice to manage my team of unappreciated ballplayers (as Morgan was until he reached Cincinnati).

1st Base – Todd Helton	C – Gary Carter
2nd Base – Frank White	LF - Vada Pinson
3rd Base – Terry Pendleton	CF – Lloyd Moseby

SS -Tony Fernandez   RF – Jesse Barfield
Pitcher - Dave Stieb/Jimmy Key

Lou Brock

Lou Brock started his career with the Chicago Cubs in 1961. Known to have great speed, Brock had to prove he could hit Major League pitching. He only got into 4 games, in 1961, as a late-season call-up. In his rookie campaign of 1962 he batted only .263 albeit 16 stolen bases that year. 1963 was also a year of mediocre statistics offensively.

Since Brock didn't have a particularly strong arm and wasn't producing offensively he was dealt by Chicago early into '64 to the St. Louis Cardinals. The change of scenery did wonders for Brock. He batted .348 in 103 games with the Cardinals that year and stole 33 bases for them. This established himself as both a hitter and a base-stealer. He led the 'Cards to a World Series Title, batting an even .300 in his first Series (against the New York Yankees).

This was only a sign of things to come for Brock. The year of 1965 saw him steal 63 bases which began a string of twelve consecutive 50+ stolen base seasons. As the pinnacle of the great St. Louis Cardinals' offense, Brock led his team to another World Series Title in 1967, a seven game victory over the Boston Red Sox. Brock managed to bat .414 and as impressive stole seven bases in those seven games.

The following year of 1968, Brock's last World Series appearance, the Cardinals lost to the Detroit Tigers in seven games (blowing a 3-1 game lead). Lou did his part though, and was probably apt to receive the WS MVP Award had St. Louis won. All he did was bat .464, with a .516 O.B.P and a .857 Slg%. He hit two home runs and had seven stolen bases in that '68 Series.

As testament to being a great leadoff hitter is the fact that he scored 107+ Runs in seven seasons, and had 92+ Runs Scored in 10 seasons.

Aside from Brock's post-season success, perhaps his greatest accomplishment was stealing 118 bases in 1974, breaking the single season stolen base record previously held by Maury Wills. He topped this record convincingly, topping Wills '61 season by 14 stolen bases.

Lou Brock was not just a stolen base threat as evidenced by his four 200+ hit seasons. Lou finished his career with 3023 base-hits and held the lifetime stolen base record (before Rickey Henderson came along) with 938 stolen bases.

Mark McGwire

Big Mac became the first Major League ballplayer of all-time to hit 52+ home runs in a year four times in a row (1996-1999). Set the all-time single season mark for home runs with

70 (until topped by Bobby Bonds) bettering Sammy Sosa (who had 66) in an epic battle in 1998. McGwire followed that up by bashing out 65 home runs the following year. McGwire finished his career with a lifetime 583 home runs. The only reason he hasn't been enshrined in Cooperstown is because he was a steroids user.

Mariano Rivera

Rivera is simply the greatest closer in MLB history. No-one comes close to him as a closer in regular season, or post-season play for that matter. What Rivera accomplished in his career will surely leave historians in awe in hundreds of years past. Rivera had nine seasons posting 40+ saves, 15 years with 30+ saves, and he led the American League in saves three times. He also had an incredible 11 sub 1.94 ERA campaigns, likewise 13 sub 2.11 ERA seasons, winning five World Series Titles with the famed New York Yankees along the way.

Here is what Rivera accomplished when looking at his average year and lifetime totals;

	W	L	ERA	G	GF	Sv	IP	H	BB	SO	WHIP	SO/9	SO/BB
Totals	82	60	2.21	1115	952	652	1283.2	998	286	1173	1.000	8.2	4.1
Avg Yr	5	4	2.21	67	58	39	78.0	60	17	71	1.000	8.2	4.1
Post Season	8	1	0.70	96	78	42	141.0	86	21	110	0.759	7.7	5.2

The reality is that regular season numbers for closers may actually improve over time with more specialization in bullpen prowess. Rivera, however, simply set the standard for ALL closers in the game from past to present to the future. The scary thing is that Rivera was the greatest set-up man to have ever played the game likewise, as he was placed in that role early in his career to accomodate the ever-effective John Wetteland (when Wetteland pitched for the New York Yankees in the early-mid nineties). Rivera's Post-Season numbers are one for the ages. Mariano will surely be enshrined in Cooperstown in his first year of eligibility.

Mickey Mantle

"The Mick" was a highly touted rookie in 1951 when he began his career. He blossomed as a Major Leaguer the following year of 1952 leading the Majors in OPS with a mark of .924 finishing 3rd in the MVP voting for that year. Mantle fufilled all expectations of him when all was said and done. In 1956 he won the prized Triple Crown, leading the American League in home runs, RBI's, and Batting Average. In fact Mantle took home three MVP

Awards in his career; 1956, 1957, and 1962. Although Mantle only won a single Gold Glove Award in his career, he was no liability in the field. Mantle played his career at the same time as other New York standout Center-Fielders Willie Mays and Duke Snider and gave the Yankees the means in which to win 7 World Series Titles during his playing career showcasing his abilities in Post-Season play with 18 HR's and a gawdy OPS mark of .908. In 1961 Mantle and Maris became the first teammates to belt 50+ HR's when Maris set the single season home run record bashing 61 HR's. Mantle had his second 50+HR season hitting 54 balls out of the yard. Mantle was feared by opponents pitchers as evidenced by his 10 years drawing 102+ Walks.

The "Commerce Comet" finished his career with 536 home runs, 952 Extra-Base Hits, 1509 RBI's, 1676 Runs, 2415 Hits, .298 Avg, 153 SB's, and an awesome .977 OPS mark. Mantle had eight consecutive 30+ HR campaigns (1955-1962) and nine in total. He led the Major Leagues in OPS 6 times and had an OPS of 1.000+ seven times. He was duly voted in to Cooperstown on his first ballot in 1974.

Mike Schmidt

Mike Schmidt started his career with the Phillies in 1972 playing in a handful of games. He won Third-Base at the start of the 1973 campaign and although he belted 18 home runs the jury was still out as he could only muster a .196 Batting Average. Schmitty answered the call for the 1974 season as he raised his Average to .282 and he hammered 36 home runs along with 116 RBI's. Over the course of his career, Schmidt managed to pop 31+ HR's an incredible thirteen times and won 8 NL home run Titles. He also had 101+ RBI's nine times in his career. Schmidt won 9 consecutive Gold Glove Awards from 1976-1984, and took home a tenth in 1986. He also won 5 consecutive Silver Slugger Awards from 1980-1984 (and a sixth in 1986). He was known to be a clutch bat as evidenced by his winning the 1980 World Series MVP Award. During his career the argument as to who the best third baseman in the game was came down to Schmidt and George Brett. Schmidt would win the argument on defense and the ability to hit the long ball during crucial times of the game.

Schmidt retired from the game with 548 home runs, 1015 Extra-Base Hits, 1595 RBI's, 1506 Runs, 2234 Hits, 174 SB's, and an OPS Mark of .908. He was so proficient at hitting the long-ball that he actually AVERAGED 37 home runs and 107 RBI's per year. Schmidt was voted into Cooperstown on his first year of eligibility, in 1995, achieving 444 votes of a possible 460 votes.

Nolan Ryan

"The Ryan Express" - His fastball was once clocked at 103MPH. Ryan finished his career with 324 Wins, and set the all-time single season record for strikeouts with 383 K's, and career marks for strikeouts with 5714 K's. Along the way he threw seven no-hitters. In-augerated in Cooperstown. Achieved 491 out of a possible 497 Hall of Fame votes in his first year of eligibility.

Ozzie "The Wizard" Smith

Ozzie started his career with the San Diego Padres in 1978. He was a good base-stealer, and had 40 steals in his rookie year.

By 1980 Ozzie was regarded by the baseball community to be the best glove-man in the game. In that year of '80 he won his first of thirteen consecutive Gold Gloves. In the off-season of the '81/'82 winter/spring, Ozzie was dealt by the Padres to the St. Louis Cardinals for hot hitting Gary Templeton (also a shortstop). This trade turned into a huge mismatch in the Cards' favour. Ozzie Smith posted 16 consecutive 20+ stolen base years. He also stole 31+ bases in year eleven times (50+ bases twice).

In 1982, Ozzie led his new team to a World Series win over the Milwaukee Brewers, in seven games. Although Ozzie never won another World Series Ring, he was instrumental in taking his Cards to the World Series two more times. They lost both Series in seven games, 1985 against the Kansas City Royals, and 1987 against the Minnesota Twins.

If I could choose a shortstop, any shortstop of all-time, my choice would be Derek Jeter, a close second is where Ozzie rates in my book.

Paul Molitor

In 1978, the Milwaukee Brewers brought a kid up from the minors. His name was Paul Molitor. He started his career as a second baseman, and teamed with Robin Yount to form one of the greatest duos of the 1980's. The "Wallbangers" of 1982 (the Milwaukee Brewers' nickname), won the American League Pennant, but lost in the World Series to the St. Louis Cardinals in seven games.

In 1993, the World Series Champion Toronto Blue Jays came calling. Toronto had lost their DH, Dave Winfield, when he became a free agent. Molitor was more than up to the challenge of replacing Winfield. In 1993, Molitor batted .332, had 64 extra base hits, and scored 121 runs. He also hit 22 HR's and stole 22 bases. This led the Blue Jays to win a second consecutive World Series title.

Paul Molitor was more than a Toronto Blue Jay, to the city of Toronto. When the local community wanted to start a youth hostel, he became their spokesperson. The youth hostel, Eva's Place, was soon approved, and has become one of the few youth hostels in the city of Toronto.

Paul has also been a generous caregiver to many hospitals. He frequented them regularly, providing support to patients in need. Giving back to the community has always been one of Paul Molitor's priorities. Molitor is a class act.

Pedro Martinez

Pedro Martinez began his career as a teammate of his brother Ramon with the Dodgers. He moved to Montreal after his rookie year and had his breakout campaign with the Expos in '97, taking home his first Cy Young Award. Pedro was coveted by a number of teams and eventually moved to the American League with the Boston Red Sox. He took home the Cy Young in back to back years of '99/'00 and even led the Red Sox (alongside Curt Schilling) to their first World Series Title in 86 years during the 2004 season.

Pedro won five ERA titles and won 20+games in a year twice. Martinez had nine 206+Strikeout campaigns and won the belt for K's three times. Martinez finished his career with 3154 Strikeouts. He also led the League in WHIP a staggering six times. Pedro was duly inducted into the Baseball Hall of Fame in Cooperstown. See his lifetime stats and average year stats in the bio written for Greg Maddux.

Pete Rose

Had ten campaigns hammering 204+ Base-hits. Holds the record for most hits in a career with 4256 Hits. Had 15 seasons bashing .301+ in Average. Was banned from the Baseball Hall of Fame in Cooperstown by the late Commissioner Bart Giamatti for gambling on games he was managing and/or playing in.

Randy Johnson

Randy Johnson was a highly touted lefty for the Montreal Expos in 1988. He voiced a desire to be traded in his rookie year and Montreal, who was looking to compete that season, traded him amongst others to the Seattle Mariners for fellow lefty Mark Langston. It was thought at the time that the Expos won the deal as Langston had superb numbers. Little did we know how great Randy Johnson would become. In 1995, Johnson won his first of five Cy Young Awards pitching with the Mariners and took them to their first post-season. The other four Cy Young's were consecutive between '99-'02, and Johnson became only the second man in the history of the game to accomplish this feat alongside Greg Maddux.

In 2001 Johnson took home the World Series MVP with Curt Schilling as their Diamondbacks won their first World Series Title.

What made Johnson so special was that he was just so overpowering. At 6'10 he was an imposing figure to any batter, especially if they were batting left. Larry Walker summed it up best during an all-star game when he literally left the batters box as the "big unit" fired one in. He was so dominating during the 2002 campaign that he took home the NL Pitching Triple Crown. Johnson won four ERA Titles and led the League in K's nine times. In fact, "The Big Unit" had eleven consecutive 204+K campaigns, 13 in total. He also had six years with 308+K's, and nine years with 290+K's. Johnson had three 20+ win seasons and finished his career with a mark of 303-166. "The Big Unit" was voted into the Basaball Hall of Fame on his first ballot. To see more of Randy Johnson's numbers refer to the bio written about Greg Maddux.

Reggie Jackson

Reggie started his career with the Kansas City A's of 1967. In '68 they moved to Oakland where Charles Finlay built a championship team. Reggie was "the straw that stirred the drink." Alongside Jackson was Catfish Hunter, Rollie Fingers, Vida Blue, and Joe Rudi. The A's won the World Series each year 1972-1974.

Reggie was considered the greatest power hitter of the 70's. He won the AL MVP in 1973 and hammered 30+ home runs/year seven times in his career. Even more impressive is the fact that Reggie hit 25+ home runs in a season fifteen times. He was also adept at stealing a base as evidenced by his four 20+ stolen base seasons. Each of these years were also 20+ home runs/20+ stolen base campaigns.

In 1976, Jackson tested Free Agency and signed with the Baltimore Orioles. In 1977, Reggie signed a mega-deal (peanuts by today's standards) to play with the New York Yankees. He led that team to two consecutive World Series in 1977/1978 giving him 5 rings in total. Reggie was World Series MVP in 1977. That series, he hit 3 home runs in Game 6 to close the Series against the Dodgers.

When all was said and done, Reggie hit 563 lifetime home runs, and will be immortalized for his role in the A's and Yankee's dynasties of the 70's.

There will also be the memories of Reggie feuding with Billy Martin. Their infamous clashes of opinion and hatred of each other was well known and in an adoring way will we remember those feuds.

Rickey Henderson

Rickey was a kid growing up in the Athletics chain back in '77. He not only exuded confidence, but boasted that he could steal on anyone in the league. . . after the dust settled he racked in 1406 stolen bases in his career. The most remarkable sub-stat that is noticeable was that his 1406 was followed by the mark of 938 set by the great Lou Brock.

Here is a list of Henderson's lifetime credentials:

1. 297 home runs   100th all-time
2. 2190 Bases on Balls   2nd all-time
3. 490.1 Power/Speed Number   2nd all-time
4. 2295 Runs Scored   1st all-time
5. 3081 Games Played   4th all-time
6. 4588 Total Bases   31st all-time
7. 3055 Hits   14th all-time

13 Seasons Posting 50+Stolen Bases
6 Seasons Posting 80+Stolen Bases
3 Seasons Posting 100+Stolen Bases

The greatest accomplishment of Henderson, was having the number of home runs that he did (297) along with all those Stolen Bases. This translated into a lifetime score of 490.41 in Power/Speed. The only player ahead of Henderson in this score is Barry Bonds.

Roberto Clemente

Joining in on the first wave of black ballplayers in essence desegregating Major League Baseball, Clemente was signed by the Brooklyn Dodgers in 1954 and left unprotected following that year by Brooklyn and signed as a free-agent by the Pittsburgh Pirates before the 1955 season. Ironically, the player Brooklyn may have thought would not matter losing (as Brooklyn won the World Series in 1955), actually was missed sorely within a few years, as Clemente established himself as one of the great stars of the game alongside Willie Mays and Henry Aaron. There was no doubting Clemente's talent. He had a rifle for an arm, had good speed, and he practically swung his way out of poverty as a youngster growing up in Puerto Rico.

When Roberto started his career in 1955 with Pittsburgh, he struggled in his inaugural season, batting a modest .255. The following year he proved himself as a force to be reckoned with batting .311. He really came into his own in 1960, when he posted a .314 batting average, hitting 16 home runs (the first time in his career belting 10+ home runs) with 94 RBI's.

It was in 1960 that Clemente became a household name, as his Pirates won the World Series on Bill Mazerowski's walk-off home run. He received due recognition for his fielding prowess in 1961, winning the first of twelve consecutive Gold Glove Awards. To go along with his Gold Glove defense that year he batted .351, leading all Major Leaguers.

In fact from 1960-1967, Clemente's lowest yearly average was .312. In an off-year, 1968, he batted only .291. Of course, in 1968, the Year of the Pitcher, nearly all batters hit below their normal averages. His .291 average was still .040 points higher than the league average of .251.

If you thought that this off-year (by Clemente's standards) was the sign of him slowing down you are sadly mistaken. The following year, Clemente hit .345, and in 1970 he bettered that mark with a .352 average. In 1971 Clemente batted .341. It seemed that Roberto could feasibly make a run at the long held career hit record of 4192, set by Ty Cobb. The 1971 campaign also saw the Pirates win their second World Series under Clemente's leadership.

Indeed, Clemente reached the milestone of 3000 Hits (on his last at-bat of the '72 campaign), while batting .312. No one realized this was to be Clemente's last hit ever. On New Year's Eve (Dec 31/72), Clemente was traveling by plane to earthquake-stricken Nicaragua with thousands of dollars worth of medical supplies, when the plane went down.

Roberto Clemente was dead at the age of 38.

In looking at Clemente's accomplishments not only was he successful when it came to his career and family relations, there was also a sense of duty to provide to the poor, where he himself had once resided.

In looking at Clemente's accomplishments we can see that he was the consummate ballplayer. He had 200+hits in a year four times. He batted .339+ six times and keep in mind that this was in a pitcher's era. His lifetime batting average of .317 was .55 points higher than the league average and he led the National League in batting average four times. Clemente won the NL MVP in 1966, and finished in the top ten in MVP voting eight times.

Roberto Clemente was coming off a .312 average and his 12th consecutive Gold Glove season after the '72 campaign. He not only produced in the regular season but in the playoffs as well as evidenced by their two World Series wins in '60 and '71 in which Roberto won WS MVP batting .414 with a .759 Slg % to latter series.

He will always be revered as a class act, not only for his professional accomplishments, but in giving back to the Pittsburgh community and to his Native Homeland of Puerto Rico.

Rod Carew

Rod Carew was signed by the Minnestota Twins in 1964. He entered the realm of Major League Baseball in 1967 and won the Rookie of the Year Award, impressing the Baseball World by batting .292.

Some people were critical when his average declined in the following year dynasties and insinuated that the sophomore slump was starting to kick in. Since Carew was a singles hitter, they reasoned, he wasn't particularly useful unless he hit .300+.

That's exactly what happened. Carew bumped his average up to .332 in 1969. This began a remarkable string of fifteen consecutive seasons of batting .305+. During this stretch, Rod won the American League MVP in 1977, and challenged to bat .400 for the season finishing with a mark of .388. Carew batted .350+ five times during this stretch and batted .331+ ten times. He won seven batting titles in his career.

Even though Carew never won a World Series ring, he was known in the baseball community to be a clutch hitter. Such was the case that Rod was either voted in, or asked to participate in, eighteen consecutive All-Star games (1967-1984).

Although Carew wasn't Gold Glove material in the field, he wasn't a liability. His speed helped somewhat in the field. In fact Carew stole 35+ bases every year from 1973-1976.

Rod Carew finished his career with 3053 hits, a .328 batting average, and had 353 lifetime steals.

Rod was elected to the Baseball Hall of Fame on his first ballot/first year of eligibility.

Roger Clemens

What can be said about Roger Clemens? Perhaps the greatest Righthanded Starter in Modern day history. Clemens won the coveted Cy Young Award a record seven times ("86,"87,"91,"97,"98,"01 in the AL and "04 in the NL) becoming the fourth man to accomplish the feat of winning the Cy Young in both Leagues; Gaylord Perry, Pedro Martinez, Randy Johnson being the others). He also won the AL MVP in '86 for his monster 24-4 season, the first of six 20+Win campaigns. Clemens won the Strikeout Title five times, and had twelve seasons in which he had 208+K's, finishing his career with a staggering 4672 K's. The Rocket led the League in WHIP three times and won two World Series Titles with the New York Yankees. He finished his career with a record of 354-184, but sadly he is languishing in the minds of Americans as a man who cheated the system by using steroids during his career. In this writer's opinion this sentiment will eventually change and Clemens will be voted into Cooperstown. The logic being that it WASN'T illegal to use steroids when he was using them. For a more complete look at Clemens numbers refer to the bio of Greg Maddux.

Rogers Hornsby

Lifetime batting average of .358. Batted .401+ in Average three times. Batted .370+ Average eight times. Is the only ballplayer in the history of Professional Baseball to bat .401+ with 42+HR's and 152+ RBI's. 1st Ballot Hall of Famer in 1942.

Roy Campanella

In 1949 Branch Rickey brought up a young "kid" catcher from their farm system. His name was Roy Campanella. The expectations were high and Campanella met them all.

In his second full season with Brooklyn, in 1950, Campanella hammered 31 home runs. He upped that in 1951 by having 33 pokes out of the yard, to go along with a .325 Batting Average, and 108 RBI's. This brought Roy his first MVP Award.

It was the year 1953, in which Campanella posted Josh Gibson type numbers. In winning his second MVP Trophy, Campanella belted 41 home runs, 142 RBI's, Batting .312 along the way.

When the Dodgers won the World Series in 1955 against the New York Yankees, Campanella led the way posting his third MVP season in a five year span.

What made Roy Campanella so special, and endeared by baseball fans is the way he played the game. He was a hustler, as evidenced by his 5.98 Career Range Factor, compared to the League Average of 4.66. This, to me, is evidence that Roy Campanella just plain and simply wanted the win more than the rest. He will forever be etched in my memory to be in the upper echelons of the greats of the game.

In 1957 Campanella was in an automobile accident that left him paralyzed. He spent the rest of his days in a wheelchair. Roy Campanella died June 26, 1993. Rest in peace.

Sammy Sosa

Sosa was only the 2nd man of all-time to post 50+ home runs in a year four times in a row doing so from 1998-2001. In fact Sosa is the only Major Leaguer to ever post three 63+ home runs years in his career, doing so in 1998, 1999, and 2001. Sammy finished his career with 609 home runs. The only reason he hasn't been enshrined in Cooperstown is his link to the steroids issue.

"Shoeless" Joe Jackson

Lifetime batting avergage was .356. Was part of the "Black Sox" scandal of 1919. Surely would have been inducted into the Hall of Fame in Cooperstown had he not been wrongly accused of gambling against his own team.

"Smoky" Joe Wood

Hall of Fame Pitcher from the turn of the 20th century.

Stan Musial

"Stan the Man" was the greatest hitter in the National League when he played. Musial finished his career with a Batting Average of .331. What made Musial so special was that he could pepper the ball to anywhere on the field. He won the NL MVP three times (1943, 1946, and 1948). Musial's' Cardinals won three World Series Titles under his guidance. He had six years with 200+ Hits and led the NL in Hits six times likewise. "Stan the Man" had 11 consecutive years with 105+ Runs (1943-1954), and he had ten seasons with 102+ RBI's over his storied career.

When Musial began to develop a problem with his throwing arm he was moved from left-field to 1st Base, he excelled in his new role and accumulated an incredible 1377 Extra-Base Hits alongside 475 home runs, 1951 RBI's, 1949 Runs, 3630 Hits and an OPS of .976. In fact Musial led the National League in OPS seven times and had an OPS above 1.021 eight times.

Steve Carlton ("Lefty")

One of the greatest left-handed starters of all-time. Carlton finished his career with 329 Wins. He was duly voted into the Baseball Hall of Fame in Cooperstown on his first ballot in 1994.

Ted Williams

When asked the goals he set for himself in his inaugural season, Williams replied "to be remembered as the greatest hitter of all time."

Shunned by the sportswriters of his day Williams still managed to win 2 MVP awards. This despite posting two Triple Crown years to which he did not win MVP, and a .406 Average in 1941 in which he finished 2nd in the voting.

Although the Red Sox didn't win the World Series in Williams' career and the sportswriters loved to hate him, Williams was adored by the fans (he is one of only 2 major leaguers to play in all-star games in 3 different decades – (Willie Mays is the other).

What makes the "Splendid Splinters" career all the more special is that he missed 5 years playing, due to WW11 and the Korean War. The fact that he was commandeered for his accomplishments as a fighter pilot distinguishes him as a success story that few sportsmen can claim.

The 5 years missed during the war were also in the prime of his career. This makes the 521 home runs all that more impressive. Williams had the highest On Base % 12 times in his storied career, and, the highest Slugging % 9 times in his career. Williams was voted on to the all-star team 17 times by the fans.

Williams projected statistics for his career (adding 5 of his "average years" to his totals for the years missed during the war).

Career Statistics + 5 Years

Games	AB	R	H	HR	RBI	BB	SO	BA	OBP%	SLG%	TB
2904	9744	2280	3360	648	2328	2552	896	.344	.482	.634	6163

Tom Glavine

First ballot Hall of Fame Pitcher. Pitched alongside John Smoltz and Greg Maddux to form a formidable threesome.

Tom Seaver

Tom Terrific was the pinnacle of the glory years of the late-sixties through the seventies. A turn of the clock takes us back to a time when social activism was at its prime. Baseball was in its glory years as the Mets were led by a young and hungry Tom Seaver in '69, becoming the Miracle Mets that fateful season in capturing the World Series.

Seaver was a known quantity from the beginning of his career, winning the 1967 NL Rookie of the Year Award. He took home his first of three Cy Young Awards in 1969 (1973 and 1975 being the other Cy Young years), leading the Mets to their first World Series Championship that year. Along the way, "The Franchise" as he was called, won 311 games with many of those games deciding whether or not his team would move into the post-season. As the Mets ace in the hole, he succeeded more often than not. Seaver won 20+games in a year 5 times and had 13 years in which he won at least 15 games. He led the National League in wins three times and also struck out 201+men in a year 10 times (9 in a row from 1968-1976), leading the league in this category five times. In this writer's opinion, Tom Terrific was the greatest pitcher of his day, on par with Bob Gibson. On the next page is a compilation of statistics of the greatest pitchers that played over the course of Seaver's career.

Ty Cobb ("The Georgia Peach")

Holds the career mark for highest career batting average with a mark of .366. Held the career record for Hits with 4189, until broken by Pete Rose in 1985. Was inducted into Cooperstown in 1936 achieving 222 votes of a possible 226.

Wade Boggs ("Chicken Man")

One of the greatest pure hitters in the game. Had 200+Hits every year from 1983-1989. Was voted into the Hall of Fame on his first ballot.

Walter Johnson ("The Big Train")

Finished his career with 417 Wins and was voted into Cooperstown the day they held their first vote in 1936, alongside Babe Ruth, Ty Cobb, Honus Wagner, and Christy Mathewson.

Pitcher	G	GS	CG	SH	Saves	IP	Hits	BB	SO	SO/9	SO/BB	Wins	Losses	Win %	ERA	WHIP
Tom Seaver	656	647	231	61	1	4783.0	3971	1390	3640	6.8	2.62	311	205	.603	2.86	1.121
Avg Year	34	34	12	3	0	250.0	207	73	190	6.8	2.62	16	11	.603	2.86	1.121
Bob Gibson	528	482	255	56	6	3884.1	3279	1336	3117	7.2	2.33	251	174	.591	2.91	1.188
Avg Year	36	32	17	4	0	262.0	221	90	210	7.2	2.33	17	12	.591	2.91	1.188
Steve Carlton	741	709	254	55	2	5217.2	4672	1833	4136	7.1	2.26	329	244	.574	3.22	1.247
Avg Year	35	33	12	3	0	245.0	219	86	194	7.1	2.26	15	11	.574	3.22	1.247
Jim Palmer	558	521	211	53	4	3948.0	3349	1311	2212	5.0	1.69	268	152	.638	2.86	1.18
Avg Year	35	33	13	3	0	249.0	211	83	139	5.0	1.69	17	10	.638	2.86	1.18
Don Sutton	774	756	178	58	5	5282.1	4692	1343	3574	6.1	2.66	324	256	.559	3.26	1.142
Avg Year	34	34	8	3	0	235.0	209	60	159	6.1	2.66	14	11	.559	3.26	1.142
Catfish Hunter	500	476	181	42	1	3449.1	2958	954	2012	5.2	2.11	224	166	.574	3.26	1.134
Avg Year	35	33	13	3	0	240.0	206	66	140	5.2	2.11	16	12	.574	3.26	1.134
Gaylord Perry	777	690	303	53	10	5350.0	4938	1379	3534	5.9	2.56	314	265	.542	3.11	1.181
Avg Year	36	32	14	2	0	248.0	229	64	164	5.9	2.56	15	12	.542	3.11	1.181
Ferguson Jenkins	664	594	267	49	7	4500.2	4142	997	3192	6.4	3.20	284	226	.557	3.34	1.142
Avg Year	36	32	14	3	0	243.0	224	54	173	6.4	3.20	15	12	.557	3.34	1.142
Luis Tiant	573	484	187	49	15	3486.1	3075	1104	2416	6.2	2.19	229	172	.571	3.30	1.199
Avg Year	37	31	12	3	1	224.0	198	71	155	6.2	2.19	15	11	.571	3.30	1.199
Vida Blue	502	473	143	37	2	3343.1	2939	1185	2175	5.9	1.84	209	161	.565	3.27	1.233
Avg Year	35	33	10	3	0	233.0	205	83	152	5.9	1.84	15	11	.565	3.27	1.233
Nolan Ryan	807	773	222	61	3	5386.0	3923	2795	5714	9.5	2.04	324	292	.526	3.19	1.247
Avg Year	35	33	10	3	0	232.0	169	120	246	9.5	2.04	14	13	.526	3.19	1.247

Warren Spahn

Had thirteen season of 20+ Wins and finished his career with 363 Wins. Was inducted into Cooperstown on his first ballot in 1973.

Willie Mays

What can I say about the "Say Hey Kid?" He was, and will always be, the epitome of what the game is about.

Starting his career playing for the Chicago American Giants of the Negro-Leagues in the late 1940's, Mays showed enormous promise. In 1951 Mays" Major League career began, playing for the New York Giants under the guidance of Leo Durocher. Mays had an awful start. Durocher, recognizing that Mays had tremendous talent, sent Mays down to the Minors for seasoning. When Mays rejoined the Giants he was ready for stardom. Not only did Willie win Rookie of the Year honours, he also led the Giants to the National League Pennant. The Giants came back from 10 games out in September against the Brooklyn Dodgers, capped by Bobby Thompson's "shot heard around the world". Mays was on deck.

Mays stardom was further evidenced by his 1954, and 1955 seasons in which he hit 92 home runs and 237 RBI's, with 32 stolen bases to boot. He won MVP honours for 1954 with his season line - .345, 119 runs scored, 41 HR's, 110 RBI's. In 1955 he batted .319, 123 runs scored, 51 HR's, 127 RBI's.

The greatest attribute of the "Say Hey Kid" was his defense, backed by 12 consecutive Gold Glove Awards 1957-1968.

He practically won a World Series Game for the Giants against the Indians in 1954 when he robbed Vic Wertz in deep center, making an incredible over the shoulder basket catch and then in one motion turning and throwing the ball back to the infield to prevent the runner on second base from scoring on a tag-up.

All in all Mays posted six 20HR/20SB years, two 30HR/30SB campaigns. He also hit 34+HR's eleven times, and posted 103+RBI's ten times, and scored 101+ runs in 12 consecutive years (1954-1965). Mays won two MVP Awards in his career, in 1954 and 1965. He also hit 51+ home runs in a year twice.

Willie Mays is what baseball is all about.

Willie McCovey

"Stretch" McCovey established himself as a bonafide Major Leaguer in 1959, his rookie campaign. He won the Rookie of the Year Honors, managing to slug 13 home runs in just 192 at-bats batting an incredible .354.

McCovey suffered from sophomore jinx and didn't seem to get his swing back until 1962, while still with the San Francisco Giants. '62 saw McCovey boom out 20 home runs in just 229 at-bats. The following year McCovey really came into his own as a superstar of the game. He hit 44 home runs and had 102 RBI's (his first 100+ RBI season).

All McCovey did from 1965-1970 was average 38 home runs/year. In 1965, McCovey teamed with Giants great Willie Mays to lead the Majors in home run twosomes with 91 combined home runs (39 by McCovey).

In 1969, Willie won the National League MVP Award belting 45 home runs, with 126 RBI's in just 491 at-bats. He batted .320 through the year to boot.

Although McCovey wasn't priveleged to have won a World Series Title, he did participate in two playoff series with the Giants. In his last playoff series in 1971 against Pittsburgh, he batted .429 with 2 home runs and 6 RBI's in just 4 games.

McCovey was traded by the Giants after the 1973 season and played three uneventful seasons in San Diego, playing for the sorry Padres. He came back to San Francisco in 1977 and won the "Hutch" Award for comeback player of the year. McCovey reminded the Baseball World of his power bashing 28 home runs and driving in 86 RBI's in just 478 at-bats.

McCovey finished his career with the San Francisco Giants in 1980 tallying 521 lifetime home runs and he made the Baseball Hall of Fame on his first year of eligibility.

Willie Stargell

Willie "Pops" Stargell was a life-timer with the Pittsburgh Pirates from 1962-1982. He started as a full-time player in 1963, and was in good company playing alongside Roberto Clemente.

In 1965, Stargell had his breakout season, clubbing 27 Dingers and driving in 107. When "Pops" connected he sent the ball a long way. Between Stargell and McCovey there were more moon shots than those sent off by N.A.S.A.

Aside from an off-year in 1968 (the year of the pitcher) Stargell was a model of consistency throughout his career.

Willie performed at the highest as evidenced by his numbers from 1970-1975. In those peak years he hit 44+ home runs twice and 31+ home runs four times.

Stargell led his Pirates to World Series Titles in 1971 and 1979. As testament to his value to the Pirates Willie finished 2nd in the National League MVP voting in 1971, and was Co-MVP (alongside Keith Hernandez) in 1979. In the 1979 World Series against the Baltimore Orioles, "Pops" rallied his Pirates (We Are Family) back from a 3-1 game deficit, winning the World Series MVP along the way.

After all was said and done Willie Stargell amassed 475 career home runs, won an MVP Award, 2 World Series Titles, a World Series MVP Award, and was duly elected into the Baseball Hall of Fame on his first ballot.

Willie was a true spokesperson for the game of baseball. Now that he is no longer with us, he may be missed, but he is not forgotten.

Yogi Berra

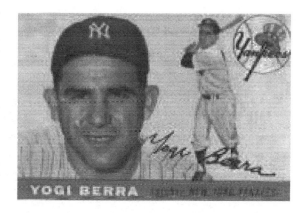

Yogi was a true baseball man in every sense. He plain out knew how to win. He won 10 World Series Titles with the New York Yankees dynasty of the late forties though the early sixties. Berra also took home 3 AL MVP Awards for his efforts. Yogi always seemed to give the sportswriters of his day a comment worth reporting.

Berra had 10 consecutive years clubbing 20+ home runs from 1949-1958, and alongside Roy Campanella they were head and shoulders above any other Catchers in the game when they played. Yogi had 5 years with 105+ RBI's and finished his career with 358 home runs, 1430 RBI's, 1175 Runs, and 2150 Hits. He surely would have taken home Gold Gloves as Catcher had they been instituted when he played. As such, Berra and Campanella were the cream of the crop during the heyday of the glory years of baseball (Post WWII - Mid-Sixties). Yogi was inducted into Cooperstown on his first ballot. He died just last year and will surely be missed for years to come.

5
Player Comparisons – Part I

Albert Pujols vs Todd Helton

These two ballplayers put up incredible statistics in their respective careers. Helton had a lifetime Batting Average of .316, Pujols is close behind with a .312 mark.

Pujols has the better statistics when it comes to post-season play. As testament to his post-season prowess, Pujols won the MVP for his role against the Houston Astros in '04, claiming the NLCS MVP batting .500 with four home runs and nine RBI's.

Helton is narrowly the better defensive 1st Baseman, winning three Gold Glove Awards to Pujols two. Helton posted two .350+ Batting Averages maxing out at .372 (in 2000). Pujols highest-mark as a hitter (his lone .350+ season) was .359 (in 2003).

Some would say that playing in Colorado at Coors Field padded Helton's lifetime statistics, but believe it or not Helton's away statistics were almost on par with his home stats.

This is a look at their 162 Game Average Seasons:

Player	AB	R	H	2	3	HR	RBI	SB	CS	BB	K	BA	OBA	SA
Helton	574	101	182	43	3	27	101	3	2	96	85	.316	.414	.539
Pujols	609	114	190	42	1	40	121	7	3	83	70	.312	.397	.581

What's impressive about these statistics is that Pujols averaged 83 Extra Base Hits per season, which is almost unheard of. It is for this reason that I would select Pujols between the two

Alex Rodriguez vs Nomar Garciaparra

Since A-Rod won only one World Series Title (none for Nomar) we'll review each player based on their average 162 Game Seasons:

Player	AB	R	H	2	3	HR	RBI	SB	CS	BB	K	BA	OBA	SA
Rodriguez	616	119	183	32	2	41	122	19	5	79	132	.297	.382	.554
Garciaparra	631	105	197	42	6	26	106	11	4	46	63	.313	.361	.521

Garciaparra carries a .016 point advantage in Batting Average to Rodriguez, but has a lower OBP and a lower Slugging %. A-Rod won two Gold Gloves at Shortstop and moved over to third base to accommodate the status quo of one Derek Jeter when he arrived in New York. Garciapara never won a Gold Glove in his career.

Garciaparra was capable of putting .350+ seasons together, doing so twice in a storied career. A-Rod had one such season. Nomar just can't compare to A-Rod's ability to hit the long ball, as shown by A-Rod's eight 40+ home run seasons, and thirteen consecutive 30+ home run campaigns. Nomar's greatest single season home run total was 35. It is interesting to note, however, that Garciaparra averaged 74 extra-base hits a year to Rodriguez' 75. Bettering Garciaparra by 15 in home runs per year, though. Quite simply, A-Rod is the more accomplished of the two.

Babe Ruth vs Henry Aaron

In 1974, Henry Aaron was chasing what was thought to be an unreachable achievement, Ruth's record for lifetime home runs of 714. Pressured by mainstream society (Aaron was bombarded with hate mail and death threats), Aaron nonetheless persevered and rewrote history. When Aaron retired in 1976 he had hit 755 home runs.

This comparison is special in many ways:

1. Both Ruth and Aaron are home run legends.
2. Both Ruth and Aaron were Right Fielders.
3. Both were outspoken throughout their careers.

When one looks at Ruth's career and compares it to Aaron we see dominance for Ruth in every area except for stolen bases. This is a very relevant statistic in this comparison. When we look at the modern day style of the game of baseball, we see that the trend to steal bases is a necessity. In order to appreciate Aaron's contribution to the game (and Ruth's for that matter) we'll post each players "best" year (by taking their best 5 years and dividing each statistic by 5).

Player	G	AB	R	H	2B	3B	HR	RBI	SB	CS	BB	SO	BA	OBP%	SLG%	TB
Aaron	155	614	119	202	34	7	41	127	15	4	62	69	.329	.388	.607	373
Ruth	150	518	157	195	39	11	52	145	13	13	149	89	.376	.518	.794	410

Player	AB	R	H	2	3	HR	RBI	SB	CS	BB	K	BA	OBA	SA
Henry Aaron	614	119	202	34	7	41	127	15	4	62	69	.329	.388	.607
Babe Ruth	518	157	195	39	11	52	145	13	13	149	89	.376	.518	.794

Numbers do not lie. Ruth was, by far, the bigger producer of the two. Keep in mind though, when Ruth played the batting average was 20 points higher than when Aaron played. Aaron may have only averaged 15 stolen bases over his 5 best years compared to Ruth's thirteen, but the margin between stolen bases – caught stealing gives Aaron an edge of eleven. Ruth has an On Base % that is 130 points higher than Aaron's mark, and a SLG % that is 187 points higher than Aaron's.

Barry Bonds vs Babe Ruth

The game of baseball changed due to the accomplishments of one man. His name was Babe Ruth. When Ruth moved from the starting rotation of the Boston Red Sox pitching staff, to Right Field he proved himself to the baseball world as "the greatest" home run hitter of all time. Ruth's record for lifetime home runs was surpassed by only one man up to 2005 (Henry Aaron with 755 Lifetime Home Runs).

At the end of his playing career Barry Bonds had 762 Lifetime home runs compared to Ruth's 714.

In comparing Bonds career to Ruth you must also take into consideration that Bonds had 514 lifetime stolen bases or an average of 30 SB a year.

Here's a look at both players' average year:

Player	AB	R	H	2	3	HR	RBI	SB	CS	BB	K	BA	OBA	SA
Bonds	534	121	159	33	4	41	108	28	8	139	83	.298	.444	.607
Ruth	544	141	186	33	9	46	143	8	8	133	86	.342	.474	.690

In trying to equate Bonds' accomplishments to Ruth's, take into account that the league batting average was .25 points higher when Ruth played. As well, Bonds' style of play changed from being a 30HR/30SB man for his first 13 years, to becoming a pure home run hitter in the mold of Ruth.

Bonds' career will surely become the yardstick of what a 5-tool player aspires to become. This is something Ruth couldn't come close to. Considering that Bonds was a better defensive outfielder than Ruth (Bonds won 9 gold gloves) and that he posted one 40 Home Run/40 Stolen Base year and five 30 HR/30 SB years. Clearly the better all-round ballplayer when compared to Ruth, Bonds has the better statistics even when comparing their yearly Home Run totals.

Barry Bonds has now surpassed Ruth and Aaron as the most prolific home run hitter the game has seen (not considering Josh Gibson), with a whopping 762 home runs. Only Josh Gibson (who clubbed 803 home runs in Negro League play, and 962 that were documented worldwide) tops Bonds.

Barry Bonds vs Ted Williams

Had stolen bases not separated the two, Williams would be the closest match to Bonds.

What made Williams career so special was that the sportswriters of his day all but abandoned him. Williams won the triple crown 2 times and in those years did not win the MVP. Saying that, Bonds had 9 places in the top 3 for MVP voting (over the span of his career), while Williams had 7 such years, Bonds was a legitimate threat to post 40HR/40SB in each of his first 13 years in the majors.

As Bonds' heyday finally ended, it would be fair to measure his career to Williams. Williams was denied 3 years of his career due to WWII (let's just say Bonds years from 2001-2004 were off the charts).

Best 5 Years

B Bonds	AB	R	H	2	3	HR	RBI	SB	CS	BB	K	BA	OBA	SA
1993	539	129	181	38	4	46	123	29	12	126	79	.336	.458	.677
2001	476	129	156	32	2	73	137	13	3	177	93	.328	.515	.863
2002	403	117	149	31	2	46	110	9	2	198	47	.371	.582	.799
2003	390	111	133	22	1	45	90	7	0	148	58	.341	.529	.749
2004	373	129	135	27	3	45	101	6	1	232	41	.362	.609	.817
T Williams	AB	R	H	2	3	HR	RBI	SB	CS	BB	K	BA	OBA	SA
1941	456	135	185	33	3	37	120	2	4	147	27	.406	.553	.735
1942	522	141	186	34	5	36	137	3	2	145	51	.356	.499	.648
1946	514	142	176	37	8	38	123	0	0	156	44	.342	.497	.667
1949	566	150	194	39	3	43	159	1	1	162	48	.343	.490	.650
1957	420	96	163	28	1	38	87	0	1	119	43	.388	.526	.731

In statistical comparison Bonds far exceeds the batting standards set by the late Ted Williams.

* Bonds' best 5 years do not include his lone 40 home run / 40 Stolen base season, nor his 4 other 30 home run / 30 Stolen base seasons.

Barry Bonds vs Ty Cobb

Barry Bonds is the greatest ballplayer of our day. Ty Cobb was the best ballplayer of his day, along with Babe Ruth.

The Georgia Peach carried a lifetime batting average of .366. He had 4192 hits and 892 stolen bases in his career. Cobb played during the Dead Ball era of the early 1900's, but was still an excellent run producer, averaging 103 RBI a season. Cobb had eight 50+ stolen base years. In 1911, Cobb won the Chalmer's award (the MVP Trophy at the time).

When Bonds came up to the majors, he had the potential to become a legitimate 30HR/30SB threat, and ultimately had five such seasons. In 2001, Bonds broke the single season home run record by hitting 73. His statistics until 2001 were superior to any other Major Leaguer in the history of the game. Barry Bonds won eight Gold Gloves over the course of his career. Cobb also played in left field. He never won a Gold Glove (the majors didn't issue them back then), but he was known to be a good defensive outfielder.

Barry Bonds recorded 514 stolen bases over his career and had 762 lifetime home runs. He also won seven MVP awards. When Cobb played (up to 1923) you could only win the Chalmers Award (the MVP Award) once, which Cobb did in 1911.

Cobb's most impressive statistic is his .366 lifetime average (the highest mark of all time), while posting three .400 seasons with nine years batting .380+.

Perhaps the most astounding statistic of Bonds is that between 2001 and 2004, he averaged 52 home runs and 189 Walks over the four years with an average yearly at bat total of only 414.

Here are each player's average 162 Game Seasons:

Player	AB	R	H	2B	3B	HR	RBI	SB	CS	BB	SO	AVG	OBP	SLG%
Bonds	534	121	159	33	4	41	108	28	8	139	83	.298	.444	.607
Cobb	610	120	224	39	16	6	103	48	10	67	19	.366	.433	.512

Player	AB	R	H	2	3	HR	RBI	SB	CS	BB	K	BA	OBA	SA
Bonds	534	121	159	33	4	41	108	28	8	139	83	.298	.444	.607
Ty Cobb	610	120	224	39	16	6	103	48	10	67	19	.366	.433	.512

Although Cobb started his career during the Dead Ball era, he did have several seasons in his prime in the live ball era of the 20's. For this reason I would start Bonds over Cobb. Bonds destroys Cobb in HR/Year. It's also interesting to note that although Cobb's lifetime BA is .068 points higher than Bonds, Bonds actually had a higher OBA.

Barry Bonds vs Willie Mays

In comparison, Barry Bonds has to be considered the better batter in every category to Mays.

Bonds started his career the same as Mays as they were both 5 tool players. In the first 13 years of Bonds' career, he posted five 30HR/30SB years. Mays posted two years of 30HR/30SB numbers in his career. In Bonds' first 13 years he posted 10 years of 20HR/20SB (9 consecutive). Mays had 6 consecutive 20HR/20SB years (6 in total).

From 2001- 2004 Bonds numbers' skyrocketed leaving all historical figures behind.

Defensively, Willie Mays has the distinction of being known as the best Center Fielder of all time. Mays won 12 consecutive Gold Glove awards (12 in his career). Bonds had won 8 Gold Gloves over his career mainly in Left-Field.

In terms of longevity, both players had great career spans. Mays played with 2 organizations for his entire career (the old New York Giants and later the San Francisco Giants and finally for the New York Mets) of 23 years, while Bonds has divided his career between the Pirates and the Giants spanning 22 years.

Barry Bonds led the Majors in lifetime home runs with 762 and holds the single season mark with 73 in 2001. Mays hammered 660 lifetime home runs, and twice bettered 50. Bonds had 514 career stolen bases, and Mays finished his career with 338 stolen bases.

There is a commonality that the two share through Barry's late father, Bobby Bonds. When Mays played in San Francisco for the Giants, they brought up a young prodigy to Mays, another five-tool player. Bobby Bonds not only played with Mays but also gave him the honor of being Godfather to his son. We now call him Barry, Barry Bonds that is.

Barry Bonds vs "Shoeless" Joe Jackson

Bonds and Jackson put up lofty numbers over their respective careers. They were each left-fielders for the most part of their careers. When Jackson played, he started with the Philadelphia A's in the "dead ball era", and was shipped to the Cleveland Indians early on in his career. It was there that he established himself as a star. In 1911 he batted .408 with 41 stolen bases. He followed that with averages of .395 and .373. In 1915 Jackson was dealt to the Chicago White Sox. He was apart of the "Black Sox" team of 1919. Ironically, his best year in the Major Leagues was in 1920, his last year, before being banned from baseball for life for being involved in the scandal.

Bonds started his career as a speedster, with the Pittsburgh Pirates. Originally a Center-Fielder, Bonds was spectacular defensively when he came up to the Majors. Moving to Left-Field, Bonds established himself to be a star in 1990, and since then never looked back.

Bonds moved from the Pirates to the San Francisco Giants in 1993. Over the course of his career he post five 30HR/30SB years (the Major League record for this feat) as well as one 40 Home Run/40 Stolen Base year. Bonds' numbers have been staggering, culminated by a 73 home run season in 2001 (the Major League record). Bonds finished his career with 762 home runs and currently holds the all-time mark.

Here's a look at Jackson's best five years. Bonds's appear on page 145.

J Jackson	AB	R	H	2	3	HR	RBI	SB	CS	BB	K	BA	OBA	SA
1911	571	126	233	45	19	7	83	41		56		.408	.468	.590
1912	572	121	226	44	26	3	90	35		54		.395	.458	.569
1913	528	109	197	39	17	7	71	26		80	26	.373	.460	.551
1919	516	79	181	31	14	7	96	9		60	10	.351	.422	.506
1920	570	105	218	42	20	12	121	9	12	56	14	.382	.444	.589

Considering that Jackson played during the Dead Ball Era, this deflates his slugging %. However, Bonds carried his weight as both a base-stealer and a home run hitter. Negating home runs and Slugging %, Jackson matches well in comparison to Bonds. Had Bonds played during the Dead Ball Era, with his speed, he could very well been the stolen base threat that Ty Cobb was. For this reason I would take Bonds over Jackson.

Barry Larkin vs Tony Fernandez

In 1984 the Toronto Blue Jays brought up a rookie from their Triple A affiliate, the Syracuse Chiefs, shortstop Tony Fernandez. Fernandez had won the starting the shortstop position for the parent club in '85. This was due to a deal in which Alfredo Griffin (Toronto's shortstop for '84) was traded alongside Dave Collins for Bill Caudill of the Oakland Athletics. In '85 the Jays seemed destined to win the World Series. In that year the Jays won the American League East and looked poised to beat Kansas City for the pennant. They were up three games to one and lost the remaining three games. Tony did his part though, batting .333 in the seven game series. Fernandez went on to post four consecutive Gold Glove awards from 1986-1989. Tony achieved the highest fielding % for a shortstop in one year, in 1989. He posted a .992% mark. (Only one man since – Cal Ripken Jr. has bettered this mark, as in 1990 he posted a mark of .996%.)

Likewise, Barry Larkin made it as a starting shortstop for the Cincinnati Reds in his second year, 1987. A great glove, Larkin won only three Gold Gloves, due to the fact that he played during the era of Ozzie Smith, the greatest defensive shortstop in the history of the Major Leagues.

Both Fernandez and Larkin were great hitters. Fernandez hit over .300 four times in his career and stole 20+ bases seven times. Larkin batted .300 or higher nine times and stole 20+ bases nine times. Larkin won the National League MVP in 1995. He batted .319 and stole 51 bases while being caught stealing only 5 times. The following year Larkin proceeded to become the first shortstop in the history of the game to hit 30+ home runs with 30+ stolen bases. Both Fernandez and Larkin batted over .300 in post-season play.

Considering that Tony was off his game when he was traded to the Padres, in the off-season of '90, until he came back to Toronto in 1993, I would say that Larkin was the better all-around shortstop.

Here's a look at their average years:

Player	AB	R	H	2B	3B	HR	RBI	SB	CS	W	SO	Avg	OBP%	Slg%
Fernandez	594	79	171	31	7	7	63	18	10	52	59	.288	.347	.399
Barry Larkin	590	99	174	33	6	15	71	28	6	70	61	.295	.371	.444

Bob Gibson vs Juan Marichal

On the surface this comparison seems to favour Gibson. After all "Gibby" was the anchor of a Cards' rotation that performed in three World Series. Gibson won two Cy Young Awards over his illustrious career and was a five time 20 game winner in the Bigs.

Marichal, on the other hand, was the cornerstone of the San Francisco Giants rotation. A good ballclub, but not Championship quality, the Giants would probably have been in the 2nd Division had it not been for the exploits of Marichal. Although he never won a Cy Young Award, Marichal did post six 20+ win seasons including 4 in a row from 1963-1966. Believe it or not, Juan had a higher career Win/Loss %, and a better career strikeout/walk ratio than "Gibby".

Marichal was a workhorse, similar to "Hoot", and pieced together 10 consecutive 200+ innings in a year from 1962-1971. Gibson was good for 12 such seasons. Both averaged 17 complete games a year, something unheard of in today's age. So evenly matched, their careers are difficult to differentiate.

Even still, "Gibby" has to receive credit for the success of the Cardinal teams in the 60's. He was truly dominating in October compiling a 7-2 record with 8 complete games in 9 starts, and a 1.89 ERA For this reason I would take Gibson if I had my choice for one must win game.

Bob Gibson vs Tom Seaver

Gibson started his career with the St. Louis Cardinals in 1959. He made the starting staff in 1961 for good. In '61 "Gibby" posted 10 complete games and the following year became the

Ace of the staff putting together his first 200+ Strikeout campaign, one of nine over his illustrious career. In 1964, Gibson led his Cards to the World Series. He won two of three starts against the Yankees, capturing the first of two World Series MVP Awards over the duration of his career. This prompted Manager Johnny Keane to remark "I had a commitment to his heart" (in reference to why he had left Gibson in the 9th inning of Game 7). "Gibby" had 31 strikeouts in three complete games in that series. The scary thing is that he was just starting to get into his zone as a pitcher, and re-affirmed his penchant for winning big games as evidenced by his 3 wins in the 1967 World Series against the Boston Red Sox. Gibson's greatest year statistically came the following year of '68. "Hoot" had the lowest modern day ERA with a 1.12 ERA that year. He completed an incredible 28 of 34 starts, and had 13 shutouts that year. The Cards looked poised to win their third World Series Title in 5 years, leading the Detroit Tigers 3 game to 1, but ended up losing the 7 Game set. '68 saw Gibson take home the first of two Cy Young Awards (his second coming in 1970). Although Bob Gibson didn't win 300 Games over his career it is still a career that carries with it awe and reverence.

Tom "Terrific" came into the Big Leagues right at the pinnacle of Gibson's career. Starting out in 1967, Seaver took home Rookie of the Year honors. By 1969 Seaver was the #1 starter in the Mets rotation, and won his first of three Cy Young Awards also leading his New York Mets to their first World Series Title. The argument of who the greatest pitcher in the National League was at that time came down to "Hoot" and "Tom Terrific".

When Gibson retired in 1975, it was obvious that Seaver was the National League's best. Taking his second and third Cy Young Awards in 1973 and 1975, Seaver supplanted Gibson as the NL's best, similar to the passing of a baton. Seaver struck out 200+ batters nine years in succession from 1968-1976 (ten times over his career) and became a 300 game winner with the Chicago White Sox in 1985. Along the path of his career, Seaver was also a mainstay in Cincinnati with the Reds (prior to Chicago), and finished up his last year in the "Bigs" pitching in Boston with the Red Sox. All told Seaver won 311 games and had 3640 strikeouts. Seaver was duly named to the Baseball Hall of Fame in his first ballot.

Comparing "Gibby" to Seaver is an interesting argument as Gibson had a higher strikeout/IP ratio and he finished his career with 3117 strikeouts. Gibson also won 9 consecutive Gold Glove Awards from 1965-1973 compared to none for Seaver. Even still, the only difference that this writer pays any credence to is Gibson's ability to win the big game. Seaver's post-season record shows that he was 3-3 with a 2.77 ERA Gibson was 7-2 with a 1.89 ERA in Fall Classics.

Cal Ripken Jr vs Tony Fernandez

Between 1978-1987 there was an influx of top-notch shortstops into the Major Leagues. From the Dominican Republic came Tony Fernandez, Alfredo Griffin, Marianno Duncan, and Julio

Franco. The United States produced shortstops Cal Ripken Jr, Alan Trammell, Ozzie Smith, and Barry Larkin.

Most baseball fans will say that Tony Fernandez was the best of the bunch coming from the Dominican Republic. Some would say that Cal Ripken Jr was the best to come from the U.S.A, during this period.

All Ripken did was play in 2632 consecutive games, breaking the old mark of 2130 games set by late Yankee great Lou Gehrig. Ripken also post twelve 20+ home run/ 80+ RBI years. Ripken also won two MVP awards for his efforts, in 1983 and 1991.

Tony Fernandez was considered the best fielding shortstop in the American League when he played. From 1986-1989 he won four consecutive Gold Glove awards. Had Fernandez stayed in Toronto he probably would have had a few more in him. When Tony was traded to San Diego in the 1989 off-season, Cal Ripken Jr took advantage and won the first of his two Gold Gloves. The reality was that Fernandez was the better defensive shortstop.

To be fair Cal Ripken Jr has to be considered the better two-way shortstop to Fernandez as testament to his batting prowess. (Side note – Ripken holds the Major League record for single season fielding %, at the shortstop position, posting a mark of .996 in 1990.)
Here's their average yearly statistics:

Player	AB	R	H	2B	3B	HR	RBI	SB	CS	BB	SO	Avg	OBP	Slg%
Cal Ripken, Jr.	624	89	172	33	2	23	91	2	2	61	70	.276	.340	.447
Tony Fernandez	594	79	171	31	7	7	63	18	10	52	59	.288	.347	.399

Carlton Fisk vs Thurman Munson

These two catchers were the best catchers that the American League had to offer in the 1970's. Munson died tragically in a plane crash, in his prime. Had he played another five or so years, he would probably have been considered to be in Johnny Bench's league. Munson did however win a MVP Award (in 1976), and played in three consecutive World Series (from 1976-1978) winning two World Series Titles.

Fisk was a mainstay with the Boston Red Sox and the Chicago White Sox over the course of his career. For this comparison we'll analyze Fisk's Boston days (as he played against Munson on several occasions when he was with the Red Sox and moved to Chicago the year after Munson died).

While Fisk never won the MVP Award he did win the Rookie of the Year Award in 1972 and Batted .284+ four times between 1972-1978. Munson Batted .280+ eight times between 1970-1979. Fisk won a Gold Glove Award in 1972 and Munson won three consecutive Gold Gloves between 1973-1975.

Let's first take a look at their average 162 Game Seasons:

Player	AB	R	H	2B	3B	HR	RBI	SB	CS	BB	SO	AVG	OBP	SLG%
Munson	608	79	177	26	4	13	80	5	6	50	65	.292	.346	.410
Fisk	568	83	153	23	3	24	86	8	4	55	90	.268	.341	.457

Player	AB	R	H	2	3	HR	RBI	SB	CS	BB	K	BA	OBA	SA
Munson	608	79	177	26	4	13	80	5	6	50	65	.292	.346	.410
Fisk	568	83	153	23	3	24	86	8	4	55	90	.268	.341	.457

These guys are pretty evenly matched. To see if we can see some discrepancies we'll look at each player's best three seasons in the seventies:

T Munson	AB	R	H	2	3	HR	RBI	SB	CS	BB	K	BA	SA	OBA
1973	'73	519	80	156	29	4	20	74	4	6	48	64	.301	.362	.487
1975	'75	597	83	190	24	3	12	102	3	2	45	52	.318	.366	.429
1975	'77	595	85	183	28	5	18	100	5	6	39	55	.308	.351	.462

C Fisk	AB	R	H	2	3	HR	RBI	SB	CS	BB	K	BA	SA	OBA
1972	'72	457	74	134	28	9	22	61	5	2	52	83	.293	.370	.538
1977	'77	536	106	169	26	3	26	102	7	6	75	85	.315	.402	.521
1978	'78	571	94	162	39	5	20	88	7	2	71	83	.284	.366	.475

These two ballplayers are extremely well matched. Based on these numbers I'd choose Fisk because of his dominance to Munson when it comes to home runs and SLG%.

Dave Winfield vs Andre Dawson

Had Winfield remained with the San Diego Padres for the duration of his career, this match-up would have carried a little more weight. As it turned out this is one of the most intriguing comparisons still. Both ballplayers were five-tool players who were excellent defensively. Winfield started his career with the San Diego Padres in 1974 and remained there until 1980. He moved to the New York Yankees and was the highest paid ballplayer at the time. Dawson was a mainstay with the Montreal Expos until taking a significant pay-cut in the off-season of 1986-87, and moved to the Chicago Cubs for most of the remainder of his career.

Winfield won seven Gold Gloves over his career while Dawson won eight Gold Gloves. Winfield posted twelve seasons with 20+HR's/80+RBI's while Dawson had eight such seasons. Dawson had five seasons in which he hit 20+HR's and had 20+ stolen bases. Winfield did so only twice. Dawson had 34+ stolen bases in a year three times. Winfield's highest yearly stolen base total was 26. Dawson also won the MVP Award in 1987 hitting 49 home runs to go along with 137 RBI's (with the Chicago Cubs). Winfield never won the MVP in his career but did win a World Series ring with the Toronto Blue Jays in 1992.

Here's a look at each player's average 162 Game Season:

Player	AB	R	H	2B	3B	HR	RBI	SB	CS	BB	SO	AVG	OBP	SLG%
Winfield	600	91	169	29	5	25	100	12	5	66	92	.283	.353	.475
Dawson	612	85	171	31	6	27	98	19	7	36	93	.279	.323	.482

The numbers are so evenly matched that neither player stands out. Dawson averaged seven more stolen bases/year compared to Winfield but his OBP was 30 points lower. With each player's average year negated we'll resort to career statistics.

Player	AB	R	H	2B	3B	HR	RBI	SB	CS	BB	SO	AVG	OBP	SLG%
Winfield	11003	1669	3110	540	88	465	1833	223	96	1216	1686	.283	.353	.475
Dawson	9927	1373	2774	503	98	438	1591	314	109	589	1509	.279	.323	.482

While Dawson's numbers are great, Winfield is just a little bit better. Had Dawson had the exposure of playing for a large market team (he was stuck in Montreal for years) he probably would have gotten the exposure that would have made him a household name, like Winfield.

Dave Winfield vs Reggie Jackson

Dave Winfield may very well be the most talented ballplayer to have ever played the game. Winfield was drafted in three sports (Baseball, Basketball and Football) upon graduating from U of Minnesota and chose Baseball (thank G-d for that), seemingly having it all. Winfield put up great numbers in his career. He had 3110 Hits, 465 home runs, and won seven Gold Gloves. Still, the feuding with George Steinbrenner cost him about 010 points in average and five home runs a year. Had Winfield not have had to waste his time and energy dealing with Steinbrenner over petty matters there could very well have been a couple of championships for the New York Yankees in the eighties.

Dave won a World Series ring with the Toronto Blue Jays in 1992. He was an outspoken leader of that team and could back it with the bat. Ironically, the man George Steinbrenner called "Mr. May" had the game winning hit in game six of the World Series (against the Atlanta Braves) to win the Series.

Reggie, on the other hand, was adored in New York (and by Steinbrenner) for his role in their back to back World Series wins against the Los Angeles Dodgers in 1977 and 1978. His greatest accomplishment came in Game six of the World Series in 1977 when he hit three home runs in the game. Reggie was also the "straw that stirred the drink" for the Oakland A's (the team he started with) and he led them to a three-peat from 1972-1974. Jackson hit ten home runs in 98 World Series At-Bats and batted .357 in those contests. As well, Jackson posted thirteen years of 25+HR's/ 80+RBI's and had 563 lifetime home runs. Winfield had nine years with 25+HR's/80+RBI's.

Surprisingly both players, big men, were 20+stolen base stealers during their primes, each doing so four times.

Here are their average 162 Game Seasons:

Player	AB	R	H	2B	3B	HR	RBI	SB	CS	BB	K	BA	OBA	SA
Winfield	600	91	169	29	5	25	100	12	5	66	92	.283	.353	.475
Jackson	567	89	148	27	3	32	98	13	7	79	149	.262	.356	.490

Even though Reggie will always be remembered as Mr. October, I'd still start Winfield due to his Gold Glove defense.

Derek Jeter vs Alex Rodriguez

These two fine ballplayers were teammates at the start of 2004. The New York media will forever have a field day in trying to evaluate who the more productive ballplayer was; A-Rod or Jeter?

Jeter had guided the Yankees to five World Series Titles while A-Rod only won once. Looking at their regular season statistics shows A-Rod dominating Jeter in every category. A-Rod won 3 MVP Awards (in 2003, 2005, and 2007) as well as 4 Hank Aaron Awards (2001, 2002, 2003 and 2007), and the Babe Ruth Award once in 2000. He had two Gold Gloves as a shortstop (none at Third Base). Jeter won 5 Gold Gloves during his illustrous career. Ironically it wasn't until 2004 (the year A-Rod appeared) that Jeter won his first. Considering the Yankees kept Jeter at shortstop and moved A-Rod to third when he came to New York shows us the confidence the New York Yankees had in Jeter's defense. Among the Awards that Jeter raked in during his Hall of Fame career were the 1996 Rookie of the Year, the 2000 WS MVP, the 2000 All-Star Game MVP, the 2000 Babe Ruth Award, the 2006 and 2009 Hank Aaron Award, the 2009 Roberto Clemente Award, and the 2010 Lou Gehrig Memorial Award.

Statistics don't lie though and here are the numbers; 162 Game Averages:

Player	AB	R	H	2B	3B	HR	RBI	SB	CS	BB	K	BA	OBA	SA
Rodriguez	616	119	183	32	2	41	122	19	5	79	132	.297	.382	.554
Jeter	660	113	204	32	4	15	77	21	6	64	109	.310	.377	.440

What we see is A-Rod being more successful hitter in the regular season. Since October is when the real season begins, let's take a look at each player's post season numbers.

Player	AB	R	H	2	3	HR	RBI	SB	CS	BB	K	BA	OBA	SA
Alex Rodriguez	278	43	72	16	0	13	41	8	3	39	77	.259	.365	.457
Derek Jeter	650	111	200	32	5	20	61	18	5	66	135	.308	.374	.465

When projected, A-Rod's post-season's statistics are on par with Jeter's. Jeter does however have a team post season series record of 22-11, while Rodriguez' teams post-season series record was 8-10.

Although the numbers count, the intangibles that Derek Jeter brought to the game of baseball were immense. He was a true ballplayer who had the clutch home run, stolen base, defense stop, or stolen base, when the situation called for it. For this reason I would name Mr. November a.k.a Captain Clutch to be the greater ballplayer between the two.

Derek Jeter vs Nomar Garciaparra

Jeter vs Garciaparra will always be an argument to a New Yorker and a Bostonian. For the years they played against each other, fans from each city were truly passionate. It may seem to be obvious to select Jeter for the fact of his winning 5 World Series Titles to none for Garciaparra but when we analyse their regular season statistics we see how good a match-up this really is;

162 Game Averages

Player	AB	R	H	2	3	HR	RBI	SB	CS	BB	K	BA	OBA	SA
Derek Jeter	660	113	204	32	4	15	77	21	6	64	109	.310	.377	.440
Nomar Garciaparra	631	105	197	42	6	26	106	11	4	46	63	.313	.361	.521

Statistically, it would seem that Garciaparra was on par with Jeter. Keep in mind though that Jeter won 5 Gold Gloves in his career while Garciaparra never won a single one. We'll have to give the edge to Jeter because of his post-season prowess. It does leave one to wonder though whether the Red Sox would have still won the World Series that year of 2004 when they traded Garciaparra and eventually broke the Bambino curse that year. Ironically it's the only World Series ring Garciaparra owns, and he wasn't even in the clubhouse to celebrate it.

Derek Jeter vs Ozzie Smith

The passing of the torch, of the greatest shortstop in the game came when Jeter started his career in 1996, taking home the AL Rookie of the Year. Ironically, this was Ozzie Smith's last year in the Majors.

All Ozzie Smith accomplished when he played was winning 13 consecutive Gold Glove Awards from 1980-1992. Smith had 16 consecutive years stealing 21+ bases (1978-1993), 5 years with 40+ SB's, and 11 years with 31+SB's. Ozzie won 1 Silver Slugger Award, and was the 1985 NLCS MVP. He took home 1 World Series Title with the St. Louis Cardinals in 1982, had 2460 lifetime hits, and had 580 SB's over his storied career. "The Wizard" was clearly the best shortstop of his day, defensively no-one in baseball could compete at his level. When Derek Jeter came to the Majors he started out with a bang winning the 1996 AL Rookie of the Year and history began to be made.

Captain Clutch never won the AL MVP Award, but that was an anomoly on his Hall of Fame Career. Jeter won the 2000 World Series MVP, and was a focal point of the great Yankee teams that he played for in the late 90's right through 2009. He won 5 Gold Glove Awards, 5 Silver Slugger Awards, and won 5 World Series Titles. Jeter had 4 seasons stealing 40+Bases, 8 years stealing 22+ Bases, 8 seasons with 202+ hits, 13 years with 183+ hits and had 13 years with 102+ runs scored. Jeter finshed his career with 260 HR's, 870 Extra-Base Hits, .310 Avg, 3465 hits, 358 SB's, and a lifetime OPS of .817.

Here is a look at their average years over the course of their careers;

Player	AB	R	H	2	3	HR	RBI	SB	CS	BB	K	BA	OBA	SA	
Derek Jeter	660	113	204	32	4	15	77	21	6	64	109	.310	.377	.440	.817
Ozzie Smith	592	79	155	25	4	2	50	37	9	67	37	.262	.337	.328	.666

Although Ozzie took home the 1985 NLCS MVP Award, it was Jeter who truly shined in Post-Season play. The reality is that Jeter was just a more complete shortstop than "The Wizard". "Captain Clutch", or "Mr November" (as Jeter was called) showed up to play most years through October. For this reason I would select Jeter as the greater shortstop between the two.

Don Mattingly vs Eddie Murray

Mattingly and Murray were considered the two top 1st Basemen in the American League when Murray was with the Baltimore Orioles. Mattingly spent his entire career with the Bronx Bombers.

Mattingly had six consecutive years batting .300+ (seven years in total). Murray, likewise, batted .300+ seven times over his career. Taking these players lifetime statistics shows Murray to be far superior to Mattingly (Murray hit 504 home runs to Mattingly's 222 and had 3255 Hits to Mattingly's 2153).

To get a truer sense of each players worth let's look at their average 162 Game Season:

Player	AB	R	H	2	3	HR	RBI	SB	CS	BB	K	BA	OBA	SA
Don Mattingly	636	91	195	40	2	20	100	1	1	53	40	.307	.358	.471
Eddie Murray	607	87	174	30	2	27	103	6	2	71	81	.287	.359	.476

Although Mattingly didn't have the career span Murray had, he still managed a lifetime Batting Average of .307. Mattingly won the American League MVP in 1985. He also won nine Gold Gloves in his career to Murray's three. For these reasons I would start Mattingly at first over Murray.

Ernie Banks vs Cal Ripken Jr.

Ernie Banks finished his career with 512 home runs. Banks was a shortstop with the Chicago Cubs from 1954-1962 (before moving to 1st base) and won a Gold Glove for his efforts in 1960. His bat netted him five seasons of 40+home runs/ 100+RBI's including four in a row (1957-1960). Ernie also won the National League MVP in 1958 and 1959.

Cal Ripken Jr. had ten consecutive years of 20+HR's/80+RBI's (twelve in total). He also set the record for most consecutive games played (at 2632), beating the old mark set by Lou Gehrig (at 2130 games). Ripken Jr. won two MVP trophies (in 1983 and 1991) and two Gold Gloves (in 1991 and 1992). He holds the record for highest single season fielding % for shortstops with a mark of .996.

Here are each player's average 162 Game Seasons:

Player	AB	R	H	2	3	HR	RBI	SB	CS	BB	K	BA	OBA	SA
Ernie Banks	604	84	166	26	6	33	105	3	3	49	79	.274	.330	.500
Cal Ripken Jr.	624	89	172	33	2	23	91	2	2	61	70	.276	.340	.447

Ripken Jr's consistency over his career makes this comparison closer than one might think. To see the impact that Banks had on his "Cubbies" let's take a look at each players' best three years.

E Banks	AB	R	H	2	3	HR	RBI	SB	CS	BB	K	BA	OBA	SA
1955	596	98	176	29	9	44	117	9	3	45	72	.295	.345	.596
1958	617	119	193	23	11	47	129	4	4	52	87	.313	.366	.614
1959	589	97	179	25	6	45	143	2	4	64	72	.304	.374	.596
C Ripken	AB	R	H	2	3	HR	RBI	SB	CS	BB	K	BA	OBA	SA
1983	663	121	211	47	2	27	102	0	4	58	97	.318	.371	.517
1984	641	103	195	37	7	27	86	2	1	71	89	.304	.374	.510
1991	650	99	210	46	5	34	114	6	1	53	46	.323	.374	.566

Although Ernie Banks' Cubs never won the World Series Title, he was a major factor (alongside Billy Williams) in Chicago having one of the best offenses in the National League in the mid-fifties to the mid-sixties. While Ripken Jr. won a World Series Title with Baltimore in 1983, I would still take Banks as my shortstop.

Ferguson Jenkins vs Robin Roberts

Both starting pitchers were extremely successful over the course of their careers, and each posted six consecutive 20+ year win seasons. They are so close in lifetime statistics that it's hard to differentiate between the two. Fergie won 284 games over his career while Roberts won 286. Roberts lifetime ERA was 3.42 while Jenkins recorded a 3.34 mark. Jenkins registered 49 shutouts to Roberts 45. The only relevant difference is that Fergie had a better strikeout/walk ratio and was a 200+ strikeout man regularly throughout his career. This was something that Roberts couldn't approach. They both pitched 200+ innings a year, Roberts did so 14 times, and Jenkins 13 times. Robin had six consecutive 300+ IP campaigns from 1950-1955, while Fergie had a string of 4 consecutive 300+ IP from 1968-1971 (and a fifth in 1974).

Although Jenkins won the 1971 Cy Young Award with the Chicago Cubs it should be noted that Robin Roberts' prime pre-dated the Cy Young Award. During his best years from 1950-1955, Roberts took home the Sporting News Pitcher of the Year (the Cy Young equivalent) twice – 1952 and 1955.

Both duly have been inaugurated into the Cooperstown.

Overall I would have to give the slight edge to Ferguson Jenkins. All things being equal, Jenkins averaged 50 more strikeouts a year over the same number of innings as Roberts, with bases on balls being on par.

Frank Thomas vs Carlos Delgado

Frank Thomas came into the Major Leagues in 1990 and quickly established himself as a star. This was nothing new to him as he'd already been recognized in the sports-world as Fullback to Bo Jackson from his Football playing days in Auburn. He also won two MVP Awards in the Majors (in 1993 and 1994). In his career Thomas had four seasons batting .309+/ 40+ HR's/ 111 RBI's. Delgado meanwhile had three seasons of 41+ HR's/ 134+ RBI's.

Had we compared the two in 2000, Thomas would have won hands down. However, from 2000 on, Delgado put together four good seasons to Thomas' one good year (in 2003).

Let's take a look at their average 162 Game Seasons:

Player	AB	R	H	2	3	HR	RBI	SB	CS	BB	K	BA	OBA	SA
Frank Thomas	572	104	172	35	1	36	119	2	?	116	97	.301	.419	.555
Carlos Delgado	580	99	162	38	1	38	120	1	1	88	139	.280	.383	.546

These are two excellent hitters and numbers don't lie. By these statistics Thomas has the advantage in almost every category, leading in Batting Average, OBP, and Slugging %.

Gaylord Perry vs Don Sutton

Two pitchers that notched more than 300 wins in their careers.

The more recognized of the two was Don Sutton. Sutton spent a large part of his career with the large market Los Angeles Dodgers. He was their #1 starter and helped guide his Dodgers to three World Series Appearances (though they lost all three). Ironically it was the year Sutton left L.A (in 1981) that the Dodgers won their first World Series since '63. While Sutton didn't dominate in the post-season, he was a respectable 6-4 with a 3.68 ERA over 100.3 innings. It is this exposure to post-season play that made Sutton a recognizable face across America. Sutton was truly consistent throughout his career and had twelve 15+ win seasons in the Majors. Surprisingly, Sutton could only muster one 20 game win season in his 23 years in the Majors. Saying this, it was still widely accepted among Baseball circles that Sutton was one of the best pitchers in the 1970's, winning 15+ games in a season eight times over the course of the decade. Sutton finished his career back in L.A with the Dodgers. Between stops saw successful tenures in Houston, Milwaukee, Oakland, and California. His lifetime stats include 324 wins, 3574 strikeouts, 58 shutouts, and a 3.26 ERA. Although Sutton never won a Cy Young Award in his career, he was considered the 'ace of a strong Dodger staff and came close to winning the Award on a couple of occasions.

Perry, in comparison, sailed in under the radar. Starting his career with the San Francisco Giants in 1962, Gaylord became part of the rotation in 1966, winning 21 games that year. From 1966-1972, Perry notched six sub 3.00 ERA campaigns, including a 1.92 mark in his first year with the Cleveland Indians. This won Perry the first of his two Cy Young Awards. It was a superb performance in that '72 season as Gaylord went 24-16, pitched 342.6 innings, striking out 234 batters, and he completed 29 of his 40 starts. Still, Gaylord was overlooked by most people outside the Baseball community, as Cleveland carried no exposure for their players. Over the course of his career Perry registered seventeen seasons of 200+ innings pitched, and six seasons of 300+ innings. After Cleveland, Perry went to the Texas Rangers putting up two decent seasons before moving to the San Diego Padres as a free agent after the '77 season. In the '78 campaign Perry took home the Cy Young Award and became the first pitcher to win Cy Young Awards in both Leagues (since equalled by Pedro Martinez, Randy Johnson, and Roger Clemens). He was an impressive 21-6 with 260.6 innings pitched and a 2.73 ERA in '78.

Perry had 4 more pit-stops that took him through NY Yanks, Atlanta, Seattle, and Kansas City before he finally called it quits. Gaylord amassed 314 wins over his career, with 3534 strikeouts and a 3.13 lifetime ERA, to go along with 53 shutouts.

This is a hard comparison to make as Sutton was a face of America playing for the gloried Dodgers and he pitched in several post-seasons while Perry did not.

I would still, however, give the nod to Gaylord for the simple reason that he could win you twenty games in a year (something he did 5 times), and the old saying is "a bird in the hand is worth 2 in the bush." It's also noteworthy that Perry won two Cy Young Awards while Sutton didn't win any.

George Brett vs Mike Schmidt

In the 1970's and 1980's the argument of who the best Third Baseman in the Major Leagues was came down to Schmidt and Brett.

Schmidt posted thirteen 30+ home run seasons and hit 40+ home runs on three occasions. Brett hit 30+ home runs in a year once. Brett did however hit .300 eleven times while Schmidt only did so once.

Believe it or not Schmidt was by far the better defensive 3rd Baseman winning nine consecutive Gold Gloves, ten over the course of his career. Brett has only one Gold Glove to his name.

Here's their average 162 Game Seasons:

Player	AB	R	H	2	3	HR	RBI	SB	CS	BB	K	BA	OBA	SA
Mike Schmidt	563	101	151	27	4	37	107	12	6	102	127	.267	.380	.527
George Brett	619	95	189	40	8	19	95	12	6	66	54	.305	.369	.487

When I grew up I always liked Brett over Schmidt. They both won the World Series once. Brett with Kansas City in 1985 and Schmidt with the Phillies in 1980 (over Kansas City, ironically enough). They were also life-timers with their respective teams.

In hindsight, Schmidt seems the more logical choice, averaging 18 more home runs a year. While Brett carries a .038 point advantage in lifetime Batting Average, Schmidt cleans up in every other category. Defensively, I'll take Schmidt's nine Gold Gloves to Brett's lone one.

1980 A.L MVP George Brett (3B) versus 1980 and 1981 N.L MVP Mike Schmidt (3B):

Player	Yr	AB	R	H	2B	3B	HR	RBI	SB	CS	BB	SO	AVG	OBP	SLG	OPS
Brett	1979	645	119	212	42	20	23	107	17	10	51	36	.329	.376	.563	0.939
Brett	1980	449	87	175	33	9	24	118	15	6	58	22	.390	.454	.664	1.118
Schmidt	1980	548	104	157	25	8	48	121	12	5	89	119	.286	.380	.624	1.004
Schmidt	1981	354	78	112	19	2	31	91	12	4	73	71	.316	.435	.644	1.080

These all-time greats are dinosaurs to where the game has gone today, with free agency permitting constant moves and changes between organizations. The Kansas City Royals and the Philadelphia Phillies couldn't have had it any better. The question baseball circles were asking in 1980 was, "Who would you start your team with, Schmidt or Brett?"

"Goose" Fingers vs "Rollie" Gossage

The real argument here comes down to who has the better moustache?

I'm serious, those are amazing looks. A "handlebar" moustache versus a "Fu-Man-Chu" moustache. Who's to say? It had to have taken them at least a year to get it down right. Keep in mind Charles Finley encouraged facial hair, while Bill Veeck did so likewise.

Now, on a serious note, did they get laid regularly when they played? A lot of people don't realize that the sexual revolution of the Seventies was an important time.

It was also a time in Baseball where the closer role became an important facet of the game. Aside from Hoyt Wilhelm and Elroy Face, baseball really didn't incorporate late inning specialists or have a recognizable closer in the game. With Fingers and Gossage, this role took shape into what we see today.

Fingers started out with the Oakland A's in 1968, and by 1972 was recognized as the best closer in the game posting 21 saves and finishing the campaign with an 11-9 record and a 2.53 ERA His A's won the World Series three years in a row 1972-1974 and Fingers was a main reason why. He took home World Series MVP in 1974 for his efforts. Fingers had 10 seasons in which he saved 20+ ballgames and took home the American League Cy Young and MVP Awards in 1981 when he was with the Milwaukee Brewers. Fingers finished his career with 341 saves, and duly voted into the Baseball Hall of Fame in 1992.

While Fingers was finesse, Gossage was pure heat. Riding a 98 MPH Fastball, the Goose dominated the late-innings like no other before him. Starting out in 1972 with the Chicago White Sox Gossage enjoyed his first successful campaign in 1975, posting 26 saves and a 1.84 ERA The 'Sox decided to put Gossage into the starting rotation in 1976 and although he was healthy, he wasn't nearly as successful as he had been the year prior as stopper. While Chicago certainly didn't give up on the Goose, they decided to go in another direction and traded him to the Pittsburgh Pirates for Richie Zisk. Playing for the Pirates in '77, Gossage enjoyed his best year ever going 11-9 with 26 saves and a 1.62 ERA over 133 innings. Goose struck out a grand total of 151 batters that year. As a free-agent following the season, Gossage signed with the New York Yankees to be co-closer alongside '77 AL Cy Young winner Sparky Lyle. The truth of the matter is that Gossage won the job as closer of the 'Yanks early into the '78 campaign and Sparky left the Yankees after the '78 season. Goose had ten 20+ save seasons and was probably the most feared pitcher the game had in his day. Highly successful during the post-season, Gossage went to the World Series three times winning one ring and finished his career with 310 saves.

 The comparison between Goose and Fingers is intriguing. In 1981, when Fingers took home the AL MVP and Cy Young, Gossage had arguably the better statistics between the two. Nevertheless, my pick of the two would have to be Goose Fingers.

Harmon Killebrew vs Eddie Mathews

Eddie Mathews teamed with Henry Aaron to form an offensive duo bettered only by Ruth and Gehrig. Mathews was a member of the Boston Braves in 1952 (their last year in Boson) and when the team re-located to Milwaukee the following year he clubbed 47 home runs to go along with 135 RBI's. Mathews finished his career with 512 home runs and finished second in the MVP voting twice. He hit 30+home runs in a season ten times over the course of his career and won a World Series ring for his efforts in the Braves championship season of 1957.

Harmon Killebrew was a very similar ballplayer to Mathews. Although "Killer" wasn't the defensive player Mathews was, he did have eight seasons of 40+home runs to Mathews four. Killebrew won the MVP Award in the 1969 campaign bashing out 49 home runs that year. Killebrew finished his career with 573 home runs.

This is a look at each players average 162 Game Season:

Player	AB	R	H	2	3	HR	RBI	SB	CS	BB	K	BA	OBA	SA
Harmon Killebrew	542	85	139	19	2	38	105	1	1	104	113	.256	.376	.509
Eddie Mathews	578	102	157	24	5	35	98	5	3	98	101	.271	.376	.509

Considering that their numbers were so close to one another, I'd give the edge to Killebrew as Mathews had more At-Bats/year and Killebrew still hit more HR's/season and more RBI's/season. Mathews also had Henry Aaron batting behind him in Milwaukee, while Killebrew was a one-man show for the Minnesota Twins.

Henry Aaron vs Roberto Clemente

These two Right-fielders were revered by all baseball fans. Clemente's life was cut short by a plane crash on New Years Eve of '72/'73. Up to that point he'd established himself as the Greatest defensive Right-fielder of All-Time. Clemente's arm was what makes for folklore and led him to twelve consecutive Gold Gloves (and probably three or four more). Although he died tragically in his prime, Clemente still managed to reach the coveted 3000 Hit-club, on his last at-bat of the '72 campaign. Clemente could hit for average and he posted six seasons of batting .339+ in a pitchers era. His lifetime batting average was .317.

While Aaron wasn't in Clemente's class defensively he was known to be a very good defensive Right-fielder, as evidenced by his three Gold Gloves. Aaron's forte was his bat. The man could flat out hit. His lifetime batting average was .305, and Aaron posted eight seasons of .322+. Aaron was not only a great hitter, he was also the most effective power hitter of All-Time (neigh Barry Bonds) finishing his career with 755 home runs (to go along with 3771 basehits). While Aaron's home runs/At bat is lower than past greats, keep in mind the era in which Aaron played (it was more pitcher friendly than in the 20's and 30's when huge power numbers were put up by many of the greats – Ruth, Foxx, Greenberg).

When we compare the two please note that in Clemente's last three seasons he batted .352, .341, and .312. Also note that Aaron stole 20+bases six times while Clemente's highest single season total was 12.

Player	AB	R	H	2	3	HR	RBI	SB	CS	BB	K	BA	OBA	SA
Henry Aaron	607	107	185	31	5	37	113	12	4	69	68	.305	.374	.555
Roberto Clemente	629	94	200	29	11	16	87	6	3	41	82	.317	.359	.475

The overall advantage goes to Aaron. Clemente could hit you .350+, but that was without BB's and very little power when compared to Aaron. Although Clemente was clearly the better defensive player, Aaron more than made up for it with his bat.

Ivan Rodriguez vs Mike Piazza

"Pudge" Rodriguez is considered the premiere catcher of our day. Not only did he call a great game (showing what he could do with a young staff- when he was with the Florida Marlins), he also had the strongest and most accurate throwing arm of all time for the Major Leagues (and probably the Negro Leagues for that matter). When it comes to offense, Rodriguez batted .300 or better in ten seasons of his storied career (eight straight from 1995-2002). "Pudge" won thirteen Gold Gloves in the Majors (ten in a row from 1992-2001). He also won seven Silver Slugger Awards (six consecutive from 1994-1999), and won the 1999 AL MVP Award as well as the 2003 NL.C.S Award while with Florida.

Piazza has the better offensive numbers when compared to Rodriguez. Piazza won the Rookie of the Year Award with the Dodgers in 1993. Over his illustrious career Pizza won ten consecutive Silver Slugger Awards

(1993-2002), and recorded eight seasons of 30+home runs/ 92+RBI's/ .300+ Average. He never captured a Gold Glove award but was not a liability in the field.

Ivan Rodriguez is clearly the best backstop of our day, and perhaps of all-time when defense is included in the mix, as he was simply dominant.

These are their average years:

Player	AB	R	H	2	3	HR	RBI	SB	CS	BB	K	BA	OBA	SA
Ivan Rodriguez	611	86	181	36	3	20	85	8	4	33	94	.296	.334	.464
Mike Piazza	586	89	180	29	1	36	113	1	2	64	94	.308	.377	.545

"Pudge" Rodriguez probably saved his 2003 World Series Champion Florida Marlins at least 110 runs. When he threw down to first base and started picking off guys with consistency, ball clubs stopped running. He probably only saw a third of the base-stealers that other catchers had to throw down for. I'm also being very conservative in his offense production. While "Pudge" didn't have a 40+home run season, he was one of the best hitters in the game when he played. Rodriguez also had a huge, positive effect on the young arms he saw in Florida (and when he was in Texas and Detroit for that matter).

If I had to choose a backstop to start my team I'd take "Pudge" over Piazza.

6
Player Comparisons – Part II

Jackie Robinson vs Rogers Hornsby

Rogers Hornsby was considered the best 2nd Baseman when he played in the Majors in the 20's and 30's. Jackie Robinson was considered the best 2nd Baseman when he played for Brooklyn between 1947-1957. Robinson broke the color barrier in 1947. All he did was win the MVP Award in his third year (1949). Between 1947-1954 it could be argued that Jackie Robinson was the best true ballplayer in the Majors. Already established in the Negro Leagues playing for the Washington Monarchs, Robinson was signed by the Dodger Organization in Brooklyn, New York City, New York. Already a star when he made "the show" in 1947, Robinson was probably the most versatile player in the Majors having started at four positions. Jackie played 1st base in 1947, 2nd Base from 1948-1952, Outfield and 3rd Base from 1953-1956.

When we look at Hornsby's numbers there is a dominance that's there that Robinson didn't reach. Keep in mind though that many ballplayers in the Negro Leagues could play at Hornsby's level. Even still, Hornsby did bat .400+ in three seasons. In probably his best year (1922) Hornsby batted .401 with 42 home runs with 152 RBI's, this was the only time in Major League History that a batter hit .400+, hit 40+HR's and had 150+RBI's in one year. Hornsby also won two MVP Awards in his career (1925 and 1929).

Considering that Robinson could very well have put up at least five more seasons at an elite level (he entered the Majors already in his prime) let's compare Robinson's best three seasons to Hornsby's three best seasons.

J Robinson	AB	R	H	2	3	HR	RBI	SB	BB	K	BA	OBA	SA
1949	593	122	203	38	12	16	124	37	86	27	.342	.432	.528
1951	548	106	185	33	7	19	88	25	79	27	.338	.429	.527
1953	484	109	159	34	7	12	95	17	74	30	.329	.425	.502
R Hornsby	**AB**	**R**	**H**	**2**	**3**	**HR**	**RBI**	**SB**	**BB**	**K**	**BA**	**OBA**	**SA**
1922	623	141	250	46	14	42	152	17	65	50	.401	.459	.722

| 1924 | 536 | 121 | 227 | 43 | 14 | 25 | 94 | 5 | 89 | 32 | .424 | .507 | .696 |
| 1925 | 504 | 133 | 203 | 41 | 10 | 39 | 143 | 5 | 83 | 39 | .403 | .489 | .756 |

It seems that Hornsby has much better statistics than Robinson, aside from stolen bases.

Keep in mind though that the league average over Hornsby's best three seasons was .295 and that the league average over Robinson's best three years was only .274. Due to his stolen base prowess, fielding ability, and versatility, I'd choose Jackie Robinson as my 2nd Baseman over Rogers Hornsby.

Jimmie Foxx vs Lou Gehrig

As Foxx and Gehrig played during the same era, let's compare their average years.

Player	AB	R	H	2B	3B	HR	RBI	BB	SO	AVG	OBP%	SLG%	TB
Foxx	569	122	185	32	9	37	134	102	92	.325	.428	.609	347
Gehrig	599	141	204	40	12	37	149	113	59	.340	.447	.632	379

The numbers seem to suggest that Gehrig was, by far, the better batter of the two. These numbers should however be quantified. When Gehrig played he had Ruth batting ahead of him in the batting order. This inflated his statistics. After Ruth retired, DiMaggio entered the scene. When Foxx started his career with the Philadelphia A's, he was their only big bat. In fact, Foxx had a big bat on his teams for only 3 years (when he played with Ted Williams in Boston). Over the course of Foxx's career he won three MVP trophies. Gehrig won two MVP's. They were considered the best two 1st Basemen in baseball when they played (and to this day, according to some people).

Foxx had eight seasons in which he had 35+ home runs, 100 runs scored, 100 RBI's, and a .300 + average, while Gehrig had 7.

The statistic that Gehrig dominated was total bases. Even at that point, Gehrig was able to be more patient than Foxx over his career, having Ruth and DiMaggio in the lineup with him.

To start my team, I would take Jimmie Foxx.

Joe Morgan vs Eddie Collins

Joe Morgan was a major cog in the wheel of the "Big Red Machine" in the seventies. Starting his career with the Houston Colt 45's, his numbers got much better when he left the Astrodome for Riverfront Stadium. Morgan won two World Series Titles with the Red's in 1975 and 1976, and was also the National League MVP in both years. Morgan also won five Gold Gloves in his career. In any given year he was capable of drawing 100+ walks/40+

Stolen Bases/20+ home runs/100+ Runs Scored. Those statistics were the norm, not an anomaly.

Eddie Collins played at the turn of the 20th Century, starting with the Philadelphia A's. He led them to three World Series Titles before moving to the Chicago White Sox in 1915. In Collins career he had ten seasons of 40+ Stolen Bases. Collins had sixteen years batting .300+. In Chicago, Collins helped the White Sox win a World Series Title (he was also on the "Black Sox" team that threw the World Series in 1919 – he wasn't in on the fix).

While Morgan won five Gold Gloves in his career, keep in mind that Gold Gloves weren't issued until 1959. Collins was known to be an excellent defensive 2nd baseman.

To capture Morgan's effect on the "Big Red Machine" let's take a look at each player's best three seasons.

J Morgan	AB	R	H	2	3	HR	RBI	SB	CS	BB	K	BA	OBA	SA
1973	576	116	167	35	2	26	82	67	15	111	61	.290	.406	.493
1975	498	107	163	27	6	17	94	67	10	132	52	.327	.466	.508
1976	472	113	151	30	5	27	111	60	9	114	41	.320	.444	.576
E Collins	AB	R	H	2	3	HR	RBI	SB	CS	BB	K	BA	OBA	SA
1912	543	137	189	25	11	0	64	63		101		.348	.450	.435
1913	534	125	184	23	13	3	73	55		85	37	.345	.441	.453
1914	526	122	181	23	14	2	85	58	30	97	31	.344	.452	.452

Since Collins played during the Dead Ball Era, during which the league leader in home runs frequently had less than 10, it's unfair to include Morgan's power numbers into the equation. Morgan was a better % base-stealer than Collins, and would have excelled during the Dead Ball Era. Also keep in mind that although his average may be lower than Collins, Morgan has a higher On-Base %. For these reasons I would choose Morgan as my second baseman over Collins.

John Smoltz vs Dennis Eckersley

Both pitchers were versatile enough to convert from their role as starter to closer.

During Dennis Eckersley's days this was unheard of. Unheralded as a starter, Eck was reliable to win 15 games, give you 240+ inning, and record a sub 3.50 ERA Starting out with the Cleveland Indians in 1975, Eckerley looked poised to be the Ace of their staff for years to come. He posted three solid years when he was unexpectedly dealt in the spring of '78 to the Boston Red Sox. Teaming with Luis Tiant and Mike Torrez, Eck almost helped lead the 'Sox to the American League East Division Title in '78 only to lose a 1 game playoff to the New York Yankees. Eck won 20 games that year and followed that up in '79 with 17 more victories. Eckersley's career started to go downhill from there and he was dealt to the Chicago Cubs during the '84 season. Neither spectacular nor dismal, Eck toiled as a solid #3 starter for three more years when his calling came. In early April of 1987 the Cubs dealt Eckersley to the Oakland A's for next to nothing. Tony LaRussa was managing the A's at the time and decided with his pitching coach Dave Duncan to convert Eckersley to the closer role. What seemed to be a desperate move to resurrect Eck's career proved huge dividends for LaRussa. Eckersley saved 16 games that year and won the closer spot for good. From 1988-1993, Eckersley saved 33+ ballgames every year, reaching a pinnacle of 51 games saved in 1992. Eckersley won the American League MVP and Cy Young Awards for that year of 1992, and although his numbers died down after the '93 campaign, his lifetime numbers are truly impressive. He averaged 35 walks in 156 Innings Pitched over the course of his career, winning 197 ballgames, and recorded 390 saves. His performance in the post season may have only been average, but he did manage to win the 1988 AL.C.S MVP and won the World Series with the Oakland A's the following year. He finished post-season play with 15 saves in 28 games. Eckersley's career may be the greatest transition move in the history of the game, and paved the way for John Smoltz.

Smoltz began his career in the Detroit Tigers Organization and was dealt to Atlanta while still a prospect. The deal brought Doyle Alexander to Detroit and most people thought the move to be in the Tigers favor as Alexander went 9-0 down the stretch for Detroit, leading the Tigers into the playoffs.

The Braves brought up Smoltz from their Farm System in 1988 and he became a fixture in their rotation in '89. Putting together five solid years (though not spectacular) helped his Braves reach the playoffs most years. Since '91 the Braves made the playoffs every year up to 2005. Smoltz came into his zone in '96, winning the Cy Young that year recording a 24-8 record. What made Smoltz truly special was his ability to win big games. In the '90's alone the Braves made the playoffs eight times winning the World Series in 1995. In post-season play Smoltz was an incredible 15-4 with a 2.67 ERA, 199 strikeouts over 209 innings pitched.

In 2001 the Braves nursed an injured Smoltz and decided to move him to closer, as the A's had done with Eckersley. Taking the role on full-time from 2002-2004, Smoltz reached 44+ saves/year each year for those three years he was their closer. The Braves turned tide and instituted Smoltz back into the starting staff. Smoltz was solid and healthy enough to rack up three more solid years in the rotation for the Bravers. He finished his career with 213 wins and 154 saves. It is clear that Smoltz will be enshrined in Cooperstown. Alongside Eckersley, Rich "Goose" Gossage, and Derek Lowe, they are the only Major League pitchers to start 29+ games in a year, and save 30+ in a year. Also, Smoltz and Eckersley are the only Major League pitchers in the history of the game to win 20 games in a year as a starter, and save 50+ games in one year as closer.

For the record, I would have to assess Smoltz numbers to be better than Eckersley's due to his panache for winning the big game.

Jorge Posada vs Javy Lopez

Both these backstops are grossly underrated. Being a Toronto Blue Jay and Boston Red Sox fan means that I love Ernie Whitt type numbers (20 HR/65 RBI's). Posada and Lopez far exceed the numbers Ernie Whitt put up.

Looking at their average 162 game season...

Player	AB	R	H	2	3	HR	RBI	SB	CS	BB	K	BA	OBA	SA
Posada	540	80	147	34	1	24	94	2	2	83	129	.273	.374	.474
Lopez	573	73	165	29	2	28	93	1	2	38	104	.287	.337	.491

It's hard to differentiate between the two. Lopez had a 14-point edge in batting average to Posada. Posada held a 37-point advantage in O.B.P to Lopez. They were both two excellent backstops for their pitchers and both had strong arms, eliminating most of the running game from opposing teams.

Lopez won 1 World Series with the Atlanta Braves, while Posada was a mainstay for the Yankees dynasty over the duration of his career winning four World Series. Lopez was a little more integral to Atlanta's offense than Posada was to the Yankees, but four World Series Titles with offense at par leads me to believe that Lopez wouldn't have been able to do much better. It is for this reason that I would start Posada if I had my choice between the two.

Josh Gibson vs Babe Ruth

Babe Ruth is known to be the epitome of home run hitters. Josh Gibson is simply the best. Not only did Gibson hit 803 home runs in Negro League competition, he hit 962 home runs when including his tours in Cuba, Mexico, Puerto Rico, Central America, and the Dominican Republic.

Ruth was a great home run hitter in the Major Leagues, but this was before the integration of "black" players in the Major Leagues. Conversely Ruth isn't necessarily the best home run hitter in the history of the Major Leagues, as ballplayers such as Barry Bonds, Alex Rodriguez, Sammy Sosa, Henry Aaron, and Willie Mays should also receive some consideration for this claim. Ruth was however, one of the most versatile ballplayers of all-time as he was a successful lefthanded pitcher when he began his career in 1914. He had four consecutive years with a sub 2.44 ERA from 1915-1918, finishing 1916 with a 23-12 record and a 1.75 ERA and 1917 with a 24-13 record and a 2.01 ERA He was 3-0 in World Series play with an ERA of 0.87 and highly successful as a starting pitcher during the regular season, but had Ruth played the outfield early on in his career, he would surely have topped 800 lifetime home runs.

When including the Negro Leagues (and any other League for that matter) the answer as to who the best home run Hitter of all time is becomes obvious, Josh Gibson. Ruth hit 714 career home runs in his Major League career. His greatest single season total was 60. Gibson's greatest single season total was 69. Gibson hit 803 lifetime home runs in the Negro Leagues bettering Bonds' mark of 762 by 41, Aaron's mark of 755 lifetime home runs by 48 and Ruth's mark of 714 by 89.

Gibson accomplished these numbers playing as a backstop, which makes his hitting ability all that more amazing as Catchers are taxed the most physically by the nature of the position. Also, Gibson was 35 when his career ended. Had Gibson been instituted into the Majors when he began his career in the mid twenties, he most surely would have at least equalled the exploits of Babe Ruth year in and year out. It is a hard argument to make that Gibson could have been topped by Ruth.

If the question comes up to whom the greatest power hitter of all-time is I find it insulting to the history of the game of baseball if the answer isn't Josh Gibson, as his 962 career home runs will never be equaled. It would have been a great story had Babe Ruth pitched and Josh Gibson caught on the Boston Red Sox team Ruth started with, had integration occurred when it should have (from day one). At that point Satchel Paige could get the next start and Ruth would have been put in right field for his off-days from the hill. The Boston Red Sox would certainly have had some World Series success in the twenties had that been the case.

Keith Hernandez vs Don Mattingly

Keith Hernandez and Don Mattingly were two similar ballplayers over the same era. Both were standouts with the glove and were both threats to drive in 90+ RBI's and hit .300+ in any given year. They both won the MVP Award once, Mattingly with the New York Yankees in 1985 and Hernandez with the St. Louis Cardinals in 1979 (in a tie with Willie Stargell).

Hernandez won a World Series ring during his playing days with St. Louis in 1982 and another one with the New York Mets of 1986.

Both were sterling with the glove. Hernandez won an unprecedented eleven consecutive Gold Gloves at first base, while Mattingly won nine Gold Gloves in his career.

Here's a look at their average 162 Game Seasons:

Player	AB	R	H	2	3	HR	RBI	SB	CS	BB	K	BA	OBA	SA
Hernandez	572	87	169	33	5	13	83	8	5	83	79	.296	.384	.436
Mattingly	636	91	195	40	2	20	100	1	1	53	40	.307	.358	.471

Based on defense and the success of his teams, I'd start Keith Hernandez over Don Mattingly at first.

Ken Griffey Jr vs Mickey Mantle

In the 1950's and 1960's the greatest Centerfielder was either Willie Mays or Mickey Mantle (I'd choose Mays). In our time the argument would probably come down to Ken Griffey Jr. and Jim Edmonds (I'd take Griffey Jr.).

All Griffey Jr. did over the course of his career is belt 630 home runs, winning the MVP award in 1997. He also won Gold Gloves every year in the 90's. From 1996-2000, Griffey Jr. hammered 40+ home runs and 118+ RBI's each year. Since moving from Seattle to the Reds organization in 2000, his numbers deteriorated. Griffey Jr. just couldn't beat out father time.

When Mickey Mantle started his career with the New York Yankees in 1951 great things were expected of him. He didn't disappoint. In just his second year Mantle batted .311. Having established himself, Mantle moved into elite status posting a Triple Crown year in 1956. During that campaign Mantle bat .353 with 52 home runs and 130 RBI's. The following year he won MVP honours again, batting .365. Mantle played on a dynasty team with the Yankees, while Griffey Jr. struggled to get his Mariners into the Post-Season, doing so only twice. Even still, Griffey Jr. did make a name for himself in 1995, when in a 5 game series against the Yankees, he hit 5 home runs. Mantle was a Post-Season standout, and for years he held the lifetime Post-Season home run mark with 18 dingers (later topped by Reggie Jackson and Manny Ramirez).

Between the two Griffey Jr won ten Gold Gloves to Mantle's one. Even in batting average with a slight edge to Griffey Jr. in career home runs, defense would have to be the deciding factor as Mantle's Yankees had the pitching that Griffey Jr's teams lacked.

Larry Walker vs Bobby Abreu

Larry Walker may seem to be the obvious choice between the two but keep in mind that it took Walker took seven seasons before he reached his peak as a hitter. Not that he wasn't productive in his early years with the Expos. Abreu quietly put up consistent numbers each year from when he first came up to the Majors (in 1996). Abreu established himself as a starter in 1998, batting .312. Since then he has posted two 30+ home run/ 30+ Stolen Bases/ 100 RBI's/ 100 Runs Scored years, and nine 20 HR/20 SB campaigns (seven in a row from 1999-2005).

Considering that Walker was a threat to hit 20 home runs/ 20 Stolen Bases each year from his first campaign, this makes these two ballplayers comparable.

This is their average 162 Game Seasons:

Player	AB	R	H	2	3	HR	RBI	SB	CS	BB	K	BA	OBA	SA
Larry Walker	563	110	176	38	5	31	107	19	6	74	100	.313	.400	.565
Bobby Abreu	566	97	165	38	4	19	91	27	9	99	123	.291	.395	.475

Both were excellent 5-Tool ballplayers who had keen eyes at the plate. Abreu won a Gold Glove in 2005 and one Silver Slugger Award in 2004 As it stands though, Walker is the more successful of the two as shown by Walker's NL MVP Award in 1997, three Silver Slugger Awards, and seven Gold Glove Awards that he won over of his career.

Larry Walker vs Manny Ramirez

Which ballplayer of the two would I choose for my team? Let's have some fun here and review each player's awards. Ramirez has won the Henry Aaron Award twice and he won the MVP for his role in the 2004 World Series. Manny won a second World Series with the Red Sox in 2007, and won eight consecutive Silver Slugger Awards (1999-2006) nine in total. Walker, on the other hand, won the NL MVP Award in 1997 and seven Gold Gloves alongside three Silver Slugger Awards (he probably should have won 7 or 8) . A paradigm in this player comparison is that Ramirez played many years of his career in Cleveland and Boston, and Walker's best years were in the friendly confines of Coors Field and the spacious Olympic Stadium in Montreal.

These are both players' 162 Game Averages:

Player	AB	R	H	2	3	HR	RBI	SB	CS	BB	K	BA	OBA	SA
Larry Walker	563	110	176	38	5	31	107	19	6	74	100	.313	.400	.565
Manny Ramiez	580	109	181	38	1	39	129	3	2	94	128	.312	.411	.585

In reviewing the statistics we see that Ramirez has the better numbers in practically every category except for stolen bases. Taking into account that Walker has won seven Gold Gloves to Ramirez' awards as World Series MVP in 2004 (and two Hank Aaron Awards), I would take Walker to start for me over Ramirez (defense prevails).

Larry Walker vs Sammy Sosa

When paired, it would seem that Sosa's power totals would dominate Walker's numbers. It is true that Sosa has averaged eleven more home runs per year. Keep in mind though that

Sosa averaged only eight RBI's/Year more than Walker and that projected over the same number of At-Bats is actually one less.

Walker also has a Batting Average that is .40 points higher than Sosa's, with an OBP that is 56 points higher and a Slugging % that is 31 points higher. Also keep in mind that Walker has won seven Gold Glove Awards in rightfield while Sosa never won a Gold Glove. While there are those that would say Sosa is the epitomy of a home run hitter and that the game of Baseball revolves around that premise is hard for me to comprehend. Yes, Sosa had seven 40+ HR seasons (including six in a row from 1998-2003), four 50+ HR seasons, and three 63+ HR seasons, he still has a lower Slugging%.

This is a look at their average years:

Player	AB	R	H	2	3	HR	RBI	SB	CS	BB	K	BA	OBA	SA
Larry Walker	563	110	176	38	5	31	107	19	6	74	100	.313	.400	.565
Sammy Sosa	607	102	166	26	3	42	115	16	7	64	159	.273	.344	.534

I'd take Walker for his defense.

Lou Brock vs Tim Raines

Both these players were speedsters that dominated games with their speed. Lou Brock was simply the pinnacle of a St. Louis Cardinals team that won two World Series with Brock on board. When Brock came to St. Louis from the Cubs, in 1964, he led that team to a World Series title, batting .348 in St. Louis that year. In Brock's three appearances in the World Series he batted .391 with a .655 SLG % with 16 Stolen Bases. Over the duration of his career, Brock managed to hold the record for lifetime steals (before Rickey Henderson came along) with a mark of 938.

Raines on the other hand didn't have the success with the teams he played for. When Raines started his career with the Montreal Expos in 1981 he stole 71 Bases in just 88 games. Raines went on to steal 70+ bases in six consecutive years. He posted 50+bases eight times in his career. Brock stole 50+ bases in twelve consecutive years. While Raines won a World Series with the New York Yankees in 1996 he wasn't the player he was in his prime. He did however mange a lofty career total of 808 lifetime steals.

These are each player's average 162 Game Seasons:

Player	AB	R	H	2	3	HR	RBI	SB	CS	BB	K	BA	OBA	SA
Lou Brock	640	100	187	30	9	9	56	58	19	47	107	.293	.343	.410
Tim Raines	574	102	169	28	7	11	63	52	9	86	63	.294	.385	.425

This is as close as it's going to get. Trying to differentiate between the two is hard. Raines has the higher stolen base percentage and he is 42 points higher in OBP. Keep in mind though, the sixties batting average was 20 points lower than when Raines played in the 80's and 90's. Brock's strength was his overall game (defensively Brock was considered to be among the best in leftfield) and considering that he led the St. Louis Cardinals to three appearances in the World Series (two Titles), I would start Brock over Raines.

Luis Tiant vs Don Drysdale

Drysdale was a flamethrower while Tiant struck out batters with both power and finesse. Both were 200 game winners and their statistics are comparable.

Drysdale was a lifetimer in the Dodger organization and started out with Brooklyn in 1956. In just his second year in the Majors, Drysdale established himself as a premier pitcher compiling a 17-9 record and a 2.69 ERA in 221 innings. It was 1959 when Drysdale posted his first of six 200+ strikeouts/year with a mark of 242, and he led LA to a World Series Title. In 1962 Drysdale won the Major League Cy Young Award with a 25-9 record, 232 strikeouts, and a 2.83 ERA over 314.3 innings. Truly consistent throughout his career Drysdale strung together 12 consecutive years of 211.6 innings or more. Drysdale finished his career with a 209-166 lifetime mark and a 2.95 lifetime ERA Alongside Sandy Koufax, many rated the Dodger starting staff of the 60's to be the best in the 'biz. They were instrumental in winning three World Series Titles (1959, 1963, and 1965).

Luis Tiant began his career in virtual obscurity with the Cleveland Indians in 1964. He could throw hard, but it was his motion that gained Tiant notoriety around the League. Tiant would contort his upper body in his pitching motion to the point of his back facing the plate, gaining torque on the release. In 1968 Tiant put up an incredible 1.60 ERA over 258.3 innings, with 264 strikeouts and a 21-9 record. Tiant still didn't take home the Cy Young Award that year though, as this was also the year Denny McClain went 31-6 (the last time a Major Leaguer has won 30+ games in a single season). Luis always seemed to be an inch away from getting an Award, or the coveted World Series Title. In '71 Tiant came to Boston from the Minnesota Twins and was an impressive versatile swingman going 15-6 with a 1.92 ERA in 179 innings pitched the following campaign. Tiant started 19 games in '72 and completed 12 of them with 6 shutouts. The following two years Tiant posted back to back 20+ win seasons. As "ace" of the Red Sox staff, Tiant almost led his Sox to a World Series Title in 1975, only to lose Game 7 against the Cincinnati Reds. In "78, Tiant, still a major cog in the Sox pitching staff, lost in a 1 game playoff against the New York Yankees for the American League East Division Title. All said and done all Tiant accomplished in his storied career was win 229 games and he struck out 2416 batters (70 less than Drysdale).

As a Red Sox fan I would have to rate Tiant slightly ahead of Drysdale for having to pitch in the tiny Fenway Park for the majority of his career, compared to the spacious Chez Ravine that Drysdale had to work with.

Manny Ramirez vs Juan Gonzalez

When comparing these two players we're looking at huge RBI totals. Gonzalez's first full season was in 1991, before the home run boom of the mid-90's-present. The next season (1992) Gonzalez put up the first of five 40+ HR / 100+ RBI's. He captured his first MVP trophy in 1996 and his second MVP in 1998. In 1998 Gonzalez had 97 extra base hits and an incredible 407 total bases.

While Ramirez never won a MVP trophy, he put up twelve 30+ HR / 100+ RBI campaigns to Gonzalez' seven. As well, Ramirez had ten seasons of 30+ HR / 100+ RBI's / .300 Batting Average to Gonzalez' five. Gonzalez is even with Ramirez in 40+ HR seasons, five apiece.

Here's their average years:

Player	AB	R	H	2	3	HR	RBI	SB	CS	BB	K	BA	OBA	SA
Manny Ramirez	580	109	181	38	1	39	129	3	2	94	128	.312	.411	.585
Juan Gonzalez	629	102	186	37	2	42	135	2	2	44	122	.295	.343	.561

For whatever reason, Gonzalez had success winning the MVP Award (winning twice), while Ramirez never did. Ramirez won two World Series Titles (both with the Boston Red Sox - 2004 and 2007) and his offensive numbers are dominant to Gonzalez in Batting Average, O.B.P, and Slugging %.

Manny Ramirez vs Sammy Sosa

Each of these players was born in the Dominican Republic. Both players put up astounding numbers respective of their careers. Sosa won the MVP Award in 1998, putting up 66 home runs and 158 RBI's to go along with a .308 Batting Average. He hit 60+home runs three times, 50+home runs four times, and posted six consecutive seasons of 40+ home runs/100+ RBI's (1998-2003). He also had nine consecutive years of 36+ home runs and 100+ RBI's (1995-2003) and two campaigns of 33+ home runs/34+ stolen bases. Ramirez had twelve seasons racking up 31+ home runs/ 102+RBI's and five seasons with 41+ home runs/ 125+RBI's.

While both players are about even in RBI totals and average home runs/year, Ramirez holds an edge in lifetime Batting Average of .39 points. Taking their average years Ramirez wins, hands down. Looking at their prime years indicates a closer indication of what Sosa has proven to the Baseball World.

M Ramirez	AB	R	H	2	3	HR	RBI	SB	CS	BB	K	BA	OBA	SA
1999	522	131	174	34	3	44	165	2	4	96	131	.333	.442	.663
2000	439	92	154	34	2	38	122	1	1	86	117	.351	.457	.697
2002	431	84	152	31	0	33	107	0	0	73	85	.349	.450	.647
S Sosa	AB	R	H	2	3	HR	RBI	SB	CS	BB	K	BA	OBA	SA
1998	643	134	198	20	0	66	158	18	9	73	171	.308	.377	.647
1999	625	114	180	24	2	63	141	7	8	78	171	.288	.367	.635
2001	577	146	189	34	5	64	160	0	2	116	153	.328	.437	.737

When Sammy Sosa began his career he was actually more of a stolen base threat than he was to hit the long ball. Sosa put up two 30HR/30SB seasons and four 20HR/20SB years over the course of his career. Since Sosa became a bona fide home run hitter there really isn't question as to whom hits the long ball better, Sosa tops Ramirez as he finished his career with 609 home runs to Manny's 555. However, Manny being Manny sees him lead Sosa in RBI's (1831-1667), base hits (2574-2408) and in OPS (.996 - .876). Ramirez also took the Red Sox to the World Series in 2004 and 2007 (winning the 2004 World Series MVP) both in victory. This comparison shows clearly that Ramirez is the offensive dynamo in comparison to Sammy Sosa. Even with Sosa being dominant defensively to Ramirez, the offensive numbers don't lie. My choice would be to carry Ramirez in left field and collect a lifetime OPS of .996.

Manny Ramirez vs Vladimir Guerrero

This match-up pairs two of the most dynamic superstars of the modern day game. Ramirez started his career with the Cleveland Indians as a late call-up in 1993. Ramirez came into his own in 1995, posting his first 30HR/ 100RBI's/ .300 year. He put up these numbers throughout the duration of his career, albeit a .294 Average in 1998 and a couple of years at the end of his career. Manny finished his career with 555 lifetime dingers.

Vladimir Guerrero came up to the majors in 1996 and by 1998 he'd put up MVP-type numbers with 38 HR's, 109 RBI's and a .324 Batting Average. Guerrero was a dynamo with the bat. What separates Guerrero from Ramirez was his ability to steal a base versus Ramirez' ability to drive in runners. Guerrero twice posted 30 HR/ 30 SB seasons (2001 and 2002) and when he moved to the American League from Montreal to play with the Angels he won an MVP Award (in his first year in the American League in 2004). He also took the

Angels into the Post-Season after missing out the year before. Guerrero was no slouch when it came to the long ball as evidenced by his 449 lifetime home runs.

The two are somewhat sloppy defensively but there is no dispute that they're great players.

This is what their average 162 game year looks like:

Player	AB	R	H	2	3	HR	RBI	SB	CS	BB	K	BA	OBA	SA
Manny Ramirez	580	109	181	38	1	39	129	3	2	94	128	.312	.411	.585
Vladimir Guerrero	615	100	195	36	3	34	113	14	7	56	74	.318	.379	.553

This is as even as it gets. Ramirez posted as high as 165 RBI's in one season (1999), while Guerrero has posted two 30 HR/ 30 Stolen Base seasons. I would have to choose Manny for the simple reason of his dominance in the post season (he holds the all-time mark for post-season dingers).

Mariano Rivera vs Trevor Hoffman

Rivera and Hoffman are considered the two greatest closers of all-time. Playing in the spotlight of New York, Rivera is a household name.

Mariano looked poised to be the Yanks' setup man for years to come. When he made the majors they already had established closer Tom Wetteland. Wetteland was signed by the Texas Rangers in the '96/'97 off-season, and Rivera inherited the role as closer. All Rivera accomplished after inheriting the closer role was 15 seasons with at least 30 saves, including 9 with at least 40. He had eleven sub-2.00 ERA campaigns and won five World Series Titles. What makes Rivera truly special was his performance in the Post-Season as he finished his career 8-1 with 42 saves with a 0.70 ERA over 141.0 Innings Pitched. His playoff success includes winning the '99 World Series MVP Award. In fact, today Rivera is the all-time save leader with his 652 lifetime saves.

Hoffman, by comparison, slipped under the radar gun playing in the small market of San Diego. Nevertheless he is currently #2 of all-time sitting with 601 career saves at the end of his illustrious career. Hoffman posted nine seasons of 40+ saves and 14 campaigns of 30+ saves. While not as accomplished as Rivera in post-season play, this may be attributed to not having nearly the same number of opportunities as Rivera had, with the juggernaut Yankees.

Deciding who to choose as closer is an obvious choice.

Let's look at each pitcher's average 162 game season;

Pitcher	Wins	Losses	Saves	IP	H	BB	SO	ERA
Rivera	5	4	39	78	60	17	71	2.21
Hoffman	4	5	39	72	56	20	74	2.87

Clearly, Rivera is the more dominant of the two based on regular season statistics. Add to that Rivera's post-season numbers, and it is safe to say that major league baseball is probably 50 years away from seeing another closer with Mariano Rivera's pedigree. Hoffman, however, still deserves a very honorable mention.

Mel Ott vs Ralph Kiner

Ralph Kiner's career started (1946) as Mel Ott's career was just ending (1947 was his last year). Ott was a mainstay with the New York Giants. Playing at the Polo Grounds for twenty-two years, Ott put up lofty numbers. Six times he hit 30+HR's/100+RBI's. Ott finished his career with 511 home runs and nine times had 100+RBI's in a season (his greatest single season RBI total was 151, in 1929).

Kiner's career was short, but the numbers he put up were staggering. Kiner started his career with the Pittsburgh Pirates in 1946. From 1946-1953 he led the National League in home runs every year. Twice Kiner posted 50+home runs (51 in 1947, and 54 in 1949). From 1947-1951 Kiner had at least 109 RBI's every year.

Although neither Ott nor Kiner won a MVP Award, they were both considered to be elite hitters. Ott was a major reason the New York Giants won the World Series in 1933, and he led the Giants to two more National League pennants. In the 1933 World Series, Ott batted .389 and slugged two dingers. Kiner's Pirates never won the pennant, nor did the other teams he played on.

These are each player's average 162 Game Season:

Player	AB	R	H	2	3	HR	RBI	SB	CS	BB	K	BA	OBA	SA
Mel Ott	561	110	171	29	4	30	110	5	0	101	53	.304	.414	.533
Ralph Kiner	573	107	160	24	4	41	112	2	0	111	82	.279	.398	.548

Although Kiner averaged eleven more home runs/year than Ott, his career Batting Average was .025 points lower. Ott and Kiner were even in just about every other offensive statistical category. All that said, Ott's contribution to the Giants winning three pennants makes him my choice to start over Kiner.

Mickey Mantle vs Duke Snider

Back in the fifties in New York, the argument of who the best centerfielder in the Majors was, came down to three men: Mays, Mantle, and Snider.

In my opinion Mays was the best, due to his defense and the fact that he was a legitimate 30 HR/ 30 Stolen Bases threat every year that he played. That leaves us with Mantle and Snider.

Between 1949-1957, Snider's Brooklyn days, he put up lofty numbers. In those eight years he batted .303+ five times and hit 40+ HR's five times as well. Once the Dodgers left the friendly confines of Ebbett Field for the spacious Chez Ravine in L.A, Snider's power numbers declined drastically.

Mantle had longevity that Snider didn't have. With Mantle, it didn't matter how far away the fences were, he could reach them. Mantle put up great numbers between 1952-1964. Mantle posted four 40+ home run years during this span as well as batting .300+ ten times over this span.

These are Mantle and Snider's average 162 Game Seasons:

Player	AB	R	H	2	3	HR	RBI	SB	CS	BB	K	BA	OBA	SA
Mickey Mantle	547	113	163	23	5	36	102	10	3	117	115	.298	.421	.557
Duke Snider	541	95	160	27	6	31	101	7	4	73	94	.295	.380	.540

Mantle wins in every category and was the greatest star on a Yankee team that won seven World Series Titles over his career.

Ozzie Smith vs Barry Larkin

Ozzie Smith was the epitome of what every shortstop strives to be when it came to defense. The man won thirteen consecutive Gold Gloves between 1980-1992.

Smith started his career with the San Diego Padres in 1978 and was traded to the St. Louis Cardinals in the 1980/81 off-season. It was a trade of shortstops, Garry Templeton for Ozzie Smith. Believe it or not, many thought at the time that Templeton was a much better shortstop.

Larkin received the torch of best shortstop in the National League once Smith retired. Ozzie recorded 16 consecutive 20+ stolen base seasons and he had 10 seasons in which he posted 30+ stolen bases. Larkin batted .300+ nine tImes and had five years in which he stole 30+ bases. Once Ozzie retired, Larkin began winning three consecutive Gold Gloves between 1994-1996. Barry Larkin was clearly the better hitters of the two and was the first shortstop in the history of the game to post a 30 home run/ 30 stolen base season.

Defense is defense though and throughout Ozzie's career his fielding % was 12 points lower than National League average. Smith's range factor was 93 points higher than the National League average. Larkin had a career-fielding % that was seven points lower than the National League average, and his range factor was only 39 points higher than the League average.

Ozzie Smith was clearly the better defensive shortstop between the two. Although Larkin was a legitimate .300 hitter with a good glove, great defense at the shortstop position wins every time.

Ozzie Smith vs Cal Ripken Jr

This is plain and simply offense versus defense. Cal Ripken was the best hitting shortstop in the game when he played. Ozzie Smith was the greatest defensive shortstop of his era (some would say in the history of the game).

Ozzie posted thirteen consecutive Gold Gloves in the National League. Ripken won two Gold Gloves in his career and was never considered the best fielding shortstop in the American League.

When it came to offense Cal Ripken dominates Smith. Ripken posted twelve years of 20+ home runs/80+ RBI. Ripken won two MVP trophies while Smith won 0.

Comparing the two defensively we see that Ozzie Smith had a career range factor that was 93 points higher than the National League average. Ripken was 55 points higher on his range factor.

There are some relevant offensive statistics that should be mentioned. Smith averaged 37 stolen bases a year, while Ripken only averaged two stolen bases a year in his career. Smith had 11 years of 30+ stolen bases, while Ripken had 0.

Ozzie vs Cal (their average season):

Player	AB	R	H	2	3	HR	RBI	SB	CS	BB	K	BA	OBA	SA
Ozzie Smith	592	79	155	25	4	2	50	37	9	67	37	.262	.337	.328
Cal Ripken	624	89	172	33	2	23	91	2	2	61	70	.276	.340	.447

All things considered, I'd have to say that Ozzie Smith is the better shortstop between the two. Ripken was capable of playing good defense. Ozzie played great defense throughout his career. While Ripken was capable of hitting 30 home runs in any given season, Ozzie was capable of stealing 50 bases in any given year.

Ozzie Smith vs Ernie Banks

Ozzie Smith was the greatest defensive shortstop of all-time. Ernie Banks was arguably the best hitter to have played the shortstop position.

Smith won an unprecedented, thirteen consecutive Gold Glove Awards (between 1980-1992). Banks won only one Gold Glove Award in his career.

Banks belted 40+ home runs five times in his career. He also posted 102 or more RBI's eight times. Smith wasn't the hitter Banks was but he was a valuable offensive player. He was a threat to steal a base any time he reached base. Smith stole 30+bases eleven times in his career.

Here are each player's average 162 Game Season:

Player	AB	R	H	2	3	HR	RBI	SB	CS	BB	K	BA	OBA	SA
Ozzie Smith	592	79	155	25	4	2	50	37	9	67	37	.262	.337	.328
Ernie Banks	604	84	166	26	6	33	105	3	3	49	79	.274	.330	.500

Taking into account Smith's contribution to the success of the St. Louis Cardinals in the eighties (winning the World Series once – getting there three times in total) and Banks' Cubbies lack of success in making the playoffs, I would choose Ozzie to start at shortstop on my all-time greatest team.

Ozzie Smith vs Tony Fernandez

It would seem that this pairing is a mismatch. Ozzie Smith won 13 consecutive Gold Glove awards, to Tony's four. However, since their primes were over the same years, let's compare Tony's four consecutive Gold Glove seasons to Smith's (he also won four consecutive Gold Gloves over the same time) over the course of 1986-1989. Over that span Smith's range factor was 82 points higher than the league average, while Fernandez carried a range factor that was 70 points higher than the league average. When it comes to their defense over this period, it's pretty even. Over those four years Fernandez had the higher batting average three times.

However, when looking at their lifetime statistics, we see that Ozzie Smith's range factor was 93 points higher than the league average, while Fernandez had a mark that was 58 points higher than the league average. As well, while Fernandez was the better batter compared to Smith, Ozzie stole more bases and drew more walks leading him to a comparable on-base %. To pick Ozzie Smith over Tony Fernandez is the smart choice.

That said, looking at it sentimentally, I'll always love Tony.

Player	AB	R	H	2	3	HR	RBI	SB	CS	BB	K	BA	OBA	SA
Smith	592	79	155	25	4	2	50	37	9	67	37	.262	.337	.328
Fernandez	594	79	171	31	7	7	63	18	10	52	59	.288	.347	.399

Paul Molitor vs Pete Rose

Most people would look at this comparison to be a mismatch. After all, Molitor is going up against the career hits leader of all-time in "Charlie Hustle." There is nothing further from the truth. While Rose had 4256 career hits and a lifetime Batting Average of .303, Molitor quietly posted 3319 hits to go alongside a .306 batting average.

Rose was a major factor in the success that the "Big Red Machine" enjoyed in the seventies, as well as the success of the Philadelphia Phillies in the early eighties.

Molitor was the glue behind the Milwaukee Brewers (Harvey's Wallbangers) and helped lead them to the World Series in 1982, and likewise was a huge factor in the Toronto Blue Jays winning the World Series in 1993 (he won the World Series MVP that year).

Neither ballplayer was very good defensively, but both wielded great bats. Rose had 200+Hits/year ten times while Molitor had 188 or more hits in a season eight times in his career (Rose did so thirteen times). Pete Rose batted .300+ fifteen times in his career to Molitor's twelve. Molitor had 504 career stolen bases to Rose's 198.

These are their average 162 Game Seasons:

Player	AB	R	H	2	3	HR	RBI	SB	CS	BB	K	BA	OBA	SA
Paul Molitor	654	108	200	37	7	14	79	30	8	66	75	.306	.369	.448
Pete Rose	639	98	194	34	6	7	60	9	7	71	52	.303	.375	.409

Molitor averaged 21 more stolen bases /year than Rose, hit for a higher average, and had twice the power. My choice between the two would have to be Paul Molitor.

Pedro Martinez vs Greg Maddux

Two of the greatest pitchers of our day. Maddux won 355 games in his career with the Atlanta Braves for the vast majority of his career. Set the bar and he climbed over it. 3371 lifetime strikeouts and nine years of 18+ wins, Maddux is surely on his way to Cooperstown.

From 1992-1995 Maddux became the first and only man who has ever won four consecutive Cy Young Awards. When looking at "Mad Dog's" career stats, no other pitcher neigh Roger Clemens or Randy Johnson of our era comes close. He also won an incredible 18 Gold Gloves (13 consecutive from 1990-2002) over his storied career .

Still, in saying this, Pedro Martinez is likewise elite, perhaps on his way to supplanting Maddux and Clemens as our era's best. Pedro started his career with the Los Angeles Dodgers, in 1992. He teamed with his brother Ramon, and in his rookie year looked to be capable of greatness, averaging over a strikeout an inning and going 10-5 with a 2.62 ERA. Perhaps the Dodgers thought that he couldn't improve on these numbers and he was traded to the Montreal Expos in the off-season of '94 for Delino Deshields. Pedro was consistent over the next three years when he broke out with a vengeance. In 1997 Martinez was the class of all pitchers in the National League (some would say in all of Baseball) striking out 305 batters in 241.3 Innings pitched going 17-8 with a 1.90 ERA Ironically it was Maddux who came second in the voting for the Cy Young that year. The Expos, being a small market franchise. Stood little chance of signing a soon to be free agent and gave him up to the Boston Red Sox for next to nothing. Martinez kept up his end of the bargain to the money Boston signed him for, and some would say a legend was born.

From 1996-2004 Pedro struck out more than one Batter/inning each year. In Pedro's first year with the Red Soxin 1998, he was an impressive 19-7 with 251 strikeouts and a 2.89 ERA Most thought it wouldn't get much better. The next year Martinez obliterated even Roger Clemens type expectations and finished the '99 season 23-4 with 313 strikeouts and a 2.07 ERA Then, as if to show that maybe he was Superman, he gave up an unprecedented 160 (Hits+Walks) in 217 IP with 284 strikeouts and lowered his ERA in the process to 1.74 winning back-to-back Cy Young Awards. Martinez will forever be commemorated by the city of Boston by leading his Red Sox to their first World Series win in 86 years, triumphant in 4 games against the St. Louis Cardinals in '04. Martinez finished his career winning 219 games, while only losing one hundred translating into a winning % of .687. His lifetime ERA was 2.93 and he finished his career with 3154 strikeouts.

This comparison will surely be scrutinized by baseball purists in years to come. It is almost painful to pick between the two as both are consummate professionals, but here goes.

Maddux is, by far, the better fielder of the two. Martinez has better post-season numbers, 6-4 with a 3.46 ERA compared with 11-14 and 3.27 ERA for Maddux.

What it comes down to, in this writer's opinion, is Won/Loss, which gives Martinez the nod, though Maddux's durability allowed him to win 136 more games.

Maddux' career Wins/Losses is 355-227 or .610. Martinez career Wins/Losses is 219-100 or .687

Just for fun, here is each pitcher's average season over their career:

Pitcher	Wins	Losses	GS	CG	SHO	IP	H	BB	SO	ERA
Maddux	16	10	34	5	2	229	217	46	154	3.16
Martinez	17	8	31	4	1	217	171	58	242	2.93

Randy Johnson vs Steve Carlton

"The Big Unit" vs "Lefty."

In their respective era's both were considered the best lefties in Major League Baseball.

Carlton started his career with the St.Louis Cardinals in 1965, a year after the 'Cards had won the World Series. Under the tutelage of Bob Gibson, Carlton joined the starting staff in 1967 and was integral to his teams success that year, starting a game against the Boston Red Sox in the World Series. Over his storied career, Lefty won 20+ games/year six times and captured four Cy Young Awards. Carlton finished his career with 329 wins and 4136 strike-outs. When he was traded to Philadelphia after the 1971 campaign, most thought that his 20 win season of '71 wouldn't get much better. His critics were silenced by a remarkable '72 season in which he went 27-9 with a 1.97 ERA and 310 strikeouts, his lone 300+ strikeout year (the 3rd lefty hurler to reach that mark aside Vida Blue and Sandy Koufax, followed by Randy Johnson). "Lefty" was the "ace" of the Phillies staff for 13 years all told, and composed seven 200+ strikout years and four 275 strikeout seasons. He guided his team to six play-off appearances, culminated by a World Series Title in 1980. "Lefty" had twelve seasons in which he post 250+ IP, and led the National League in complete games three times, culmi-nated by a max of 30 in 1972, his first year with Philly. Carlton took home the NL Pitching Triple Crown and the Cy Young that year. Carlton was so revered in Philly that he had his own personal catcher in Tim McCarver.

During his years in Philly, Carlton and Tom Seaver were considered the best the National League had to offer.

"The Big Unit" started his career as a highly touted southpaw in the Montreal Expos farm system. He wanted southern exposure and was dealt to the Seattle Mariners during the 1989 season in a package deal for Mark Langston. Many thought the Expos got the better of the deal. Johnson's potential was never in question, but there were skeptics who thought he'd have problems harnassing his control.

In 1993 Johnson silenced all his critics as he finally had his breakthrough season, fin-ishing with a 19-8 mark and 308 strikeouts (becoming the 4rth lefty to record 300 k's in a season). Although Johnson was still walking his share of batters, he was never the less over-powering, as evidenced by his career strikeout/walk ratio of 3:1. Over the duation of his career Johnson won 5 Cy Young Awards including four in a row between 1999-2002. Randy Johnson is talked about in Baseball circles as perhaps the best starter of our era. Johnson had six 300+ strikeout campaigns (max-ing out at 372 – 11 short of the record, in 2001) and 14 consecutive years from 1991-2004 where he had more than a strikeout an inning. Johnson had mixed performances in post-season play, but did win the World Series MVP in 2001 (a tie with fellow pitcher Curt Schilling) winning 3 games with a 1.04 ERA against the New York Yankees. "The Big Unit had fourteen 200+ strikeout seasons and 303 lifetime wins. What separates Johnson from Carlton, would have to be the fact that Johnson has an incredible .646 winning % compared to Carlton's mark of .574. It does make one wonder of what if. What if Johnson had to pitch in the 70's? Would going deeper into the game, as was the tradition for your starting pitcher, have an hinderence on his overall numbers. Therefore was Johnson's winning % of .646 inflated by the newly fashioned element of "the closer?"

Reggie Jackson vs Reggie Smith

This was a great argument to have in the late sixties through the seventies.

Reggie Smith was a standout when he cracked the lineup for the Boston Red Sox in the late sixties as their starting Center-Fielder. He pronounced himself as a dangerous bat in the 1967 World Series with 2 HR's in the Series. He played standout ball with the Red Sox from the time he came up to the Majors finishing second in the Rookie of the Year voting in 1967 and winning a Gold Glove in 1968 for his play in Centerfield. Through the seventies, Smith put up great numbers including 6 years in a row hammering 21+ HR's (8 in total). After his tour to duty with the Red Sox, Smith moved on to the St. Louis Cardinals Chain and moved to Right-Field for two more solid years including his first 100 RBI season in 1974. In 1976 Reggie Smith was traded again this time to the Los Angeles Dodgers. He resumed in Right and in 1977 had his career year hammering 32 HR's, with an OPS of 1.003. In the 1977 World Series it came down to the Reggie's. Reggie Smith with the Dodgers and Reggie Jackson with the New York Yankees. All Reggie Smith did in the '77 Series was hammer 3 home runs with 5 RBI's. There was magic in the air in Yankee Stadium for Game Six of the Series and Reggie Jackson simply stole the show before everyone World-Wide clubbing 3 home runs in the game making the Yankees the World Series Champs.

This was the story of the Reggie's. Jackson was the catalyst of the teams he played for and although Reggie Smith was a bonafide slugger in the mold of Jackson, he was just second best.

Reggie Jackson started his career with the Kansas City Athletics putting in a handful of games in the 1967. Kansas City re-located to Oakland, and with the Athletics in 1968 Reggie Jackson made a name for himself banging 29 home runs along with 74 RBI's. In 1969 Reggie Jackson came second in the Majors with 47 HR's and had 118 RBI's with 123 Runs Scored.

In 1972 the Oakland A's played in their first World Series and although Reggie was injured for the Series, he was a known quantity. In 1973 the A's resurfaced to the big dance once again and this time a healthy Jackson showed the World that he was 'the straw that stirred the drink' of the A's offense winning the "73 World Series MVP with a Homer, 6 RBI's, a .310 Avg, and a .941 OPS. As the A's three-peated in '74, Reggie once again had a strong showing. However, it wasn't until he came to the New York Yankees in 1977 that he became the household name that he is today. In that '77 World Series against the Los Angeles Dodgers he hammered 5 home runs with 8 RBI's, 10 Runs Scored, a .450 Avg, and an OPS of 1.792. In '78 when the Yankees repeated Jackson once again lit up pitchers in the Post-Seasonk clubbing 4 home runs in the playoffs. 2 in the ALCS against the Kansas City Royals, and 2 more against Reggie Smith's' Dodgers. In total Reggie Jackson had 18 home runs and 48 RBI's with an OPS of .885 in Post-Season play. His panache for a timely home run was also seen in the regular season shown by his leading the AL in home runs 4 times. Jackson won the AL MVP in 1973, had four 23+HR/22+SB seasons, seven 32+HR campaigns, and fifteen 25+home run years. He finshed his career with 563 home runs, 1702 RBI's, 1551 Runs, an OPS of .846, and 2584 Hits. Reggie Smith by comparison had 314 Career home runs, 1092 RBI's, 1123 Runs, 2020 Hits, with an OPS of .855. Although Smith played better defense than Jackson, and even had a higher lifetime OPS, Jackson truly was "the straw that stirred the drink" of the teams he played for and deserves to be rated the higher of the two.

Rich Gossage vs Sparky Lyle

Sparky started his career with the Boston Red Sox in 1967 and looked poised from the start of his career to be their closer for years to come. He was their main man for 4 years, topping out with 20 saves in 1970. Although Lyle wasn't flashy or spectacular, he was consistently good. In spring training of '72 Sparky was dealt by the Red Sox to the New York Yankees for next to nothing and it was there that he shined. In his first year with the 'Yanks he had a sub 2.00 ERA and saved 35 games. New York was rebuilding their franchise and by '76 they were a team to be reckoned with. Alongside Munson, "Catfish", Chambliss, and Randolph, Lyle was an integral part of a soon to be mini-dynasty. They lost the '76 World Series to the Cincinnati Reds "Big Red Machine" in four straight but showed the Baseball World that the 'Yanks had the talent to re-emerge. They did just that the following year adding Reggie Jackson and Mickey Rivers, while Ron Guidry joined the starting staff in '77 as well. In perhaps Sparky's best year of his career, the Yankees won the World Series that year in six games against the Los Angeles Dodgers. In '77, during the regular season, Lyle went 13-5 with a 2.17 ERA and had 26 saves taking home the Cy Young Award.

Probably thinking that he'd be a fixture in New York for another six years, Steinbrenner did the unthinkable and signed another closer, Rich Gossage. The plan was to use Gossage against righty hitters late in the game and Sparky against lefties. The move backfired, and even though the Yankees repeated as World Champs it cost the team its chemistry. Lyle quietly left New York as a free-agent after the '78 campaign and joined the Texas Rangers, where he finished his career.

Rich "Goose" Gossage started his career with the Chicago White Sox in 1972. A flame-thrower, "Goose" came into his own in 1975 compiling 26 saves to go along with a nifty 1.84 ERA over 141.6 innings. The 'Sox tried to put Gossage into the starting rotation the following year, and although Gossage wasn't a complete bust it was evident that he was more effective as a closer. "Goose" was traded after the year to Pittsburgh, in a deal that brought Richie Zisk to Chicago. "Goose" was put back into the closer role and he was un-hittable over the '77 campaign, compiling 26 saves in 133 innings with a 1.62 ERA Granted free agency at the end of the year it was then that the 'Yanks came calling. The truth of the matter is that Gossage was the closer on the '78 Yankees and Sparky Lyle was their set-up man. 'Goose put together five 20+ save seasons in New York in only 6 years, topping out at 33 saves (1980). His ERA was under 3.00 every year over the course of his tenure in the "Big Apple".

Gossage moved on to the San Diego Padres with his friend/teammate Graig Nettles and had a couple more effective years as a closer before he lost a few miles off his dominating fastball.

When we compare Sparky to Goose, let's take a gander (get it?) at their average 162 game season:

Pitcher	Wins	Losses	Saves	IP	Hits	BB	SO	ERA
Gossage	8	7	20	118.3	97	47	98	3.03
Lyle	7	5	18	105	97	36	66	2.88

The numbers are so close we'll have to see how they performed in the post-season.

Sparky was 3-0, with 1 save in 21.3 innings and a 1.69 ERA

Gossage was 2-1, with 8 saves in 31.3 innings and a 2.87 ERA

Simply put, it would be unfair to try and quantify one over the other as there are redeeming qualities in both players' statistics. This begs the question, why the hell did Steinbrenner sign a closer for the '78 season when his '77 closer won the Cy Young Award?

Rickey Henderson vs Lou Brock

Henderson is considered, in the baseball world, to be the greatest base-stealer the game has ever seen. Prior to Henderson, Brock carried that distinction. Brock had twelve consecutive years of 50+ stolen bases (twelve in total). Henderson had thirteen such years. They both had 3000+hits over their respective careers. Brock was considered to be the better defensive leftfielder of the two. Henderson drew more walks and was the better leadoff man.

This is what their average 162 Game Season looked like:

Player	AB	R	H	2	3	HR	RBI	SB	CS	BB	K	BA	OBA	SA
Rickey Henderson	576	121	161	27	3	16	59	74	18	115	89	.279	.401	.419
Lou Brock	640	100	187	30	9	9	56	58	19	47	107	.293	.343	.410

Brock was a major factor in the Cardinals success in the sixties. He helped them make it into the World Series three times (in 1964, 1967, and 1968) and win two of them (1964 and 1967). He batted .391 in those three World Series, very much the pinnacle of their offense. Henderson never won a World Series ring.

I would still take Henderson as my leftfielder. His stolen base prowess superceded Brock's and his On-Base % was .058 points higher, making him better suited to bat leadoff.

Rickey Henderson vs Manny Ramirez

Both ballplayers played leftfield. One a speed "demon", and the other a great pure hitter.

While Ramirez is recently retired, likewise so to is Henderson,,and this leads to a good argument.

All Henderson did in his career was steal 1406 bases. He also holds the season mark for stolen bases with 130 in 1982. Henderson is first in lifetime stolen bases by an incredible 468 over second place Lou Brock. He was the defining leadoff hitter in Major League history, and ignited offenses on every team he played for. His lifetime On Base % was a superlative .401. Henderson stole 52+ bases in a year an incredible 13 times over the course of his career.

Manny Ramirez covers a completely different area when it comes to offense. He's the guy who brings runners in. Topping out with a mark of 165 RBI's in 1999. Ramirez started his career with the Cleveland Indians. In his third season in the 'bigs Ramirez came into his zone. Putting up George Bell type numbers with 31 home runs, 107 RBI's, and a .308 batting average, Manny's numbers only got better. While Rickey played for nine organizations (mainly the A's and the Yankees), Ramirez had been a mainstay with the Red Sox since 2001, until he was traded to the Los Angeles Dodgers.

Although Henderson won only one MVP Award (in 1990) over the course of his career and Ramirez' never did, both are deserving of more awards.

From 1998 to 2008, Ramirez post 33+ home runs, 107+ RBI's and a .294+ Batting Average every year aside from 2007. With these power numbers Manny Ramirez is simply dominant in offensive numbers like RBI's and Slg%. Rickey Henderson was a table setter though, and his dominance in stolen bases and OBP leaves this writer to believe that if you were starting a Major League Franchise Rickey would be the logical choice. I'll take my chances with a guy who can get to third base when your team needs a run, versus a player like Manny who has great power numbers but who can be pitched around if first base is open. Plus, Rickey Henderson could go deep as evidenced by his 297 home runs. He also collected over 3000 hits (3055) over his illustrious career. Not that Ramirez' 555 lifetime home runs is anything to sneeze at but I'd take 20 home runs, 100-150 runs scored and 50-100 stolen bases a year over a guy that can bring in 100-150 runs a year but can't steal you a base or play great defense (sub-par some would say).

Rickey Henderson vs Tim Raines

Many baseball fans wouldn't take this match-up seriously. After all Henderson is the all-time leader in stolen bases with 1406 thefts. Raines however was as dominant as Henderson, between 1981-1987. Over this span Raines batted .300+ five times (During this period Henderson batted .300+ only twice). During these years Raines stole 50+ bases every year (Henderson did so six of the seven years). Over this period the question of which player was the better leadoff man was left ambiguous.

When we look at each player's entire career, we start to see Henderson's dominance. Henderson had 3055 career hits to Raines 2605. Henderson had 1406 stolen bases to Raines 808. Henderson had 50+ stolen bases thirteen seasons to Raines eight. Neither was very good defensively, but they were the catalysts for their teams' offense.

Here are their average 162 Game Seasons:

Player	AB	R	H	2	3	HR	RBI	SB	CS	BB	K	BA	OBA	SA
Rickey Henderson	576	121	161	27	3	16	59	74	18	115	89	.279	.401	.419
Tim Raines	574	102	169	28	7	11	63	52	9	86	63	.294	.385	.425

The fact that Henderson averaged 19 more runs scored/year and 22 more stolen bases per year makes Henderson the deserving choice for leadoff man.

Roberto Alomar vs Ryne Sandberg

Ryne Sandberg was a truly complete ballplayer. He was great defensively and a pure hitter. In any given year Sandberg could hit you 20+home runs and/or steal you 20+bases. In 1984 he won the National League MVP, leading his Cubs to the playoffs for the first time since

1945. Sandberg won nine consecutive Gold Gloves between 1983-1991. He also had nine seasons in which he scored 100+ runs.

While Roberto Alomar has never won an MVP Award, he is a very similar five-tool player in the mold of Sandberg. Alomar has won ten Gold Gloves to this point of his career and is a lifetime .300 hitter. When he came to the Toronto Blue Jays in 1991 via trade (alongside Joe Carter for Tony Fernandez and Fred McGriff) he established himself as a superstar, playing Gold Glove defense, stealing 53 bases, and recording 61 Extra-Base Hits. He was the "glue" behind the Jays back to back championships of 1992-1993. Alomar won the ALCS MVP in 1992 for his role against the Oakland A's, including a clutch three-run home run that he hit off Dennis Eckersley (in Oakland).

Here are their average 162 Game Seasons:

Player	AB	R	H	2	3	HR	RBI	SB	CS	BB	K	BA	OBA	SA
Roberto Alomar	618	103	185	34	5	14	77	32	8	70	78	.300	.371	.443
Ryne Sandberg	628	99	179	30	6	21	79	26	8	57	94	.285	.344	.452

Taking into account that Alomar tops Sandberg in both average (by .15 points) and O.B.P (by .027 points). I'd put Alomar at second base to start my team.

Roberto Clemente vs Kirby Puckett

Clemente and Mays were the best defensive outfielders of their time. In our time (1984-Present) that distinction would go to Puckett and Griffey Jr.

Clemente had an awesome throwing arm and gunned down many from rightfield. Mays was arguably the best defensive centerfielder the Majors has ever seen. Clemente was the best defensive rightfielder of all-time.

Kirby Puckett batted .314+ in eight seasons in his twelve-year career. He posted six seasons of 20+HR's/89+RBI's. Puckett also won six Gold Gloves and played in ten consecutive All-Star Games, retiring early at the age of 34.

Clemente won twelve consecutive Gold Gloves including his last year (the year he died in a plane crash). He batted .311+ thirteen times.

Their average years are almost identical.

Player	AB	R	H	2	3	HR	RBI	SB	CS	BB	K	BA	OBA	SA
Roberto Clemente	629	94	200	29	11	16	87	6	3	41	82	.317	.359	.475
Kirby Puckett	658	97	209	38	5	19	99	12	7	41	88	.318	.360	.477

Clemente was capable of putting together another four good years had he not died in a plane crash (plus another four Gold Gloves in all likelihood as well). He also finished his career with precisely 3000 Hits. Both players were the pinnacles of their respective teams. Puckett's Minnesota Twins were champions in 1987 and 1991. He won the ALCS MVP for his role against the Toronto Blue Jays in 1991. Clemente's Pirates won the World Series in 1960 and 1971.

If I had to choose between the two, I'd flip a coin.

Rod Carew vs Don Mattingly

When Rod Carew played he was considered the best batter in all of baseball. Carew won seven batting titles in his day. Mattingly seemed poised to win several batting titles when he came up to the "show", winning the batting title in his rookie campaign (1984). Mattingly didn't have the longevity that Carew did. He did however play a much better defensive 1st Base than Carew and won nine Gold Gloves in his career. Carew didn't win a Gold Glove in his career.

Taking their average 162 Game Seasons is the fairest comparison as Mattingly doesn't compare offensively to Carew when looking at lifetime statistics.

Here are their statistics:

Player	AB	R	H	2	3	HR	RBI	SB	CS	BB	K	BA	OBA	SA
Rod Carew	611	93	200	29	7	6	67	23	12	67	67	.328	.393	.429
Don Mattingly	636	91	195	40	2	20	100	1	1	53	40	.307	.358	.471

What's interesting to note is that even though Carew had over 900 more hits over his career than Mattingly, Mattingly's average hits/year is just five lower than Carew's average hits/year. Carew was a legitimate stolen base threat throughout his career (Mattingly wasn't), has a higher yearly average by .21 points, and a higher OBP than Mattingly by .35 points. Mattingly however was a power threat, averaging 14 more home runs/Year than Carew and averaged 33 more RBI's a year.

If I had to choose between the two I'd take Mattingly for his power and defense (very similar to the Brett vs Schmidt comparison).

Roger Clemens vs Tom Seaver

Roger Clemens started his career seemingly as a Red Sox life-timer. In just his third season he was an astonishingly superb 24-4 with a 2.48 ERA Guiding his Red Sox into the playoffs it looked inevitable that he would win his first World Series ring. In the ninth inning of the sixth game against the New York Mets, the Sox had a 1 run lead dissipate needing only the third out to win the World Series. With 2 out and two strikes on Mookie Wilson. Wilson hit a routine groundball right at Bill Buckner and it went through his legs into right-field allowing Lenny Dykstra to score the winning run from 3rd base. As the Mets won the 6th game, unbelievably, Boston squandered another late lead in game seven in a total team collapse.

A very young Roger Clemens

With years of dominance on the mound, Clemens registered three Cy Young Awards while pitching in Boston for 13 years. The Toronto Blue Jays stunned the Baseball World by signing Clemens in 1997. All Clemens did in Toronto was win back to back Cy Young Awards, in what some speculated to be years past his prime. Clemens regained his youth and left Toronto after the '98 campaign signing with the New York Yankees to pursue the coveted World Series Title for the dynasty driven Yanks. He won back to back World Series Titles in his first two years with them. In his 3rd and 5th years, still a major cog in arguably the best starting staff in baseball, Clemens narrowly missed out on two more titles as the 'Yanks lost both Series in seven games. Clemens has been successful on every team he's played for and had three successful years pitching for the Houston Astros (including a World Series appearance in '05) before finally retiring with the 'Yanks in '07 at the age of 46. He was so successful even as recent as '05, posting a career low 1.87 ERA over 211 1/3 Innings with a record of 13-8. Over his career, Clemens captured seven Cy Young Awards, and is second of All-Time in strikeouts with 4672 K's. He won 354 games in his caree to only 184 losses, translating into a winning % of .658.

Tom Seaver began his rookie year with the New York Mets in 1967 and took home Rookie of the Year Honours. In Seaver's third year with the Mets he won a World Series ring and was the pinnacle of the Mets Rotation, winning his first of three Cy Young Awards. Over the course of his career Seaver had 5 -20+ win seasons. 'Tom Terrific' compiled 3640 strikeouts, 311 wins, and a 2.86 ERA Although Seaver won only one World Series he almost won a second in 1973 with the Mets, and was the Cincinnati Reds' top hurler when he moved there in 1977.

Both hurlers were deemed as the best in baseball over their careers, with respect to their ERA's, and to distinguish one over the other is a hard call to make. Clemens has 351 wins to date and a 3.10 ERA, compared to Seavers 311 wins and 2.86 ERA

The difference between the two would have to come down to personal achievements. Clemens holds the single game mark for strikeouts in a game with 20 (ironically Seaver held the old mark of 19), posted 4 No-Hitters, and won seven Cy Young Awards, compared to Seavers' three Cy Youngs. It is this dominant edge in Clemens' favour that leads me to favour him over "Tom Terrific."

Roy Campanella vs Johnny Bench

This is a fun matchup. Campanella was thought to be the best catcher of his time, Bench likewise.

All Campanella did was win three MVP Awards, and he took his team (the Brooklyn Dodgers) to a World Series Title in 1955. Bench meanwhile won two MVP Awards and helped the "Big Red Machine" win back to back World Series Titles (in 1975 and 1976).

Both players spent their entire careers with one organization. Campanella played with the Brooklyn Dodgers and Bench with the Cincinnati Reds. They were also known to be excellent defensively. Bench won ten consecutive Gold Glove Awards (ten in total). The league didn't issue Gold Gloves when Campanella played.

Similar players, Campanella and Bench were both capable of hitting 30+HR's/100+RBI's in any given year.

This is what their average 162 Game Seasons looked like:

Player	AB	R	H	2	3	HR	RBI	SB	CS	BB	K	BA	OBA	SA
Campanella	561	84	155	24	2	32	114	3	2	71	67	.276	.360	.500
Bench	575	82	154	29	2	29	103	5	3	67	96	.267	.342	.476

The slight edge goes to Campanella. It should also be noted that while Bench won ten Gold Gloves, Campanella defensive numbers were awesome. When Campanella played the average range factor in the National League at the catcher position was 4.66. Campanella's range factor in his career was 5.98.

7
Player Comparisons – Part III

Sammy Sosa vs Vladimir Guerrero

Both these ballplayers have established themselves to be great rightfielders. Sosa and Guerrero are five-tool players with enormous power, Sosa a little more-so to the power game, as evidenced by his three 63+ home run seasons and four consecutive 50+ home run seasons (1998-2001). Sosa also had seven seasons of 40HR/ 100+ RBI's compared to Guerrero's two. Guerrero had ten years batting 27+ home run with 108+ RBI's. He also won eight Silver Slugger Awards compared to Sosa's six (five consecutive 1998-2002)

Sosa and Guerrero both had two 30+HR's/ 30 Stolen Base seasons. Guerrero won the 2004 AL M.V.P Award, while Sosa won the NL M.V.P Award in 1998.

Here's what their average 162 Game Seasons look like:

Player	AB	R	H	2	3	HR	RBI	SB	CS	BB	K	BA	OBA	SA
Sosa	607	102	166	26	3	42	115	16	7	64	159	.273	.344	.534
Guerrero	615	100	195	36	3	34	113	14	7	56	74	.318	.379	.553

What surprises me is how close Guerrero is in his average home runs/year to Sosa. After all, Guerrero maxed out at 44 home runs (2000). Taking this into consideration and the fact that Guerrero's lifetime Batting Average is .45 points higher than Sosa and has a higher slugging % believe it or not. This makes this comparison a tough call. I would have to choose Sammy Sosa for the accomplishment of hammering 50+ home runs in four consecutive seasons, as well as 49+ home runs in five consecutive years 1998-2002, and 609 lifetime home runs (to Guerrero's 449 mark)

Ted Williams vs Babe Ruth

When Ted Williams was asked what goals he set for himself, he replied,

"To be remembered as the greatest hitter who ever played the game."

The man who earned that distinction before him was Ruth. Both Williams and Ruth were great ballplayers right from the start of their careers. Ruth, starting out as a lefty starting pitcher for the Boston Red Sox, moved to right field for good in 1919. Williams started his career in Right Field with the Boston Red Sox in 1939.

When Ruth moved to New York to play with the Yankees in 1920, he was considered the greatest hitter in the league and carried that accolade throughout his career.

Williams missed a minimum of 3 years due to WW11 and the Korean War. Let's have some fun and speculate what his average year may have looked like had he played in those years that were in the prime of his career.

Player	G	AB	R	H	2B	3B	HR	RBI	BB	SO	BA	OBP %	SLG %
Williams	150	518	141	181	35	7	37	130	150	47	.349	.498	.658
Ruth	162	544	141	186	33	9	46	143	133	86	.342	.474	.690

Ted Williams vs Jimmie Foxx

These two Hall of Famers were both considered great hitters throughout their careers.

When Williams played he was considered the best hitter in the Major Leagues. When Foxx played, many considered him to be on par with the greatest bat of all, Ruth.

Foxx was a threat every year in his career to hit 50+ home runs. He did so twice (along with 8 other years of 35+ home runs). Williams was not the power threat that Foxx was, but he did hit 30+ home runs 8 times in his career.

When comparing Williams to Foxx let's take their 5 best years totals (divide by 5 to get their average 'best' year.

Player	G	AB	R	H	2B	3B	HR	RBI	AVG	BB	SO	OBP %	SLG %	TB
Williams	146	496	133	181	34	4	38	125	.367	146	43	.513	.686	338
Foxx	151	569	133	198	33	8	48	156	.348	109	92	.454	.688	392

Williams was clearly the better of the two in terms of getting on base (he drew 37 more bases on balls and batted 19 points higher than Foxx). Foxx was clearly the better home run hitter. The statistic that surprises me the most is Foxx' ability to drive in runners. He was 31 RBI's better than Williams in their average 'best' years.

Foxx and Williams played together in Boston from 1939 – 1942. (They were both regulars in Boston between 1939 – 1941). Having an established hitter in the lineup from the start of his career only made things easier for Williams.

Ted Williams vs Stan Musial

In the 1940's the argument as to who was the best hitter in baseball came down to Williams and Musial.

Since there was bias on the sports-writers part when it came to Williams' career,   I would negate the fact that Musial won three MVP awards in comparison to Williams two. Williams could have easily won 5 MPV awards. Williams had two 'Triple Crown' years in which he didn't win an MVP award, as well as one year when he hit .406and didn't take home top honors. Williams and Musial both placed in the top 5 in MVP voting 9 times each over their respective careers.

Taking into account that Williams was away at war while Musial played 2 years over that span, leaves me to believe that Williams lifetime statistics would only be that much more impressive in comparison to Musial's

Player	G	AB	R	H	2B	3B	HR	RBI	BB	SO	BA	OBP%	SLG%	TB
Williams	162	545	127	188	37	5	37	130	143	50	.344	.482	.634	345
Musial	162	587	104	194	39	9	25	104	86	37	.331	.417	.559	328

'Teddy Ballgame' cleans up in every statistical category. Williams, simply put, was the better offensive machine.

Tom Glavine vs David Cone

An 'ace' lefty versus a strikeout 'ace'. On the surface one would automatically suffice that Glavine is the better pitcher. After all, Glavine reached the milestone 300 finishing his career with 305 wins and captured two Cy Young Awards. Alongside Greg Maddux and John Smoltz in Atlanta, Glavine was perhaps a member of the greatest pitching staff ever assembled. Glavine had five 20+ win seasons and was a main reason the Atlanta Braves made the playoffs eight times in the 90's, and in 11 of his 15 years with them. Since moving to the New York Mets to start the 2003 season, Glavine, while not spectacular as he was with Atlanta, put up decent numbers while there. Glavine was reliable for 200+ IP and 15 wins throughout his career. Glavine pitched 200+ innings/year fourteen times in his career, falling 2 innings short twice. Consistency was truly what Glavine's' game was about.

David Cone, ironically enough, made his name with the same Mets that Glavine played for five years (before returning to the Braves). Dealt by Kansas City to the Mets, Cone had his breakthrough year in the 'Bigs in 1988, posting a 20-3 record, a 2.22 ERA, and notched 213 strikeouts in 231.3 IP. Although Cone had only one other 20+ win season over the duration of his career, he was usually considered the 'ace' of the staff among the teams he pitched for.

Taking the ten years in which Cone pitched 193.3 Innings Cone struck out 177 batters at his worst and notched seven 200+ strikeout campaigns. It was his '94 season that brought Cone his only Cy Young Award (the strike season), a year he pitched 171.6 innings, among the leaders in that category. Cone was a hired gun twice over his career, helping guide both the Toronto Blue Jays (1992), and later the New York Yankees to World Series Titles. Cone compiled an 8-3 record in the post-season, alongside a 3.80 ERA. Perhaps the most interesting aspect of his post-season success was that his teams won all 5 World series he participated in going 2-0 in 5 starts in the Fall Classic (a 2.12 ERA to boot).

While Glavine was certainly not a bust in post-season play, his Braves were, as evidenced by only one World Series Title in eleven post-season trips. Glavine's post-season numbers were 14-16 with a 3.30 ERA overall. He was 4-3 with a 2.16 ERA in World Series play performing as a consummate professional when Braves needed a strong performance in the World Series matches they were in. In this player comparison Glavine is on par with Cone with respect to post-season prowess.

To negate Glavine's performance in the World Series compared to Cone would be unfair as it was the result of an entire team collapse, Glavine was actually a bright spot.

To differentiate between the two I'll put up each pitcher's average year;

Pitcher	Wins	Losses	GS	CG	SH	IP	H	BB	SO	ERA
Glavine	15	10	34	3	1	220	214	75	130	3.54
Cone	15	10	33	4	2	227	196	89	209	3.46

I'll take Cone for his ability to get the strikeout when needed with all other statistics being on par.

Tom Seaver vs Jim Palmer

Seaver and Palmer were amongst the greatest pitchers of their day. In fact during the 70's each was considered the best of their Leagues. Palmer with the American League Baltimore Orioles, and Seaver with the National League New York Mets (and later the Cincinnati Reds). Palmer was named to the All-Star team six times, while Seaver played in the mid-season classic 12 times. It would seem that Seaver was the more successful pitcher of the two.

Jim Palmer was however as respected as Seaver due to his uncanny ability to simply win. Although he won 43 fewer games over his career compared to Seaver, Palmer reached the 20 win/year mark eight times (all during the 70's). Both Palmer and Seaver won 3 Cy Young Awards and were the 'Aces' of the teams they played for. Seaver had five 20 win/year campaigns and posted 12 sub 3.00 ERA seasons. Palmer did so nine times. Palmer posted a better wins/losses % and finished his career with, ironically enough, the exact same ERA as Seaver (a 2.86 ERA). Let's also take into account the fact that the American League brought in the DH rule in 1972, and this added 1more tough bat into the opposing teams lineup for Palmer to face. Seaver didn't have this in the NL and saw the DH only in the last three years of his career.

Another factor in this comparison is that Seaver was the Franchise when he played for the Mets (his first 11 years in the Majors), while Palmer had a more talented Ball-club to work with. For this reason I wouldn't emphasize Palmers' Post Season success (Palmer has three World Series rings compared to Seavers' one). Also keep in mind that the Orioles of Palmers' heyday had the best starting rotation in Baseball, and had the only ever 4-man rotation where each starter won 20 games during the 1971 campaign (Palmer, Dobson, Cuellar, and McNally).

My ranking between the two will be obvious as soon as you see their average year.

Pitcher	Wins	Losses	GS	CG	Sho	IP	BB	SO	ERA	Hits Allowed
Seaver	16	10	33	12	3	249.3	72	189	2.86	207
Palmer	16	9	32	13	3	248.6	82	139	2.86	211

With the two carrying almost identical numbers it is simply impossible to rank one over the other. Seaver=Palmer. Flip a coin.

Tony Gwynn vs Dave Winfield

Dave Winfield started his career with the San Diego Padres, the team Tony Gwynn played his entire career for. Both Winfield and Gwynn had outstanding careers. Winfield finished his career with 3110 base-hits and 465 home runs. He also won seven Gold Gloves. Winfield was much traveled throughout his career playing stints in New York (with the 'Yanks), California, Toronto (winning his only World Series ring), and finally for his hometown Minnesota Twins to finish a spectacular career.

Gwynn had 3141 base-hits in his career and batted .309+ in every year he played aside from his rookie campaign in which he had only 191 at-bats. Gwynn won five Gold Gloves in his career, so essentially defense between the two is a wash. Winfield had eleven campaigns in which he posted 20+home runs/80+RBI's. Gwynn didn't have Winfield's power but boy could he hit for average. Gwynn posted seven years batting .350+. He also stole 40+bases twice in his career. Although Gwynn never won the coveted World Series Title he did guide his Padres to the Grand Finale twice (1984 and 1998).

This is a look at their average 162 game seasons;

Player	AB	R	H	2B	3B	HR	RBI	SB	CS	BB	SO	AVG	OBP	SLG%
Gwynn	617	92	209	36	6	9	76	21	8	52	29	.338	.388	.459
Winfield	600	91	169	29	5	25	100	12	5	66	92	.283	.353	.475

Purely going by the numbers the nod goes to Gwynn. It's surprising how dominating Gwynn is to Winfield in stolen bases O.B.P, Average and also being only .16 points lower in slugging percentage in comparison to the brute Winfield. This may be a statement of Winfield having to play years for the toughest market in Market in Baseball (New York) and constantly feuding with 'Yanks Owner George Steinbrenner. Even still, Gwynn clearly has the better overall offensive numbers.

Ty Cobb vs Rickey Henderson

Ty Cobb is considered by many to be the best pure hitter the game has ever seen. Not only did he hit for average, he also stole bases in great numbers (for a total of 892 stolen bases in his career). Rickey Henderson stole 1406 bases in his career and accumulated 3055 hits in his career. Cobb held the record for career hits with 4189, until Pete Rose broke his long-standing record in 1986. Cobb also carries the highest lifetime batting average with a .366 mark.

These are their average 162 Game Seasons:

Player	AB	R	H	2	3	HR	RBI	SB	CS	BB	K	BA	OBA	SA
Cobb	610	120	224	39	16	6	103	48	NA	67	19	.366	.433	.512
Henderson	576	121	161	27	3	16	59	74	18	115	89	.279	.401	.419

Henderson carries a better mark for stolen bases/year than Cobb. Cobb however, is truly dominating in every other statistical category. Taking into account that Cobb played during the Dead Ball Era makes his lifetime Slugging % of .512 that much more impressive.

Had the Negro Leaguer's played during the Dead Ball Era, Cobb would still probably been the dominant player he was. Choosing between the two, I would take Cobb.

Vladimir Guerrero vs Juan Gonzalez

Guerrero won his first and only MVP Award in 2004. He established himself as one of the best players of all-time (even when including the Negro Leagues). While Gonzalez has won two MVP Awards, his superstar status was devalued for the fact that he didin't have a long career (perhaps Don Mattingly like).

Gonzalez did however put up great offensive numbers between 1991-2001.

Let's see their 162 Game Average Season and then do some breakdowns:

Player	AB	R	H	2	3	HR	RBI	SB	CS	BB	K	BA	OBA	SA
Guerrero	615	100	195	36	3	34	113	14	7	56	74	.318	.379	.553
Gonzalez	629	102	186	37	2	42	135	2	2	44	122	.295	.343	.561

Gonzalez has a large advantage in RBI's, averaging 22 more a year than Guerrero. Guerrero dominates every other category except SLG%. What impressed me the most about Guerrero was that he never really had an off-year over the duration of his career, producing thirteen campaigns of .300 or better and two 30+ HR/30+ SB seasons. He also led Gonzalez in career home runs (449-434) and career basehits (2590/1936). I'm on the fence on this one.

Vladimir Guerrero vs Larry Walker

Both of these players were products of the Montreal Expos. Walker came on to the scene towards the end of the 1989 campaign. He was a legitimate 20+ HR / 20+ SB / .300 Batting Average player until he left for Colorado in the off-season of '94-'95. From that point on Walker caught fire. Playing at Coors Field helped boost Walker's numbers and he had four seasons in which he hit .350 or greater. Walker also won seven Gold Glove Awards over his career, proving that he was a five-tool ballplayer.

Once Walker left the Expos, another young phenom came along. Vlad Guerrero showed in his first full campaign of 1998 that he could put up Walker type numbers. From 2000 – 2004 Guerrero batted .330+ in four of those five seasons. From 1998 – 2004 Guerrero put up six seasons in which he hit 34+ HR / 108+ RBI's / .316+ Batting Average.

In comparison let's look at each player's prime years (Guerrero's prime– 1998-2004, Walker's prime- 1997-2002):

Player	Year	AB	R	H	2B	3B	HR	RBI	SB	CS	BB	SO	AVG	OBP	SLG%
Guerrero	1999	610	102	193	37	5	42	131	14	7	55	62	.316	.378	.600
	2000	571	101	197	28	11	44	123	9	10	58	74	.345	.410	.664
	2001	599	107	184	45	4	34	108	37	16	60	88	.307	.377	.566
	2002	614	106	206	37	2	39	111	40	20	84	70	.336	.417	.593
	2004	612	124	206	39	2	39	126	15	3	52	74	.337	.391	.598

Player	Year	AB	R	H	2B	3B	HR	RBI	SB	CS	BB	SO	AVG	OBP	SLG%
Walker	1997	568	143	208	46	4	49	130	33	8	78	90	.366	.452	.720
	1998	454	113	165	46	3	23	67	14	4	64	61	.363	.445	.630
	1999	438	108	166	26	4	37	115	11	4	57	52	.379	.458	.710
	2001	497	107	174	35	3	38	123	14	5	82	103	.350	.449	.662
	2002	477	95	161	40	4	26	104	6	5	65	73	.338	.421	.602

In looking at their best year one would concede that Walker is by far the better ballplayer of the two (that's why average 162 game averages and prime years are used in my analysis).

Here's a look at their average 162 game season:

Player	AB	R	H	2	3	HR	RBI	SB	CS	BB	K	BA	OBA	SA
Guerrero	615	100	195	36	3	34	113	14	7	56	74	.318	.379	.553
Walker	563	110	176	38	5	31	107	19	6	74	100	.313	.400	.565

Looking at their prime years, one would conclude that Guerrero is overmatched. Their average year seems to indicate that the two are on par with each other. Considering that Walker won seven Gold Gloves to go along with his amazing bat, I'd say overall that Walker is the better ballplayer of the two.

Walter Johnson vs Christy Mathewson

On the surface it would seem that 'Big Train' was the better pitcher of the two. Not only did Johnson win 44 more games in his career, he also fanned 1007 more batters than Mathewson.

Johnson won 20+ Games/year twelve times in his career (ten consecutive from 1910-1919). He also posted ten campaigns of 256.3 IP and sub 2.00 ERA Mathewson had 5 such seasons, however, he won 20+ games in a season 13 times over his career (12 consecutive from 1903-1914). Matty accomplished this in four fewer years pitched. In fact, Matty topped Johnson in 30+ win seasons 4-2, and in lifetime ERA (2.13 compared to Johnson's 2.17 mark). Both were known as hard throwers of their day, Johnson dominates in this category as evidenced by his seven consecutive 200+ strikeout years to Mathewson's 5. This edge should be quantified though as each player's average year is listed;

Pitcher	Wins	Losses	GS	CG	SHO	IP	Hits	BB	SO	ERA
Johnson	19	12	30	24	5	273.6	227	63	162	2.17
Mathewson	21	10	31	24	4	274	241	48	143	2.13

What history deemed is now clearly dispelled. Johnson is clearly not dominant to Mathewson. In actual fact, Mathewson has the edge in nearly every category when looking at their average year line, albeit by a narrow margin (while Johnson holds a 19 strikeout/year edge over Matty, keep in mind that Matty actually holds an edge in strikeout/walk ratio 2.98-2.57).

Both hurlers won a World Series ring with their respective Ball-clubs. Let's look at how each pitcher fared when they took the hill in the post-season;

Johnson was 3-3 with a 2.16 ERA Mathewson was 5-5 with a 0.97 ERA

Even though the 'Big Train' won two MVP Awards to Matty's 0, the statistics clearly show a slight edge of performance in Mathewson's favour, especially when including his post-season dominance.

Willie Mays vs Henry Aaron

Mays and Aaron were both pioneers for 'blacks' in the Major Leagues. Mays started his career in 1951, Aaron in 1954. They were both 5-tool players, capable in any year of hitting 30+ home runs and stealing 20+ bases.

The fact is Mays and Aaron, both National Leaguers, were candidates to win the MVP award each year they played. As they played in the same era let's compare the two yearly, from 1955 (Aaron's first year as a starter) – 1966 (Mays' last strong year).

Player	Year	G	AB	R	H	2B	3B	HR	RBI	SB	BB	SO	BA	OBP%	SLG%
Mays	1955	152	580	123	185	18	13	51	127	24	79	60	.319	.400	.659
Aaron	1955	153	602	105	189	37	9	27	106	3	49	61	.314	.366	.540
Mays	1956	152	578	101	171	27	8	36	84	40	68	65	.296	.369	.557
Aaron	1956	153	609	106	200	34	14	26	92	2	37	54	.328	.365	.558
Mays	1957	152	585	112	195	26	20	35	97	38	76	62	.333	.407	.626
Aaron	1957	151	615	118	198	27	6	44	132	1	57	58	.322	.378	.600
Mays	1958	152	600	121	208	33	11	29	96	31	78	56	.347	.419	.583
Aaron	1958	153	601	109	196	34	4	30	95	4	59	49	.326	.386	.546
Mays	1959	151	575	125	180	43	5	34	104	27	65	58	.313	.381	.583
Aaron	1959	154	629	116	223	46	7	39	123	8	51	54	.355	.401	.636

Player	Year	G	AB	R	H	2B	3B	HR	RBI	SB	BB	SO	BA	OBP%	SLG%
Mays	1960	153	595	107	190	29	12	29	103	25	61	70	.319	.381	.555
Aaron	1960	153	590	102	172	20	11	40	126	16	60	63	.292	.352	.566
Mays	1961	154	572	129	176	32	3	40	123	18	81	77	.308	.393	.584
Aaron	1961	155	603	115	197	39	10	34	120	21	56	64	.327	.381	.594
Mays	1962	162	621	130	189	36	5	49	141	18	78	85	.304	.384	.615
Aaron	1962	156	592	127	191	28	6	45	128	15	66	73	.323	.390	.618
Mays	1963	157	596	115	187	32	7	38	103	8	66	83	.314	.380	.582
Aaron	1963	161	631	121	201	29	4	44	130	31	78	94	.319	.391	.586
Mays	1964	157	578	121	171	21	9	47	111	19	87	72	.296	.383	.607
Aaron	1964	145	570	103	187	30	2	24	95	22	62	46	.328	.393	.514
Mays	1965	157	558	118	177	21	3	52	112	9	76	71	.317	.398	.645
Aaron	1965	150	570	109	181	40	1	32	89	24	60	81	.318	.379	.560
Mays	1966	152	552	99	159	29	4	37	103	5	70	81	.288	.368	.556
Aaron	1966	158	603	117	168	23	1	44	127	21	76	96	.279	.356	.539

Bearing the fact that Mays won 12 Gold Gloves compared to Aaron's 3 leads me to believe that Mays was the better all-round ballplayer of the two.

Willie Mays vs Joe DiMaggio

This is a comparison that will be heartfelt by most baseball fans. Both Mays and DiMaggio were 'dynamo's' with the bat. They were also considered the best Center Fielders of their time. (DiMaggio in the 30's and 40's, Mays in the 50's and 60's). Since Mays won 12 consecutive Gold Gloves I'll give the edge to Mays. (When DiMaggio played, MLB didn't authorize Gold Gloves, he did however have competition from his brother Dom in Boston).

Looking at their offensive numbers leads the average fan to believe that DiMaggio was, by far, the better bat of the two. To quantify choosing Mays numbers over DiMaggio's- Mays was a threat to steal 30+ bases in any given year. DiMaggio only averaged 3 stolen bases a year. Saying this here is a look at their 'average' year.

Player	AB	R	H	2	3	HR	RBI	SB	CS	BB	K	BA	OBA	SA
Willie Mays	589	112	178	28	8	36	103	18	6	79	83	.302	.384	.557
Joe DiMaggio	637	130	207	36	12	34	143	3	1	74	34	.325	.398	.579

DiMaggio dominates in every statistical category except for Home Runs and Stolen Bases. His numbers however were posted at a time when the league batting average was 13 points higher than when Mays played. As well, Mays had 6 consecutive 20 home run / 20 stolen base years, while DiMaggio had none. Mays revolutionized the way players were cultivated. Mays, was at the very least as productive as DiMaggio with the bat. Adding defense to the equation makes Mays selection in Center Field over DiMaggio a safe bet.

Willie Mays vs Ken Griffey Jr.

This is a fun comparison. Both being Gold Glove five-tool players, Mays and Griffey Jr were the dominant centerfielders of their time (Griffey Jr. was the more recent player). If Griffey Jr. had played over Mays' career it would be a tough choice as to who would win the Gold Glove. All Griffey Jr accomplished was winning a Gold Glove every year in the 90's. From 2001 until the end of his career, Griffey Jr. was plagued by injuries. In his first twelve seasons Griffey Jr. was clearly the best centerfielder that the Major Leagues of today had to offer. Time ended Griffey Jr.'s career, however he was still one of the game's elite. Even still, Griffey Jr. posted six seasons of 40 HR's/ 109+ RBI's, Mays likewise had six such seasons.

In Mays' career he won twelve Gold Glove Awards and won the MVP Award in 1954 and 1965. Griffey Jr. won ten Gold Glove Awards to this point of his career and won the MVP Award in 1997. Mays posted two 30HR/ 30 Stolen Base seasons and six 20HR/20 Stolen Base years. Griffey Jr. had only two 20HR/ 20 Stolen Base years to this point of his career.

Here's a look at each player's average 162 Game Seasons:

Player	AB	R	H	2	3	HR	RBI	SB	CS	BB	K	BA	OBA	SA
Willie Mays	589	112	178	28	8	36	103	18	6	79	83	.302	.384	.557
Ken Griffey, Jr.	599	107	175	32	3	41	117	14	5	80	107	.292	.377	.560

The numbers seem almost interchangeable from one player to the other. On the merits of having two more Gold Gloves, and considering Mays played in a much tougher era for batters, my choice for centerfielder on my all-time 'Greatest Team' would have to be Mays.

Willie Mays vs Mickey Mantle vs Duke Snider

Willie Mays and Mickey Mantle were known to be the greatest Center-Fielders in the 50's and 60's. Alongside Duke Snider the three started out as New York's finest.

Although Snider put up great numbers, he did so in a small ballpark at Ebbots Field. Once Snider moved to the larger confines of Chez Ravine in Los Angeles his power numbers faded and this takes him out of the equation.

All Mays did over the course of his career is the following:

1. Won the 1951 NL Rookie of the Year Award
2. Post 9 seasons of 34+ home runs 103+ RBI's
3. 13 consecutive seasons with 29+ home runs and 84+ RBI's
4. Consecutive seasons with 35+ home runs and 38+ Stolen Bases
5. 6 consecutive seasons with 29+ home runs and 24+ Stolen Bases
6. 12 consecutive seasons with 101+ runs scored
7. 10 seasons batting .304+
8. Hit 51+ home runs in a year twice (1955 and 1965)
9. Hit 40+ home runs in a year 6 times
10. Hit 34+ home runs in a year 11 times
11. Won 12 consecutive Gold Glove Awards (1957-1968)
12. Won two NL MVP Awards in 1954 and 1965
13. Won the 1963 and 1968 All-Star MVP Awards
14. Played in 20 consecutive All-Star Games (1954-1973)
15. Won the 1971 Roberto Clemente Award
16. Won a World Series in 1954 with the New York Giants
17. Finished his career with 660 home runs, a .302 Avg, 3283 base hits, 2062 runs scored, and 1903 RBI's

All Mantle did over the course of his career is the following:

1. Won 7 World Series with the famed New York Yankees
2. Hit 18 home runs in World Series play
3. Won three AL MVP Awards; 1956,1957, and 1962
4. Won the AL Triple Crown in 1956
5. Hit 52+ home runs in a year twice (1956 and 1961)
6. Had 30+ home runs in a year 8 times in succession (nine in total)
7. Had 11 consecutive years of 21+ home runs/75+ RBI's (12 in total)
8. Finished his career with 536 home runs
9. Batted .300+ in a year 9 times

All Snider did over the course of his career was the following:

1. Won 2 World Series, 1with the Brooklyn Dodgers in 1955 and again in 1962 with the Los Angeles Dodgers
2. Had 5 consecutive 40+HR campaigns from 1953-1957
3. Had 4 HR's in two separate World Series; 1952 and 1955
4. Had 3 consecutive seasons batting .309+. with 40+HR's and 126+RBI's
5. Had 7 seasons batting .303 or higher
6. Finished second in 1955 NL MVP voting to teammate Roy Campanella
7. Had 6 seasons with 101+RBI's
8. Had 9 years with 92+RBI's
9. Finished his career with 407 HR's, 1333 RBI's, 1259 Runs .295 Avg

The reality is that all three were tremendous leaders for their ball clubs. Mays didn't have nearly the supporting cast that Mantle had. The Yanks always had top-notch pitching, and playing alongside Yogi Berra, Roger Maris, Phil Rizzuto, and Elston Howard, Mantle had an offense that he could lead. Mays was not surrounded by the level of teammates needed to take his Giants to the World Series (He was 1-2 in World Series play, with both losses coming to the Yankees). It seemed that San Francisco was going to do some damage when sluggers like Bobby Bonds, Willie McCovey, and Orlando Cepeda came up to the show, but their pitching was rarely strong enough to put them over the top.

Snider was simply a poor man's Willie Mays and Mickey Mantle. From 1953-1955, the case could be made that Snider was the best of the bunch. Losing his power numbers once the Dodgers re-located to Los Angeles prevented Snider from consideration as the greatest of the three as Mays and Mantle had longevity in sustaining their power numbers.

For the simple reason of defense I would choose Mays as the greater center fielder when comparing him to Mantle, with Mantle second best, and Duke Snider third.

Willie Stargell vs Eddie Murray

Both of these players are in Cooperstown. Stargell played his entire career with the Pittsburgh Pirates and finished his career with 475 home runs. He helped lead the Pirates to World Series Titles in 1971 and 1979. Stargell won the National Leage MVP Award in 1979 (in a tie with Keith Hernandez) and also the World Series MVP Award in the same year.

When Stargell's career was winding down Murray's was just beginning. Although Murray never won the MVP Award, he did finish his career with 504 home runs and 3255 hits. Murray also won a World Series ring for his role with the Baltimore Orioles of 1983. Ironically it was Murray's Orioles that blew a three games to one lead to Stargell's Pirates in 1979. They were each regarded, in their day, to be at the top of the list at first base.

Murray was a truly consistent player and he posted fourteen seasons of 20+HR's/80+RBI's. Stargell managed to put together eleven such seasons and he had six 30+HR years to Murray's five.

Murray also won three Gold Gloves while Stargell never won a Gold Glove.

These are their average 162 Game Seasons:

Player	AB	R	H	2	3	HR	RBI	SB	CS	BB	K	BA	OBA	SA
Stargell	544	82	155	29	4	33	106	1	1	64	133	.282	.360	.529
Murray	607	87	174	30	2	27	103	6	2	71	81	.287	.359	.476

Stargell clearly has the better numbers. He put up better power numbers in fewer At-Bats. Based on this fact, and because he carried his Pirates to a huge comeback against Murray's Baltimore Orioles in 1979, I would pick Stargell over Murray as my first baseman.

Willie Stargell vs Willie McCovey

Willie Stargell spent his entire career with the Pittsburgh Pirates. Stargell and McCovey were considered by most baseball people to be the best 1st Basemen in the Majors between 1963-1979. They were both dangerous left-handed power hitters. Stargell posted six 30+HR years and McCovey seven such years.

Both players won a MVP Award. McCovey in 1969 and Stargell in 1979 (a tie with Keith Hernandez). Stargell was the leader of the World Series Champion Pittsburgh Pirates of 1979, winning the World Series MVP Trophy (he also won a World Series Title with the 1971 Pirates). McCovey never achieved a World Series Title. Although McCovey never won a World Series Title he did better Stargell 521 to 475 in lifetime home runs and 1555 to 1540 in lifetime RBI's.

This is their average 162 Game Season:

Player	AB	R	H	2	3	HR	RBI	SB	CS	BB	K	BA	OBA	SA
Willie Stargell	544	82	153	29	4	33	106	1	1	64	133	.282	.360	.529
Willie McCovey	513	77	138	22	3	33	97	2	1	84	97	.270	.374	.515

Although these two players are closely matched, I would give the nod to Stargell based on the leadership he provided to the 1979 'We Are Family' World Series Champion Pittsburgh Pirates.

8

A History of the Canadian Teams, and the Greatest Blue Jays and Expos of All Time

Many people think that Professional Baseball began for Montreal and Toronto when they were granted Major League Franchises in 1969 and 1977 respectively. This is false.
The reality is that although the Expos were formed in Montreal in 1969 and the Jays Franchise began in Toronto in 1977, both cities have deep ties into Professional Baseball, dating back to 1912 when both the Toronto Maple Leafs and the Monteal Royals joined the International League. In fact, Toronto had a Team in the first two years of the International League in 1886 and 1889 (owned by the Toronto Ferry Company), when they were known as the "Canucks" and they became the Maple Leafs in 1900.

There was even a team in Hamilton, Ontario, Canada in 1886, known by the name the Hamilton Clippers (who resurfaced under the name of "Hams" for 1889 and the "Tigers" in 1918). In 1951 the Ottawa Giants (another Canadian Team) came into the League and they became the Athletics for the 1952 and 1953 seasons. The Montreal Royals were in the International League from 1912-1917 and 1928-1960, and the Toronto Maple Leafs were in the League from 1900-1967. A noteable Manager of one of the first Toronto Maple Leafs' team was Nap Lajoie, who played in Major League Baseball from 1896-1916 and whose lifetime Major League Batting Average was .338. Lajoie ended up playing some ball as a Player/Manager for the Leafs after his Major League playing career in 1917 and batted .380 at the age of 42 with the Maple Leafs.

There were many famous ballplayers that played a year or more with the Toronto Maple Leafs or the Montreal Royals during their time in Professional Baseball including; Willie Keeler (Toronto Maple Leafs), Nap Lajoie (Toronto Maple Leafs), Burleigh Grimes (Toronto Maple Leafs), Tony Lazzeri (Toronto Maple Leafs), Charlie Gehringer (Toronto Maple Leafs), Carl Hubbell (Toronto Maple Leafs), Ralph Kiner (Toronto Maple Leafs), Jackie Robinson (Montreal Royals), Roy Campanella (Montreal Royals), Sam Jethroe (Montreal Royals), Don Newcombe (Montral Royals), Roberto Clemente (Montreal Royals), Duke Snider (Montreal Royals), Don Drysdale (Montreal Royals), Johnny Podres (Montreal Royals) Elston Howard (Toronto Maple Leafs), Rocky Nelson (Montreal Royals and Toronto Maple Leafs), Ernie Broglio (Toronto Maple Leafs), Dick Williams (Toronto Maple Leafs), Sparky Anderson (Montreal Royals and the Toronto Maple Leafs), Tommy Lasorda (Montreal Royals), Rico Carty (Toronto Maple Leafs) and Sparky Lyle (Toronto Maple Leafs) to name but a few. The Maple Leafs and the Royals were sometimes independant of affiliation with a Major League team, but most of the time they were affiliated. Most notably the Montreal Royals were affiliated with the Brooklyn Dodgers and the Toronto Maple Leafs were affiliated with many teams including the Philadelphia Athletics and the Boston Red Sox.

The history of baseball in Toronto is very deep as it was where Babe Ruth hit his first Professional home run, on Center Island at Hanlan's Point Staudium against the Toronto Maple Leafs in 1914. The Montreal Royals played their games (from 1928 to 1967) at Delorimier Downs (a.k.a Montreal Stadium), and the Maple Leafs played their games at Maple Leaf Stadium in Downtown Toronto (Bathurst Street/Lakeshore Blvd) from 1926-1967.

The Greatest Toronto Blue Jays of All-Time

Catchers

1. Russell Martin
2. Ernie Whitt
3. Darrin Fletcher
4. Pat Borders
5. Greg Myers
6. Bengie Molina
7. Dioner Navarro
8. Greg Zaun
9. Buck Martinez
10. Rick Cerone

First Basemen

1. Carlos Delgado
2. Fred McGriff
3. John Olerud
4. Edwin Encarnacion
5. Willie Upshaw
6. Adam Lind
7. Lyle Overbay
8. John Mayberry
9. Chris Colabello
10. Doug Ault

Second Basemen

1. Roberto Alomar
2. Damaso Garcia
3. Aaron Hill
4. Manny Lee
5. Orlando Hudson
6. Homer Bush
7. Ryan Goins
8. Devon Travis
9. Nelson Liriano
10. Kelly Johnson

Third Basemen

1. Josh Donaldson
2. Troy Glaus
3. Scott Rolen
4. Kelly Gruber
5. Tony Fernandez

6. Tony Batista
7. Ed Sprague
8. Rance Mulliniks
9. Garth Iorg
10. Roy Howell

6. Mookie Wilson
7. Colby Rasmus
8. Rajai Davis
9. Rick Bosetti
10. Bob Bailor

Shortstop

1. Tony Fernandez
2. Alfredo Griffin
3. Troy Tulowitzki
4. Jose Reyes
5. Manny Lee
6. Tony Batista
7. Alex Gonzalez
8. Yunel Escobar
9. Marco Scutero
10. Ryan Goins

Right Fielders

1. Jose Bautista
2. Jesse Barfield
3. Shawn Green
4. Joe Carter
5. Alex Rios
6. Raul Mondesi
7. Junior Felix
8. Otto Velez
9. Reed Johnson
10. Mark Whitten

Left Fielders

1. George Bell
2. Rickey Henderson
3. Shannon Stewart
4. Dave Collins
5. Candy Maldonado
6. Michael Saunders
7. Ben Revere
8. Reed Johnson
9. Frank Catanolotto
10. Ron Fairly

DH

1. Paul Molitor
2. Dave Winfield
3. Edwin Encarnacion
4. Cliff Johnson
5. Jose Canseco
6. Brad Fullmer
7. Rico Carty
8. Otto Velez
9. Rance Mulliniks
10. Matt Stairs

Center Fielders

1. Lloyd Moseby
2. Devon White
3. Vernon Wells
4. Kevin Pillar
5. Jose Cruz Jr.

Starting Pitchers

1. Roger Clemens
2. Roy Halladay
3. Dave Stieb
4. Jimmy Key
5. Doyle Alexander

6. Jack Morris
7. Aaron Sanchez
8. David Cone
9. Juan Guzman
10. Pat Hentgen
11. David Wells
12. J. A. Happ
13. Mark Buehrle
14. David Price
15. Dave Stewart
16. Todd Stottlemyre
17. Marcus Stroman
18. Jim Clancy
19. Mike Flanagan
20. R. A. Dickey

Relief Pitchers

1. Tom Henke

2. Duane Ward
3. B.J Ryan
4. Mark Eichhorn
5. Roberto Osuna
6. Pete Vuckovich
7. Aaron Sanchez
8. Casey Janssen
9. Billy Koch
10. Scott Downs
11. Victor Cruz
12. Kevin Gregg
13. Dennis Lamp
14. Brett Cecil
15. Mike Timlin
16. Gary Lavelle
17. Bill Caudill
18. Jason Grilli
19. Roy Lee Jackson
20. John Cerutti

The Greatest Montreal Expos of All-Time

Catchers

1. Gary Carter
2. Darrin Fletcher
3. Mike Fitzgerald
4. Michael Barrett
5. John Bateman

First Basemen

1. Andres Galarraga
2. Rusty Staub
3. Tony Perez
4. David Segui
5. Al Oliver

Second Basemen

1. Jose Vidro
2. Delino DeShields
3. Mike Lansing
4. Rodney Scott
5. Doug Flynn

Third Basemen

1. Tim Wallach
2. Larry Parrish
3. Bobby Bailey
4. Tony Batista
5. Sean Berry

Shortstops

1. Orlando Cabrera
2. Wil Cordero
3. Hubie Brooks
4. Mark Grudzielanek
5. Chris Spier

Left Fielders

1. Tim Raines
2. Moises Alou
3. Ron LeFlore
4. Henry Rodriguez
5. Warren Cromartie

Center Fielders

1. Andre Dawson
2. Marquis Grissom
3. Rondell White
4. Otis Nixon
5. Dave Martinez

Right Fielders

1. Vladimir Guerrero
2. Larry Walker
3. Andre Dawson
4. Ken Singleton
5. Ellis Valentine

Starting Pitchers

1. Pedro Martinez
2. Steve Rogers
3. Dennis Martinez
4. Bill Gullickson
5. Livan Hernandez
6. Jeff Fassero
7. Charlie Lea
8. Scott Sanderson
9. Mark Langston
10. Ross Grimsley
11. Ken Hill
12. Bryn Smith
13. David Palmer
14. Javier Vazquez
15. Bill "Spaceman" Lee

Relief Pitchers

1. John Wetteland
2. Jeff Reardon
3. Mike Marshall
4. Chad Cordero
5. Mel Rojas
6. Tim Burke
7. Rudy May
8. Elias Sosa
9. Scott Stewart
10. Woodie Fryman
11. Joey Eischen
12. Claude Raymond
13. Scott Stricklande
14. Stan Bahnsen
15. Bob James

After careful analysis of the two franchises, The Toronto Blue Jays and The Montreal Expos, I have compiled a list of the greatest ballplayers (by position) who played north of the border from 1969 to the present. (These guys make up my dream roster and may differ from the actual rating for their individual teams).

Catchers

>**Gary Carter** - The best Catcher in Baseball during his day. In the top ten of all-time in my book (tenth to be precise)

16. **Russell Martin** - Probably the best at throwing out runners in the game today. He's good for 20+home runs/70+RBI's with enough AB's.
17. **Ernie Whitt** - Whitt anchored the early success of the Blue Jays from '83-'89. Was a good run producer.
18. **Darrin Fletcher** - A well rounded Catcher. Was a very effective bat in the lineups he played for in both Toronto and Montreal.
19. **Pat Borders** - He was the Jays Catcher in our back to back World Series Titles of '92 and '93.
20. **Greg Myers** - One of my favorites, Myers could flat out hit.
21. **Bengie Molina** - A great defensive Catcher.
22. **Dioner Navarro** - A dynamo with the bat.
23. **Greg Zaun** - Was a solid backstop who enjoyed success with the Florida Marlins, winning the World Series with them before he came to Toronto.
24. **Buck Martinez** - A class act. Anyone remember his infamous double play against the Mariners, when he tagged out Gorman Thomas flat on his back?

First Basemen

1. **Carlos Delgado** - Proto-typical 40+HRS 120+RBI's/Year
2. **Fred McGriff** - Hit the ball into the Upper Fifth Deck in 1987 against Rick Rhoden at old Yankee Stadium in the Bronx. The ball was measured to be hit 560 Feet. True story!!! Hammered 493 home runs over his illustrious career. Won a World Series with the Atlanta Braves in 1995 as their starting first baseman. Enjoyed many successful campaigns in Toronto before he was dealt to the Padres in the winter of 1990.
3. **John Olerud** - Could throw 80+MPH with both his right and left arms. Batted .363 in 1993. Was a consummate ballplayer who just knew the game.
4. **Andres Galarraga** - The Big Cat. Known as the best defensive 1st Baseman of his day. A clutch RBI producer in his years in the 'bigs.
5. **Edwin Encarnacion** - Perhaps the most underrated of the bunch.

Second Basemen

1. **Roberto Alomar** - 1992 ALCS MVP. Probably deserved a couple of AL MVP Awards for all his offensive prowess, when including all his stolen bases plus Gold Glove defense. THE GREATEST DEFENSIVE 2ND BASEMAN OF ALL-TIME.

2. **Jose Vidro** - Helluva 2nd baseman. Was as dynamic as Alomar offensively, and was solid defensively.
3. **Delino DeShields** - Could steal you 40+ in practically any season.
4. **Mike Lansing** - Played some good years in Montreal.
5. **Damaso Garcia** - Was 2nd Base for the Toronto Blue Jays glory years' 1982-1988.

Third Baseman

1. **Josh Donaldson** - THE BEST. The 2015 AL MVP (I would give him MLB Player of the Year as well).
2. **Troy Glaus** - 40 home run man. Solid defense.
3. **Tim Wallach** - One of the most complete third basemen of all time.
4. **Kelly Gruber** - Great RBI guy. Should have gotten credit for a triple play in the 1992 World Series. With today's instant replay review it's a done deal.
5. **Tony Fernandez** - Started his career as a shortstop and won 4 Gold Glove Awards at that position with the Toronto Blue Jays. After stints in San Diego and New York, he joined the Cincinnati Reds and played 3rd Base for them. He owns the all-time highest fielding % for a single season at 3rd posting a mark of .991, committing 2 Errors in 87 GP. This was the year after he came back to Toronto to win his first and only World Series ring as their starting Shortstop!!! Believe it or not, he actually played 2nd Base for the Indians in 1995, taking Cleveland to the World Series before bowing out to the Atlanta Braves. He should be enshrined in Cooperstown. With 2276 lifetime hits, Fernandez batted .300+ for 5 seasons.

Shortstops

1. **Tony Fernandez** - THE BEST. Almost on-par with Derek Jeter and Ozzie Smith. Defensively it's a possibility for Fernandez to be rated #1, based on his versatility.
2. **Alfredo Griffin** - A wizard with the glove. Won the 1979 AL Rookie of the Year Award in Toronto with the Blue Jays and a Gold Glove with the Oakland A's in 1985.
3. **Orlando Cabrera** - Played some good years for the Expos. Excellent defense with some pop offensively.
4. **Troy Tulowitzki** - It was sad to see Tulowitzki injured at Yankee Stadium in the Jays-Yankees Game in early September of this past year. Didn't make an error in Toronto. His bat will always be dangerous.

5. **Jose Reyes** - Reyes had a short stint in Toronto but he showed that he can be one of the more dynamic offensive ballplayers in the game (irrespective of position), while he was here.

Left Fielders

1. **Tim Raines** - One of the most prolific stolen base leaders of all-time. Good glove, great bat. He could hit in any spot in the batting order, neigh cleanup, yay to the third spot.
2. **George Bell** - Perhaps the best pure hitter in the game when he played (1981-1993).
3. **Moises Alou** - Was a polished ballplayer, a true 5-tool talent.
4. **Shannon Stewart** - The only flaw in his game was that he didn't have a strong arm. An excellent lead-off hitter with tremendous speed.
5. **Ron LeFlore** - Was the fastest player of the five. He stole 97 bases in his lone year with the Expos in 1980.

Center Fielders

1. **Andre Dawson** - The best pure ballplayer of all the positions alongside Josh Donaldson in my book. Dawson was a five tool ballplayer who was a deserving Gold Glove recipient throughout his career winning eight Gold Gloves. He won the 1977 NL Rookie of the Year Award, and the 1987 MVP Award (in Right-Field with the Cubs). His years in Montreal showed that he could dominate both defensively in Center (great arm and great range) and he had one of the best bats in the game.
2. **Marquis Grissom** - An excellent glove in Center, Grissom could steal 2nd and 3rd Base with the best of them. He won 4 Gold Gloves over his storied career.
3. **Lloyd Moseby** - Was perhaps the most talented of the bunch. Would have been a contender for the 1983 AL MVP Award had the Blue Jays been closer to the playoff picture at the end of September in that year.
4. **Devon White** - Alongside Gary Pettis, White was the best defensive Center-Fielder in the Majors when he played. He was also a great table setter for the Jays during his years in Toronto.
5. **Vernon Wells** - A great overall Center-Fielder. Toronto and Montreal have always boast great Outfields throughout each proud history, so fifth on this list is a very high ranking.

Right Fielders

1. **Vladimir Guerrero** - Offensively Guerrero gives the most bang for your buck.
2. **Jose Bautista** - The only man on this list to have hit 50+ home runs in a single season. A true spolesman for the game of Baseball.
3. **Larry Walker** - Would rank #1 except his best years were with the Colorado Rockies. In Montreal, Walker was a Gold-Glover with 20+HR/20+SB numbers.
4. **Jesse Barfield** - THE BEST DEFENSIVE RIGHT-FIELDER I"VE EVER SEEN PLAY FOR OR AGAINST US. Jesse was the first Toronto Blue Jay to lead the AL in home runs with 40 in 1986.
5. **Shawn Green** - A 35+HR/35+SB campaign with the Blue Jays in 1997, and in 1998 with Toronto he hammered 42 dingers with 87 XBH, 123 RBI's and 20 Stolen Bases alongside a .309 Avg. He took home his lone Gold Glove that year as well.

Starting Pitchers

1. **Roger Clemens** - Back to back Cy Young Awards in his two years in the "Big Smoke". Won 7 Cy Youngs over his illustrious career.
2. **Pedro Martinez** - Won a Cy Young in Montreal in 1997. Captured 4 Cy Young Awards during his time in the Majors.
3. **Roy Halladay** - Won two Cy Young Awards in his career, one with the Blue Jays, and one with the Phillies. Threw a no-hitter during the NLDS of '10.
4. **David Price** - Won a Cy Young Award with the Tampa Bay Rays.
5. **Dave Stieb** - A great competitor.
6. **Steve Rogers** - Solid, if not spectacular.
7. **Dennis Martinez** - Great talent who fulfilled his days as an elite starting pitcher.
8. **Jimmy Key** - Mr. Consistant.
9. **Doyle Alexander** - Had at least a dozen different pitches.
10. **Bill Gullickson** - A fabulous flamethrower.
11. **Pat Hentgen** - Won the 1996 AL Cy Young Award. Was 20-10 with a 3.22 ERA in 1996.
12. **Juan Guzman** - Had an .824 Winning % in 1993. Was 5-1 with an ERA of 2.44 in post-season play, winning back to back World Series in 1992 and 1993.
13. **Mark Langston** - Had seven 15+ win campaigns in the 'bigs.
14. **Charlie Lea** - A leader in the Expos glory years of the early eighties.
15. **David Palmer** - Was a standout 10-2 in his rookie campaign.

Relievers Pitchers

1. **Tom Henke** - The Terminator.
2. **John Wetteland** - Great closer.
3. **Jeff Reardon** - The other "Terminator".
4. **Duane Ward** - Had the best slider of the bunch.
5. **Mike Marshall** - Was perhaps more valuable a pitcher than the modern day pitcher based on how many games he played on average yearly.
6. **B.J. Ryan** - Great 'lefty closer.
7. **Roberto Osuna** - On his way to greatness. He looks like he'll be a steady closer for many years to come.
8. **Mark Eichhorn** - Was the best pitcher in the Majors in '88, while with Toronto. Eichorn would have led the American League in ERA in 1986 had he accrued five more innings on the year. He had a sidearm delivery that made it hard for a batter to pickup where the ball was coming from.
9. **Mel Rojas** - Was one of the best set-up men early on in his career before being used as a closer.
10. **Brett Cecil** - Started his career as a starting pitcher and has evolved into a dominating lefty from the 'pen.
11. **David Wells** - Was a great lefty pitcher. He was a valuable starter AND reliever in his storied career.
12. **Al Leiter** - A great swingman who became a great pitcher once he left Toronto for the Marlins in 1996.
13. **Mike Timlin** - A solid set-up man for the Jays.
14. **Aaron Sanchez** - On his way to greatness. Could mature into either a set-up man/closer, or as a starter.
15. **Rudy May** - A great swingman who passed some time with the Expos in their glory years.

Ex-Blue Jays Still Playing in the Majors in 2016

1. Jose Reyes
2. Noah Syndergaard
3. Eric Thames (KBO)
4. Adam Lind
5. Melky Cabrera
6. Alex Rios
7. Brett Lawrie
8. Colby Rasmus
9. Sam Dyson
10. Travis d'Arnaud
11. Anthony Gose
12. Henderson Alvarez
13. Yan Gomes
14. Adeiny Hechavarria
15. Kendall Graveman
16. 16. Casey Janssen
17. J.A. Happ
18. J.P. Arencibia
19. Jake Marisnek
20. Daniel Norris
21. Justin Nicolino
22. Moises Sierra
23. Matt Boyd
24. Kelly Johnson
25. Sean Nolin
26. Ryan Schimpf
27. Rajai Davis

Canadian-Born Ballplayers

1. Jeff Heath
2. Ferguson Jenkins
3. Claude Raymond
4. Dr. Ron Taylor
5. John Hiller
6. Reggie Cleveland
7. Dave McKay
8. Terry Puhl
9. Kirk McCaskill
10. Rob Butler
11. Rich Butler
12. Paul Quantrill
13. Larry Walker
14. Erik Bedard
15. Rheal Cormier
16. Jason Bay
17. Eric Gagne
18. Matt Stairs
19. Justin Morneau
20. Jeff Francis
21. Ryan Dempster
22. Russell Martin
23. John Axford
24. Rich Harden
25. Pete Orr
26. Jesse Crain
27. Joey Votto
28. Shawn Hill
29. Scott Richmond
30. Jim Henderson
31. Scott Mathieson
32. Phillippe Aumont
33. Chris Leroux
34. Michael Saunders
35. Brett Lawrie
36. James Paxton
37. Jim Adduci
38. Andrew Albers
39. Adam Loewen
40. Dalton Pompey

9

Player Evaluations: Rating Baseball's Best

The Hitters

Batting Formula

Plug in a player's average production per 162 games into the following equation:

$$\frac{1000*[(Avg+OBP+SLG\%)]}{3}+[3(SB-CS)]+\frac{[(BB-SO)]}{2}+Extra\ Base\ Hits+RBI+Runs]$$

Based on average performance per 162 games

Note 1 - Player Adjustment % is made on basis of league, era, and home park

Note 2-750 + First-tier Hall of Famer

        700-749 Second-Tier Hall of Famer

        650-699 Third-Tier Hall of Famer

        600-649 Excellent Hitter

        550-599 Very Good Hitter

1. Barry Bonds $\frac{1000[(.298+.444+.607)]}{3}$ + [3(28-8)] + $\frac{[(139-85)]}{2}$ + 78 + 108 + 121 = 845

2. Lloyd Moseby [584]
3. Vladimir Guerrero [715]
4. Ted Williams [873 + 5% = 917]
5. Mickey Mantle [726 + 5% = 762]
6. Willie Mays [735 + 5% = 772]
7. Duke Snider [665 + 5% = 698]
8. Henry Aaron [729 + 5% = 765]
9. Rickey Henderson [773]
10. 1Sammy Sosa [652]
11. Joe Morgan [704 + 5% = 739]
12. Manny Ramirez [738]
13. Roberto Alomar [672]
14. Ken Griffey Jr. [688]
15. Johnny Bench [599 + 5% = 629]
16. Willie Stargell [610 + 5% = 641]
17. Ernie Banks [607 + 5% = 637]
18. Stan Musial [742 + 5% = 779]
19. Frank Robinson [707 + 5% = 742]
20. Mike Schmidt [673 + 5% = 707]

21. Larry Walker [743-3% = 721]
22. Roy Campanella [640 + 5% = 672]
23. Tony Gwynn [665]
24. Joe DiMaggio [815 + 5% = 856]
25. George Brett [669 + 5% = 702]
26. Frank Thomas [730]
27. Alex Rodriguez [740]
28. Jackie Robinson [719 + 5% = 755]
29. Mark McGuire [699]
30. Nomar Garciapara [696]
31. Derek Jeter [640]
32. Rafael Palmeiro [671]
33. Carlos Delgado [674]
34. Jason Giambi [647]
35. Tim Raines [740]
36. Vince Coleman [663]
37. Eric Davis [663]
38. Ryan Braun [713][a]
39. Jose Bautista [623][a]
40. Matt Kemp [618 + 5% = 649][a]
41. Rod Carew [618 + 3% = 637]
42. George Foster [578 + 5% = 607]
43. Jim Rice [633 + 3% = 652]
44. Fred Lynn [611 + 3% = 629]
45. Don Baylor [602 + 3% = 620]
46. Reggie Jackson [601 + 3% = 619]
47. Reggie Smith [630 + 5% = 662]
48. Pete Rose [583 + 5% = 612]
49. Ichiro Suzuki [595][a]
50. Vernon Wells [588]
51. Roberto Clemente [610 + 10% = 671]
52. Juan Gonzalez [679]
53. David Ortiz [686][a]
54. Albert Pujols [768][a]
55. Ralph Kiner [714 + 5% = 750]
56. Roger Maris [601 + 5% = 631]
57. Ryan Howard [610][a]
58. Johnny Mize [722 + 5% = 758]
59. Cecil Fielder [575]
60. Prince Fielder [646][a]
61. Brady Anderson [611]
62. Luis Gonzalez [624]
63. Albert "Joey" Belle [726]
64. Greg Vaughn [592]
65. Jim Thome [665]
66. Andruw Jones [596]
67. Jeff Bagwell [739]
68. Willie McCovey [615 + 5% = 646]
69. Orlando Cepeda [628 + 5% = 659]
70. Bobby Bonds [663 + 5% = 696]
71. Harmon Killebrew [625 + 5% = 656]
72. Kirby Puckett [635]
73. Eddie Murray [630]
74. Don Mattingly [639]
75. Keith Hernandez [604]
76. Dave Winfield [628 + 3% = 647]
77. Willie Upshaw [528]
78. John Olerud [624]
79. Fred McGriff [631]
80. Paul Molitor [671]
81. Tony Fernandez [555]
82. Cal Ripken Jr. [588]
83. Barry Larkin [664]
84. Ozzie Smith [568]
85. Craig Biggio [623]
86. Ryne Sandberg [631]
87. Robin Yount [595]
88. Alan Trammell [581]
89. George Bell [587]
90. Jesse Barfield [537]
91. Todd Helton [706-5% = 671]
92. Lance Berkman [693]
93. Mike Piazza [660]
94. Ivan Rodriguez [578]
95. Carlton Fisk [574 + 5% = 603]
96. Thurman Munson [541 + 5% = 568]

97.   Gary Carter [549 + 5% = 576]
98.   Andre Dawson [587 + 3% = 605]
99.   Carl Yastremski [628 + 5% = 659]
100. Dwight Evans [601]
101. Andy Van Slyke [603]
102. Bobby Bonilla [587]
103. Julio Franco [579]
104. Lou Brock [640 + 5% = 672]
105. Kenny Lofton [697]
106. Joe Carter [606]
107. Mo Vaughn [636]
108. Tony Perez [563 + 5% = 591]
109. Cecil Cooper [601]
110. Alfonso Soriano [626][a]
111. Willie McGee [539]
112. Tony Conigliaro [566 + 5% = 594]
113. Travis Hafner [609][a]
114. Troy Glaus [609]
115. Scott Rolen [640]
116. Matty Alou [510 + 10% = 561]
117. Felipe Alou [538 + 10% = 592]
118. Bobby Abreu [678]
119. Eddie Mathews [654 + 5% = 687]
120. Al Kaline [642 + 5% = 674]
121. Shawn Green [631]
122. Billy Williams [640 + 5% = 672]
123. Steve Garvey [567 + 5% = 595]
124. Yogi Berra [638 + 5% = 670]
125. Joey Votto [687][a]
126. Miguel Cabrera [711][a]
127. Josh Hamilton [634][a]
128. Buster Posey [614][a]
129. Brooks Robinson [521 + 5% = 547]
130. Maury Wills [555 + 5% = 583]
131. Miguel Tejada [597]
132. Elston Howard [504 + 5% = 529]
133. Jacoby Ellsbury [674][a]

134. Larry Doby [644 + 5% = 676]
135. Al Rosen [671 + 5% = 705]
136. Troy Tulowitzki [649][a]
137. Cesar Cedeno [660 + 5% = 693]
138. Davey Lopes [637 + 5% = 669]
139. Robinson Cano [591][a]
140. Dale Murphy [595]
141. Johnny Damon [657]
142. Bill Madlock [608 + 5% = 638]
143. Carlos Beltran [683][a]
144. Jermaine Dye [595]
145. Greg Luzinski [581 + 5% = 610]
146. Wade Boggs [635]
147. Richie "Dick" Allen [668 + 5% = 701]
148. Ken Griffey Sr. [582 + 5% = 611]
149. Mark Teixeira [656][a]
150. Mark Grace [618]
151. Ken Caminiti [575]
152. Rico Carty [579 + 5% = 608]
153. Joe Mauer [623][a]
154. Justin Morneau [602][a]
155. Andres Galarraga [587]
156. Kirk Gibson [633]
157. Jimmy Wynn [598 + 10% = 658]
158. Chipper Jones [714]
159. Jorge Posada [584]
160. Javy Lopez [561]
161. Yoenis Cespedes [592][a]
162. Evan Longoria [611][a]
163. Adam Jones [559][a]
164. Nelson Cruz [597][a]
165. Giancarlo Stanton [628][a]
166. Josh Donaldson [629][a]
167. Paul Konerko [596]
168. Lorenzo Cain [575][a]
169. Adrian Gonzalez [667][a]
170. Jose Altuve [610][a]

171. Victor Martinez [615][a]
172. Adrian Beltre [594][a]
173. Mike Trout [751][a]
174. Andrew McCutchen [675][a]
175. Edwin Encarnacion [614][a]
176. Jose Reyes [684][a]
177. Jayson Werth [606][a]
178. Jimmy Rollins [632][a]
179. Chase Utley [654][a]
180. Michael Brantley [601][a]
181. Yasiel Puig [584][a]
182. Brian Giles [691]
183. Gary Sheffield [708]
184. Joe Torre [567 + 5% = 595]
185. Jose Canseco [654]
186. Rusty Staub [561 + 5% = 589]
187. Jeff Kent [635]
188. George Scott [528 + 5% = 554]
189. Chris Davis [554][a]
190. Jose Abreu [636][a]
191. Bernie Williams [657]
192. Paul O'Neill [620]
193. Edgar Martinez [685]
194. David Justice [637]
195. Mike Greenwell [634]
196. Ruben Sierra [579]
197. Tino Martinez [591]
198. Chuck Knoblauch [667]
199. Lou Whitaker [590]
200. Willie Randolph [567]
201. Bryce Harper [641][a]
202. Nolan Arenado [589][a]
203. Manny Machado [570][a]
204. Eric Hosmer [564][a]
205. Paul Goldschmidt [700][a]

206. Dee Gordon [589][a]
207. Anthony Rizzo [583][a]
208. Carlos Gonzalez [655][a]
209. Todd Frazier [542][a]
210. J.D. Martinez [528][a]
211. Torii Hunter [582][a]
212. Carl Crawford [651][a]
213. Rocky Colavito [622 + 5% = 653]
214. Kevin Mitchell [621]
215. Richie Zisk [562 + 5% = 590]
216. Jack Clark [615 + 5% = 646]
217. Glenn Davis [576 + 5% = 605]
218. Boog Powell [568 + 5% = 596]
219. Pedro Guerrero [611 + 5% = 642]
220. Hal McCrae [582 + 5% = 611]
221. Joe Adcock [563 + 5% = 591]
222. Norm Cash [597 + 5% = 627]
223. Jackie Jensen [662 + 5% = 695]
224. Will Clark [647]
225. Ted Kluszewski [622 + 5% = 653]
226. Mike Sweeney [634]
227. Lou Boudreau [601]
228. Ray Boone [569]
229. Bret Boone [558]
230. Aaron Boone [544]
231. George Kell [588]
232. Al Oliver [592 + 5% = 622]
233. Jose Cruz Sr. [577 + 5% = 606]
234. Jose Cruz Jr. [552]
235. Michael Young [584]
236. Rico Petrocelli [515 + 5% = 541]
237. Frank Howard [573 + 5% = 602]
238. Lenny Dykstra [654]
239. Magglio Ordonez [663]
240. David Wright [664]

a - denotes active

1927 Babe Ruth vs Lou Gehrig

Lou Gehrig

$$\frac{[(.373 + .474 + .765)]}{3} + [\ 3(10\text{-}8)] + \frac{[109\text{-}84]}{2} + 117 + 173 + 149$$

= 537 + 6+ 13 + 117 + 173 + 149 = 995

Babe Ruth

$$\frac{[(.356 + .486 + .772)]}{3} + [3(7\text{-}6)] + \frac{[137\text{-}89]}{2} + 97 + 165 + 158$$

= 538 + 3 + 24 + 97 + 165 + 158 = <u>985</u>

Let's now analyse Babe Ruth's monster year of 1921;

$$\frac{[(.378 + .512 + .846)]}{3} + [3(17\text{-}13)] + \frac{[145\text{-}81]}{2} + 119 + 168 + 177$$

= 579 + 12 + 32 + 119 + 168 + 177 = <u>1087</u>

Statistical Analysis of Batters (Yearly Numbers)

Batting Formula

$$1000\left[\frac{AVG + OBP + SLG\%}{3}\right] + [3(SB\text{-}CS)]\left[\frac{BB\text{-}SO}{2}\right] + \text{Extra Base Hits} + RBI + RUNS$$

750 +	1st Tier Hall of Fame Level
700 – 749	2nd Tier Hall of Fame Level
650-699	3rd Tier Hall of Fame Level
600-649	Excellent Batsman
550-599	Very Good Batsman

1. a) Barry Bonds 2001 Stats

$$1000\left[\frac{.328 + .515 + .863}{3}\right] + [3(13\text{-}3)] + \left[\frac{177 - 93}{2}\right] + 107 + 137 + 129$$

b) Barry Bonds 2004 Stats

$$1000\left[\frac{.362 + .609 + .812}{3}\right] + [3(7\text{-}1)] + \left[\frac{232 - 41}{2}\right] + 75 + 101 + 129$$

$$= \frac{[1783]}{3} + 18 + 96 + 75 + 101 + 129$$

$$= 594 + 18 + 96 + 75 + 101 + 129$$

$$= 1013$$

c) 1990 Stats - 832

d) 1992 Stats - 873

e) 1993 Stats - 905

f) 1994 Stats + 15% = 879

g) 1995 Stats - 799

h) 1996 Stats - 959

i) 1997 Stats - 852

j) 1998 Stats - 847

k) 2000 Stats - 838

l) 2002 Stats - 987

m) 2003 Stats - 875

2. Lloyd Moseby 1983 Stats

$$\frac{[.315 + .376 + .499]}{3} + [3(27-8)] + \frac{[(51-85)]}{2} + 56 + 81 + 104$$

$$= 397 + 3(19) - 17 + 56 + 81 + 104$$

$$= 678$$

3. a) Vladimir Guerrero 2002 Stats - 811

b) 1999 Stats - 766

c) 2000 Stats - 769

d) 2001 Stats - 764

e) 2004 Stats - 797

f) 2005 Stats - 734

g) 2006 Stats - 718

h) 2007 Stats - 714

4. a) Ted Williams 1941 Stats + 5% = 994

b) 1947 Stats + 5% = 910

c) 1948 Stats + 5% = 916

d) 1949 Stats + 5% = 992

e) 1957 Stats + 5% = 875

5. a) Mickey Mantle 1956 Stats + 5% = 926

b) 1955 Stats + 5% = 810

c) 1957 Stats + 5% = 915

d) 1958 Stats + 5% = 823

e) 1961 Stats + 5% = 902

f) 1962 Stats + 5% = 864

g) 1964 Stats + 5% = 748

6. a) Willie Mays 1955 Stats + 5% = 904

b) 1954 Stats + 5% = 844

c) 1956 Stats + 5% = 793

d) 1957 Stats + 5% = 849

e) 1958 Stats + 5% = 867

f) 1959 Stats + 5% = 851

g) 1960 Stats + 5% = 776

h) 1961 Stats + 5% = 823

i) 1962 Stats + 5% = 881

j) 1963 Stats + 5% = 763

k) 1964 Stats + 5% = 824

l) 1965 Stats + 5% = 816

7. a) Duke Snider 1954 Stats + 5% = 843

b) 1953 Stats + 5% = 826

c) 1955 Stats + 5% = 811

8. a) Henry Aaron 1963 Stats + 5% = 872

b) 1957 Stats + 5% = 798

c) 1959 Stats + 5% = 858

d) 1960 Stats + 5% = 764

e) 1961 Stats + 5% = 823

f) 1962 Stats + 5% = 839

g) 1965 Stats + 5% = 777

h) 1966 Stats + 5% = 784

i) 1967 Stats + 5% = 770

j) 1969 Stats + 5% = 761

k) 1970 Stats + 5% = 775

l) 1971 Stats + 5% = 799

m) 1973 Stats + 5% = 726

9. a) Rickey Henderson 1985 Stats - 913
    b) 1980 Stats - 827
    c) 1981 Stats + 15% = 739
    d) 1982 Stats - 832
    e) 1983 Stats - 849
    f) 1984 Stats - 748
    g) 1986 Stats - 842
    h) 1988 Stats - 826
    i) 1989 Stats - 790
    j) 1990 Stats - 874
    k) 1993 Stats - 779

10. a) Sammy Sosa 2001 Stats - 885
    b) 1998 Stats - 800
    c) 2000 Stats - 756
    d) 1999 Stats - 724
    e) 2002 Stats - 715

11. a) Joe Morgan 1976 Stats + 5% = 969
    b) 1972 Stats + 5% = 817
    c) 1973 Stats + 5% = 880
    d) 1974 Stats + 5% = 839
    e) 1975 Stats + 5% = 941
    f) 1977 Stats + 5% = 820

12. a) Manny Ramirez 1999 Stats - 799
    b) 1998 Stats - 742
    c) 2000 Stats - 775
    d) 2001 Stats - 698
    e) 2002 Stats - 731
    f) 2003 Stats - 749
    g) 2004 Stats - 737
    h) 2005 Stats - 741
    i) 2006 Stats - 700
    j) 2008 Stats - 742

13. a) Roberto Alomar 1999 Stats - 846
    b) 1991 Stats - 692

c) 1992 Stats - 743
d) 1993 Stats - 796
e) 1996 Stats - 763
f) 2000 Stats - 745
g) 2001 Stats - 787

14. a) Ken Griffey Jr. 1997 Stats - 819
    b) 1996 Stats - 815
    c) 1998 Stats - 800
    d) 1999 Stats - 792

15. Johnny Bench 1970 Stats + 5% = 757

16. a) Willie Stargell 1973 Stats + 5% = 773
    b) 1966 Stats + 5% = 674
    c) 1971 Stats + 5% = 743
    d) 1972 Stats + 5% = 657
    e) 1974 Stats + 5% = 685
    f) 1979 Stats + 10% = 612

17. a) Ernie Banks 1958 Stats + 5% = 779
    b) 1955 Stats + 5% = 750
    c) 1957 Stats + 5% = 747
    d) 1959 Stats + 5% = 768
    e) 1960 Stats + 5% = 712

18. a) Stan Musial 1948 Stats + 5% = 959
    b) 1949 Stats + 5% = 888
    c) 1950 Stats + 5% = 821
    d) 1951 Stats + 5% = 845
    e) 1953 Stats + 5% = 868
    f) 1954 Stats + 5% = 840
    g) 1957 Stats + 5% = 769

19. a) Frank Robinson 1962 Stats + 5% = 901
    b) 1959 Stats + 5% = 785
    c) 1960 Stats + 5% = 736
    d) 1961 Stats + 5% = 865
    e) 1966 Stats + 5% = 831

20. a) Mike Schmidt 1981 Stats + 15%
      = 818
    b) 1977 Stats + 5% = 753
    c) 1979 Stats + 5% = 749
    d) 1980 Stats + 5% = 779
21. a) Larry Walker 1997 Stats - 5%
      = 906
    b) 1994 Stats + 15% = 780
    c) 1998 Stats - 5% = 725
    d) 1999 Stats - 5% = 789
    e) 2001 Stats - 5% = 770
    f) 2002 Stats - 5% = 686
22. a) Roy Campanella 1953 Stats +
      5% = 803
    b) 1951 Stats + 5% = 734
    c) 1955 Stats + 5% = 712
23. a) Tony Gwynn 1987 Stats - 828
    b) 1984 Stats - 660
    c) 1989 Stats - 650
    d) 1993 Stats - 646
    e) 1994 Stats + 15% = 797
    f) 1995 Stats - 680
    g) 1997 Stats - 756
24. a) Joe DiMaggio 1937 Stats + 5%
      = 960
    b) 1941 Stats + 5% = 891
    c) 1948 Stats + 5% = 838
25. a) George Brett 1980 Stats +
      10%=902
    b) 1977 Stats + 5% = 722
    c) 1979 Stats + 5% = 801
    d) 1983 Stats - 673
    e) 1985 Stats - 796
26. a) Frank Thomas 1994 Stats +
      15% = 948
    b) 1993 Stats - 796
    c) 1995 Stats - 770
    d) 1996 Stats - 808

    e) 1997 Stats - 796
    f) 2000 Stats - 811
27. a) Alex Rodriguez 2007 Stats - 891
    b) 1996 Stats - 834
    c) 1998 Stats - 801
    d) 2000 Stats - 813
    e) 2001 Stats - 818
    f) 2002 Stats - 788
    g) 2003 Stats - 779
    h) 2005 Stats - 804
28. a) Jackie Robinson 1949 Stats +
      5% = 908
    b) 1950 Stats + 5% = 741
    c) 1951 Stats + 5% = 799
    d) 1952 Stats + 5% = 741
    e) 1953 Stats + 5% = 774
29. a) Mark McGuire 1998 Stats - 882
    b) 1999 Stats - 814
    c) 1996 Stats - 795
    d) 1997 Stats - 712
30. a) Nomar Garciapara 1999 Stats -
      778
    b) 2000 Stats - 758
    c) 1997 Stats - 710
    d) 1998 Stats - 740
    e) 2002 Stats - 701
    f) 2003 Stats - 724
31. a) Derek Jeter 1999 Stats - 772
    b) 1998 Stats - 700
    c) 2000 Stats - 693
    d) 2001 Stats - 683
    e) 2002 Stats - 674
    f) 2004 Stats - 660
    g) 2005 Stats - 631
    h) 2006 Stats - 756
    i) 2007 Stats - 616
    j) 2009 Stats - 687
32. Rafael Palmeiro 1999 Stats - 788

33. a) Carlos Delgado 2000 Stats - 851
    b) 1998 Stats - 690
    c) 1999 Stats - 710
    d) 2003 Stats - 769
34. a) Jason Giambi 2001 Stats - 838
    b) 1999 Stats - 738
    c) 2000 Stats - 830
    d) 2002 Stats - 766
35. a) Tim Raines 1983 Stats - 870
    b) 1981 Stats + 20% = 826
    c) 1984 Stats - 805
    d) 1985 Stats - 804
    e) 1986 Stats - 807
    f) 1987 Stats - 833
36. a) Vince Coleman 1987 Stats + 5% = 795
    b) 1985 Stats + 5% = 743
    c) 1986 Stats + 5% = 709
    d) 1990 Stats + 5% = 675
37. Eric Davis 1987 Stats - 819
38. Ryan Braun 2011 Stats - 802
39. a) Jose Bautista 2010 Stats - 756
    b) 2011 Stats - 752
    c) 2014 Stats - 686
    d) 2015 Stats - 702
40. Matt Kemp 2011 Stats - 797
41. a) Rod Carew 1977 Stats + 5% = 842
    b) 1973 Stats + 5% = 732
    c) 1974 Stats + 5% = 706
    d) 1975 Stats + 5% = 763
    e) 1976 Stats + 5% = 758
    f) 1978 Stats + 5% = 692
42. George Foster 1977 Stats + 5% = 824
43. a) Jim Rice 1979 Stats + 5% = 798
    b) 1978 Stats + 5% = 783
    c) 1977 Stats + 5% = 736

44. a) Fred Lynn 1979 Stats + 5% = 825
    b) 1975 Stats + 5% = 753
45. Don Baylor 1979 Stats + 5% = 798
46. a) Reggie Jackson 1969 Stats + 5% = 806
    b) 1973 Stats + 5% = 740
    c) 1974 Stats + 5% = 721
    d) 1977 Stats + 5% = 730
    e) 1980 Stats + 5% = 716
47. a) Reggie Smith 1977 Stats + 5% = 747
    b) 1971 Stats + 5% = 668
    c) 1974 Stats + 5% = 683
    d) 1978 Stats + 5% = 689
48. Pete Rose 1969 Stats + 5% = 723
49. Ichiro Suzuki 2001 Stats - 760
50. Vernon Wells 2003 Stats - 721
51. a) Roberto Clemente 1961 Stats + 5% = 716
    b) 1966 Stats + 10% = 741
    c) 1967 Stats + 10% = 772
    d) 1969 Stats + 10% = 729
52. Juan Gonzalez 1998-765
53. a) David Ortiz 2007 Stats - 797
    b) 2004 Stats - 723
    c) 2005 Stats - 781
    d) 2006 Stats - 786
    e) 2016 Stats - 741
54. a) Albert Pujols 2009 Stats - 890
    b) 2001 Stats - 759
    c) 2002 Stats - 740
    d) 2003 Stats - 830
    e) 2004 Stats - 839
    f) 2005 Stats - 840
    g) 2006 Stats - 853
    h) 2007 Stats - 725
    i) 2008 Stats - 825

j) 2010 Stats - 800

55. a) Ralph Kiner 1949 Stats + 5% = 863

    b) 1947 Stats + 5% = 733

56. Roger Maris 1961 Stats + 5% = 821

57. Ryan Howard 2006 Stats - 767

58. Johnny Mize 1947 Stats + 5% – 846

59. Cecil Fielder 1990 Stats - 679

60. Prince Fielder 2007 Stats - 734

61. a) Brady Anderson 1996 Stats - 786

    b) 1992 Stats - 708

62. Luis Gonzalez 2001 Stats - 859

63. a) Albert Belle 1994 Stats + 15% = 886

    b) 1995 Stats - 825

    c) 1996 Stats - 848

    d) 1998 Stats - 830

64. Greg Vaughn 1998 Stats - 724

65. Jim Thome 2002 Stats - 756

66. Andruw Jones 2005 Stats - 675

67. a) Jeff Bagwell 1994 Stats + 15% = 976

    b) 1996 Stats - 810

    c) 1997 Stats - 829

    d) 1998 Stats - 777

    e) 1999 Stats - 864

    f) 2000 Stats - 824

    g) 2001 Stats - 770

68. a) Willie McCovey 1959 Stats + 60% = 923

    b) 1969 Stats + 5% = 843

    c) 1966 Stats + 5% = 697

    d) 1968 Stats + 5% = 687

    e) 1970 Stats + 5% = 822

69. Orlando Cepeda 1961 Stats + 5% = 775

70. a) Bobby Bonds 1973 Stats + 5% = 783

    b) 1969 Stats + 5% = 739

    c) 1970 Stats + 5% = 773

    d) 1971 Stats + 5% = 717

    e) 1972 Stats + 5% = 712

    f) 1975 Stats + 5% = 672

    g) 1977 Stats + 5% = 733

    h) 1978 Stats + 5% = 679

71. a) Harmon Killebrew 1969 Stats + 5% = 834

    b) 1961 Stats + 5% = 754

72. a) Kirby Puckett 1988 Stats - 693

    b) 1986 Stats - 691

73. a) Eddie Murray 1985 Stats - 727

    b) 1983 Stats - 714

74. a) Don Mattingly 1985 Stats - 766

    b) 1986 Stats - 765

75. Keith Hernandez 1979 Stats + 5% = 769

76. a) Dave Winfield 1979 Stats + 5% = 768

    b) 1983 Stats - 679

    c) 1984 Stats - 676

    d) 1988 Stats - 690

    e) 1992 Stats - 642

77. Willie Upshaw 1983 Stats - 652

78. John Olerud 1993 Stats - 792

79. a) Fred McGriff 1994 Stats + 15% = 779

    b) 1992 Stats - 664

    c) 1993 Stats - 676

80. a) Paul Molitor 1987 Stats - 809

    b) 1993 Stats - 767

81. a) Tony Fernandez 1987 Stats - 636

    b) 1999 Stats - 601

82. a) Cal Ripken Jr. 1991 Stats - 737

    b) 1983 Stats - 670

83. a) Barry Larkin 1996 Stats - 800
    b) 1995 Stats - 759
84. Ozzie Smith 1987 Stats - 716
85. Craig Biggio 1997 Stats - 802
86. a) Ryne Sandberg 1990 Stats - 732
    b) 1984 Stats - 723
87. Robin Yount 1982 Stats - 788
88. Alan Trammell 1987 Stats - 774
89. George Bell 1987 Stats - 744
90. Jesse Barfield 1986 Stats - 659
91. a) Todd Helton 2000 Stats - 5% = 871
    b) 2001 Stats - 5% = 827
    c) 2003 Stats - 5% = 787
92. a) Lance Berkman 2001 Stats - 771
    b) 2006 Stats - 756
93. a) Mike Piazza 1997 Stats - 786
    b) 2000 Stats - 713
94. Ivan Rodriguez 1999 Stats - 728
95. Carlton Fisk 1977 Stats + 5% = 708
96. a) Thurman Munson 1977 Stats + 5% = 629
    b) 1976 Stats + 5% = 621
97. a) Gary Carter 1982 Stats - 648
    b) 1984 Stats - 620
98. a) Andre Dawson 1983 Stats - 708
    b) 1987 Stats - 685
99. a) Carl Yastremski 1970 Stats + 5% = 856
    b) 1967 Stats + 5% = 823
100. Dwight Evans 1987 Stats - 733
101. a) Andy Van Slyke 1992 Stats - 674
     b) 1988 Stats - 673
102. Bobby Bonilla 1995 Stats - 672
103. Julio Franco 1991 Stats - 710
104. a) Lou Brock 1974 Stats + 5% = 821
    b) 1964 Stats + 5% = 667
    c) 1965 Stats + 5% = 700
    d) 1966 Stats + 5% = 685
    e) 1967 Stats + 5% = 709
    f) 1968 Stats + 5% = 695
    g) 1969 Stats + 5% = 676
    h) 1970 Stats + 5% = 702
    i) 1971 Stats + 5% = 769
    j) 1973 Stats + 5% = 735
105. a) Kenny Lofton 1994 Stats + 15% = 907
     b) 1996 Stats - 794
106. a) Joe Carter 1986 Stats - 722
     b) 1993 Stats - 618
107. a) Mo Vaughn 1996 Stats - 755
     b) 1995 Stats - 695
108. Tony Perez 1970 Stats + 5% = 775
109. Cecil Cooper 1980 Stats - 738
110. a) Alfonso Soriano 2002 Stats - 732
     b) 2006 Stats - 725
111. a) Willie McGee 1985 Stats - 757
     b) 1990 Stats - 631
112. a) Tony Conigliaro 1970 Stats + 5% = 636
     b) 1965 Stats + 5% = 597
113. Travis Hafner 2006 Stats - 755
114. Troy Glaus 2000 Stats - 722
115. a) Scott Rolen 2004 Stats - 736
     b) 1998 Stats - 711
     c) 2003 Stats - 698
116. Matty Alou 1969 Stats + 10% = 678
117. a) Felipe Alou 1966 Stats + 10% = 733
     b) 1968 Stats + 10% = 609
118. a) Bobby Abreu 2004 Stats - 824
     b) 1999 Stats - 772
     c) 2001 Stats - 770

119. a) Eddie Mathews 1953 Stats + 5% = 817
     b) 1959 Stats + 5% = 777
120. Al Kaline 1955 Stats + 5% = 761
121. a) Shawn Green 1999 Stats - 785
     b) 2001 Stats - 783
     c) 2002 Stats - 707
     d) 1998 Stats - 675
122. a) Billy Williams 1970 Stats + 5% = 841
     b) 1972 Stats + 5% = 785
     c) 1965 Stats + 5% = 776
123. a) Steve Garvey 1978 Stats + 5% = 690
     b) 1974 Stats + 5% = 653
     c) 1977 Stats + 5% = 658
     d) 1979 Stats + 5% = 663
124. a) Yogi Berra 1950 Stats + 5% = 782
     b) 1954 Stats + 5% = 700
     c) 1956 Stats + 5% = 717
125. a) Joey Votto 2010 Stats - 759
     b) 2011 Stats - 692
     c) 2015 Stats - 705
126. a) Miguel Cabrera 2013 Stats - 793
     b) 2004 Stats - 638
     c) 2005 Stats - 696
     d) 2006 Stats - 748
     e) 2007 Stats - 690
     f) 2008 Stats - 648
     g) 2009 Stats - 682
     h) 2010 Stats - 775
     i) 2011 Stats - 766
     j) 2012 Stats - 768
127. a) Josh Hamilton 2010 Stats - 733
     b) 2008 Stats - 695
     c) 2012 Stats - 676
128. Buster Posey 2012 Stats - 663

129. Brooks Robinson 1964 Stats + 5% = 698
130. Maury Wills 1962 Stats + 5% = 858
131. a) Miguel Tejada 2004 Stats - 732
     b) 2002 Stats - 685
     c) 2006 Stats - 658
132. a) Elston Howard 1961 Stats + 5% = 614
     b) 1963 Stats + 5% = 614
133. a) Jacoby Ellsbury 2011 Stats - 772
     b) 2009 Stats - 718
     c) 2013 Stats - 675
134. a) Larry Doby 1950 Stats + 5% = 761
     b) 1952 Stats + 5% = 707
135. a) Al Rosen 1953 Stats + 5% = 855
     b) 1950 Stats + 5% = 735
136. a) Troy Tulowitzki 2010 Stats - 679
     b) 2009 Stats - 676
     c) 2011 Stats - 668
     d) 2013 Stats - 609
137. a) Cesar Cedeno 1972 Stats + 5% = 805
     b) 1973 Stats + 5% = 770
138. a) Davey Lopes 1979 Stats + 5% = 764
     b) 1975 Stats + 5% = 742
139. a) Robinson Cano 2010 Stats - 689
     b) 2011 Stats - 687
     c) 2012 Stats - 681
     d) 2013 Stats - 668
140. a) Dale Murphy 1983 Stats - 796
     b) 1982 Stats - 688
     c) 1984 Stats - 682
     d) 1985 Stats - 705
     e) 1987 Stats - 743

141. Johnny Damon 2000 Stats - 807
142. a) Bill Madlock 1982 Stats + 5% = 709
     b) 1975 Stats + 5% = 636
     c) 1976 Stats + 5% = 680
     d) 1979 Stats + 5% = 680
143. a) Carlos Beltran 2004 Stats - 815
     b) 2006 Stats - 785
144. a) Jermaine Dye 2006 Stats - 721
     b) 2000 Stats - 707
145. a) Greg Luzinski 1977 Stats + 5% = 747
     b) 1975 Stats + 5% = 680
146. a) Wade Boggs 1988 Stats - 774
     b) 1983 Stats - 688
     c) 1985 Stats - 691
     d) 1986 Stats - 686
     e) 1987 Stats - 761
147. a) Dick Allen 1972 Stats + 5% = 774
     b) 1964 Stats + 5% = 711
     c) 1966 Stats + 5% = 759
     d) 1967 Stats + 5% = 714
148. Ken Griffey Sr. 1976 Stats + 5% = 727
149. a) Mark Teixeira 2005 Stats - 747
     b) 2008 Stats - 728
     c) 2009 Stats - 713
150. Mark Grace 1995 Stats - 693
151. Ken Caminiti 1996 Stats - 778
152. a) Rico Carty 1970 Stats + 5% = 753
     b) 1964 Stats + 5% = 649
153. Joe Mauer 2009 Stats - 730
154. a) Justin Morneau 2006 Stats - 697
     b) 2008 Stats - 684

155. a) Andres Galarraga 1996 Stats - 5% = 713
     b) 1997 Stats - 5% = 707
     c) 1998 Stats - 690
     d) 1993 Stats - 5% = 625
156. a) Kirk Gibson 1985 Stats - 699
     b) 1986 Stats - 686
     c) 1988 Stats - 677
     d) 1984 Stats - 670
     e) 1987 Stats - 639
157. a) Chipper Jones 1999 Stats - 859
     b) 2008 Stats + 10% = 770
     c) 2000 Stats - 768
     d) 2007 Stats - 756
     e) 1998 Stats - 751
     f) 2001 Stats - 750
     g) 1996 Stats - 741
     h) 2002 Stats - 712
     i) 2006 Stats - 682
158. Yoenis Cespedes 2015 Stats - 629
159. a) Adam Jones 2013 Stats - 620
                    2012 Stats - 615
160. a) Nelson Cruz 2010 Stats - 635
     b) 2014 Stats - 600
     c) 2015 Stats - 613
161. a) Giancarlo Stanton 2014 Stats - 674
     b) 2012 Stats - 613
162. a) Josh Donaldson 2013 Stats - 633
     b) 2015 Stats - 729
163. a) Paul Konerko 2010 Stats - 678
     b) 2006 Stats - 671
     c) 2005 Stats - 645
     d) 2004 Stats - 638
     e) 2011 Stats - 626
164. Lorenzo Cain 2015 Stats - 657

165. a) Adrian Gonzalez 2011 Stats - 713
    b) 2009 Stats - 675
166. Jose Altuve 2015 Stats - 645
167. a) Adrian Beltre 2004 Stats - 753
    b) 2012 Stats - 662
    c) 2010 Stats - 660
168. a) Mike Trout 2012 Stats - 803
    b) 2013 Stats - 783
    c) 2014 Stats - 710
    d) 2015 Stats - 682
169. a) Andrew McCutchen 2013 Stats - 695
    b) 2014 Stats - 693
    c) 2012 Stats - 689
170. a) Edwin Encarnacion 2012 Stats - 701
    b) 2015 Stats - 670
171. a) Jose Reyes 2006 Stats - 776
    b) 2007 Stats - 759
    c) 2008 Stats - 745
    d) 2011 Stats + 5% = 736
172. a) Jimmy Rollins 2007 Stats - 798
    b) 2006 Stats - 737
    c) 2004 Stats - 680
    d) 2005 Stats - 676
173. a) Chase Utley 2007 Stats - 723
    b) 2009 Stats - 722
    c) 2006 Stats - 713
    d) 2008 Stats - 713
    e) 2005 Stats - 692
174. Michael Brantley 2015 Stats - 650
175. a) Brian Giles 2000 Stats - 801
    b) 2002 Stats - 793
    c) 1999 Stats - 768
176. a) Gary Sheffield 2003 Stats - 845
    b) 1996 Stats - 841
    c) 2000 Stats - 762

177. a) Joe Torre 1971 Stats + 5% = 790
    b) 1966 Stats + 5% = 683
    c) 1970 Stats + 5% = 675
    d) 1964 Stats + 5% = 663
178. a) Jose Canseco 1988 Stats - 789
    b) 1991 Stats - 731
179. Rusty Staub 1969 Stats + 5% = 701
180. a) Jeff Kent 2000 Stats - 772
    b) 2002 Stats - 694
    c) 1998 Stats - 681
    d) 2005 Stats - 669
181. a) George Scott 1973 Stats + 5% = 679
    b) 1975 Stats + 5% = 650
182. a) Chris Davis 2013 Stats - 713
    b) 2015 Stats - 625
183. Jose Abreu 2014 Stats - 653
184. a) Bernie Williams 1998 Stats + 10% = 791
    b) 2000 Stats - 741
    c) 1999 Stats - 728
    d) 1996 Stats - 726
    e) 1997 Stats - 714
185. a) Paul O'Neill 1994 Stats + 20% = 820
    b) 1998 Stats - 696
    c) 1997 Stats - 682
186. a) Edgar Martinez 1995 Stats - 821
    b) 1996 Stats - 786
    c) 2000 Stats - 765
    d) 1997 Stats - 734
    e) 1998 Stats - 708
    f) 1999 Stats - 692
187. a) David Justice 1997 Stats - 693
    b) 2000 Stats - 692
188. Mike Greenwell 1988-747

189. a) Ruben Sierra 1991 Stats - 708
     b) 1989 Stats - 696
190. a) Tino Martinez 1997 Stats - 735
     b) 1995 Stats - 662
     c) 1998 Stats - 651
191. a) Chuck Knoblauch 1996 Stats - 814
     b) 1994 Stats - 785
     c) 1997 Stats - 740
     d) 1995 Stats - 714
192. a) Lou Whitaker 1991 Stats - 638
     b) 1983 Stats - 630
193. a) Willie Randolph 1987 Stats + 15% = 727
     b) 1980 Stats - 670
194. Bryce Harper 2015 Stats - 781
195. Nolan Arenedo 2015 Stats - 664
196. Manny Machado 2015 Stats - 652
197. Eric Hosmer 2015 Stats - 609
198. Paul Goldschmidt 2015 Stats - 760
199. Dee Gordon 2015 Stats - 621
200. a) Anthony Rizzo 2014 Stats - 610
     b) 2015 Stats - 679
201. a) Carlos Gonzalez 2010 Stats - 749
     b) 2015 Stats - 593
202. Todd Frazier 2015 Stats - 573
203. a) J.D. Martinez 2014 Stats - 559
     b) 2015 Stats - 596
204. a) Torii Hunter 2002 Stats - 639
     b) 2007 Stats - 647
205. a) Carl Crawford 2004 Stats - 683
     b) 2005 Stats - 698
     c) 2006 Stats - 721
     d) 2007 Stats - 689
     e) 2009 Stats - 697
     f) 2010 Stats - 730

206. a) Rocky Colavito 1958 Stats + 5% = 733
     b) 1961 Stats + 5% = 825
207. a) Kevin Mitchell 1989 Stats - 733
208. a) Richie Zisk 1977 Stats + 5% = 614
209. a) Jack Clark 1987 Stats + 5% = 736
210. a) Glenn Davis 1986 Stats + 5% = 658
211. a) Boog Powell 1970 Stats + 5% = 725
     b) 1964 Stats + 10% = 719
     c) 1966 Stats + 5% = 625
     d) 1969 Stats + 5% = 713
212. a) Pedro Guerrero 1985 Stats + 10% = 751
     b) 1982 Stats + 5% = 731
     c) 1983 Stats + 5% = 720
     d) 1987 Stats + 5% = 697
     e) 1989 Stats + 5% = 666
213. a) Hal McCrae 1982 Stats + 5% = 743
     b) 1974 Stats + 5% = 633
     c) 1976 Stats + 5% = 668
     d) 1977 Stats + 5 % = 730
214. a) Joe Adcock 1956 Stats + 10% = 688
215. a) Norm Cash 1961 Stats - 863
216. a) Jackie Jensen 1958 Stats + 5% = 744
     b) 1954 Stats + 5% = 729
     c) 1955 Stats + 5% = 718
     d) 1956 Stats + 5% = 718
     e) 1957 Stats + 5% = 656
     f) 1959 Stats + 5% = 743
217. a) Will Clark 1989 Stats - 715

b) 1987 Stats - 609

c) 1991 Stats - 633

d) 1998 Stats - 655

218. a) Ted Kluszewski 1954 Stats + 5% = 839

b) 1953 Stats + 5% = 744

c) 1955 Stats + 5% = 778

219. 226.a) Mike Sweeney 2000 Stats - 746

b) 1999 Stats - 699

c) 2001 Stats - 699

d) 2002 Stats - 706

220. a) Lou Boudreau 1948 Stats - 775

b) 1940 Stats - 658

c) 1944 Stats - 642

d) 1947 Stats - 603

221. a) Ray Boone 1953 Stats + 10% = 729

b) 1956 Stats + 10% = 692

222. a) Bret Boone 2001 Stats - 728

b) 2003 Stats - 712

223. a) Aaron Boone 2002 Stats - 612

b) 2003 Stats - 627

224. a) George Kell 1949 Stats - 652

b) 1950 Stats - 718

c) 1953 Stats + 10% = 612

225. a) Al Oliver 1982 Stats - 688

226. a) Jose Cruz Sr. 1977 Stats + 5% = 711

b) 1978 Stats + 5% = 717

c) 1983 Stats + 5% = 680

d) 1984 Stats + 5% = 708

227. a) Jose Cruz Jr. 2001 Stats - 668
2000 Stats - 580

228. a) Michael Young 2005 Stats - 677

b) 2006 Stats - 629

c) 2009 Stats - 603

d) 2011 Stats - 646

229. a) Rico Petrocelli 1969 Stats + 5% = 737

b) 1970 Stats + 5% = 627

c) 1971 Stats + 5% = 609

230. a) Frank Howard 1962 Stats + 5% = 663

b) 1968 Stats + 5% = 635

c) 1969 Stats + 5% = 755

d) 1970 Stats + 5% = 727

231. a) Lenny Dykstra 1993 Stats - 788

b) 1990 Stats - 713

232. a) Magglio Ordonez 2007 Stats - 809

b) 1999 Stats - 683

c) 2000 Stats - 746

d) 2001 Stats - 743

e) 2002 Stats - 764

f) 2003 Stats - 690

233. a) David Wright 2005 Stats - 687

b) 2006 Stats - 712

c) 2007 Stats - 798

d) 2008 Stats - 743

Note: Player Adjustment % is made on basis of League, Era, and Home Park (1981 and 1994 strike seasons were given a + 10% to 20% raise as they were shortened seasons)

Starting Pitchers

The Starting Pitcher Formula

$$[(W-L) \times 15] + \frac{300}{ERA} + [10(SO/9 - BB/9)] + \frac{200}{WHIP}$$

1. Clayton Kershaw $[(16-8) \times 15] + \frac{(300)}{2.43} + [10(9.8-2.6)] + \frac{[200]}{1.033} = 509.1$[a]

2. Pedro Martinez $[(17-8) \times 15] + \frac{(300)}{2.93} + [10(10-2.4)] + \frac{[200]}{1.054} = 503.2$

3. Gerrit Cole 485.2[a]
4. Sandy Koufax 470.5
5. Jacob deGrom 468.9[a]
6. Randy Johnson 455
7. Juan Marichal 446.5
8. Roger Clemens 443.7
9. Hisashi Iwakuma 443.4[a]
10. David Price 441.8[a]
11. Johan Santana 438.5
12. Whitey Ford 433.7
13. Adam Wainwright 432.3[a]
14. Roy Halladay 428.8
15. Ron Guidry 423.1
16. Stephen Strasburg 422.3[a]
17. Madison Baumgarner 419.7[a]
18. Max Scherzer 419.3[a]
19. Chris Sale 415.7[a]
20. Jered Weaver 414.8[a]
21. Sonny Gray 414.6[a]
22. Justin Verlander 412.3[a]
23. Don Gullett 407.5
24. Mike Mussina 405.3
25. Curt Schilling 403.6
26. Greg Maddux 402.9
27. Felix Hernandez 402.3[a]
28. Tom Seaver 400.3
29. Cliff Lee 399.4
30. Jim Palmer 399.4
31. Roy Oswalt 397.5
32. Noah Syndergaard 394.6[a]
33. Dwight Gooden 392.7
34. Zach Greinke 392.5[a]
35. Tim Hudson 388.2
36. Bob Gibson 387.5
37. Jon Lester 386.4[a]
38. Bret Saberhagen 383.1
39. Mark Fidrych 383.1
40. C.C Sabathia 382.8[a]
41. Gary Nolan 381.1
42. John Tudor 378.1
43. Sal Maglie 376.2
44. Tanner Roark 375.0[a]
45. Cole Hamels 373.0[a]
46. J.R Richard 372.1
47. Kevin Brown 371.2
48. John Smoltz 370.8*
49. Denny McClain 370.5
50. David Cone 368.9
51. Andy Pettite 368.9
52. Jimmy Key 368.2
53. Don Newcombe 367.6
54. Corey Kluber 365.6[a]

55. Bob Feller 364.4
56. Jordan Zimmerman 364.0[a]
57. Don Drysdale 363.9
58. Teddy Higuera 361.9
59. Jake Arrieta 360.7[a]
60. Warren Spahn 358.5
61. John Candalaria 358.0
62. James Shields 357.7[a]
63. Andy Messersmith 356.9
64. Jake Peavy 356.1[a]
65. Chris Carpenter 355.5
66. Jim "Catfish" Hunter 355.3
67. Dave McNally 355.3
68. Ferguson Jenkins 353.9
69. Johnny Cueto 353.2[a]
70. Steve Carlton 352.6
71. Julio Teheran 352.1[a]
72. Luis Tiant 351.7
73. Vida Blue 350.9
74. Jim Bunning 350.3
75. Don Sutton 350.1
76. Mike Cuellar 348.5
77. Gaylord Perry 346.8
78. Bartolo Colon 346.1[a]
79. Bob Welch 345.9
80. David Wells 344.6
81. Larry Jansen 344.2
82. Tim Lincecum 343.8[a]
83. Lamar Hoyt 342.9
84. Preacher Roe 342.4
85. Carlos Zambrano 341.3
86. Josh Beckett 339.7[a]
87. Jack McDowell 339.5
88. Ramon Martinez 339.3
89. Mike Garcia 334.4
90. Tom Glavine 333.9
91. Orel Hershiser 333.8
92. Eddie Lopat 333.1
93. Bob Lemon 332.5

94. Bert Blyleven 330.5
95. Jason Schmidt 330.2
96. Dennis Leonard 327.6
97. Hal Newhauser 326.6
98. Jose Rijo 326.1
99. Mel Stottlemyre 326.1
100. Mickey Lolich 323.2
101. Freddy Garcia 321.8
102. Milt Pappas 321.5
103. Dallas Keutchel 318.8[a]
104. John Lackey 318.7[a]
105. Mike Scott 318.7
106. Chris Archer 318.5[a]
107. Nolan Ryan 317.4
108. Billy Pierce 317.4
109. Robin Roberts 316.9
110. Lew Burdette 316.9
111. Kevin Appier 316.8
112. Jack Morris 316.2
113. Dean Chance 315.7
114. Dennis Eckersley 313.1*
115. Dave Stieb 312.8
116. Mario Soto 311.0
117. Doug Fister 311.0[a]
118. Mark Buehrle 310.8[a]
119. Jim Perry 307.4
120. Phil Hughes 307.3[a]
121. Steve Blass 306.9
122. Dennis Martinez 306.7
123. Phil Niekro 303.3
124. Jim Kaat 302.9
125. Scott Sanderson 302.5
126. Al Leiter 298.2
127. Frank Viola 296.1
128. Jerry Koosman 295.2
129. Jaime Moyer 294.9
130. Steve Rogers 294.9
131. Tommy John 294.8
132. Dave Stewart 294.7

133. Pete Vuckovich 293.6
134. Wilbur Wood 292.9
135. Ken Holtzman 292.2
136. Dick Donovan 291.2
137. Scott MacGregor 291.1
138. Early Wynn 290.8
139. Larry Gura 290.1
140. Sam McDowell 289.5
141. Mark Langston 289.3
142. Chuck Finley 289.2
143. Burt Hooton 288.7
144. Doug Drabek 288.3
145. Scott Kazmir 288.3[a]
146. Rick Reuschel 287.9
147. Rick Rhoden 286.8
148. Mike Boddicker 285.4
149. Bill Gullickson 285.3
150. Bobby Ojeda 284.4
151. Barry Zito 283.5
152. Johnny Sain 282.8
153. Rick Sutcliffe 282.7

154. Jerry Reuss 282.3
155. R.A. Dickey 282.1 a
156. Charlie Liebrandt 280.4
157. Fernando Valenzuela 280.2
158. Kenny Rogers 279.9
159. John Denny 278.3
160. Mike Hampton 276.6
161. Mike Flanagan 275.8
162. Frank Tanana 272.5
163. Dan Petry 271.6
164. Derek Lowe 270.8
165. Jim Lonborg 269.6
166. Ron Darling 268.3
167. Joaquim Andujar 267.5
168. Pat Hentgen 265.2
169. Doyle Alexander 264.5
170. Joe Niekro 262.2
171. Mike Caldwell 258.3
172. Charlie Hough 250.6
173. Mike Torrez 244.7

a - denotes active

* analyzed as a Starting Pitcher and as a Reliever

Closers

Pitching Formula for Closers

$$[(\text{Wins} - \text{Losses}) \times 10] + [\frac{300}{\text{ERA}}] + [(\text{SO} / 9 - \text{BB} / 9) \times 10] + [\frac{100}{\text{WHIP}}] + (\text{Saves} \times 3)$$

1. Craig Kimbrel
$$[(4 - 2) \times 10] + [\frac{300}{1.63}] + [11.1 \times 10] + [\frac{100}{0.927}] + [43 \times 3] = 551.9[a]$$

2. Kenley Jansen 446.2[a]
3. Aroldis Chapman 439.6[a]
4. Billy Wagner 431.1

5. Mariano Rivera 424.7
6. Jonathan Papelbon 422.5[a]
7. Greg Holland 405.0[a]

8. John Smoltz 387*
9. Bryan Harvey 384.2
10. Huston Street 379.5[a]
11. Koji Uehara 375.4[a]
12. Trevor Hoffman 375
13. Joakim Soria 374.9[a]
14. Francisco Rodriguez 374.1[a]
15. Tom Henke 372.1
16. Joe Nathan 371.7
17. Dennis Eckersley 368.7*
18. John Wetteland 360.5
19. Robb Nen 359.1
20. Troy Percival 339.9
21. Mark Melancom 339.1[a]
22. Kazuhiro Sasaki 338.8
23. Eric Gagne 335
24. Bruce Sutter 333.7
25. Rafael Soriano 328.6[a]
26. Trevor Rosanthal 327.5[a]
27. Rob Dibble 319.4
28. David Robertson 319.4[a]
29. Jose Velvarde 319.3
30. Armando Benitez 318
31. Lee Smith 317.6
32. J.J. Putz 316.2
33. Dick Radatz 314.6
34. Bobby Jenks 313.9
35. Rod Beck 313.8
36. Jeurys Familia 313.3[a]
37. Todd Worrell 311.2
38. Chad Cordero 308.6
39. Keith Foulke 306.1
40. Ugueth Urbina 305.4
41. Rollie Fingers 304.9
42. Shawn Tolleson 304.5[a]
43. Jeff Reardon 304.3
44. Brad Boxberger 303.7[a]
45. Brad Lidge 303.2
46. Hoyt Wilhelm 302.9

47. Brian Wilson 299.7[a]
48. Dan Quisenberry 297.8
49. Randy Myers 296.7
50. Dave Smith 296.7
51. Doug Jones 296.3
52. Jeff Montgomery 294.1
53. Rick Aguilera 291.5
54. Mike Henneman 291.1
55. John Franco 290.8
56. John Axford 290.7[a]
57. Rich "Goose" Gossage 289.9
58. Billy Koch 282.6
59. Francisco Cordero 282.1
60. Heath Bell 281.8
61. Duane Ward 278.1
62. Bobby Thigpen 275.9
63. John Hiller 272.9
64. Sparky Lyle 272.6
65. Jay Howell 272.5
66. Glen Perkins 272.3[a]
67. Al Holland 271.6
68. Brian Fuentes 271.3
69. B.J Ryan 270
70. Zach Britton 269.4[a]
71. Gregg Olsen 266.1
72. Grant Balfour 264.0[a]
73. Kelvin Herrera 261.8[a]
74. Jason Isringhausen 260.7
75. Casey Janssen 259.0[a]
76. Wade Davis 258.3[a]
77. Tug McGraw 258.2
78. Dave Righetti 257.4
79. Fernando Rodney 257.4[a]
80. Jeff Brantley 257.2
81. Roberto Hernandez 256.2
82. Roy Face 254.6
83. Jesse Orosco 250.1
84. Todd Jones 248.4
85. Bob Wickman 248.4

86. Ron Perranoski 247.6
87. Steve Howe 246.6
88. Guillermo Hernandez 246.1
89. Steve Bedrosian 245
90. Dan Plesac 243.2
91. Tippy Martinez 243.1
92. Gary Lavelle 241.5
93. Jeff Shaw 241.1

94. Kevin Gregg 240.1
95. Kent Tekulve 240
96. Lindy McDaniel 239.6
97. Donnie Moore 238.8
98. Mike Marshall 237.8
99. Gene Garber 235.9
100. Bill Campbell 232.9

a - denotes active

10
Players From Around the World

Leagues of Nations

1. U.S.A (including the Negro Leagues) - Satchel Paige, Josh Gibson, Babe Ruth, Joe DiMaggio, Ted Williams,"Cool Papa" Bell, Sandy Koufax, Mickey Mantle, Willie Mays, Henry Aaron, Derek Jeter, Roger Clemens, Ken Griffey Jr., Barry Bonds, and Alex Rodriguez to name but a few...

2. Dominican Republic - Juan Marichal, Manny Mota, Rico Carty, Matty, Felipe, and Jesus Alou, Victor Cruz, Alfredo Griffin, Damaso Garcia, George Bell, Tony Fernandez, Joaquin Andujar, Juan Samuel, Julio Franco, Pascual, Melido and Carlos Perez, Sammy Sosa, Manny Ramirez, Ramon and Pedro Martinez, Moises Alou, Mel Rojas, Miguel Tejada, Roberto Hernandez (a.k.a Fausta Carmona), Albert Pujols, David Ortiz, Jose Bautista, Edwin Encarnacion, Robinson Cano, Johnny Cueto, Jose Reyes, Yordana Ventura...

3. Puerto Rico - Roberto Clemente, Jose Cruz Jr. and Sr., Matty, Jesus, Felipe and Moises Alou, Willie Montanez, Roberto, Sandy Jr. and Sandy Alomar Sr., Jose, Bengie, and Yadier Molina, Orlando Cepeda, Bernie Williams, Ivan Rodriguez, Juan Gonzalez, Carlos Delgado, Roberto Hernandez, Carlos Beltran, Alex Rios, Carlos Correa...

4. Japan - Sadaharu Oh, Masanori Murakami, Eiji Sawamura, Ichiro Suzuki, Hideki Matsui, Daisuke Matsuzaka, Kasahiro Sasaki, Koji Uehara, Hisashi Iwakuma, Masahiro Tanaka, Yu Darvish, and Kenta Maeda to name but a few...

5. Cuba - Minnie Minoso, Sandy Amoros, Tony Oliva, Mike Cuellar, Luis Tiant, Tony Perez, Bert Campaneris, Orlando and Livan Hernandez, Aroldis Chapman, and Jose Abreu to name but a few...

6. Venezuela - Jose Altuve, Luis Aparicio, Bobby Abreu, Tony Armas Jr. and Sr., Dave Concepcion, Luis Leal, Andres Galarraga, Ozzie Guillen, Felix Hernandez, Johan Santana, Manny Trillo, Omar Vizquel, Miguel Cabrera, Carlos Zambra-

no, Marco Scutaro, Magglio Ordonez, Anibal Sanchez, Salvador Perez, Alcides Escobar...

7. Mexico - Fernando Valenzuela, Teddy Higuera, Esteban Loaiza, Marco Estrada, Roberto Osuna, Francisco Rodriguez, Vinny Castilla, Joakim Soria, Ismael Valdez, Sid Monge, Yovani Gallardo, Jorge Orta, Hector Torres, Aurelio Rodriguez...

8. Canada - Jeff Heath, Ferguson Jenkins, Larry Walker, Joey Votto, Jason Bay, Eric Gagne, Russell Martin, Justin Morneau, John Hiller, Erik Bedard, Ryan Dempster, Dr. Ron Taylor, Reggie Cleveland, Claude Raymond, Kirk McCaskill, Rheal Cormier, Rob and Rich Butler, Paul Quantrill, Terry Puhl, John Axford, Michael Saunders, Dalton Pompey...

9. Italy - Babe Herman Ruth (Half-Italian/Half German), Tony Lazzeri, Joe, Vince, and Dom DiMaggio (each had a Confirmation), Yogi Berra, Sal Maglie, Rocky Colavito, Johnny Antonelli, Ernie Broglio, Tony and Billy Conigliaro, Rico Petrocelli, Joe and Frank Torre, Dave Giusti, John Candelaria, Steve Balboni, Mike Piazza, Joe Girardi, Jason Giambi, Paul Sorrento, Frank Catalanotto, Joey Votto, Jake Arrieta, Chris Colabello, Gene Rye (Eugene Marcerelli - had a Confirmation)...

10. Israel - Mordecai "Three Finger" Brown, Henry Greenberg, Sandy Koufax, Rod Carew, Shawn Green, Ryan Braun, Al Rosen, Lou Boudreau, Heinie Zimmerman, Larry Sherry, Mike Epstein, Steve Yeager, Oren Nuremberg, Mark Clear, Kevin Pillar (had a Bar Mitzvah), Ken Holtzman, Walt Weiss, Steve Stone, Kevin Yuekilis, Brad Ausmus, Ian Kinsler, Ryan Zimmerman, Ira Smith, Ricky Green, I.J Schecter, Colin Halperin, Rick Litwin, Les Bernstein, and Robbie Cooper...

Henry Greenberg with a young Tigers fan

11. Korea - Eric Thames (U.S.A), Seung Yuop Lee, Byung-ho Park, Chan Ho Park, Byung-Hyun Kim, Shin-soo Choo, Han-jun Yu, Sung-Bum Na, Hyeon-soo Kim, Sok-min Park, Hyoung-woo Choi, Min-ho Kang, Jim Adduci (Canada), Jun-suk Choi, Yamaica Navarro (Dominican Republic), Brett Pill (U.S.A), ...

12. Panama - Rod Carew, Mariano Rivera, Carlos Lee, Manny Sanguillen, Omar Moreno, Juan Berenguer, Roberto Kelly, Ben Oglivie, Rennie Stennett, Carlos Ruiz, Hector Lopez, Bruce Chen...

13. England - Eddie Collins, Lefty "Moses" Grove, Jeff Heath, Larry Walker, Joey Votto, Jason Bay, Justin Morneau, Russell Martin, Danny Cox, Ferguson Jenkins...

14. France - Nap Lajoie, Justin Morneau, Bruce Bochy, Charlie Lea, Eric Bedard, Eric Gagne, Claude Raymond, Rheal Cormier, Steve Jeltz...

15. Greece - Nomar Garciaparra, Milt Pappas, Nick Markakis, Mike Moustakas...

16. Netherlands - Honus Wagner, Johnny "Double No-Hit" Vander-Meer, Bert Blyleven, Jerry Koosman, Andy Van Slyke, Jacob deGrom, Didi Gregorius...

17. Colombia - Orlando Cabrera, Edgar Renteria, Julio Teheran, Jackie Gutierrez, Orlando Ramirez, Yhonathan Barrios...

18. Ireland - Tommy Bond, Mickey "Black Mike" Cochrane, Mark McGwire, Andrew McCutchen...

19. Taiwan - Wei-Yin Chen, C.C Lee, Chin-hui Tsao, Chien-Ming Wang, Wei-Chung Wang...

20. Jamaica - Chili Davis, Devon White, Justin Masterson...

21. Curacao - Andruw Jones, Hensley Meulens, Kenley Jansen, Jonathan Schoop...

22. Germany - Lou Gehrig, Harry Heilmann, Orel Hershiser, Von Hayes, Ron Gardenhire, Craig Lefferts, Mike Blowers...

23. China

24. Poland - Ted Kluszewski, Moe Drabowsky, Troy Tulowitzki (best Shortstop in the game today), A.J Pierzynski...

25. Australia - Joe Quinn, Dave Nilsson, Grant Balfour, Graeme Lloyd, Liam Hendriks, Peter Moylan...

26. Brazil - Yan Gomes, Paolo Orlando, Andre Rienzo...

27. Scotland - Bobby Thomson (hit the "Shot Heard Around the World" in the 1951 Playoff Game for the New York Giants against the Brooklyn Dodgers)

28. Spain - Alfredo Cabrera, Bryan Oelkers, Alberto Pardo, Daniel Rios...

29. Portugal - Duarte Pimentel, Steven Souza...

30. New Zealand - Scott Richmond
    Nicaragua - Dennis Martinez (El Presidente), David Green

31. Russia - Al Simmons (a.k.a Aloys Szymanski)

32. Belgium - Brian Lesher

World Baseball Classic

2006

1. Japan
2. Cuba
3. South Korea
4. Dominican Republic
5. Puerto Rico
6. Mexico
7. Venezuela
8. U.S.A
9. Canada
10. Italy
11. Netherlands
12. Chinese Tai Pei
13. Australia
14. Panama
15. China
16. South Africa

Tournament MVP - Daisuke Matsuzaka

All-WBC Team

Player	Nation
C - Tomoya Satozaki	Japan
1B - Seung-Yeop Lee	South Korea
2B - Yulieski Gourriel	Cuba
3B - Adrian Beltre	Dominican Republic
SS - Derek Jeter	U.S.A
OF - Ken Griffey Jr.	U.S.A
OF - Jong-Beom Lee	South Korea
OF - Ichiro Suzuki	Japan
DH - Yoandy Garlobo	Cuba
P - Yadel Marti	Cuba
P - Daisuke Matsuzaka	Japan
P - Chan-Ho Park	South Korea

2009

1. Japan
2. South Korea
3. Venezuela
4. United States

5. Puerto Rico
6. Cuba
7. Netherlands
8. Mexico
9. Dominican Republic
10. Italy
11. China
12. Australia
13. Canada
14. Chinese Tai Pei
15. Panama
16. South Africa

Tournament MVP - Daisuke Matsuzaka

All-WBC Team

Player	Nation
C - Ivan Rodriguez	Puerto Rico
1B - Tae-Kyun Kim	South Korea
2B - Jose Lopez	Venezuela
3B - Bum-Ho Lee	South Korea
SS - Jimmy Rollins	U.S.A
OF - Norichika Aoki	Japan
OF - Frederich Cepeda	Cuba
OF - Yoenis Cespedes	Cuba
DH - Hyun-soo Kim	South Korea
P - Jung-Keun Bong	South Korea
P - Hisashi Iwakuma	Japan
P - Daisuke Matsuzaka	Japan

2013

1. Dominican Republic
2. Puerto Rico
3. Japan
4. Netherlands
5. Cuba

6. U.S.A
7. Italy
8. Chinese Tai Pei
9. South Korea
10. Venezuela
11. Mexico
12. Canada
13. China
14. Brazil
15. Spain
16. Australia

Tournament MVP - Robinson Cano

All WBC Team

Player	Nation
C - Yadier Molina	Puerto Rico
1B - Edwin Encarnacion	Dominican Republic
2B - Robinson Cano	Dominican Republic
3B - David Wright	U.S.A
SS - Jose Reyes	Dominican Republic
OF - Nelson Cruz	Dominican Republic
OF - Angel Pagan	Puerto Rico
OF - Michael Saunders	Canada
DH - Hirokazu Ibata	Japan
P - Nelson Figueroa	Puerto Rico
P - Kenta Maedo	Japan
P - Fernando Rodney	Dominican Republic

World Baseball Leagues and Organizations

Leagues and League Rankings

1. Major League Baseball
2. Korean Baseball Organization
3. Japanese Central and Pacific Leagues

4. AAA Class Minor Leagues to the Majors
5. Mexican League (AA Class equivalent)
6. AA Class Minor Leagues to the Majors
7. High A Class Minor Leagues to the Majors
8. Low A Class Minor Leagues to the Majors
9. Major League Baseball Winter-Ball (consisting of prospects just finishing College and even some recent High School graduates)

The 2015 World Professional Baseball M.V.P

1. MVP - Eric Thames
2. Josh Donaldson
3. Bryce Harper
4. Jake Arrieta
5. Zach Greinke
6. Mike Trout
7. Lorenzo Cain
8. Nelson Cruz
9. Byung-ho Park
10. David Price

By deduction the 2015 All-World MVP is Eric Thames and the MLB MVP is Josh Donaldson. In my opinion, this rating is socially relevant as a ballplayer in Korea, Japan, the Dominican Republic, Canada, Puerto Rico, Mexico, and Cuba, would feel somewhat appreciated within the U.S.A as they would see they were socially relevant in the same context as an American within America.

The reality is that Worldwide exposure can't just be confined to within America and/or outside America. It's Universal as has been defined by the Freedom of Information Act in Canada (in est. 1977).

Seung Yuop Lee vs Byung-ho Park: The two greatest Korean hitters of our day

Seung Yuop Lee a.k.a "the Lion King" started his career with Samsung in the Korean Baseball Organization belting 54 home runs in his rookie year of 1999 winning Rookie of the

Year and MVP honours. Four years later (in 2003) he hammered 56 dingers with 144 RBI's leading the KBO in both categories taking home his second MVP Award. Also in his pedigree Yuop Lee has nine years with 30+ home runs and four years with 41+ home runs. He's also had 101+RBI's to date in his career and six years with 101+runs scored. He went to Japan to play there from 2004-2011 before coming back to the KBO. He looks poised to put together a few more good seasons. Lee has 483 lifetime home runs and 1367 RBI's in his illustrious career to date.

Byung ho-Park began his career in the KBO in 2005 and was a utility player until 2012 when he bacame a fixture at First Base with Nexen. In each year between 2012 to Present, Park has produced 31+home runs and 105+RBI's. Byung has batted .303+ in each of the last three years and has hit 52+home runs and 124+RBI's in each of the last two years winning the MVP in the KBO in 2014 and coming second in the 2015 KBO MVP vote (to Eric Thames). Park's' lifetime OPS is .951. He was just signed by the Minnesota Twins and the consensus within the Twins organization is that Park will produce early and often in adjusting to Major League pitching.

If we're to compare the two ballplayers it should be noted that each play First Base, they're both power hitters, and they both started their careers in the KBO. I'll abstain from choosing one over the other until I see what Byung ho-Park does in his years' to come in MLB.

Statistical Analysis of Hitters in the Korean Baseball Organization

1. Eric Thames' 2015 Stats

$$\left[\frac{.381 + .497 + .790}{3} \right] + 94 + 140 + 130 + [3(40\text{-}8)] + \left[\frac{103\text{-}91}{2} \right]$$

$$= 556 + 94 + 140 + 130 + 96 + 4 = 1020$$

2014 Stats - 780

2. a) Byung-ho Park 2012 Stats - 675
   b) 2013 Stats - 736
   c) 2014 Stats - 786
   d) 2015 Stats - 842

3. a) Seung Yuop Lee 1999 Stats - 865
   b) 2002 Stats - 810
   c) 2003 Stats - 841
   d) 2006 Stats (in Japan) - 699

4. a) Han-jun Yu 2014 Stats + 15% = 720
   b) 2015 Stats -740

5. a) Hyeon-soo Kim 2008 Stats + 10% = 765
   b) 2009 Stats + 10% = 811
   c) 2010 Stats + 10% = 711
   d) 2014 Stats + 10% = 682
   e) 2015 Stats - 750

6. a) Sung-Bum Na 2014 Stats + 10% = 746
   b) 2015 Stats - 741

7. a) Sok-min Park 2012 Stats + 15% = 725
   b) 2013 Stats + 20% = 714
   c) 2014 Stats + 25% = 794
   d) 2015 Stats + 10% = 767

8. a) Hyoung-woo Choi 2011 Stats + 10% = 799
   b) 2014 Stats + 15% = 843
   c) 2015 Stats - 689

9. a) Jim Adduci 2015 Stats - 705

10. a) Min-ho Kang 2010 Stats + 20% = 668
    b) 2015 Stats ı 25%= 793

11. a) Jun-suk Choi 2010 Stats + 20% = 700
    b) 2015 Stats - 645

12. a) Yamaico Navarro 2014 Stats + 5% = 800
    b) 2015 Stats - 815

13. a) Brett Pill 2015 Stats - 642

14. a) Tae-Kyun Kim 2001 Stats + 60% = 965
    b) 2003 Stats + 10% = 712
    c) 2004 Stats + 10% = 712
    d) 2005 Stats + 10% = 718
    e) 2008 Stats + 20% = 829
    f) 2012 Stats + 20% = 781
    g) 2014 Stats + 20% = 786
    h) 2015 Stats + 20% = 799

15. a) Jung-ho Kang 2012 Stats + 20% = 828
    b) 2014 Stats + 20% = 956
    c) 2015 Stats (with the Pittsburgh Pirates) + 20% = 594

16. a) Jeong Choi 2008 Stats + 25% = 758
    b) 2010 Stats + 25% = 799
    c) 2011 Stats + 25% = 769
    d) 2012 Stats + 10% = 714
    e) 2013 Stats + 20% = 794

17. a) Tae-in Chae 2013 Stats + 50% = 882
    b) 2014 Stats + 5% = 618
    c) 2015 Stats + 40% = 682
18. a) Ah-seop Son 2011 Stats + 15% = 715
    b) 2013 Stats + 5% = 712
    c) 2014 Stats + 5% = 740
19. a) Ji-wan Na 2014 Stats + 20% = 658
20. a) Ho-jun Lee 2003 Stats + 5% = 693
21. a) Geon-chang Seo 2014 Stats - 818
22. a) Ju-chan Kim 2015 Stats + 50% = 899
23. a) Byeong-heon Min 2014 Stats + 10% = 697
24. a) Chi-hong Ahn 2014 Stats + 15% = 749
25. a) Jae-won Lee 2014 Stats + 20% = 714
26. a) Seong-hun Chung 2014 Stats + 25% = 766
27. a) Jae-gyun Hwang 2014 Stats + 5% = 620
    b) 2015 Stats - 614
28. a) Dae-ho Lee 2010 Stats + 10% =
    b) 2006 Stats + 10% =
    c) 2007 Stats + 10% =
    d) 2011 Stats + 10% =

Analysis of Hitters in the Japanese Central League for the 2015 Season

1. Tetsuto Yamada 2015 Stats - 825
2. Yoshitomo Tsutsugo 2015 Stats - 623
3. Shingo Kawabata 2015 Stats - 562

Stats Analysis of Hitters in the Japanese Pacific League for the 2015 Season

1. Yuki Yanagita 2015 Stats - 829
2. Shogo Akiyama 2015 Stats - 647
3. Ikuhiro Kiyota 2015 Stats + 10% = 651
4. Kensuke Kondo 2015 Stats + 10% = 640
5. Nobuhiro Matsuda 2015 Stats - 593
6. Dae-ho Lee 2015 Stats - 592
7. Takeya Nakamura 2015 Stats - 630
8. Sho Nakata 2015 Stats - 565

Stats Analysis of Hitters in the Mexican League for the 2015 Season

1. Cyle Hankerd 2015 Stats + 50% = 1032
2. Jesse Castillo 2015 Stats +15% = 821
3. Jesus Valdez 2015 Stats + 15% = 736
4. Japhet Amador 2015 Stats + 20% = 910
5. Jorge Cantu 2015 Stats + 20% = 838
6. Henry Rodriguez 2015 Stats + 20% = 734
7. Saul Soto 2015 Stats + 20% = 822
8. Felix Perez 2015 Stats + 20% = 725

Stats Analysis of Starting Pitchers in the Korean Baseball Organization for the 2015 Season

$$[(W - L) \times 15] + \frac{300}{ERA} + [10(SO / 9 - BB / 9)] + \frac{200}{WHIP}$$

1. Eric Hacker - 556.2
2. Gwang-hyun Kim - 470.3
3. Hui-gwan Yu - 470.1
4. Hyeon-jong Yang - 458.7
5. Seong-hwan Yoon - 446.3
6. Woo-chan Cha - 437.3
7. Andy Van Hekken - 397.9

Stats Analysis of Starting Pitchers in the Japanese Leagues for the 2015 Season

Pacific League

1. Shohei Otani - 587.9
2. Rick van den Hurk - 553.5
3. Shota Takeda - 420.4
4. Yuki Nishi - 418.9

5. Hideaki Wakui - 368
6. Takahiro Norimoto - 338.8

Central League

1. Miles Mikolas - 581.3
2. Kenta Maeda - 503.9
3. Kris Johnson - 487.7
4. Shintaro Fujnami - 456.1
5. Shunta Wakamatsu - 446.4
6. Hiroki Kurada - 385.1
7. Tomoyuki Sagano - 373.5
8. Yudai Ono - 372.9

Stats Analysis of Closers in the Japanese Leagues for the 2015 Season

$$[(W-L) \times 10] + \frac{300}{ERA} + [10(SO/9 - BB/9)] + \frac{100}{WHIP} + (Saves \times 3)$$

Pacific League

1. Dennis Sarfate - 713.6
2. Yuki Matsui - 658
3. Yuj Nishiro - 450.3

Central League

1. Tony Barnette - 540.5
2. Hirokazu Sawamura - 512.8
3. Yasuaki Yamasaki - 449.2
4. Seung-hwan Oh - 374.6

11
The Final Analysis

The Race Card

The whole argument comes down to this; When does Major League Baseball come to terms with its blatant racism of the "Black" ballplayer. I say "Black", because blood is Red, not white, nor black. Had Major League Baseball instituted a 20% share to the Negro-Leagues in 1947, we'd all be looking at a different sphere. 20% in todays' Market would translate into roughly $100 Billion U.S.D annually. The Annointments that I made to the NLBPA, the N.B.A and the N.F.L are heartfelt. These are not fly by decisions made under rash circumstances, they are well thought out solutions to the Civil unrest within a Continent that hasn't been so alive since the mid-sixties. Would Cito Gaston and Dave Winfield make a good Ownership Team in Toronto, Ontario, Canada? I do believe so, likewise that of Michael Jordan in Chicago with the Bulls, and Tony Dorsett with the Dallas Cowboys. Worldwide, this would make our Continent seem to be less racist to the plain eye. When a Canadian (as I happen to be) travels to Europe, or Africa for that matter, it is inevitable that you're a known quantity as to the Pop-Culture of that Nation. A baseball player from the U.S in Japan is an easy sell, likewise, of a Japanese player to the U.S.A. What about a Pakistani' ballplayer in America? Will America shoot that down?

In fifty years people will still be asking where are the best ballplayers from? Are we to honesty expect that answer to be singularly defined and answered? As if by cosmosis, an American was the standard given for Worldwide Baseball talent. This will be an anomoly for eternity. Is there truth to an American having more Baseball saavy than any other Nation, so help us G-D? I would imagine that Gehrig was heralded by Germany the same as Israel heralded Koufax. I will say, that Eiji Sawamura would have been on-par with Satchel Paige had they barn-stormed together in the 30's. What had those barnstorms been reported in Tokyo, 1937?

The reality of America in 1947 was that Baseball returned to its glory after a long arduous battle of World War 2. The fact that the Nazi's had been defeated lent us to remember the likes of Henry Greenberg and Satchel Paige. The guilt played its way into Branch Rickey's famous speech "What would I have told my maker had I not signed Jackie Robinson (I paraphrase, 'Black' ballplayer)?" Is that really enough compensation? , a realization that things weren't "fair" before the integration of a "Black" ballplayer into the Majors. What about practicality and business, two other distinct' American principles.

Free Agency in the Early Years

Curt Flood should have been the first free-agent in 1971. The reality was that Flood hadn't played for the Cardinals for the entire 1970 Baseball season, making his one year contract from 1969 null and void. Some have speculated that Major League Baseball didn't want to end slavery in Baseball (as the Reserve Clause bound a player to a team for life, and even though the Courts rejected this claim in the late fifties, describing the Reserve Clause as slavery is still accurate). The reality was that the establishment wasn't about to give this freedom first, to a "Black" ballplayer. Andy Messersmith (a good-looking Caucasian) became the first free-agent in 1975/76, as Marvin Miller - Head of the MLBPA, pushed the challenge of the "Reserve Clause" once again, and this time an arbitrator ruled in the MLB-PA's favor. Bowie Kuhn was the Commissioner of MLB at the time, and looked like he saw a ghost when interviewed after the arbitrator's decision.

Roberto Clemente was a free-agent signing of the Pittsburgh Pirates in 1955, after he was put on waivers by the Brooklyn Dodgers. This was the only way a player could be drafted by another team up until Expansion. Expansion Teams were largely responsible for the revision towards Free Agency, as when they surface, each Major League Team can only protect 40 men, hence the 40-Man Roster.

Once the Reserve Clause was challenged and defeated, this essentially ended slavery in Professional Baseball as the Owners' had to negotiate in good faith through Collective Bargaining, from that point on. It also enabled ballplayers to market their abilities to a wider audience giving flexibility in a player determining his own fate should he become a free-agent.

Economic Restructuring Within Major League Baseball

What would happen if Major League Baseball instituted a minimum salary of $60,000 U.S.D/ Year and maximum salary of $10 Million U.S.D/ Year within the signings of all ballplayers within each chain of MLB (including the Minor Leagues, and all aspects of the Players Association and Front Office positions)?

1. IF the ultra-rich within MLB (the Owners and Marquee players) are taxed accordingly, the guy selling peanuts is a happy camper making $35,000 U.S.D/ Year. The least paid position at the ballpark would be $35,000 U.S.D/ Year.
2. The player in A-Ball is seeing $60,000 U.S.D/ Year
3. The player on the average level sees $1,000,000 U.S.D/ Year
4. The marquee player sees $10,000,000 U.S.D/ Year

The reason I stipulate is for this reason. No team has 25 superstars. I repeat no team has 25 superstars. No hitter will ever bat 1.0000 with any consistency, and no pitcher will ever achieve a perfect record with any consistency. You might have a guy who finishes his career 1 for 1 with a grand slam to boot, but try to repeat that over and over again... It's the same thing for the pitchers within the game. A pitcher is always trying for the perfect game. Does he achieve this? No.

The game of baseball is an institution for this reason. The guy selling the peanuts and cracker jacks, the soda and the beer, the baseball and the jersey, all need to make a buck to bring enough chicken bacon home to feed the wife and kids. The stories we tell after the game has been played is part and parcel of what North American cities and towns need. Something to grow on that makes life worth living. A reason to wake up in the morning. When we look back on our lives as a baseball fanatic, we realize that success happens, mistakes happen, you roll with the punches. You play the game and roll the bones whether in America, Korea, Cuba, Japan, or even Pakistan for that matter.

The Steroids Issue

The reality behind the hocus pocus guilt complex that MLB threw at its players will be looked at in the future for what it was, a scam. The U.S Government knew they had a steroids issue as far back as 1978, when famous boxer Ken Holmes was shown to be on anabolic steroids. From there it spread to Pro-Football players and Sprinters who attended the Olympics (Ben Johnson at the 1988 Olympic Games in Seoul, South Korea comes to mind). Everyone knew that the majority of these athlete's were juiced up. Why didn't the U.S Government ban anabolic steroids from use way back then? Once they realized that they couldn't put it off any longer they tried to discredit the users from MLB to set an example. Where was the Steroids testing in the late eighties is what I'd like to know. Canada came down hard on its athlete's that were caught using, why didn't the U.S.A follow suit in 1988?

Many MLB players in the nineties were using steroids. The steroids testing that's being done was put into place after the 2004 Baseball season. I do not believe in punishing a Major Leaguer that was caught using steroids from before 2005 for this reason; You can't punish a man for smoking a cigarette yesterday. If it is legal yesterday and not today than you adapt to the change in Law. It was a very dangerous precedent to punish players for their steroid use before 2005 (from before the Law was put in place). This becomes a question of morality. When does the Government (Owners from a hierachy perspective) take responsibily for ITS negligent inaction as far back as 1978 when Holmes admitted that he was on the juice. This whole argument makes me question the ethics of every Owner in the game today.

Instant Replay Review

The fact is that Umpires will never get every call right. A bad call on balls and strikes is something that we'll always have to deal with, but as long as the Umpire is consistent with his strike zone, I'm okay with that. It is the call at the Plate in a crucial time of the game when instant replay is a valuable commodity. To make sure that the call is gotten right. In first year of existence instant replay was used quite a bit, especially on stolen base attempts (as many are close calls). I would say to make it a harder practice for a Manager to challenge a call during the game. Make it so that each team has three possible challenges per game, and that if a challenge is unsuccessful it takes away one of the remaining challenges. Other than that, I'm all for a Manager having some leaway in challenging an Umpires call at a crucial time of the game.

Blocking the Plate

It has just been changed this year as to a Catcher not being allowed to block the plate when the runner is in the vicinity of home-plate at the same time as the ball arriving. I'm totally against this rule change as I'm a purist of the game of baseball. Having played the game at a high level in baseball at the Catcher position, I always took pride in my postioning when a runner was bulling into the plate. I'm a firm believer that if a Catcher does his job right in blocking the plate there would be fewer injuries. It's when a Catcher doesn't have a good position in blocking the plate when injuries arise (like the Buster Posey incident). Conversely, the change in the rule of a Catcher not being allowed to block the plate will make it harder on the defense to do job once the ball is in play. Done correctly, the chance of a runner scoring when the ball arrives at the same time at the bag or the plate is practically nil.

Breaking Up the Double Play

I'm also a purist when it becomes reviewable to see if the runner made intentional contact when trying to break up the double play. It's an oxymoron, explainable in itself. How the hell else are you supposed to "break up the double play", and isn't the runner just as vulnerable in going in hard to the bag, not knowing if the middle infielder that's turning the two is going to fire one at his head? When are people just going to accept that pro ball can be a contact sport? Instead of being so politically correct, the players should just be able to play the game hard and to the best of their abilities without having to question their innate abilities to do their job politically correct at the exact time when being politically correct is the last instinctive reaction to the protocol of BREAKING UP THE DOUBLE PLAY.

Conclusion

In the World today there are many team sports that people follow. Whether that be Baseball, Soccer, Football, Basketball, or Hockey, the fans' interest is what is relevant. Professional Baseball isn't just limited to the U.S.A, it has become a fixture in many Nations (including Cuba, Mexico, Puerto Rico, Venezuela, Japan, Korea, and the Dominican Republic). Will there ever be a MLB Franchise in Mexico? What about another MLB Franchise in Canada?

The reality is that economics and popular culture dictate to a large degree what we digest in this realm. MLB is an institution and needs to be with the times, and for this reason I would say that it's a Global Market. The New York Yankees, St. Louis Cardinals, Boston Red Sox, Chicago Cubs, Chicago White Sox, Cincinnati Reds, and the Los Angeles Dodgers will always be in the League. It's the teams like the Miami Marlins and Milwaukee Brewers that would be expendable if they weren't drawing crowds in their ballparks.

When the fans have final say in determining a Global Market is when MLB will flourish like European Football (on a Global scale). This writer believes that a couple of teams in Canada, Mexico, Puerto Rico, Venezuela, Cuba, and the Dominican Republic are in order to Globalize the game. Could the National League and the American League go with a North, South, East, Central, West format where division rivals face each-other less, to accommodate the two new Divisions?

Made in the USA
Lexington, KY
29 November 2016